THE NEW FRONTIER OF WAR

Political Warfare, Present and Future

THE NEW FRONTIER OF WAR

Political Warfare, Present and Future

by

William R. Kintner

with

Joseph Z. Kornfeder

HENRY REGNERY COMPANY

Chicago: 1962

CONTENTS

CONTENTS

PREFACE

WHILE LIVING IN FRANCE IN 1958, I RECEIVED A LETTER FROM Joseph Z. Kornfeder asking me to collaborate with him in writing a book on communist political warfare. The request seemed natural because both he and I had devoted a good part of our lives to the understanding of communist ideology, organization, and strategy. Kornfeder attended the Lenin School in the period 1927 to 1930. Benjamin Gitlow, a leading former member of the Communist Party, U.S.A., stated that Kornfeder knew Stalin better than any other member of the American Communist Party. After receiving his training at the communist political-warfare school, Kornfeder helped to organize the Communist Party in Venezuela and Colombia. He left the movement in the mid-thirties when it became apparent that the Party had abandoned all the ideals which attracted him to it and had been transformed into a power apparatus.

In part this book represents a memoriam to Mr. Kornfeder's wife, Eva, and his son, Spartac, who along with untold numbers of other victims perished in Stalin's purges during the thirties.

My own interests in the study of communism began after World War II as a result of my service in the Intelligence Division of the Army's General Staff. Subsequently, I have had the opportunity to study and write extensively on many facets of the confrontation between communism and the Free World—a condition which the Communists now describe as a "conflict of systems." Service in the C.I.A., the National Security Council Planning Board, the Executive Office of the President (as an assistant to Nelson A. Rockefeller), and, finally, in the Office of the Chief of Staff of the United States Army gave me a privileged insight into the totality of the communist effort to undermine the Free World, as well as the nature of the American response to this challenge. In particular, I have sensed a decreasing American willingness to wage the struggle in the realms of psychological, ideological, and political warfare. It is in these areas that the Communists have laid the foundation for the successes they have achieved. I became convinced that our failure to understand the inner logic of communism and communist political warfare lies behind many of our difficulties in coping with the communist challenge. I therefore accepted Mr. Kornfeder's suggestion to undertake this study.

Because we were moving into as yet uncharted seas, the writing of this book was a time-consuming and demanding task. The book has benefited from the advice, assistance, and critical comment of many knowledgeable people. In its early stages, Richard G. Stilwell and Paul C. Davis helped to establish the book's subsequent focus. Keith Wheelock's provocative criticisms of the initial draft were also helpful in developing the final formulation. Subsequently, Walter and Lorna Hahn contributed editorially to simplifying its presentation. Later, many individuals contributed to the development of specific chapters. These included Alda Raffa, who made available some penetrating observations regarding "The Expanding Conflict of Systems"; Tai Sung An, who helped shape "Communist China in Political Warfare: Past, Present, and Future"; and Genevieve Linebarger, who helped to prepare the first draft of "Southeast Asia: Confused Battleground" and assisted in its final formulation. Among the many individuals whose knowledge was put to use in "The Latin American Way" were Nathaniel Weyl, Sig Synnestvedt, William Doherty, Jr., and John Caldwell. Allen Grant's thorough investigation of the inadequacies in the training of the American people with regard to the theory and practice of communism is largely reflected in "Training for Political Warfare." "Conflict Management" has benefited from the suggestions of Gregory L. Higgens, Edwin F. Black, John Cushman, and John Stutesman. Betty Macafee helped with the notes concerning Africa in the introduction to Part Two. Vladimir Petrov's unusual background as a former citizen of the Soviet Union and a staff member of the U.S.I.A. made his knowledge of present-day Soviet society very helpful in writing "Target: Communist Vulnerabilities."

Stefan T. Possony, a colleague and my associate in many endeavors, strengthened the entire manuscript with his incisive critique and suggestions on many points of fact and interpretation. The study in its book form has also benefited immeasurably from the editorial skill and substantive knowledge of Paul M. A. Linebarger, whose competence did much to clarify the content and make it more readable. Paul Ambrose assisted with the indexing and with the bibliography.

I have benefited throughout the preparation of this book from my association with the Foreign Policy Research Institute. Dr. Robert Strausz-Hupé, the Director, and many of the associates and members of the staff have contributed much in thought, time and effort. The book would not be what it is without their unstinting cooperation.

The book's argument gained force and thrust through the clarity of view, perseverance, and deep insight of my colleague, Joseph Z. Kornfeder. The final formulation, however, was largely my own. And, as with any book, someone had to make choices when points of difference arose. I assume full responsibility for what actually appears on these pages.

This preface would not be complete—in fact, the book would never have been written—were it not for the secretarial help of Margaret Capotrio, Kay Christiansen, Patricia Hawes, Jacqueline Ketcham, Diane Kressler, Ruth Yeuell, and Joy Cottrell.

WILLIAM R. KINTNER

INTRODUCTION

LENIN ASKED OF HISTORY: "WHO IS STRONGER?" HIS QUESTION becomes more crucial as time passes. Despite the hopes and wishes of good men everywhere, the confrontation of two antagonistic systems becomes plainer and sharper every day. The Free World, to its sorrow, has learned that men cannot dispose of armed enemies by simply wishing that they were not hostile. Reconciliation, like war or love, is a process which requires two partners; it cannot be effected by one side alone.

The doctrines and stresses of the communist system have made the system and the leaders within it the blind captives of their own belief. Their human intelligence and their moral qualities function, but they function only within the postulates of the dramatic, dangerous theories to which they are now irretrievably committed.

On both sides, the sense of impending climax is sharp. President Kennedy said, after the Cuban fiasco, "I am equally convinced that history will record the fact that this bitter struggle reached its climax in the late Nineteen Fifties and the early Nineteen Sixties."[1] Khrushchev, characteristically, was even more blunt: "Our epoch is the epoch of the triumph of Marxism-Leninism." In his basic-policy statement of January 6, 1961, he explained this in detail: "An analysis of the world situation as it had shaped by the beginning of the sixties of this century is bound to give all champions of the great Communist movement a feeling of deep satisfaction and legitimate pride. Indeed, comrades, reality has far exceeded the boldest and most optimistic predictions and expectations."[2] He added, grimly

1. See the *New York Times*, April 20, 1961.

2. *For New Victories for the World Communist Movement*—Report by N. S. Khrushchev on the results of the meeting of Representatives of the Communist and Workers' Parties, delivered at a General Meeting of Party Organizations of the Higher Party School, Academy of Social Sciences, and Institute of Marxism-Leninism of the C.C. C.P.S.U. (*Kommunist*, No. 1, 1961); published by Soviet Information Bureau, Maly Putlinkovsky Pereulok, Moscow, p. 3; cited hereafter as *Report by N. S. Khrushchev*.

but realistically, that "the triumph of Communism" was itself a "jolt" to the enemies of communism; victory was close enough to become a factor in its own achievement.[3]

A billion people are mustered under the banner of communist statism. The last stage of the communist plan is simple: displace the United States as the leading world power. That done, the other countries will be vulnerable victims of communist intimidation or seduction. But to conquer the United States in open battle still poses dangers for communism itself. A final period of alternate nuclear blackmail and peaceful coexistence is necessary in order to assure the conquest of the U.S.A.; this is the assignment given the Kremlin's masters of political warfare. The danger for America will grow as the Communists increasingly link bold political operations with the terror of thermonuclear power encased in ICBM warheads.

As the communist threat enters this decisive phase of the struggle the leaders of the free peoples react in various ways to the challenge. Some are swayed by the communist doctrine of the inevitability of the new world order. Others do not believe in the near victory of communism but think it is possible to coexist peacefully with the communist bloc; they believe that permanent coexistence is possible via agreement. Still other leaders recognize the reality of the communist danger; they believe that free countries must increase and coordinate their efforts to achieve defense on an effective scale.

Unfortunately, there are very few who recognize that beyond military defense, communism must be met on "the new frontier of war"—the battlefields of political warfare. Although nothing is altogether new, novel political operations have increased enormously in the last few decades. New weaponless "armies" have been organized for the purpose of conquest away from the fields of open, recognizable battle.

Though the Fascists, Nazis, and Japanese paced them for a while, the Communists have always led in these new techniques of mass manipulation. A little over forty years ago, the Communist Party had less than thirty thousand Russian members. It now commands an empire of one billion subjects and in addition directs the activities of millions of party members outside the boundaries of the Sino-Soviet bloc. Much of that empire was conquered in the aftermath of war, gathered less by marching armies than by political warfare. To "conquest from within" has been added the ex-

3. *Ibid.*, p. 44.

ternal power of Soviet military technology, itself growing at immense speed. If communist growth continues at the same rate, in forty years the earth can become a huge chain of communist prison-commonwealths, ready to fight each other with the capitalists out of the way. The Free World's billions will have been spent in vain if communist growth is not understood, met, and stopped.

The non-military weapons system of communism may be described in various terms: political warfare, "psywar," institutional conflict, psychosocial combat.[4] By any name, its primary purpose is to disorient and disarm the opposition. At the grass-roots level, political warfare seeks to induce the desire for surrender—in opposing peoples. At the strategic level, political warfare seeks to corrode the entire moral, political, and economic infrastructure of a nation, particularly by affecting governmental decisions.

"The new frontier of war" defines political warfare as a form of conflict between states in which a protagonist nation seeks to impose its will upon its opponents without the direct use of armed force. Political warfare combines the operations of diplomacy and propaganda frequently backed by the threat of military force. Political warfare aims to weaken, if not to destroy, the enemy by use of diplomatic proposals, economic sorties, propaganda and misinformation, provocation, intimidation, sabotage, terrorism, and by driving a wedge between the main enemy and his allies. The communist bloc, in waging political warfare, frames its total policy in such

4. Murray Dyer has proposed the term "political communication" in his book *The Weapon on the Wall*. This has the advantage of combining several existing terms, but it dissociates the mass-communications output of "political warfare" from the conspiratorial. It is precisely the linkage of these two items which gives Soviet doctrine much of its flexibility and penetrating power. The term "political warfare" itself is, of course, British in origin, having been developed as a cover label for interdepartmental activities during World War II; the term "psychological warfare," on the other hand, is American in derivation and seems to stem from a section in General Pershing's headquarters. Both terms have undergone repeated amendment and modification in the course of practical use. Reference to "political warfare" in the present book does not signify a direct connection with this label as it has been used in times past; it merely happens to be the phrase most current.

However, defined, "the purpose of political warfare may be to strengthen some competing groups or to weaken others; to organize forces whose activities can be directed toward desired ends; to support groups for as long as their objectives conform to one's own; and to help fully controlled and semi-controlled groups and personalities to reach positions of power and influence and eventually to take over the government. These methods can range all the way from simple manifestations of sympathy to the financing, organizing, and equipping of political movements, and from personal friendships between statesmen to the infiltration or capture of politically important agencies in the target country and the fomenting of mutinies, civil wars, and revolutions." Robert Strausz-Hupé and Stefan T. Possony, *International Relations*, p. 423.

a way as to obtain the by-products of political power from propaganda coups, orbital space rides, military deployments, economic pressures, or even from the political decisions of opposing governments. "Political warfare" as practiced by the Communists covers more than mass communications or the exploiting of weapons in order to undermine the will to resist. With them, all instruments of policy need constant and sustained correlation.

Political warfare has been defined as consisting of diplomacy, international commerce, information, and other civilian activities, governmental and non-governmental, as well as military action. But there is something lacking in this classic statement, for with the possible exception of military action, the definition fails to recognize the dynamism inherent in the intense hostility and competitiveness of the bipolar conflict. The higher frequency and intensity of present-day actions call for new descriptive labels. Let us therefore substitute new terms: for diplomacy, *political action;* for commerce, *economic warfare;* for information, *psychological warfare.* And let us extend the term "military action" beyond its traditional scope to include intervention to aid foreign governments and populations, and guerrilla and partisan warfare.

These definitions apply to both the Free World and the communist nations. We do not suggest, however, that in the Free World conventional diplomacy should no longer serve its customary function or that legitimate commerce has no further place in international affairs. Many of the traditional activities of interstate relations continue. But superimposed upon these, and often crucial to the struggle, is a pattern of conflict. Conflict concerns mainly the great protagonists, but it also involves those countries seeking "uncommitted" status, whose ultimate destiny will affect the global struggle of East and West.

It is not possible to visualize the interrelationship of the various instruments of political warfare unless one recognizes that their employment is guided by certain basic principles. In the first place, political warfare requires a durable ideological position. This should be as true for American political warfare as it is for the Soviet variety. Soviet ideology is complemented by an amazingly integrated philosophy of action, a combination which has, by and large, been successful. Ideology or faith and application or deeds—have been important in all religious and cultural history and are still important in the creedal struggles of today's world politics.

Communists find their own tenets persuasive. While individuals may doubt certain elements of the ideology from time to time (just as a Christian sectarian may question a particular article of his faith without putting his entire religion in question), the typical Communist finds the general Marxist-Leninist prescription convincing. This is not just because it proves successful; it is essential to the Communist to believe, since he cannot maintain the integrity of his personality or his methods without faith in the unprovable myths of Marxism. Among their beliefs is the view that imperialism, which they call "the last stage of capitalism," will reveal its inner contradictions and lead to its own collapse and the triumph of "socialism." It is the message which the Party carries to those who will listen and who may thereby be induced to become true converts. The communist doctrine of *imperialism* is both an end sought and, since it has persuasiveness, a means.[5]

In view of the fact that communist writings abound in political-warfare concepts, it is paradoxical that this doctrine is so rarely comprehended as a distinct entity. In Western Europe, where the intellectuals have long since become disenchanted with communism proper, clever political-warfare doctrine—using other symbols—has enabled the Communists to weaken European defense. These trends have seemed so natural and so inevitable that the catalytic role of the Communists has often been overlooked. The West has taken entirely too casual an approach to the evaluation of the weapons of political conflict with which the Communists are expertly armed and to which the free nations are often vulnerable.

A prerequisite for the formulation of an adequate Western strategy is an understanding of the communist political-warfare doctrine of conflict management. Reams have been written about communism as an ideology, as a political power structure, and as an international organization. Less attention, however, has been paid to the communist concept of concrete political operations.

Expediency and success, in communist working doctrine, are the only relevant measuring devices for techniques which are designed to contribute toward political conquest. Since whatever aids the Party is moral, if the political weapons which are selected for use in a specific situation produce

5. In this book, other somewhat technical terms relating to the communist movement, its operational techniques, and its sociological concepts will be used. Among them are: psychological warfare, propaganda, infiltration, subversion, Marxism, Leninism, Stalinism, the proletariat, the bourgeoisie, the intelligentsia, capitalism, socialism, communism, feudalism, liberalism, the Communist International, the Communist Party, and secret police.

victory, they are *a posteriori* vested with morality. Communist organization is geared for conflict. Force, either actual or threatened, is the cutting edge of communist operations. War and politics form a continuum; this permits a high degree of integration of military and political goals and methods.

Communists often try "peaceful" political tactics to win an engagement by non-military action. The violent and the non-violent, the military and the political, flow into and alternate with one another. The Communists understand expansion in political, organizational dimensions without overtly violating geographical frontiers. In the Weimar Republic and in the French Fourth Republic, for example, the communist parties entered into a tacit working agreement with extreme rightist elements to paralyze the parliamentary mechanism, thereby preparing the way for popular acceptance of a radical solution.

The Communists do not, of course, openly spell out their operational doctrines for the benefit of the West. Although they discuss strategic and tactical problems profusely, they have kept most of their central concepts esoteric. While some of the rudiments are taught in party schools to ordinary comrades, the extent of the disclosure generally depends on party rank, the full doctrine being reserved for the communist high command and its staffs.[6]

Communism embraces studied, calculated deception. In power acquisition, theory is the servant of strategy, and slogans are the executors of tactics. To understand communist literature and speeches, one must not be content with literal meanings of words but must seek instead to discover the context in which the Communists have used and heard them. The Kremlin, for example, has repeatedly declared that it is "against interference in the internal affairs of other nations" and at the same time is actively committed to interference within the internal affairs of every nation on earth. The Kremlin has also declared itself on many occasions to be the champion of peace, while its political-warfare armies (the communist parties) carry on their internal war of conquest around the clock.

---

6. In the narrow, technical sense of "occult"—namely, operating in the dark or from behind the cover of darkness—the communist movement is a worthy successor to the various fanatical or revolutionary movements which used occult religious or organizational vehicles in the European past. The Communists have reconciled the techniques of occultism and mystery with those of mass propaganda, achieving results which the Illuminati, the Masons, and others never accomplished in the politics of Continental Europe.

In short, the Communists interfere in the name of noninterference and carry on war in the name of peace.

The communist concept of "peaceful coexistence" is historically a code term for concealed aggression. As the Twentieth Congress of the Communist Party of the Soviet Union stated in 1956, "it does not at all follow from the fact that we stand for peaceful coexistence and economic competition with capitalism that the struggle against bourgeois ideology, against bourgeois survivals, can be relaxed. Our task is tirelessly to expose bourgeois ideology, reveal how inimical it is to the people, and show up its reactionary nature." The meaning of "peaceful" coexistence has been demonstrated in such local crises as Quemoy, the Middle East, Berlin, Cuba, Laos, and The Congo. Coexistence opens the road to disengagement and to new avenues of political penetration. Neither disengagement nor coexistence is a device to encourage an authentic relaxation of tension; they are, instead, methods of political deception.

A key element in the Soviet political-warfare arsenal is an enormous propaganda machine, a gigantic apparatus employing hundreds of thousands of paid or voluntary agents and costing more than a billion dollars annually. The Soviets owe much to this machine. In the future, their propaganda effort will be increasingly combined with nuclear blackmail, as it was during the Suez invasion and the Lebanon crisis and, more recently, in Cuba and Berlin. Although past atomic blackmail has been a huge bluff, future Soviet policy will have the megatonnage to back the bluff.

The Soviet propaganda effort is not merely external; by far the greater part of it is internal, directed to communist audiences, accusing the West of war preparations or encirclement of the U.S.S.R. or portraying the United States as an imperialistic power bent upon political and economic domination of her allies.

In the Soviet Union, responsibility for and control of the media of communication are concentrated in the hands of the Communist Party. The Soviet government, for example, does not include any agency which serves the functions of a ministry of public information. The organization which fulfills those functions in the U.S.S.R., as well as in international communism, is known as the Department of Propaganda and Agitation; it is a part of the Communist Party apparatus under the direct and immediate supervision of the Central Committee of the Party. Under the Party's direction, millions of dollars are spent yearly on jamming radio frequencies to prevent Western broadcasts from reaching Soviet citizens, and So-

viet, satellite, and Chinese Communist press and radio alike serve the
monotonous but hypnotic repetitions of the Party line to their captive audiences. When they cannot insure belief in their own communications, their
purposes are still well served if the audiences disbelieve all mass communications; this cuts off the threat of truth seeping in from the outside.

Efforts to mold or brainwash these captive audiences thus make use of a
large and capable apparatus which enjoys monopoly of communication.
Even when it cannot inculcate communist ideas, it can exclude effectively
information and ideas that might undermine the impact of the Party's
efforts. The internal message is simple: "Work harder, trust the Party, hate
those the Party defines as enemies of the regime within and without, and
believe in the future." The same message is repeated endlessly in a thousand contexts.[7]

Outside the territory it controls, communism fights in the "war zone"—
the camp of the West. All available tools are used to further its cause. The
campaign is controlled and directed by the presidia in Moscow and Peking.
Obviously, communism does not intend to play the contest by outmoded
bourgeois parliamentary rules. Establish power within a country, organize
the one-party state, crush all opposition, and rule—this is the way of modern totalitarianism.

Beyond propaganda and military effort, communist pressure may be
expected to expand even further in the next decade into the economic
and diplomatic fields. Khrushchev, in embracing neutral countries, particularly in Asia, Africa, and the Middle East, has reversed a basic tenet of
the Marxian dialectic. The acceptance into the "camp of peace" of friendly
neutrals marks a new phase of the offensive launched at the 1955 Bandung
Conference. Economic penetration into traditional Western markets,

7. The Communists' capacity to brainwash their own subjects through internal indoctrination and propaganda and to change the minds of people outside their control
through manipulation of mass communications owes much to the studies made by I. P.
Pavlov and published in a book entitled *Conditioned Reflexes*, London: Oxford University Press, Humphrey Milford, 1927. For a critical analysis of this problem, see *Battle
for the Mind*, by William Sargant, who has succinctly stated the importance of brainwashing and over-all communist political warfare: "Politicians, priests and psychiatrists
often face the same problem: how to find the most rapid and permanent means of
changing a man's beliefs. . . . [There is] enormous importance now attaching to the
problem—because of an ideological struggle that seems fated to decide the course of
civilization for centuries to come.

"Great Britain and the U.S.A. therefore find themselves at last obliged to study seriously
those specialized forms of neuro-physiological research which have been cultivated with
such intensity by the Russians since the Revolution, and have helped them to perfect
the methods now popularly known as 'brainwashing' or 'thought control.' "

coupled with hints and promises of vastly increased trade—seductive to some Western businessmen—is a new capability in the Soviet roster, made possible by increased Soviet production and by the accumulation of the gigantic Soviet gold hoard. Gold is not even used for dentistry in their socialist economy; thus many billion rubles' worth of uncommitted bullion gives Soviet economic maneuvers both range and impact capacity. Promises of economic aid, with no obvious strings attached and no questions asked, concentrated in crucial areas rather than spread over the globe, have been effective.

Marxism-Leninism imposes certain restrictive long-range strategic goals on communist-bloc foreign policy, but the tactical methods are varied and diversified. The communist system of conflict management gives a choice of alternatives, constantly shifting fields of battle, the utilization of military and non-military weapons systems, subversion, propaganda, and sustained pressure. The communist system of conflict provides that, if political warfare cannot deliver by itself, military war is an accepted alternative. Lenin's views of "just" and "unjust" wars, reaffirmed by Khrushchev, rationalize communist military attack on an "inferior" social system as defense and not aggression. Communist political warfare is based on the exploitation of sociological contrasts. It is pragmatically sociological in approach. All groups are considered for vulnerability; the Communists could not possibly care less about "left" and "right" as we know them.[8]

The Communist Party organization and its tactical practices are conducive to a high degree of maneuverability: The Communists manage to take advantage of any opening in the defenses of the target society, to penetrate and subvert it. The Trojan horse practice of operating under false labels has become general. It gives the Communists an easy entry into the enemy camp.

It is conceivable that in time political warfare, as the new frontier of war, will completely replace military warfare between nations and become the primary weapon in international struggles for power. It is also likely that the political warfare of the future will not be based on the philosoph-

---

8. The reader, whether liberal, conservative, or socialist, should not feel offended when it is pointed out how the Communists exploit liberal "idealism," the "rigidities" of conservatism, or the "contradictions" of parliamentary socialism. It is all in the course of a day's work in communist political warfare. This book, in tracking down communist techniques, will follow the Communists in their search for Western vulnerabilities; this does not mean that it seeks to stigmatize one group as being more vulnerable than another.

ical rhetoric of today. The class warfare source of communist ideological motivation is probably too narrow to serve much longer as a base for conflict strategy. Man may abandon general military warfare, for its growing destructiveness may make it altogether irrational; but, unless man completely abandons conflict, he will engage in variations of political warfare. For the present, military and political warfare are likely to exist side by side. It is probable that those most capable of their combined use will achieve victory.

In the last decade there has appeared a vast amount of critical literature analyzing one or another aspect of communist movements. What is still needed, however, is an analysis of communist political warfare. *The New Frontier of War* is an effort to meet this need.

PART ONE

The Communist Machine

THE COMMUNIST MACHINE

THE CONFLICT MANAGEMENT OF COMMUNIST POLITICAL WAR-
fare long ago established certain ground rules: (1) there must be an over-all
theory for orientation, setting goals and establishing guide lines; (2) there
must be an organization, both adequate and capable, to work for the realization of these goals; and (3) there must be operational methods suited
to the purpose.

In the context of political warfare, a nation is not a monolithic abstrac-
tion represented only by its governmental heads. It is a myriad of social,
economic and political subgroupings, each with its own part in the conflict
of the epoch and each influencing, and being influenced by, the great
sociopolitical trends and decisions. Today's struggle is taking place in
all corners of the earth. It involves use of the instruments of power available to a state—diplomacy, psychological warfare, and economic warfare—
to influence directly or indirectly the components of the adversary's
politico-social fabric and through them to influence the policies and debil-
itate the power of the adversary nation. Political warfare also shapes
the hostile nation's "intelligence," its picture of the meaning of events, and
hence brackets the decision-making process.

The "cold war," which is really pure political warfare, results from the
expansionist techniques which the U.S.S.R. initiated and with which the
United States has been more and more compelled to cope.

Communists achieve successes through organizational skills welded to a
practical concept of power accumulation. The Communist will join in any
fight, support any cause which gives him the chance of getting at the levers
of power. Khrushchev told us in his revealing January, 1961, speech that
"Communists are revolutionaries" and that it would be a bad thing if they
failed to spot newly arising opportunities or to find new ways and means
leading most surely to the realization of their set goal.[1]

1. *Report by N. S. Krushchev*, p. 32.

This helpful information was preceded by advice drawn from Lenin and incorporated in the statement of the eighty-one Marxist-Leninist parties, which called "for the maximum utilization of the revolutionary possibilities of the various classes and social strata and for drawing all allies, no matter if inconsistent, shaky and unstable, into the struggle against imperialism."[2]

With such marching orders the Communist may find himself shoulder to shoulder with pacifists, race minorities, nationalists, peasants or proletarians, right-wing socialists or left-wing socialists, just as, at the national level, he can tolerate an alliance with bourgeois democracies or with rightist dictators. Thus does he seek to win, step by step, not just opinions and popular support, but the control of organizations beyond his own party, its front groups, and captive organizations.

The communist machine did not spring full born from the mind of Lenin in a single night. But its genesis influences directly the operational pattern of communist political warfare. The first three chapters of Part One trace this evolution: The initial party structure has been modified by successive communist dictators, and the recruiting base has been opportunistically broadened so that all but the most hard-bitten capitalists can be enticed into the movement. Stalin's reign transformed the movement from an initially idealistic conspiracy into a monolithic party, easily copied by the Fascists and Nazis, in which members are motivated primarily by the urge to power. Success attracts success. Communist party leaders throughout the Free World seek constantly to master the many roads that lead the true believer to power.

Part One examines the sociological character of communist political warfare demands and the contrast between propaganda and agitation; the nature of the ideological attack on non-communist symbols and the range of social targets considered to be accessible to communist penetration.

Finally, Part One surveys the role of the Communist state, as contrasted to the world-wide network of parties, in political warfare operations, with emphasis on the Soviet Union. The principal kinds of Soviet operations are analyzed, the role of military power and its companion—disarmament—is then set forth preliminary to describing post-Stalin organizational innovations in what the Communists call "the conflict of systems."

2. *Ibid.*

CHAPTER I

THE COMMUNIST PARTY STRUCTURE AND RECRUITING BASE

COMMUNIST POLITICAL WARFARE IS HIGHLY DEPENDENT UPON the party system of organization. The recruiting base of the Party is in turn sensitive to shifts in communist strategic doctrine.

The special role of the Party as a functioning mechanism is not well understood in the West. The Party, whatever it is, is not a "party" in the sense outlined by Paul Ostrogorski about 1900 in his classic *La Democratie et l'Organization de la Partie Politique*. The Communists organize a party to destroy all other parties, not a fraction to contend with other fractions within the limits of a genuine democracy. In this sense, the Hitlerites were more brutal and more honest than the Communists in their nomenclature when they insisted that their *Partei* was not really a *Partei* but a *Bewegung*—a "movement" which would sweep all other movements before it. Neither the economic ideas attached to the theory of communism nor the statist realities applied by communist governments in power matter as much as the dynamism of their self-styled "party." The communist organization and operation of the "party" is the most revolutionary innovation which political technology has seen since Machiavelli. It is the "party" which has transformed communism from an occult parlor game of intellectuals into a chain of empires bigger and fiercer than anything ever erected by Genghis Khan.

The communist "party" develops in two distinctive stages. It changes like those insects which metamorphose as they leave the larval stage. Before gaining power, the Party is a power-seeking mechanism of considerable versatility and strength. The moment it obtains power, it becomes a policing mechanism without parallel in the modern world. There is an organic

3

connection between communist party structure and methods prior to and after seizure of power.

We turn now to the Communist Party of the U.S.S.R., which still plays the commanding role in the world movement.

Mao Tse-tung stated in late 1957: "Our Socialist camp should have a leader, and this is the Soviet Union. The enemy also has a leader, and this is America. If there is no leader, the strength will be weakened."[1] Khrushchev made the same point more obliquely:

> It should be noted that the delegation of the Communist Party of the Soviet Union stated at the meeting [November, 1960 meeting in Moscow of eighty-one Marxist-Leninist parties] its point of view that the Soviet Union stands at the head of the Socialist camp and the C.P.S.U. at the head of the Communist movement. . . . There has always been complete equality and solidarity of all the Communist and Workers' Parties. . . . The Communist party of the Soviet Union does not lead other parties. There are no "superior" and "subordinate" parties in the Communist Movement.[2]

After this tribute to equality, Khrushchev continued: "The Communist Party of the Soviet Union has always been the universally recognized vanguard of the world Communist movement."[3] In order that all parties can keep in step with the vanguard:

> We need to set our watches, so that our mighty army should keep in step and march confidently towards Communism. Putting it figuratively, Marxism-Leninism, the jointly prepared documents of international Communist meetings, are our time-piece.
>
> Now that all the Communist and Workers' Parties have adopted unanimous decisions at the Meeting, each Party will strictly and undeviatingly abide by these decisions in everything it does. . . .
>
> The unity of every Communist Party, the unity of all the Communist Parties is what makes up *the integral world Communist movement*, which is aimed at achieving our common goal—victory of Communism throughout the world.[4]

It is noteworthy that the United States Supreme Court, in an epochal 5 to 4 decision on June 5, 1961, likewise concluded that the Communist

1. Doak Barnett, *Communist China and Asia*, pp. 361-2. From a speech by Mao Tse-tung, November 17, 1957, reported by New China News Agency.

2. *Report by N. S. Khrushchev*, p. 46. This assertion was somewhat tarnished by Khrushchev reading the Albanian Party leaders out of the movement at the 22nd Party Congress held in Moscow in October 1961.

3. *Ibid.*, p. 41.

4. *Ibid.*, p. 43; italics added.

Party, U.S.A., was part of "the integral World Communist Movement" and noted, accordingly, that it would have to register as an agent of a foreign power.

The Communist Party represents a complete departure from the political organizations developed in democracies. It comprises a new system, a political elite which aims at total power over society. It seeks not to compete with other parties but to do away with them. The Communist Party's organizational structure, weapons system, and operational methods are constructed to serve that purpose. The communist one-party state formed after the seizure of power is foreshadowed in the organization, structure, and methods of any communist party seeking power.[5]

Transformations in the structure and strategy of the vanguard Communist Party of the Soviet Union inevitably influence the conduct of communist political warfare, both inside and outside the communist orbit. Analysis of communist political warfare must therefore begin with the present party machine.

Toward the second half of the nineteenth century, the communist-type political party began to emerge. Its essential principles were embodied in the *Communist Manifesto,* authored by Karl Marx and Friedrich Engels. The *Manifesto* advocated the abolition of the existing free democratic society in favor of one in which all property would be owned by the state. The state would become a "dictatorship of the working class," pending transformation into a new form of society. In view of the cultural backwardness of the working class, an elite party would be needed to lead them toward that goal.

It is significant that the architects of the totalitarian-type organization, of which the Communist Party is now pre-eminent, were all former Socialists.[6] Most noteworthy were Nicolai Lenin and his associates, former Socialist Benito Mussolini of Italy, and, later, Hitler and others who, although not Socialists, used or imitated the pattern set by Lenin.

Lenin's concept of a party first appeared in 1902 in a pamphlet entitled *What Is to Be Done?* Subsequently he called for a party of "professional revolutionaries" who were to devote their lives to the conquest of power:

5. For analysis of the Communist Party's evolution and structure, see William R. Kintner, *The Front is Everywhere.*

6. The only exceptions to this are the Kuomintang leaders of China, who followed their chief, Dr. Sun Yat-sen, in giving their party the complete Soviet apparatus in 1924 without undoing its deeply Chinese principles and character.

a party centrally directed and highly disciplined; a party of "democratic centralism." In time, the democracy faded and only the centralism remained.

Lenin incorporated into his party program some of the anarcho-syndicalist concepts of the use of labor unions for revolutionary purposes. Lenin conceived the idea, not envisaged by Marx, of an alliance with the small-property element, the peasants, without which seizure of power in Russia would have been impossible. Outside these modifications in organization and strategy, Lenin adhered in the main to Marx's socialist concepts of a party based on the working class. Out of the womb of Marx's socialist movement was born a new party which departed more and more from the earlier democratic tendencies of the Western European socialist movement.

The seed of totalitarianism was present in Marx's theories of a class dictatorship and a class party, but until Lenin, two paths of development were still possible: one toward limited democracy and the other toward the one-party state, or totalitarianism. Lenin took the latter path.

Lenin's party resembled the conventional democratic parties in only one respect: it put up candidates during parliamentary-election campaigns. But even that was done largely for the purpose of propaganda and agitation, and if any of its candidates were elected and took the oath of office, they were to sabotage the parliamentary system, not serve it. In every other respect, Lenin's party—and later Stalin's—was as different from democratic parties as fire is from water.

Lenin's party came into power as a result of the collapse of the Czarist monarchy in World War I. Lenin had had little to do with the actual overthrow of the Czars, but, with the aid of Imperial Germany, he helped to destroy the democratic government which succeeded it. Among the first acts of Lenin's Bolshevik Party was the forcible dissolution of the newly elected Constituent Assembly, the only freely elected parliament in the entire history of Russia.

According to Trotsky and others, Lenin's supposed goal was the birth of a superior democracy, a birth at which his party's dictatorship was to serve as midwife. In reality, the Russians had real democracy stolen from under their noses by talk of an allegedly superior new democracy—an ingenious ideological hoax. This ideological confidence game was repeated years later in Czechoslovakia, China, and Cuba with the same totalitarian results. It appears, therefore, that just as individual rights lead to democracy, so party dictatorship, which is a denial of those rights, leads to totalitarianism.

A century of "Marxist" propaganda has created the impression that communist doctrine—and hence strategy—is, and was, always the same. It is quite true that Marx's principal writings still provide the basic philosophy of dialectical materialism. Karl Marx, however, conceived of the socialist revolution only in highly industrialized countries where the working class was in a majority. Lenin, on the other hand, conceived of the possibility of a "socialist-led" revolution in a country like Russia, where the factory working class was a small minority compared to the peasants. He did this by devising a theory which he called the "Bourgeois Democratic Revolution carried out by the Proletariat," a theory which required a strategy entirely different from that envisioned by Marx, although the ultimate goal was the same: political power. Lenin's theory about the metamorphosis of the bourgeois revolution into a proletarian revolution is dealt with in his thesis on "Two Tactics," in which he forges the bourgeois democratic revolution and the socialist revolution as two links in one chain. In Lenin's words:

The course of the revolution has confirmed our view. First of all, the proletariat marched with the peasantry as a whole; against the monarchy, against the landlords, against the vestiges of medievalism (and up to this point the revolution was still bourgeois, was still bourgeois democratic). Then the proletariat marched with the poorer peasants, with the semiproletarians, with the exploited; against Capitalism, and against its embodiment in the countryside, the Kulaks, the speculators so that now the revolution became a socialist revolution.[7]

This theory made possible the communist alliance of the worker with the peasants. Marx saw the peasants only as property owners to be expropriated. Lenin offered them land to induce them to back his ride to power, only to take it away from them, in stages, later on.

Lenin thus saw two types of revolution: the socialist revolution in the industrialized West and the bourgeois democratic revolution in more agrarian societies. As a Hegelian, he conceived of revolution's thesis and antithesis as being led and manipulated by the same organization: the Communist Party. By this theoretical twist, Lenin subsequently linked, in a new synthesis, the revolutionary movement in the then quiescent colonies with the socialist revolutionary movement in the West.

Lenin's concept of the power of the Communist Party as a professional, disciplined organization also varied considerably from the views held by Marx. During his stay in England in the mid-nineteenth century, Karl Marx developed a rather high opinion of the bourgeoisie as a ruling class.

7. Nicolai Lenin, *Collected Works* (Russian edition), Vol. XV, pp. 508-509.

Lenin, on the other hand, considered the bourgeoisie to be poor in social vision and cohesive leadership. He believed that they were a class of people forever feuding for individual gain and, consequently, that a highly disciplined party of agitators and tacticians could outmaneuver the bourgeoisie.

Stalin Ousts Trotsky and Revises Lenin

Karl Marx and Friedrich Engels, as "prophets" and founders of the communist movement, did not have to concern themselves with problems of a working socialist society. They merely conceived a theory opposing existing society. There was little in their writings, except vague speculation, regarding the role of the proletariat after the seizure of power.

Lenin and Trotsky were forced to reinterpret Marx in order to rule in Russia. Lenin, however, lived only long enough to guide his political-warfare machine through the civil war and to preside over the initial stages of the new Soviet government. It was left to Stalin, after he eliminated Trotsky, to blaze the trail to be followed by communism in power. It took Stalin seven years (1923–1930) to become the pivot in the Soviet power machine and another eight years to become its absolute ruler.[8] But his style of political warfare became manifest very soon.

In the realm of foreign affairs, Stalin soon showed himself to be an "Asia" man, concentrating his main attention on the Chinese Communist Party. As early as 1928, the emphasis there was switched from the proletariat to the peasantry as "the axis of the colonial revolution." This extended Lenin's wide departure from Marxism, and, although Mao is generally credited with the shift from the urban proletariat in China, the switch to the peasants as "the axis of the colonial revolution" was adopted at the Sixth Congress of the Comintern (1928), held in Moscow. The idea of Mao's alleged independence from Stalin's Comintern line is dubious.[9]

8. Khrushchev, a generation later, required the same period of time to consolidate his position.

9. "A Mao Tse-tung who viewed entrenchment in the countryside as a permanent principle and not as a temporary strategic device would be no deviant Communist, but merely a fool. He would be like the man who always prefers a stick to a gun, because once in the woods he had only a stick to fight with.

"But Mao is no fool. He and his followers never considered themselves leaders of a peasant party [Lattimore claimed that during the ten years preceding the Sino-Japanese War, the Chinese Communists, 'cut off from cities and urban workers, had become a peasant party.'], whose actions were motivated, and limited, by the interests of the villages. When the conditions of the civil war forced the Chinese Communists to operate in the countryside, they always expected to return to the cities. And when they seized the cities, they did exactly what the Bolsheviks had done after the October revolution." Karl A. Wittfogel, *Oriental Despotism*, p. 442.

The two may not always have seen eye to eye, but Stalin was the main architect of the design for the "colonial[10] revolution," for which China was to be the foundation. His reputed indifference to Mao during the crucial post-World War II period will be discussed in a separate chapter. Stalin fully supported the Chinese Communist Party and even founded a large college, Sun Yat-sen University in Moscow, for its benefit.

Asia was considered by Stalin as the "soft underbelly" of world capitalism. Because of this strategic orientation, Stalin sabotaged the German Communist Party when it reached its showdown with Hitler. Long before the advent of Hitler, Stalin feared the politically sophisticated European proletariat, which could be influenced more easily by rival socialist parties and trade-union movements than by the Communists. In Asia there was no such competition. To build the kind of power machine he sought— in and out of Russia—Stalin needed Asians more than Europeans.

More important to Stalin than these considerations, however, were his plans for Russia itself and its role in world revolution. Bear in mind that the men around Lenin expected to see the world revolution occur in their own time. Stalin pushed the development of Russia first and China second, with everybody outside this central orbit to be used as political cannon fodder. Trotsky—Stalin's rival for Lenin's mantle—had a different view of the world revolutionary situation and a more urgent sense of timing with regard to when the revolution must be carried out abroad. In their intramural discussions, in spite of major conceptual differences, both Trotsky and Stalin agreed that Russia had to be strengthened immensely, both industrially and militarily—that she must march at a fast pace through a period of "primary capital accumulation." Stalin and Trotsky split, however, over who was to carry the main burden of that accumulation and the pace of the forced march.

At the time these discussions were held, Russia, primarily a peasant country, was worn out by civil war. Her industries were completely ruined. The idea of a campaign to make such a country into a major industrial and military power in one lifetime seemed outright fantasy. There is no doubt that Trotsky's more cautious views were much closer to the departed Lenin's views than were those of Stalin. The bolder plans of the latter were a product of overwhelming ambition and barbaric ignorance.

The impression, however, that Stalin won these decisions on the merits

10. The Communists use this term in referring to underdeveloped countries not yet under communist control.

of objective, ideological discussion is a false one. This does not mean that all discussions of ideology are merely a "veneer" in Russia or that idealism, as well as cynicism, does not enter into communist decisions. But ideology is not the sole motivation of communist leaders, at least not of such men as Stalin and Khrushchev.

The struggle for power between Stalin and Trotsky was cloaked as an ideological battle between "socialism in one country," Stalin's sloganized formula, and world revolution as the precondition to socialism in any country, which, according to the Soviet press, was Trotsky's formula. Stalin's faction controlled the press, and Stalin, a pupil of Lenin no matter how much he departed from his master, always quoted Lenin's "scriptures" in defense of his actions. The management of this "discussion" resulted in a verbal lynching of Trotsky, who was then still a member of the Central Committee of the Soviet Communist Party. It revealed much of Stalin's future method of political deception, both at home and abroad.

Stalin's War for Internal Power

British capitalism has been described by many socialist writers as the original sin. Yet in comparison to what Stalin did after 1928 in the name of "building socialism," Britain's period of primary capital accumulation was a humanitarian venture.

The problem of primary capital accumulation was discussed in Moscow in 1928, but Stalin's plan for tackling this problem in Russia was not fully known, even within his immediate entourage. Now, many years later, it has become possible to reconstruct Stalin's design.

Primary capital accumulation for the purpose and at the pace desired by Stalin could be accomplished in only one way: force, more force, and still more force. Propaganda appealing for sacrifice, no matter how clever and intense, could not do the job. Force had to be used against a working class and a peasantry who considered themselves the victors in the civil war and who had been taught to regard themselves—the proletariat in particular—as the ruling class.

Stalin's plan called for *a war against the Russian peasants*, reducing them to the status of serfs of the state. The peasants were to be the primary victims of the process of capital accumulation, a group of "inner colonials"[11] exploited by the new ruling class. They were selected because they possessed the only wealth that could be exported in exchange for Western

11. Trotsky's term.

technology. During this phase of the plan, the proletariat was to be mobilized psychologically against the peasants, the alliance between the workers and the peasants, the basis of Lenin's formula for the seizure of power, irrevocably sundered.

This new civil war, conducted by Stalin, had an enormous impact on Russia. It claimed millions of victims in death, and millions more filled Stalin's slave-labor camps. The food supplies for the cities dried up, necessitating a rigid system of food rationing. Even in the privileged Lenin College, the rations were reduced. The conflict shook the Party to its foundations, but Stalin held his course. The war against the peasants also gave Stalin the opportunity to build up his favorite instrument, the secret political police, particularly its military branch. After the backbone of the peasant resistance had been broken in 1935, he was ready to turn on the working class itself.

Primary accumulation at Stalin's rate could not be realized without a type of exploitation which reduced the living conditions of the working population to the bare subsistence level. Stalin's forced march toward industrialization required the physical means to command large forces of cheap labor. Lenin's party, which Stalin inherited, could not be used to carry on a sustained war against the working class whose embodiment and "historical" representative it claimed to be. Lenin's party, therefore, had to be superseded by another organ, the secret and militarized political police which Stalin had built up for his war against the peasants. Secret police, of course, were a heritage from Imperial Russia, but Stalin employed this instrument far more ruthlessly than any Czar.

The purge of the Party, the initial phase of the war against the working class, was carried out by the political police. By 1936, this phase was in full swing, with thousands of executions and hundreds of thousands of arrests. By 1938, when the terror had come to an end, most of the old communist elite, who had carried through the civil war and set up the Soviet government, were either dead or in slave-labor camps. Resistance had been broken on this front, too, and Stalin and his political police had the field to themselves. He had won the war against his own people.

A new war, this time against the proletariat, began in 1938 with a decree reducing the Soviet labor unions to complete servility to the state, abolishing even the toothless bargaining status that they had retained until then. Liberty of movement from plant to plant and from town to town was abolished. The statutes on sabotage were broadened and redefined. Even

late arrival for work was subject to heavy penalties, including imprisonment.

By these multiple campaigns against the peasants, the Party, and the
workers, Lenin's party was destroyed, although its form was maintained.
Once again this was done in the name of Lenin and in the name of the
Party. Stalin attacked his enemies in the name of their own ideological
gods. His political maneuvering was, at least on the surface, in consonance
with communist scriptures. While his victims were confused and disori-
ented, he struck.

A New Soviet Class Structure

In consequence of these internal developments, a new social stratification
emerged in Soviet society. The present class structure consists of (1) the
political elite (Communist Party); (2) the management class; (3) the workers (proletariat); (4) the collectivized peasants; and (5) forced laborers.
Each of these major strata is further divided into substrata, such as skilled
workers, semiskilled, unskilled, etc. The new ruling class is new in every
respect—new titles, new privileges, large salaries, and increased authority
over the underdog. The characteristics of the new class have been succinctly
described by Milovan Djilas, former leading theoretician of the Yugo-
slavian Communist Party:

> The theory that contemporary communism is a type of modern totali-
> tarianism is not only the most widespread, but also the most accurate. How-
> ever, an actual understanding of the term "modern totalitarianism" where
> communism is being discussed is not so widespread.
>   Contemporary communism is that type of totalitarianism which consists
> of three basic factors for controlling the people. The first is power; the
> second, ownership; the third, ideology. They are monopolized by the one
> and only political party, or—according to my previous explanation and
> terminology—by a class; and, at present, by the oligarchy of that party or
> of that class. No totalitarian system in history, not even a contemporary
> one—with the exception of communism—has succeeded in incorporating
> simultaneously all these factors for controlling the people to this degree.[12]

Internal Soviet developments have been briefly reviewed here because
of their relationship to external political warfare. Marxist-Leninist psychological warfare, as we have shown, first concentrated on winning over
the factory workers, then the peasants, then the intelligentsia. The Communists have a much broader appeal now that they no longer use just the

12. Milovan Djilas, *The New Class*, pp. 166-7.

proletariat or the peasants. And despite the fact that the peasants and factory workers inside the communist empire are far down the social scale, the Communists still manage to lure workers and peasants in many countries into their fold.

Summary

Communist political warfare was and is basically social in its content; it aims at the liquidation of all social relations based on private property. The instrument through which that warfare is carried on is the Communist Party, its fronts, and captive organizations. Outside these three relatively stable factors, however, much has changed. Communist political warfare is no longer rooted or based on only one class, namely the working class, but is now multiclass, with growing emphasis on the managerial group. And communist political warfare now probes far more thoroughly than ever before for weaknesses among the bourgeoisie proper, not only in the dependent and semi-independent nations, but also in the advanced industrial countries.

To the extent that the regime in Russia itself has departed from its previous class basis, communist political warfare has been freed of its former constraints. To be sure, outside its own state domain it still exploits the illusions and grievances of the masses of both West and East for its own purposes, but it is not bound by any of the old class loyalties and is free to roam the whole social field. This new opportunism, a major departure from Marxism, and even Leninism, is one of the principal legacies Stalin left to communism.

Despite Khrushchev's campaign posthumously to degrade Stalin, culminating with the removal of his body from the mausoleum shrine in Moscow's Red Square, the indispensable role which Stalin played both in political warfare and in laying the foundation of Soviet industrial and military power should not be ignored.

CHAPTER II

PARTY POWER IN RUSSIA

THE PROCESS BY WHICH THE COMMUNIST PARTY FIRST MONOPO-
lized power in Russia and then throughout the vast lands now called
the Soviet Union has been followed with local adaptation everywhere the
Communists have seized control. It divides into three phases: political domination through police power, economic domination by expropriation of
the property-owning classes, and liquidation of bourgeois ideology, particularly those parts pertaining to the theoretical rights of the individual.

In the Soviet Union,[1] complete political domination by the Communist
Party had been achieved as early as 1923; full economic control, however,
was not reached until the expropriation of the peasants more than ten
years later. The liquidation of the remnants of bourgeois ideology, better

---

1. It is important to recognize that the Soviet Union itself is not a monolithic structure
but an enforced federation dominated by the Russian element—in turn dominated by
the Communist Party. The Russian ethnic element in the U.S.S.R. comprises little more
than half of the total population. In reality, according to Edward Crankshaw, "Russia
is also one of the great colonial powers; and, unlike Britain or France, Russia has never
given up an inch of the territory she has taken from small nations. The conquest of
Siberia proceeded almost unnoticed by the outside world: the Russians, over the centuries,
moved slowly east until they got to the Pacific. But it was a conquest nonetheless,
involving innumerable small wars and the subjugation and reduction of innumerable
Asiatic tribes and nationalities. . . . The grandfathers of the present-day inhabitants
of Uzbekistan, Kazakhstan, Turkmenia, Khirgizia, to say nothing of the Georgians and
the Azerbaidjans, and Armenians of the Caucasus, did not submit themselves to Moscow
of their own free will. . . . When the Revolution came the process in many cases had to
be repeated. With the collapse of central authority, there was an empire-wide move
toward separatism. This included not only the Asiatic nationalities, but also the Ukrainians and the peoples of the little Baltic nationalities. Of all these, only the last managed
to preserve their separate identities—until they were reoccupied once more by the
Russians in 1940. For the rest there was no hope at all, though the proud and high-
spirited Georgians gave the Russians a grueling time before they finally surrendered to
their great compatriot Stalin." From the *London Observer*, 1956.

defined as conditioning men not to believe in their own rights, has not yet
been fully achieved and is not likely to be.

Communist political warfare operates simultaneously against non-communist countries and the people in countries under its domination. In
communist-controlled states, a continuous war of consolidation is carried
on by the communist hierarchy. Outside the Sino-Soviet bloc the war is
waged by the legal or illegal communist parties in opposition to existing
governments, with the tacit backing of communist states. Both fronts are
under the same command. During the Stalin era, the concentration of
effort was mainly on the internal Soviet front, but this emphasis gradually
shifted after World War II.

Communist warfare on the "internal" front influences actions on the
"external" front. Since warfare against the people in a country in which
the Communists have seized power has affected both the style and content
of communist political warfare abroad, a brief recapitulation is in order
here.

The Impact of Stalin

Stalin conceived the war on the internal front, and despite de-Stalinization his impact on the Communist Party is unmistakable.[2] The measures
which played the biggest role in the transformation of the Party during the
reign of Stalin were: (1) the liquidation of open discussion within the
Party; (2) the building up of the secret police; (3) the purging of the
Party; and (4) innovations concerning the admission of new members.

Stalin was not a theorist. He participated in theoretical discussions only
to the extent necessary to safeguard his manipulations for control of the
party apparatus. Stalin conceived clearly that in a one-party regime, he who
controls the apparatus of that party will eventually control all power.

The concentration of more and more power in the hands of Stalin's
bureaucratic apparatus began with the usurpation of control in the name
of the Central Committee of the Party, then in the name of the Politburo,
then in the name of the Secretariat and the Organization Department of
the Party. Internal democracy in the Party disappeared in proportion to
the concentration of power in Stalin's hands. Everything took place under
the façade of the Party's constitution and under the aegis of the Central

2. "To expect [therefore] a fundamental mellowing in the political system of the
U.S.S.R. is to show a great misunderstanding of the nature of totalitarianism and to
engage in a dangerous underestimation of the compelling logic of totalitarian rule."
Zbigniew K. Brzezinski, *The Permanent Purge*, p. 173.

Committee, which met less and less frequently as the years rolled on. When it did meet, it was merely to approve Stalin's actions. Party conventions, too, became rare and were held only to approve what Stalin already had done.

Stalin was notorious for his lack of faith in individuals. He built up the secret police as an enforcement agency to insure his control over the Party. Like Hitler's Gestapo, the secret police were a select militarized, highly trained force entirely obedient to Stalin as General Secretary of the Party. The secret police were originally used against the "class enemy," but continued to grow and flourish long after the "class enemy" had been crushed. Eventually they served to subjugate the Party itself. The secret police had clandestine units everywhere: in the factories, on the railroads, in the armed forces, even at party headquarters. The slave-labor camps were entirely their domain, as was the guarding of the frontiers.

Even with the party apparatus and the police in his hands, Stalin did not feel entirely secure. The armed forces were a constant worry. With good reason, Stalin assumed that the servicemen conscripted from among the people bore to him and his regime the same hatred as the people themselves. Stalin could not dispense with the army, navy, and air force, but he could subject them to political control by creating the political administration which tied together the party cells within the armed forces and installed political commissars as watchdogs over the officers and men. As a final precaution, the armed forces were deprived of control over munitions, which were put under custody of the military units of the state police. Stalin thus made certain that no successful revolt against him could be staged by the armed forces.

By the time Stalin was through reorganizing, he controlled three parallel power apparatuses: the Party, the police, and the armed forces. The heads of each group and its subdivisions were chosen by Stalin. This, in the main, is the pattern of domination subsequently followed by the leaders of all communist parties after the seizure of power.

The Shift to Power

Various communist parties have used several means of seizing political control. But whatever method is employed, each communist party is so constructed that it is easily converted into an apparatus of power.

The Central Committee, with slight rearrangement, becomes the gov-

ernment. The departments of the Party, with equally slight rearrangement, become the administrative arms which exercise the power of government. The trade-union department and its fractions seize the labor
unions and become the "Federation of Labor," the youth department organizes all youth, and the cultural department and its fractions seize the
educational system.

The secret nuclei in the armed forces form the "commandos" or combat
forces which spearhead the physical seizure of power and the reorganization of the armed forces into a "People's Red Army." The control commission becomes the political police, charged with the immobilization or
extermination of actual or potential opposition.

The agitation and propaganda department seize control over all newspapers and radio and TV stations, while the organization department and
its cadre division supervise the staffing of these operations. If the Party
has united front allies during the initial stages of the seizure of power,
prior to consolidation, some of the less strategic posts may be distributed
among these allies.

If the seizure of power is more gradual, by infiltration into the government and into non-communist political parties, "allies" may have to be
tolerated initially in some important posts. But the long-range purpose of
garnering all power into the Party's hands remains, and the Party is designed to be the framework upon which to build totalitarian state power.

The seizure is a physical process in which (1) all elements deemed hostile
are liquidated; (2) all organizations, governmental or private, are taken
over by force so that competing political parties and other organizations
considered useless for the purposes of the new party-state are disbanded
and their leaders arrested;[3] (3) a completely new police system is created,
staffed, and commanded entirely by Communists and the bearing of arms
becomes a monopoly of the Communists, except for the armed forces, which
are thoroughly reorganized to assure their loyalty to the Party; and (4) all
major enterprises and land and subsoil resources are formally declared
nationalized and the wealthier bourgeoisie rapidly expropriated.

During the first phase, only people considered actively hostile are arrested or executed. Those allied with or neutral toward the Communist

3. In communist "multiparty" states, such as East Germany or mainland China, minor
parties are compelled to survive and to operate on terms dictated by the Communists and
with programs approved by the communist center as being suitable to their inferior status.

Party are exploited or left to be dealt with later. This is particularly true
when the Communist Party lacks influence and numbers and is temporarily dependent on allies, as during the first year in Castro's Cuba.

Judicial processes are either dispensed with during this period or are
replaced by revolutionary justice, which relies upon kangaroo courts comparable to drumhead courts-martial.

Of the three major phases of the communist revolution, the political
phase is the easiest. During it, the accumulated wealth and property of the
bourgeoisie and other enemies are taken over, with the party members, collectively and individually, becoming the principal beneficiaries. Allies, if
any, obtain some of the spoils, particularly if the distribution of landed
estates to the peasants is involved.

To give the reader a more concrete idea of how the Communists operate
when they take power, we cite a list of people marked for arrest, slave-
labor camps, or execution by the secret police following the Baltic States
take-over:[4]

(1) All former members of anti-Soviet political parties, organizations,
and groups: Trotskyists, right-wingers, Mensheviks, Social Democrats, an-
archists, etc.

(2) All former members of nationalistic, chauvinistic, anti-Soviet parties,
nationalists, Christian Democrats, the active members of student organizations, the National Guard, etc.

(3) Former policemen, officers of the criminal and political police and
of the prisons.

(4) Former army officers and members of all military courts.

(5) Persons who were dismissed from the Communist Party and communist youth organizations for various offenses against the Party.

(6) All refugees, political emigrants, immigrants, repatriates, and con-
trabandists.

(7) All citizens of foreign states, representatives of foreign firms, employees of foreign-state institutions, former citizens of foreign states, former
employees of foreign legations, concessions, and stock companies.

(8) Persons who maintain personal contact or are in correspondence
with foreign countries, legations, and consulates, with philatelists and
Esperantists.

(9) Former officials of ministerial departments.

(10) Former Red Cross officials.

(11) The clergy of religious communities, orthodox priests, Roman
Catholic priests, sectarians, and active members of religious congregations.

4. Order issued by Beria, acting through Serov, on November 28, 1940, following the
take-over of the Baltic States by the Soviet Union.

(12) Former noblemen, estate owners, merchants, bankers, businessmen, owners of factories and shops, owners of hotels and restaurants.

Industrialization

Once the initial political "cleansing" is accomplished, the second and more difficult phase, the economic revolution, begins. Having appropriated and consumed the ready goods of the former regime, the new regime must begin to produce. To produce anew there must be not only order and discipline but also skill. The theories of Marx, Engels, and Lenin contain no advice on that subject.

With the management and engineering personnel dispersed and equipment worn out, production in Russia was difficult. The factory committees who took over during the political revolution were debating societies and could not manage. Authority with knowledge and experience was needed. The authority was soon provided in the form of factory directors appointed from the top, while the committees were reduced in 1925 to a mere advisory capacity and were eventually abolished altogether. In subsequent years, unions inside the U.S.S.R. were shoved aside and the party-state took over the exclusive function of fixing working conditions, wages, and prices.

The Soviet effort at industrialization started in 1928 with the first five-year plan, which envisaged the building of hundreds of new plants, government offices, and other enterprises. Until then, all the Soviets had been able to do was to recondition a good part of the factory equipment inherited from the Czarist regime. The war against the peasants wrecked most of the five-year plan. Nevertheless, for the benefit of the outside world, the plan was declared fulfilled, and a second five-year plan was announced in 1935. This one, coinciding with the great blood purges, also fell far short of its goals. At the end of the allegedly successful fulfillment of the two five-year plans there was less to eat than ever and civilian goods were scarcer than before. In spite of all of this, however, armament production had increased steadily. A third five-year plan was announced in 1939 but was never fulfilled because World War II intervened. Only after World War II was Stalin, with the aid of vast stores of loot captured or obtained as war indemnities, able to pursue his five-year plans in earnest.

Characteristic of the entire period of pre-war plans was the disappearance of all real data about Soviet economy. All of the alleged successes of the five-year plans were given out in the form of percentages. In this man-

ner, the plans appeared to have been not only successful but even overful-
filled. The enemy—the non-communist world—was thus both kept in the
dark about what was really taking place inside the U.S.S.R. and systematically misinformed. Even among the Communists, only a few knew the facts.

The Expropriation of Rights

The path toward communist totalitarianism is one of constant power
accumulation into fewer and fewer hands, with the Party not only expropriating all enemy classes but also assuming the power of all social organizations. Finally, the Party itself ends up being dominated by the huge
internal police apparatus which it has created.

In the third phase of communist-party revolution, the rights of the multitude—as a mass and as individuals—are taken away. Initially the revolution is made in the name of expropriating the rich. The masses, filled with
propaganda-produced illusions, see only a chance for revenge. Those having small property expect, not to lose it, but to gain more. Those having
no property expect to be enriched. They do not care what the rich lose or
how they lose it.

When the second phase of the revolution came in Russia, those who had
no property were not overly concerned when the small owners lost theirs.
In fact, many of them, especially Communist Party members, expected to
profit from this as well. It was the third phase which brought about their
awakening. The Communists practice "liquidate and rule"—a staggered
liquidation, one category at a time. Only when everyone has lost his property does there arise the question of who truly benefits from the party-
state's possessing all property.

The final phase brings a struggle for the right to participate in the
exploitation of the new state property. This struggle, which corrodes the
whole society, is a battle for the highest salaries, the best jobs and living
quarters and privileges, and positions of authority and power. In the new
stratification the political autocrats are on top, the managers and directors
next in rank, and so on down the line, with the working man once again
at the bottom—except for a new category below the previous base level:
slave or forced labor.

Communist inequality is based not on property but on the privileges
which go with rank and position. The right to convert the results of one's
labor and ability into property is a far more basic right than is generally
realized. When this right is abolished both *de jure* and *de facto,* all polit-

ical rights are undermined.[5] This stage was reached in Soviet Russia by the mid-thirties. If one still wanted to profit from another's labor, one had to make a place for oneself in the party-state, the holder of all rights and property and the appropriator of the fruits of all labor.

At first, those who lost no property did not consider themselves deprived of any basic value; on the contrary, they thought themselves enriched, if not actually, at least potentially. They expected to assert their individual rights through the mass organizations which bloomed in the wake of the revolution. Only when those organizations themselves were deprived of their status did the people begin to sense the absence of individual rights in the new party-state.

The loss of rights in the Soviet Union came in the following stages:

(1) Abolition, in stages, of all property rights;
(2) Abolition of the right to leave the country;
(3) Abrogation of the rights of the unions in the determination of wages and working conditions;
(4) Abolition of the right to strike;
(5) Abolition of the right to change jobs or travel freely inside the country;
(6) Abolition of the semi-autonomy of the co-operatives and their incorporation into the state trading apparatus; and
(7) Constriction of the rights of the village soviets and their virtual abolition as a result of enforced collectivization.

Civil liberties, such as the right to assemble, organize, and speak freely, were restricted during the initial phase of the political revolution and were finally done away with altogether.

The Party, as created by Lenin and Trotsky, had been ideologically primed for the expropriation of all property owners, but not for expropriating the masses from their collective rights. On the contrary, the rights of the masses under party-state ownership were supposed to increase, not diminish. The Party, having grown in numbers, considered itself a trustee of the masses and not their expropriator. After all, if their rights were to disappear, whose state was it? Who owned it, and for whose benefit? These questions are still unanswered.

The issues at stake were not seen as clearly then as they are now with

5. A socialist commonwealth is not incompatible per se with individual property rights, as the experiences of Mexico, Australia, and Sweden have shown. When property deprivation becomes a means of political entrapment, the process has crossed the line which separates democratic socialism from totalitarian captivity.

the benefit of hindsight. They were first sensed within the Party as early as 1921, when the so-called workers' opposition demanded the right of dissent or democracy within the Party. The dissenters were forbidden to join in presenting their views within the Party, but individual dissent was still allowed. The dissenters who then raised the issue of rights and authority over collective property barely avoided expulsion from the Party. Lenin would tolerate no tampering with the authority of the party-state over property, either collective or private.

We omit discussion of the trickery and cruelty involved in the long fight over oppressive party bureaucratization, which terminated with the purges of 1935–1938. By the time it was over, the Communist Party of the Soviet Union had become a bureaucratic instrument subject to the political police it had created. The mass organizations, bereft of all power, were reduced to surveillance of the workers. Political and economic power were held in one fist. The Soviet Union had become a police state operating under the flag of the continually purged, reorganized, and degraded Communist Party.

A process similar to communist power accumulation in the Soviet Union, compressed in time, has occurred in the communist parties of the satellite countries and Red China. The same is true of Yugoslavia, except that after Tito's expulsion from Moscow's inner sanctum a relaxation occurred and mass-organization rights were partially restored. In 1961, communist state control appeared to have been established in Cuba.

History will tell whether the complete strangulation of political rights is inevitable under the party-state. Thus far it appears to be so, regardless of whether the party-state is red, brown, or black. In a communist party-state, however, the process seems to be the most thorough.

The forced conversion of all private property into state property leads to the liquidation of basic rights. Without the protection which private property can provide, it is difficult for the individual to resist the state; if deprived also of his rights over collective property, he becomes a mere pawn of the government. The communist version of socialism is a process of expropriating the individual of both private property and of his rights over collective property.

In the long run, communist power hinges on its novel method of control over the masses. When in opposition, Communists will incite and array people against the non-communist leaders and, by getting control of mass organizations, will bring individuals into the orbit of the Party. After the seizure of power, these mass organizations become tools of oppression of the Party and its government.

Whereas all former political systems sought to prevent or impede the organization of the masses in order to facilitate control, the Socialists, following Marx's doctrines, started the opposite process. The Communists transmuted that process into a means of, first, aligning the masses against democracy in the name of a new and superior democracy, and then, once in power, of transforming them into a new instrument of oligarchy.

The new system, which places all social and political organizations under the Communist Party, permits the Communist Party a degree of control over the masses that is unprecedented in history.

Purging

Among the most mystifying characteristics of a communist regime is the bloodletting, or purge. After a communist party comes to power, a steady parade to the executioner and the concentration camp or exile begins. As the old "capitalist" enemy diminishes, the prison population grows; so does the police system which fills the prisons. The phenomenon is inherent in the communist system and is present in all communist regimes, including those of Red China and Cuba.

A perusal of the purges in Russia reveals that they followed closely the various changes in policy which reflected the various phases of the communist-party revolution. The part of the purge process least understood in the West was the constant elimination of Communists, culminating in the huge purge of 1935–1938. This purge was almost entirely motivated by the internal situation; counterrevolutionary penetration by Germany had very little to do with it.

Stalin usually purged one apparatus at a time. When the party apparatus was purged, the police and the army were left alone. When the military apparatus was purged, the party and police apparatus provided support. Least touched under Stalin was the police apparatus. That purge came after Stalin's death, with the party and military apparatus used as backing. The full story of the purging of the police apparatus under Khrushchev is not yet known, but it included the execution of Beria, the dismissal of Serov, and the reorganization of the Ministry of the Interior.

According to Lenin, the Party was to arrive at collective decisions by discussion and carry out these decisions through discipline. There was a time, even after the seizure of power in Russia, when this was more or less true. The system now operates to some extent within the Presidium; else-where, decisions are imposed from the top. The purges are necessary for the execution of these decisions. The Party does not give the opposition a chance to congeal into a force: warned by reports from the secret police, it is the first to act. Before the opposition can reveal itself, its members are on the way to exile or prison—the only place in the communist orbit where any sort of frank discussion is held. Contrary to the still propagated fables that decisions in the Communist Party are arrived at freely, the Party is a prisoner of its own system of government. Decisions are made by conspir-acy or caprice. Ratification is by panic. Differences are resolved by force. Hungary and Poland, in 1956, have provided the only instances thus far where the opposition has succeeded in challenging, temporarily, the lead-ership.

Another reason for the purges was what Stalin called "the changing of the guard." This involved the elimination of the revolutionaries who had joined the movement during the period of destruction of the old capitalist system, either prior to or after the political seizure of power. Having made the revolution, they expected much from it. The habit of criticism became a negative, if not destructive, force during the period of reconstruction which follows every revolution. Stalin aimed to do away with the profes-sional revolutionaries and replace them with constructive careerists who were interested only in place and position and would be loyal to him. Stalin's last politically motivated purge, which was gaining momentum when he died, bore an anti-Semitic stamp and was dramatized by the arrest in the Kremlin of several Jewish doctors charged with a conspiracy against Stalin and his aides. One can only speculate as to what might have come of the anti-Semitic purge if Stalin had lived longer.

The purge is so important to communist rule that it is hard to conceive how the Communists can govern without it. In an undramatized form, it goes on continually; if it did not, a multifraction system would inevitably arise. The bureaucracy in an industry or plant may be purged because it fails to perform according to the current five-year plan. The food sector of the administration may be decimated because of shortages in meat or potatoes. A bureau for the transportation of supplies may be purged because of too much stealing in transit or at the terminals. It does not mat-ter who is at fault; the blame must be placed on somebody, and it cannot be placed on the Presidium, whose mystique of prestige must be main-tained. Purges are also a means of diverting the hatred of the population from the top command of the Party to the lower ranks of the party-state bureaucracy. They are, finally, a means of replacing, on a large scale, worn-out or inefficient human material and promoting other people from the ranks.

In summarizing the purge process, we can see distinct stages. The first accompanies the political revolution (expropriation), in which enemy elements are purged from the state apparatus and possibly from the party apparatus as well. The second stage is the usurpation of all authority over collective property and the abolition of the rights of the masses. The purge process during this stage is aimed at the old Communists and represents a crisis, a change in purpose of the Party from revolution to governing. The third phase, after the abolition of rights, consists of the use of the purge as a method of governing. According to Z. K. Brzezinski of the Columbia University Research Center:

There is no indication that the latest regime [Khrushchev's] is yielding even in the remotest respects any of its political power. As long as it continues in its present form, the conditions precipitating the purge and ultimately giving it its violent character will also continue. Their consequences may no longer be a mass purge, which is not so necessary given a pliable and silent membership which has been politically neutralized. The purge will continue to liquidate, violently if necessary, those who tend to disrupt the unity of the top strata. The Stalinist era is over, but it has left the Stalinist purge as a lasting heritage.[6]

Jurisprudence

The rule of law simply does not exist in the Soviet system. When the state pre-empts all rights for itself, there is no room for justice as we know it; there is room only for punishment.

Where there is an absence of individual rights, administrative procedure supplants justice. The political police mete out the sentences and execute them. In the Soviet Union the police, proceeding in secrecy, are the judge, jury, and executioner. Since the proceedings are secret, the West learns little except from the few escapees.

A country ruled by the Communist Party does not have a government of laws; it has a government of men who rule arbitrarily. Decrees made at the pleasure of the dictator can be withdrawn, changed, or interpreted. When the dictator is the supreme judge, judges are part of the appointive apparatus of the state, removable at any time and, like all other officials,

6. *The Permanent Purge*, pp. 166-67.

subject to purge. The idea of an independent judiciary is the most Western of Western ideas. It is strongest in the United States, where, under
the doctrine of division of power, the judiciary is not only equal to the
legislative and executive branches of the government but often overrides
them in interpretation of the Constitution.

Under communism there is no separation of powers. There is, nevertheless, a judicial apparatus, with prosecutors, judges, and even attorneys to
handle felonies. Common criminals are released after they serve their
sentences, but political offenders are subject to administrative decisions.

Justice under the Communist Party is variable. During the civil war,
its main interest was the extermination of class enemies, and it paid little
attention to common criminals. During the big political purges, it hunted
mainly for anti-Stalinist dissenters among the Communists. The political
deportees were always the great majority among state prisoners because
almost any offense could be declared political. Theft of state property,
assault on officials, even inefficiency at work can be declared sabotage, and
all such cases are adjudicated by the police apparatus.

The quality of justice in a nation is, as a rule, the measure of its civilization. By this yardstick a nation under communism retrogresses into barbarism.[7] Nothing is as consistently veiled from Western view as the workings of Soviet justice, and nothing portrays as starkly the true nature of
communism as the fate of justice under its control.

Bread and Circuses

Political liberty cannot exist without economic liberty. A total dictatorship requires the elimination of both. Under communism, the most complete form of dictatorship in history, the party-state alone decides who
eats, who has living quarters, and who enjoys other privileges of life. Food
supplies and other necessities are made available to people, not according

---

7. Significantly enough, the head of the Chinese Communist judicial system, Tung
Pi-wu, pleaded for the creation of communist law and communist courts as a means
of regularizing the "people's government" on the mainland. Himself a very old man,
old enough to have been reared in the rigid but humane traditions of Confucianist
ethics and propriety, Tung was appalled at the risks taken by his government in trying
to operate forever without law. He was persuaded to cease his complaints after 1960,
and he never was undiplomatic enough to predict, in flat terms, what would happen
to Red China if law did not stiffen and regularize the processes of government. Tung,
as a veteran Communist, apparently knew enough to suspect that the regime would
develop inner weaknesses if dependable laws, enforceable on cadres and people alike,
were not enacted. The regime, instead of heeding Tung, launched a campaign to teach
the communist leaders "tenderness" in their handling of the people.

to their needs, but according to their importance to the party-state. Among the most privileged are the political police and the higher party bureaucracy, who buy at the lowest prices in stores reserved for them. Next come the armed forces, in particular the officers, then the higher personnel in strategic industries, then the less important members of the political bureaucracy and management. Workers, too, receive supplies according to the category of importance of the enterprise or institution for which they work, the ones in light industry being the least favored.

This system of privilege permits the government to manipulate the supply of food and other necessities in accordance with policy. It assures a supply to the personnel essential to the maintenance of power, no matter how great the scarcity. It can be used to subdue rebellious areas through a complete cut-off of food. It was, and can be, used to punish purged people who were not arrested simply by driving them and their families into a search for food so desperate as to leave no time free for thinking, let alone discussion.

In addition to the captive-store system, there are, particularly in the big cities, general stores where one can buy certain unrationed goods. There, too, the supply can be tightened or relaxed according to the convenience of the Kremlin. Moscow has a high priority on food supplies because of the large number of governmental personnel located there and because it is treated as a comparative show place.

The system of food controls was born of the necessities of the civil war and was then developed into an instrument of domination over the populace. Full control could not be established without the complete subjugation of the peasant, for as long as the peasant was in charge of the original production of food, the cities remained dependent upon his good will. Only after the defeat of the peasant could Stalin add food control to his methods of absolute domination.

The system of highly organized controls over the population was imposed gradually. Class differentiation, so roundly condemned in capitalism by the Communists, was reborn in a more vicious form under their rule. Under capitalism, in order to own property one must earn it and retain it by one's own effort; under communism, rank and position are entirely dependent on the whims of many people, most of them personally unknown to their victims, who staff the dictator's bureaucratic control apparatus. Whatever his rank, privileges, or possessions, the holder has no vested right to them; the one who gives can arbitrarily take away.

Beginning in the late twenties, limitations on earnings, which were originally confined to those of a skilled worker, were gradually lifted or ignored for the upper brackets of the new ruling strata. By the mid-thirties and thereafter, there was practically no limit to the amount one could accumulate through bureaucratic promotion, except that no one could invest in productive enterprise and become independent of the pleasure of the government.[8] Salaries rose to ten or twenty times those of workers and were often supplemented by bonuses and extra emoluments for various achievements and profits from black-market operations. The government deigned to see this only when it served governmental purposes during purges and other shake-ups. In other words, one could be dishonest at the convenience of the government. This type of extra enrichment could not be fully controlled, but it never got completely out of hand.

The upper layers of management bureaucracy and the Party acquired the comforts of fine homes, servants, and cars. Title to these remained in government or party departments; their exclusive assignment to individuals gave the users all the privileges of ownership and none of the responsibilities. While at work these people ate in privileged eating places, and they took their vacations in summer resorts or villas, usually at the expense of the government. They were also permitted to wear distinctive uniforms and to display their rank with great ostentation. Stalin was willing to be very generous to subordinates in material matters as long as every one of them obeyed his commands.

The policies toward the workers also changed, but not toward increased individual well-being. The influence of the labor unions had been broken by 1936, and the hourly wage system had earlier been replaced by piecework throughout the country. A deceptive propaganda campaign was launched to sell the workers on the merits of piecework as a means of building socialism. Through piecework, it was alleged, everyone could earn according to his ability; there would be no limitations on earnings. In reality, things turned out quite differently. The piecework rates might have increased the earnings—if the rates had not been reduced constantly as production increased, if the management had been efficient, and if conditions in the country had been normal. Many of the managers were inex-

8. The Communists and their sympathizers abroad claim that the greatest extremes under communism were still less than the greatest extremes in the non-communist world. This argument omits the elementary arithmetic on the contrasts which prevail within any given Western country, where extremes as radical as those in the Soviet Union are seldom found.

perienced amateurs, most of the plants had old equipment which frequently broke down, and raw materials for processing often did not arrive
in time or were deficient. All of this resulted in a great deal of waste, which
was not paid for under the piecework system. The lack of co-ordination,
the lack of efficiency, and other shortcomings of communist management
were unloaded on the worker.

Increased armaments and the material privileges of the new managerial
elite had to be earned and paid for by somebody. Piecework made the worker pay. This was the socialism of the Communist Party a generation after
the seizure of power.

Cultural Mobilization

The many peoples of the Soviet Union, peasants or of peasant origin,
are—as groups—open, hard working, and frolicsome; they know how to
relax with music, song, and dance. The classic Russian opera and ballet
were borrowed from abroad and perfected. During the revolution and the
civil war which followed, much of this deeply rooted culture was sterilized
or damaged.

After the civil war, when political and economic conditions began to
stabilize, the arts were under the same cloud as everything else inherited
from the days of Czarism. They were soon replaced by "proletarian art."
No one knew precisely what should constitute proletarian art, except that
it should be opposed to bourgeois tastes. As it turned out, proletarian art
was simply a theatrical expression of the anti-Czarist, anti-capitalist propaganda of the civil war with an added glorification of the new Soviet
regime. True art usually is a product of the culturally superior segment of
the population and should be unfettered by political motivation. Proletarian art was virtually the opposite.

It did not take long for the new Soviet ruling class to transform proletarian art into "people's art," which meant the use of real art for new
purposes. Old operas were rewritten and produced; the ballet came into
its own again; painting and sculpture were used to glorify the new society
and its leaders. The artistic intelligentsia were made part of the upper
stratum of Soviet society. In time, new productions were added to old art,
and some capitalistic art was used or converted to Soviet purposes. In
short, the new upper classes wanted to be entertained, and Stalin was
quite willing to provide entertainment for them.

The development of the Soviet *kino,* or cinema, was a new contribution to mass culture. Soviet movies, particularly in the late twenties, combined political propaganda with amusement. Mass entertainment and relaxation also became available in the "parks of culture," which provided music bands, sports, and circuses.

Under communism there is no such thing as art for art's sake. Art is used to embellish propaganda and agitation, to slander the enemy and enemy concepts, to lionize communist achievements and leaders. It is the refined element in the personality-conditioning process. In the Soviet Union it required the prolific use of police power to force artists to conform to the various switches of the party line. No one is more hounded than the "workers of the cultural front," as they are called, to make art under the Soviets a tool of ideology. A factory manager or engineer can work and hide his thoughts, but a cultural worker, a "people's artist," must openly work with his.

Real thoughts were often hidden behind extravagant flattery of the Soviet leaders and their doings. Stalin, in particular, was described as the source of all knowledge, master theorist, savant, and supreme military genius. He was built up into a godlike colossus who "makes the grass grow and the sun shine." The country was dotted with monuments to Stalin during his lifetime. No artist or writer was ever reprimanded for gross flattery, but any writer or artist who did not quote Stalin as an authority at least once in his product was suspect. Flattery of the leader thus became a *sine qua non* for promotion and extra insurance for survival. Few survived without thus prostituting themselves. Purges were severe for those who refused, and many artists wound up in slave-labor camps.

Summary

Our analysis of a communist party after the seizure of power has been drawn largely from the long Soviet experience. The same pattern of events, however, has been repeated in every country in which a communist dictatorship has been established. The fact that the communist movement has become, at its core, a cynical power elite does much to explain its ability to draw ruthlessly ambitious men to its banners. The communist idealism of the twenties has been replaced by the lure of power in the sixties. The politically ambitious can be told that if they win power for a communist state, they need not suffer the privations which many of the original Communists had to endure in Russia but will obtain automatically all the prerogatives of the communist elite.

CHAPTER III

THE ROAD TO EXPANDED POWER

THE KEY TO COMMUNIST CONTROL AND CONQUEST IS THE formation of an elite which first exploits the latent class divisions and then, after seizure of power, establishes itself as the dominant caste or class. "Classes," as such, have seldom ruled in history; they have merely reigned, the actual rule having been exercised by the elite of the time. The royal elites of feudalism often acted against the interests of the lower aristocracy and allied themselves with the then rising bourgeois leaders. These, in turn, allied themselves with the rising labor movement, despite the opposition of large sections of the bourgeoisie. This kind of interclass alliance has been most recently typified by Roosevelt's "New Deal" and by the present balance between the British "establishment" and the working-class majority in the electorate.

Classes are seldom able to agree on fundamentals, much less on strategies and tactics which are decided by the leadership. Marx's theory of the rule of classes throughout history is largely an unwarranted extrapolation or at best a half-truth. Least of all is it applicable to the bourgeois democratic system, probably the most varied and flexible of social systems.

The communist concept that there can be a working class which is also a ruling class is entirely theoretical. Whenever the theory has been tried, the working class has carried its new masters on its back from the very beginning. In practice, then, the scheme results in a new servant-master relationship.

The vanguard elite of Marx and Lenin aims at ruling all society. Whereas the aims of the bourgeois democratic elite are limited, those of the

Communists are totalitarian. Keeping these chief characteristics of Lenin's vanguard elite in mind, we shall now examine its organizational workings.

The Role of Moscow in the Global Communist Organization

Each communist party is part of a world-wide organization with supreme authority in Moscow.[1] At the Second World Congress of the Third International, held in Moscow in 1920, Lenin arranged the organization of communist parties in every country of the world. Lenin himself drafted the twenty-one conditions for the acceptance by the Comintern of the affiliation of any communist party. The most important of these conditions of membership was absolute compliance with the Comintern's orders.

The world-revolutionary organization established in Moscow in 1920 continues to function.[2] Gone are the days in which international delegations paraded in broad daylight, insolently announcing their purpose to the world. The old Comintern, with all its drama, has passed into history. To put the Comintern together again would be more difficult than repairing Humpty Dumpty: the component parts are not only broken apart, they are scattered, for the purposes of secrecy and cover, into dozens of party and governmental subdivisions of the U.S.S.R. The only sure control of them—perhaps even the only certain knowledge of them—lies with the boss of the Soviet Communist Party and the high ministers of the Soviet government. The Kremlin is aware that a world communist parliament, no matter how docile, presents risks. The world organization is kept in fractions for the security of the Soviet Union, but it is operationally integrated for the sake of the world-wide communist movement. Moscow thus has the advantage of ostensibly presiding over no world-wide organization at all—except for some harmless correspondence between "fraternal parties"—and commanding a very real organization operating at various levels of camouflage.

Although the old Comintern has lost its public title, the basic organizational structure remains with its essential purpose and nature unchanged. The program adopted at the Sixth World Congress of the Comintern in 1928 reaffirmed century-old communist aims: "The Communist International . . . openly comes out as the organizer of the international proletarian revolution."

1. For a more detailed account, see *The Front Is Everywhere*, pp. 75-83.
2. For an understanding of the Soviet Union's vanguard role in the world communist movement, see *Report by N. S. Khrushchev.*

Stalin sanctioned the draft of the program of the Sixth World Congress. "The draft provides a program not for any one or other of the national communist parties together, embracing what is general and basic for all of them. Hence, its character is a program of principles and theory. . . . Hence the all embracing profoundly international character of the draft program."

The Comintern carried on world-wide revolutionary operations until 1943, when, for the alleged purpose of promoting wartime unity between the Soviet Union and the West, it was abolished—but never dissolved. Igor Gouzenko, former code clerk in the Soviet Embassy in Ottawa, has stated that the fictitious abolition of the Comintern was staged for political and deceptive purposes.

The communist parties of the world did not grow up spontaneously, but were planted and nursed by Moscow. As they took root in foreign soil, however, the need for the Comintern to send Russian organizers and recruiting agents abroad gradually decreased. Native-born but Kremlin-trained communist leaders rose to command the local operations in every country.

Central control is facilitated by the fact that each party has been patterned on Lenin's organization. The *Party Organizer,* the official internal organ of the American Communist Party, intended for indoctrination of party members only, has carried articles from time to time which confirm this fact. Ever since the conquest of power by Lenin's Bolsheviks, the Russian Communist Party has actively manipulated the affairs of the Communist International and those of each affiliated party. It has run into difficulties with factions in some parties and has occasionally competed with Peking for control of others, such as Albania in 1961.

Before the Comintern was officially abolished, Communists were proud to assert that it had grown into a true "world party" and had reached the stage "where all communist parties are carrying out the single line of the Comintern." The policies it established became the guiding principles for all communist parties, not just for the Russian.

For many years there was legitimate doubt that a direct-command relationship existed between Moscow and the various national communist parties. By now, the evidence overwhelmingly confirms Moscow direction. Proof of Moscow's domination of world communism can be shown in a number of ways, although the Communists themselves will either deny or affirm this domination, depending on the "line" of the day.

Every Communist since Lenin has rejected "spontaneity" in the revo-

lutionary movement. Hence the world, if it cannot be won by "spontaneity," must be won by an organized plan which requires a world organization to execute it. And a militant world organization requires central
world headquarters.[3]

Defectors from the communist system have reported the existence of a
center in Moscow which keeps abreast of world-wide developments and
co-ordinates Soviet, satellite, and communist-party activities. It is difficult
to see how the varied communist operations can be conducted without
the existence of some such mechanism to facilitate the co-ordination of
activities. The conflict which the Communists wage against us in the diplomatic, economic, political, and military spheres—appears to be carried out
according to a systematically and centrally directed strategy.

The following description of the role and operations of the Moscow
headquarters is based on personal experience.[4] Since this evidence was
garnered many organizational changes have undoubtedly been made. New
problems have arisen for the world-communist movement and supplemen-
tary machinery has been created to handle them. Certain of these innovations will be discussed subsequently.

Despite the changes that have taken place, the following report gives an
important insight into the role of the Moscow headquarters in communist
political warfare. All the organized departments in any communist party,
vertical or horizontal, have a tie-in with corresponding departments in
Moscow. All parties, even the minor ones, consequently have in their organization agit-prop, trade-union, youth, and underground or secret departments. In addition, the Moscow headquarters has a number of secretariats
which specialize in and co-ordinate the activities of the various parties in
their respective political areas: the Far Eastern Secretariat for Asiatic countries, the Latin American Secretariat for South American countries, etc.
Moscow also has a number of geopolitical field headquarters located outside Russia, such as the Central European Bureau and the Latin American
Bureau. These bureaus and secretariats are staffed by Moscow's top experts

3. Gene D. Overstreet and Marshall Windmiller, in *Communism in India*, do a
marvelous job of detective work from open, scholarly sources in showing Moscow's
guidance of the unfortunate Indian Communist Party, which constantly got itself into
difficulty with factionalism and with "spontaneity." Overstreet and Windmiller show
that the Indian Communists became slavishly obedient to Moscow when they were sure
it was Moscow speaking but that the heat of their internecine quarrels sometimes kept
them from agreeing on what was an important Moscow message and what was not.

4. The personal experience mentioned was that of Joseph Z. Kornfeder, who visited
the Moscow headquarters hundreds of times.

on political warfare. Every communist party is obliged to send to Moscow
a representative "consultant," usually a member of its central committee.
The major parties also send one or more report analysts to handle the
stream of reports and minutes coming in from that party. The representatives attend department and committee meetings, and, while in Moscow,
are members of the geopolitical secretariat established for the area in
which their country is located. The geopolitical field bureaus are usually
headed by Russians. The membership of a field bureau, however, is composed of representatives of the parties of the area.

To execute the directives of the departments, secretariats, and field
bureaus, representatives and instructors are attached to each communist
party. These may include a political representative, plus specialists in
organization, agit-prop, trade-union, and youth. These operate behind the
official façade of the Party. Generally, they are not citizens of the countries
in which they work or members of the party whose activities they direct,
but rarely are they Russians. The Russian directors, for obvious reasons,
have learned to stay in the background.

Tying together all these activities at Moscow's headquarters is an over-
all general secretariat working directly under the Presidium of the Soviet
Communist Party. While the other secretariats or field bureaus may be
staffed (or occasionally even headed) by trusted non-Russians, the general
secretariat is always composed of Soviet citizens. The same is true of the
heads of key departments in Moscow, such as organization, agit-prop, trade-
union, youth, and the underground-activities department. Dmitri Manuilsky, who presided over the United Nations in 1948, headed the general
secretariat for many years.

Among the least-known features of Moscow's headquarters is the leadership training and placement system, or cadre division, of the Soviet Communist Party. The cadre division supplies the personnel for the political-
warfare colleges and libraries which train personnel for the Soviet Communist Party and other parties. The curriculum is the same in each college,
but with special emphasis on the geographical areas in which these elites
are destined to operate. The students must learn fluently at least one major
foreign language.

The colleges train non-Russian communist-party personnel from special
geopolitical areas, as in the Far Eastern University for Asia, the Western
University for Eastern Europe, the Lenin University for the highly developed industrial countries, and a new institute for Africa and Latin Amer-

ica called "People's Friendship University." Located in Moscow, the latter
was opened by Khrushchev himself to "train leaders for new countries of
Africa and the poorer, older ones of Latin America." These colleges concentrate on psychological-political warfare. They do not teach sabotage
or espionage beyond indicating the role the latter plays in the total configuration of political warfare. Intelligence, sabotage, coded communications, and the more intricate arts of underground operations are taught in
special schools operated by the foreign division of the secret police.

The range of subjects taught in communist political-warfare colleges
includes:

General

(1) The doctrines of Marx and Lenin concerning the role of government
(the state, the Party, and their roles in society);
(2) The Communist Party insurrectionary organization, its structure
and methods;
(3) Labor unions as an instrument of economic and political warfare
against capitalist democratic society;
(4) The strategy of neutralizing or demoralizing the middle classes;
(5) The strategy of winning over or neutralizing the farm population
of the advanced countries;
(6) Communist colonial policy, based on the teachings of Lenin as elaborated by Stalin; and
(7) The peasants as a main base for igniting the colonial revolution.

Underground Warfare

(1) The role of Communists in case of war against the Soviet Union;
(2) Infiltration of armed services;
(3) The relation between aboveground (legal) and underground (illegal)
activities and the necessity of carrying on both at the same time;
(4) The purpose and methods of infiltrating government departments;
and
(5) The role of sabotage and espionage in political warfare.

Armed Insurrection

(1) How to form a paramilitary combat force;
(2) Means and methods of arming such a force;
(3) The role of such a force in case of war against the Soviet Union;
(4) The general scheme of seizing a city;
(5) How to hold a city after seizure;
(6) The supremacy of surprise in carrying out a successful insurrection;
(7) Techniques and objectives of guerrilla warfare;
(8) Probable countermeasures of the government sensing an insurrection
and methods of overcoming same; and
(9) The consolidation of power.

In the foreign political-warfare colleges, a number of the students are Russians, who, as a rule, are assigned to the Soviet Foreign Service. A higher percentage of Soviet citizens attend the secret-police schools and the general-staff college. All foreign communist-party members attending these colleges and residing in Russia for more than six months become members of the Soviet Communist Party by transfer.

At the time of these personal observations, the cost of all training operations was defrayed by the Soviet treasury. The floor space and personnel represented by these institutions and by the Soviet government departments entirely or principally engaged in political warfare, plus the Comintern headquarters in Moscow, was equivalent to that of the Pentagon. This gives an idea of the role that political warfare plays in the operations of the Soviet government.

The communist pattern of organization, in theory and practice, embodies old and new ideas. The Party is both hierarchical and flexible: it is rigid with regard to over-all strategy (party line), yet flexible with regard to means of application. In pursuing the general strategy, the party members in various countries interpret in their own way instructions from Moscow. They have much leeway in choosing tactics, and every nucleus or fraction has to decide how to deal with its problems on the local level. All that is required is that the tactics be executed in general consonance with the strategy laid down by Moscow.

On the subject of high strategy, individual party members have no say. Every member is obligated to gather intelligence for his superior, and the information thus obtained is taken into consideration in the determination of strategy. The lower echelons may thus influence the top, but only indirectly. On matters of strategy, centralization dominates.

Concentrating the Elite

Let us now examine the utilization of the trained manpower in the vast communist political-warfare machine. Since the colleges were first established, tens of thousands of men and women have been trained and assigned to various posts on five continents. About 30 per cent of the graduates remain under the general supervision of the cadre division; the rest are put at the disposal of the various communist parties from which they came, but can be called in by Moscow at any time. All assignments are made in the name of the Central Committee.

Graduates are used to man the political warfare headquarters in Moscow and its field bureaus, working as field representatives, instructors, and consular and other specialists in capitalist countries. They also fill the leading positions in the communist parties in the countries from which they came. Originally, the leadership of the Communist Party in most countries was not Moscow trained, but as Moscow trainees became available, they replaced the others. A rough estimate of American Communists trained in Moscow would be eight hundred, not enough as yet to man all the ranking positions in the American Communist Party. The others are either self-educated or trained in the more limited indigenous schools each party maintains.

The training of officer or elite personnel for this type of operation does not tell the full story. A trained force must be mobile to be utilized fully. Organizational mobility means that a force can be concentrated at a strategic spot at the proper time. In the twenties, when Germany and China were the prime targets, a high percentage of Moscow's resources in the way of organizers, funds, and even arms moved into those areas. When in the thirties Germany was given up as the primary target area, major resources were concentrated upon China. It is known, for instance, that American Communist Party personnel played a role in the conquest of China, both by infiltrating the United States government and influencing its policy to serve Soviet aims and by operating within the Nationalist-held territory. Earl Browder himself served his final communist apprenticeship on Chinese territory, running dangerous errands in the deep interior.

Moscow assigns priorities to its political-warfare machine on the basis of both long-range and immediate considerations. The United States, for instance, has now become the *primary target,* on the basis of long-range considerations; countries adjacent to the Iron Curtain are always considered top priority target areas, even though they cannot be taken immediately. A secondary target area is one, such as Indonesia, where a breakthrough by infiltration seems feasible, even though the country is far away from Soviet borders. The flow of Moscow-trained and Moscow-directed personnel, resources, and arms into these areas will depend on both the local opportunity and the over-all communist strategy.

A key target area can expect a major inflow of Soviet diplomatic and trading personnel, guerrilla and military specialists, and psychological-political warfare personnel. They will have funds to corrupt officials, buy into local newspapers, and provide operational cover in the form of businesses, farms, and export and import firms, arms smuggling and the procuring of arms from local sources. As internal infiltration of government proceeds, all of these processes will be facilitated and augmented, and eventually the Soviet Union will take a more direct hand in the matter through its Embassy.

In countries which are long-term targets, the same process will be followed, but the emphasis will be on political-warfare operations and espionage.

In order to be able to concentrate its trained political-warfare elite in any desired area, Moscow headquarters maintains a large organization for forging identity papers. This passport center can equip anyone with a passport for any country, with the necessary seals and stamps. It also fabricates birth and baptismal certificates, police permits, and entry and exit visas. Biographies of party members from all over the world are used to create a "legal" personality.[5] False papers to hide his origin or identity are used for a Russian who speaks a foreign language or for other nationals who would expose themselves by using their own identities or who could not obtain their own traveling papers. Agents are commonly instructed to obtain their own papers on someone else's identity.

American, British, and German Communists have used forged bona fides, particularly in Asia and Latin America, India, and North and South Africa, where they worked hand in glove with Soviet diplomatic or other clandestine party personnel. Soviet diplomatic personnel travel with Soviet passports, of course, but the identity stated thereon is not always a true one.

The general pattern of concentrating the elite in accordance with the strategic pattern also prevails within a particular country. Each national communist party aims to influence strategic industries and transportation and communications centers and to infiltrate the government and its armed forces. It often happens that in these key spots communist-party recruiting is the weakest. The American Communist Party's recruiting in its early years was mostly in the East Coast garment trades and other light industries, an undesirable base. In such a case, Moscow will insist that the able and trained personnel be shifted gradually to take up residence and develop activity in strategic target areas. This, in party language, is called "colonizing." Thus the West Coast, originally among the least-pene-

5. For a real-life account of how this worked out in one particular case, see the comical but frightening description given by Richard Hirsch in *The Soviet Spies*, chap. 12, "Two Ignacy Witczaks." The original Witczak was a Canadian farm hand; the second was a Soviet agent using the farm hand's passport. The agent was no farm hand at all; he earned a Phi Beta Kappa key at the University of Southern California.

trated areas, was developed into one of the strongest centers of party activity in the United States.

When any actual or potential trouble spot or weak link in the social system exists, such as the sitdown strikes in Detroit in the thirties, an elite reinforcement will be moved into that area. Within the concentration of the communist elite according to strategic areas there is also an internal distribution. There may be only a weak nucleus of four party members in a steel or automobile plant. These four may be of less than average ability and represent a tiny toehold. They will be reinforced by an organization or agitation specialist, who will preoccupy himself with conditions in that one plant.

The specialist seeks to improve the quality of communist work. He will utilize every bit of information he gets to fashion suitable agitation leaflets and suggest effective demands. The leaflets will be distributed at the gates by members of party units not working in the plant. The impact on the workers may be considerable; they will feel that there is a secret, inside organization trying to do them some good. The management may engage in blind retaliation or do just the wrong thing, which the Party will, of course, use for its own purposes. Even if the Communist Party, posing as the Samaritan, does not organize the plant or produce a strike, its ideological and even organizational inroads may be considerable.

Versatility

According to the instructors in the Lenin College, Moscow's "West Point" for this type of warfare, the vanguard elite must be capable of operating in all social sectors. The Party's role is not only to be a catalytic energizer of the masses but also to determine the direction toward which the masses are to be moved.

The creation of a communist party first requires gathering together the active elements among discontented or frustrated intellectuals and indoctrinating them in the long-range objectives of Marxism-Leninism. Once indoctrinated and trained, they can be organized into the vanguard elite used for the seizure of power. Unlike conventional parliamentary parties which organize their members solely by geographical areas, the Communist Party also organizes on the basis of the place of employment: in factories, mines, colleges and universities or government offices.

Place-of-work cells seek to organize the employees under communist influence if unorganized or to capture the employees' organizations and influence them from within if these are already formed. It is the duty of such units (in the party language called "nuclei") to familiarize themselves thoroughly with the place of work, its technology, and its personnel, exploit whatever discontent may exist, and create more. If the place is strategic, they plan for the interruption of its operations through strikes and sabotage. Intelligence regarding the place of work is reported to the local party and, if significant, the information is relayed from there to Moscow.

As a rule, the membership of this type of unit, especially in a strategic place, is secret. The unit is kept small. If the party membership in a large plant or enterprise grows, the cells or nuclei are subdivided according to the natural subdivisions or departments. If they are still too large, they may be further subdivided and then co-ordinated through secret committees. Small cells are a precaution against penetration by hostile elements.

The nucleus or "industrial branch" in this type of warfare plays the same role the infantry plays in conventional warfare; that is, it penetrates and occupies the "ground." Psychological-warfare, both short range and long range, softens up the enemy ideologically, knocking down resistance, and generally preparing the way for advance. Without the nuclei, however, the propaganda and agitation barrages could not be exploited—just as in military warfare the infantry seizes ground softened up by artillery fire.

Giving flank support to the activities of the nuclei are the captive and front organizations. The front organization is an instrument which organizes fellow travelers and sympathizers around certain limited objectives. In the scheme of organization taught at the Lenin School, fronts serve as support points for party nuclei. The nuclei are the basic attack units of communist-party organization; fronts and captive communist unions are auxiliaries.

The secondary basic attack unit of the Party is the "fraction." A fraction is a unit composed of party members inside a non-party organization, regardless of whether that non-party organization is friendly or hostile. A Communist may be a member of four or more organizations and thus belong to four or more fractions at the same time. Fractions are even formed within party fronts as a control apparatus for the Party.

The party fraction operating in hostile or potentially hostile non-communist organizations—a union, a veteran's association—opposes any moves that may be hostile to the Communist Party's objectives. Its more remote goal is to obtain control of the organization within which it operates. For this purpose, it seeks, with the help of fellow travelers and sympathizers plus any disgruntled elements, to place pro-communists in office. In hostile organizations, fractions operate secretly. The closest they come to operating in the open is to form front committees or groups to advocate "progressive" goals or reforms. If a particular campaign succeeds, they may sponsor a new slate of officers to take over the organization in its behalf. In the case of labor unions, the same party members who form the nuclei or industrial branches are also members of the fraction of the union. When they meet as a fraction, they preoccupy themselves with the relatively limited objectives of the union and the problems of party control over it. When they meet as a party nucleus, however, the activities of the Communist Party come under focus.

The fraction system also serves as the medium of co-ordinating party activity within a national non-communist or anti-communist organization. For this purpose a leading fraction is appointed by the politburo (of a given communist party) from among the ablest party members within the organization to be captured. If the national organization is already controlled by the Communist Party, then its national officers, who are party members are included in the leading fraction. Each lower fraction has a committee and a secretary, which it elects, subject to the approval of the corresponding superior-party committee. Co-ordination takes place through these committees and their secretaries from the leading or top fraction down, all under the direction of the Politburo of the Communist Party.

All the activities of Communists in the water-front unions throughout a nation—and even internationally—are co-ordinated through a committee (leading fraction) specializing in that field. The same is true for activities within veterans', youth, or women's organizations. Thus it happens that when Moscow conducts a "peace" campaign or a campaign against Chiang Kai-shek or nuclear tests or Congressional investigating committees, resolutions similar in content appear simultaneously in many organizations throughout the country. By examining in detail any one of these campaigns, one can find the hand of the Communist Party's fraction apparatus.

The nuclei-and-fractions system described above comprises the communist-party network designed to marshal and win over the masses. Its inner workings are secret or semisecret. The more hostile the environment in which it operates, the more secret the methods of work and the more ingenious the camouflage under which it operates.

The most secret of party nuclei are in the armed forces, strategic government offices, the police, and the government's intelligence and counterintelligence agencies. This type of unit is very small and only communicates through the secret apparatus of the Party, and via that channel, with Moscow's intelligence and counterintelligence agencies. Many of Moscow's intelligence agents outside the Iron Curtain are recruited from these units. These are "sleeper" units; that is, they engage in little, if any, political activity until the time is propitious. The time is favorable when the country involved loses a major war, or has an economic or political crisis, or when the government becomes friendly with the Kremlin. In such a case, the top-secret sleeper nuclei come to life politically, albeit cautiously, to help swing the government's policy in a direction favorable to Moscow or to aid in the paralysis and demoralization of the government machinery.

The nuclei may then pose as adherents of the party in power and seek to organize the government employees into unions the Communists might control, or seek to penetrate existing goverment employees' associations. They may also increase their organized party following by forming "study" or "friendship" groups. During what General Dean aptly described as our "strange alliance" with the Soviet Union, groups and nuclei like these helped organize the "bring the boys home" demobilization demonstrations at the end of World War II, enjoyed considerable influence in the Troop Information and Education program, penetrated our atomic-science laboratories, and scored some successes in the O.S.S. and in the State, Treasury, and other departments in Washington.

Even while "sleeping," these units are of great value to the Communist Party in keeping it informed about what is going on inside the government. They are the eyes and ears of the Party and of Moscow, the intelligence apparatus of the party. And when the proper time comes, they can also be utilized to influence, shift, or sabotage government policy. In brief, these special party nuclei are not only intelligence units, but political weapons as well.

Specialization and Co-ordination

In addition to the ability to concentrate its resources where needed, communist political warfare also exploits specialization. To gain the most from skilled specialization, there must be both horizontal and vertical co-ordination. The horizontal co-ordination is effected through section or county committees and, on a higher level, through district or state committees. On a still higher level, it takes place through the central or national committee, with the political bureau of the party central committee in charge. There is also international co-ordination through committees in Moscow. The horizontal committees co-ordinate on a geographical basis the activities of the nuclei and fractions which deal with general issues, be they local, regional, national, or even international in character.

A vertical apparatus is one that directs a specialized political-warfare activity at all levels. We have already described how the fractions operating within a particular industry or non-communist organization are co-ordinated so that all communist activity follows a concerted uniform pattern. The trade-union commission, or department, of the Party, the chairman or secretary of which will be a member of the Central Committee, supervises all of the activities in the unions. The activities of party fractions within non-communist women's organizations will be directed by the women's department. Directing the activity in the movie studios, theaters, and related fields is the so-called cultural commission. The work of this commission can often be seen not only in the entertainment and cultural fields. During May and June, 1961, a few months before the building of the wall in Berlin, over fifty TV and radio shows concerning Nazi Germany appeared in the New York metropolitan area. Perhaps this splurge of revived interest in the Nazis was coincidental. But a communist fraction may well have sparked the revival since it is in Moscow's interest to link present-day Western Germany with the Nazi past. In the field of education communist ideas and disruptive doctrine are sometimes skillfully woven into training films produced for schools, industry, and the armed forces. The top secret activity among the armed forces is monitored through the anti-militarist committee. Other departments are created to direct the activities in special fields. These are semi-open in the sense that their existence is publicly known, but their activities, like those of the fractions they direct, are always shrouded in secrecy.

Youth activity is a distinct department of the Party and is run through a special organization known as the Young Communist League. In the United States, this later became known under the title of "American Youth for Democracy," of which the *American Student Union* was a relative. To infiltrate the schools and colleges the League had its own fraction or unit system, guided by party adults. It is assisted by a dual co-ordination with the teachers' fractions and fractions inside the parent-teacher associations.[6]

6. For a specific illustration of this particular penetration, see "Communist Appeal to Youth Aided by New Organizations," Hearing before the Subcommittee to Investigate the Administration of the Internal Security Act and Other Internal Security Laws of the Committee on the Judiciary, United States Senate, 87th Cong., 1st Sess., April 25, 1961.

The Party may also have a department or commission on sports activities. In Europe, where there are large mass-sports organizations, such as the "Sokols" in Czechoslovakia, the aim is to penetrate these organizations and co-ordinate the fraction activities within them. Behind the cover of alleged sports activities and the organization of sports and hikers' clubs, the physically fit and combat-trained elements of the movement are organized, ready for use in such strong-arm activities as the Party may direct. They may be used to protect communist demonstrations and meetings, raid enemy union headquarters, play the strong-arm role on picket lines, beat up defectors or anti-communist leaders, or engage in sabotage.

Analogous activity was illustrated in the United States in September, 1949, when an alleged defense corps of two thousand men commanded by Louis Strauss, a former officer in the United States Army, showed up to "protect" a Paul Robeson meeting in Peekskill, New York. Several double lines of the defense corps surrounded this open-air meeting and the approaches to it. The arms found in their possession were long can openers, baseball bats, knives, and blackjacks. Sports club or "defense" activity may be organized as an adjunct to party-controlled labor unions and fronts.

Operating under the cover of patriotism in the Maquis and the Communist Party Partisans, the communist sports or defense units revealed their power in France after World War II. As the Germans retreated and local authority broke down, they moved in and, under the pretense of punishing collaborators, liquidated their opponents, took over newspapers, raided banks, occupied union headquarters and public offices, and established themselves as police forces in many towns. Considerable armament fell into their hands. These groups created much havoc and might have taken over the government except that France was within the Anglo-American sphere and Soviet troops were far away. In Italy, a comparable operation took place under the cover of the resistance. It proceeded under the blanket of Allied operations against the common enemy, which the Communists, posing as friends, used for their own ulterior purposes. These activities account to a large extent for the rapid post-war growth of the communist parties in both France and Italy.

In Czechoslovakia, the Communists controlled a large, armed workers' defense corps. The 1947 take-over here showed how the force element, essential in any communist seizure of power, can be organized under an innocent-looking camouflage and be ready to operate when the time comes. In industrially backward countries, similar instruments are organized through peasants' leagues. Even when the Communists infiltrate army regiments or a general staff, they still organize politically reliable armed-forces units of their own to facilitate their seizure of power.

The Communist Party also has departments through which it controls and directs organization and agitation and propaganda. Departments controlling these activities are the first to be organized in any party. Others may be formed and dissolved, depending on circumstances, but these two are always present.

The organization department specializes in organization techniques and strategy relating to all phases of the movement, both open and secret, nuclei and fractions, fronts and unions. It teaches these techniques in party schools and conferences. Every district of the Party has an organization department whose activities are synchronized through the national organization department. This agency, which publishes its own special bulletin (the *Party Organizer*), is under the direction of the international organization department in Moscow. Because of the wide scope of their activities and techniques, the Communists have produced the most extensive literature on organization of any political movement.

Agitation and propaganda support all communist organizational efforts. The Agitprop Department, as it is known in the Party, plans both the over-all strategy and the tactics of psychological-warfare campaigns. It co-ordinates the Party's press and publishing outlets, its training schools, bookstores, lectures, and indoctrination activities. Like the National Organization Department, Agitprop also has its district departments. The result is a uniform pattern of communist agitation propaganda on both national and international scales.

The Underground

Moscow requires that every affiliate party have an underground (secret) department. The affairs of this department are under the direction and supervision of the particular party's national secretary and are known to only a few persons. It is a "no questions asked" department. Normally, when the Party operates in the open, this department handles only the top-secret phases of the Party's activity, such as liaison with the Soviet secret services. It transfers suitable party personnel to aid or staff those services and works with secret infiltration cells in strategic government departments or services.

The underground also handles the Party's secret communication with

Moscow and within the country, whether by radio, coded communications, or couriers. This communication system bypasses the official headquarters or known personalities of the Party and uses instead names and addresses of people whose party affiliations are not suspected.

The secret department also makes preparations for the party to go underground in case of war against the Soviet Union or the outlawing of the Party. In the event of war, the Party expects that all known Communists who can be caught will be arrested and interned. It hopes, however, that some of its key personnel, through appropriate planning, may be able to elude arrests. Its main reliance is on a sleeper apparatus composed of party members and trusted fellow travelers whose communist connections are not publicly known or suspected. In the United States, "sleepers" present the F.B.I. with an extremely difficult problem. This apparatus lies in reserve and is ready, aided by the secret-communications system, to operate in case of wartime suppression of the Party.

In case the Party should be outlawed in peacetime, the underground plans for the Party's general apparatus to operate under suitable camouflage, so that the activities of the party nuclei and fractions will be hidden.

The underground is also charged with hiding printing and duplicating facilities and radio-communication equipment which may be difficult to obtain in time of war.

Psychological-political warfare requires an overt apparatus. One must agitate and propagandize in order to recruit. For that reason, the Party will use every loophole to operate through fronts or captive organizations. If need be, it will use camouflage and water down its program to exist as an overt, legal party. If it is unable to maintain a legal status, it will place its varied activities under a myriad of camouflages co-ordinated through the underground. In that case, the underground will become, in effect, the Party, and the open organizations will be the transmission belts to the masses. The 1961 decision of the Supreme Court, declaring the Communist Party, U.S.A., to be an agent of a foreign power may force it to operate in this fashion.

Another function of the communist underground is to provide the base for Soviet espionage and potential sabotage. The Soviet Union commands the largest network of foreign espionage in the world. At least 90 per cent of its agents are nationals of target nations. It is a costly network, not because of the pay received by the agents, most of whom work without compensation, but because of the operational overhead.

In dealing with the Communists, one must discard the view of spies betraying their country for "thirty pieces of silver." Anyone who thinks of Soviet espionage in that way does not begin to understand the foundations upon which it rests.

Soviet espionage is effective because it is a built-in feature of Soviet political warfare. A Harry Dexter White, a Pontecorvo, a Fuchs, an Allan Nunn May, a Rosenberg, or an Alger Hiss is first converted to the cause of communism; his betrayal stems from ideology. Soviet espionage also buys information when necessary, but that is only a minor aspect of the total operation. Soviet espionage will occur again and again so long as communism as an ideology has any attraction.

Throughout history, man has had many loyalties: to his family, then to his tribe, clan, or feudal lord, then to his church or monarch, and, in more recent times, to the nation-state of which he is a citizen. The Communist, however, has only one loyalty and that is to communism. Loyalty is not to the nation but to the Party. The Soviet Union itself is portrayed as the heart of international communism and as such is supposed to command first loyalty from Communists everywhere. If the state or nation is non-communist or anti-communist, the Party commands its members to work for the destruction of the state. As to this point, the initiation pledge of new party members in New York during the thirties was quite revealing:

I pledge myself to rally the masses to defend the Soviet Union. I pledge myself to remain at all times a vigilant and firm defender of the Leninist line of the Party, the only line that insures the triumph of Soviet power in the United States.

Communist loyalty is not a divided loyalty, but an undivided, monolithic loyalty hostile to the United States. Blatant declaration of intended treason was in vogue among the Communists up to World War II. Although since toned down for tactical reasons, the Party's intent and purpose remain the same.

Not every party member or fellow traveler is a spy; but he is mentally conditioned to become one, if asked. The Kremlin does not call upon all party members to do so; on the contrary, Soviet intelligence is very selective. But every communist party is a reservoir from which to recruit agents. Nor is espionage the only service which a party can render its Soviet masters. It is only part of the manifold work of subversion, and often not the most important part.

A less-known operation of the Soviet underground is sabotage, not the sabotage of amateurs but that of professionally trained personnel who combine a knowledge of modern technology and science with the art of large-scale organization. Except for some occasional trial runs, sabotage has not been much in vogue since World War II. If the time for it should ever become ripe, however, we are likely to be surprised by the extent and the thoroughness of its preparation. The saboteurs, too, are recruited mainly from the ranks of the various communist parties.

Ethnic Groups

Another apparatus or department—one unique to the American Communist Party—is the Nationalities Groups Commission of the Central Committee of the Communist Party, U.S.A. Within every nationality organization in the United States the Party operates a fraction system, aiming to influence and capture the existing organizations and create separate fronts for that purpose. The party activities within each organization are co-ordinated through the Commission and group secretaries, directed by a member of the Central Committee.

Party activities in nationality groups have been largely overlooked or underestimated. The fact is that at one time the American Communist Party controlled eleven daily newspapers in different languages, some of which now exist only as weeklies. Even the smallest of these language-fraction systems published at least one weekly paper. Some even had monthlies in addition to dailies and weeklies, and each of these contained large amounts of communist literature in a particular foreign language, printed on its presses or received from foreign communist sources.

During the first ten years of the Party's existence in the United States, at least 80 per cent of its membership and funds (not counting Moscow's subsidies) came from foreign-language groups. Even today the Party counts heavily upon its overlooked empire among the foreign-language groups. In accordance with the Party's general strategy, interest is concentrated upon those nationality groups who work in the steel and automobile industries, in coal, iron, and copper mines, and in other strategic industries.

The fraction system employed among nationality groups played a major role in the early history of the C.I.O. By supplying speakers and organizers in various languages the Communist Party's infiltration among workers in the C.I.O. was made easier. The network still exists, but with the defection of several communist-controlled national unions and the expulsion of the others by the C.I.O., this operation is now less significant.

Pressured by Moscow, the American Communist Party also created a special department for dealing with Negroes, the National Negro Commission. The Commission began its activities by stressing the special grievances of the Negroes, advocating social equality, and generally fanning race hatred based on inequalities and prejudices. In 1928, Stalin invented the "theory of racial nationalism," which held that the American Negroes were a nation and should be recognized as such. According to Stalin's theory, the Negroes in the more than two hundred Southern counties in which they had a majority should have formed an independent Negro state ("Black Republic"). Behind the theory was the strategic concept of utilizing the American Negro, as the most advanced element of his race, to stimulate nationalist movements in Africa and the Caribbean area. Similar departments, staffed mainly by white Communists, were created in the British and French communist parties for operations in Africa.

An enormous amount of propaganda literature was produced on the subject. To the surprise of Moscow, however, the American Negro was not enthusiastic about the idea of a "Black Republic" in the South. Even the few American Negro Communists were either hostile to or lukewarm on the subject. The segregation of the American Negro into a "Black Republic" was considered both undesirable and impracticable. Its realization presupposed a bloodbath in the South and widespread racial strife in the North. Immersing the United States in race warfare was undoubtedly desirable from the point of view of Moscow, but it did not make good sense to the American Negro; what he wants is to be equal to other American citizens, not to be segregated further from them in a political and social sense. Most of the white Communists, too, had their doubts about this theory, but so subservient was the American Communist Party to Moscow's orders that Stalin's dictum on the Negro question remained as a guiding principle in the Party as long as Stalin lived.

Party Negro activities hit their stride only in the thirties. The Party believed that the unorganized Negroes could be corralled into communist fronts and that it could penetrate whatever non-communist organizations existed among the Negroes. It therefore set up a deceptive front, called the League of Struggle for Negro Rights, and worked with a front organization of Negroes, known as The National Negro Congress, in order to unite its own fronts with other willing Negro organizations. That was the Party's high point in trying to capture the American Negro.

The united front collapsed with the announcement of the Soviet-German alliance, and from then on, The National Negro Congress became little more than just a party front, until its demise at the close of World War II. The Party's voluminous racial propaganda and agitation did, however, have an impact on large sections of the Negro intelligentsia and, through them, on the Negro masses. A large number of Negro workers were influenced by communist fronts to join communist-controlled unions, thus bolstering the Party's strength in the labor field.

On the whole, however, the Negro remained suspicious of communist motives. He stayed away from the communist Negro fronts and preferred to join liberal-type Negro organizations, such as the N.A.A.C.P. or the Urban League. The Party therefore switched its policy and concentrated upon infiltrating the growing non-communist Negro organizations, seeking to capture them or split them from within through its secret-fraction system. The main target at the present is the National Association for the Advancement of Colored People, which has operated with care to exclude communist organizational penetration.

In addition to trying to organize the Negroes the Communists have sought vigorously to use the American Negro question to emphasize to Asiatics and Africans the "cruel repression of the colored races in America." One Soviet propaganda film shown throughout the world depicts a riotous nightclub scene in which drunken GIs in Europe not only barred Negro servicemen from their festivities but went out on the streets to beat them up for sport.

Control Commission

The most unusual of the major departments of the Party is the Control Commission, which enforces party discipline and keeps out enemy elements. The Control Commission (C.C.) is unique in that, unlike the other departments of the Party, it has nothing to do with mass activity. It is the police department of the Party. It reflects the police complex which is inherent in the communist mind. While the Party is in opposition, however, the Control Commission confines itself to the policing of party members. When the Party is in power the Control Commission continues as the special police, co-ordinating its activities, when needed, with the regular political police of a Soviet-type government. Party purges, for instance, are the responsibility of the Control Commission.

In the Soviet Union, the Control Commission was originally supposed to catch anti-communist spies within the movement, watch morality within the Party, and try deviators from the changing party line. Its jurisdiction stopped at the doors of the Central Committee, which, in the party organization, has supremacy. Cases involving Central Committee members were tried by the Committee itself.

The fratricidal struggle within the communist movement which accompanied Stalin's rise to power transformed the Control Commission into a tool of the ruling Stalinist faction. Party members were supposed to spy upon each other and report to the Control Commission. If a party leader was suspect, the Control Commission furnished him with an assistant whose task was to "frame" his boss. Party members of the higher rank were asked to furnish their complete biographies. Information regarding their past activities and associations, their families and friends, the stand they took in various party controversies, and their attitude toward deviators or defectors with whom they might have associated in the past could thus be checked and used against them if they defected or became suspect.

In free countries control commissions have no jails or slave-labor camps at their disposal, but they can arrange for an expelled individual to be deported or otherwise legally harassed. There have been cases of physical manhandling through the third degree and even some unsolved assassinations. As a rule, however, in free countries a control commission limits itself, if possible, to ostracism, smearing, and hounding the expelled individual from the job. One can join the Party freely, but one can quit it only at a risk. Deviationists from the party ranks are more greatly feared than any others openly hostile to the Communists.

The Party's Financial System

If the layman knows little about the inner workings of the Communist Party's organizational system, he knows far less about the methods of financing its far-flung operations. It is generally assumed that the costs of some of the Party's activities are met by collections, such as dues in the party of each country, or that Moscow pays for most of them. Moscow does pay, as already indicated, for the headquarters and elite training operations in Russia. Most of these expenses are defrayed from an international assessment imposed upon party and trade-union members *in Russia*. But subsidies from Moscow to the various communist parties outside the Iron Curtain usually average only about 20 per cent of the total cost of operation of these parties. In other words, Moscow expects these parties to raise 80 per cent of their costs from within the country in which they operate.

The policy is to "let Capitalism pay for its own destruction." The 20 per cent cannot be paid in rubles because the Soviet monetary unit is worthless outside the Iron Curtain; it must be paid in dollars or other foreign currency.

The 20 per cent subsidy to parties in capitalist countries is doled out in the form of *strategic* subsidies; that is, Moscow prescribes how the money should be spent and through its field representatives sees to it that it is so spent. The general pattern for allocating these monies is as follows:

(1) For maintenance of the central apparatus of the Party, its propaganda activities, and such central newspapers as the *Daily Worker,* Moscow does not pay all the expenses; it merely covers the deficit, thus assuring the continuance of the central apparatus of the Party;
(2) Strategic subsidies for infiltrating or organizing activities among communications workers and for penetration of key seaports, railroad workers, etc.;
(3) Subsidies for infiltrating strategic industries, such as coal and iron ore, copper mining, oil and chemical works, and steel plants;
(4) Subsidies for the infiltration of armed services and youth activities; and
(5) Subsidies for ideological and organizational infiltration of key white-collar personnel in government offices, laboratories, newspapers, etc.

Many of these activities are very expensive in their initial stages, and returns are slow in coming. Moscow's subsidies are used to pave the way, while subsequent costs may be paid out of party dues. What is or is not strategic varies from country to country. In backward countries, more of the subsidies may go for operations among the peasants, the students, and the intelligentsia and less for operations among the workers.

If a country becomes a primary target, the Moscow subsidies will be increased; they may then be limited only by the capacity of the organization to absorb them effectively. Even more will be forthcoming if the country becomes an immediate target for conquest. In that case, funds may be made available to buy up desirable newspapers through third parties, to corrupt minor competing parties and leaders, and to procure arms. Conversely, if a country becomes less important, the subsidy may be reduced to the point of assuring only the maintenance of the central apparatus of the Party. Moscow's subsidy policy toward the various communist parties is very flexible and adjusts itself to the over-all strategy.

Despite the size of the headquarters organization in Moscow, only the Soviet Communist Party pays dues to support it. Officially, the present-day

world-wide communist movement parades as a loosely fraternal world federation of autonomous or semi-autonomous communist parties which are
independent of the Soviet government. In 1928, there was inserted in the
Comintern constitution a proviso stating that all parties should contribute
dues. It was added to bolster that fiction, but it was never enforced. This
should make it clear that the communist parties and their world headquarters are dependent on and operate as tools of the Soviet government.
This is the only world-wide political organization which pays no dues for
the maintenance of its world headquarters and whose affiliates are sub-
sidized.

We shall now indicate briefly how money is raised by the local parties.
Keep in mind that although all activities in the communist movement are
directed activities, most of them are carried out voluntarily; that is, the
individual member donates his time and even contributes financially.
This is not figured in the cost. Only the elite working full time in the party
apparatus receive a salary, which in capitalist countries is approximately
that of a skilled worker, sometimes less. Even part of that, as we shall see,
is often made the responsibility of captive organizations and fronts.

Funds raised by the Party cover expenditures for propaganda and agitation, headquarters, salaries for the elite, mass meetings and campaigns,
concentration on strategic operations and areas, and legal defense.

A substantial amount of party income is derived from dues and assess-
ments, which amount to about 5 per cent of the member's earnings, or
about $100 a year on an average. Some pay less, others considerably more,
according to their earnings. The dues system varies from party to party.
In poor countries, the income per member from that source is considerably less. It is, however, a steady income. Thus a party of 100,000 employed
members would have an income of about $10,000,000 a year from dues
alone. The major part of this would go to the Central Committee, and the
rest would be divided among the lower echelons of the Party.

Another source of income are the endless special campaigns, in which
the members are asked to contribute to the party press, to defend arrested
Communists, and to help other so-called class-war victims. At every mass
meeting a maximum effort is made to "milk" the audience: direct collections, pledges, and sales of literature. The income above the expenses is
then divided among the higher echelons of the Party according to the purpose of the meeting and the party echelon arranging it. The party members present at these meetings are supposed to set a good example and

contribute accordingly. The Central Committee may cut itself in on the profits of large meetings, to the tune of 20 per cent or more, but as a rule, the profits from smaller meetings go to the district or local organizations arranging the meeting.

Periodically, the Party will clothe itself in Samaritan robes and carry on a huge national campaign on behalf of persons the Communists assert were unjustly condemned to death. It thus launched the Sacco-Vanzetti campaign in the late twenties, the Scottsboro boys campaign in the thirties, and the Rosenberg campaign in the fifties. In such cases, the whole machinery is mobilized—the Party, its fronts, and captive organizations. Large amounts of agitation literature will be turned out. Mass meetings will be arranged from coast to coast. Speakers will visit all possible non-communist organizations. Picket lines will march and street demonstrations will take place. Tag days will be held to collect funds on the streets and everybody within reach will be tapped to help the victims of the alleged class or racial injustice. These emotional campaigns, aside from their psychological-political value, are also staged for their always-considerable financial worth to the Party.

Similar types of campaigns are periodically conducted around certain strikes which the Party chooses to dramatize—strikes led by party members. The campaign will collect funds to aid and relieve the strikers. All party-controlled unions will be milked to the maximum for that relief, and all other unions will be worked over for help. A large part of the relief always finds its way into the party treasury.

In certain countries, as in Italy, Party operated businesses also provide a source of income. In Italy the Communist Party runs agricultural whole-sale and brokerage firms for East-West trade.

One of the best ways to raise large amounts of money for the Party in the United States is to loot the treasuries of captive unions, fronts, and other organizations controlled by the Party. The income from that source may equal or even exceed the income from dues and all other sources, depending upon the extent of the Party's control and influence at the time. Several subterfuges may be used for that purpose.

If a wealthy union is on strike and donations are being made, the Party's take is always substantial. Its share will come under the cover of strike expenditures. Another method is for a front of the Party to take a loan from the wealthier union or front. In time, the loan is written off as uncollectable, the money finding its way into the Party's coffers. The fronts

are also used to obtain donations or loans from liberal foundations dedicated to worthy causes or from rich and sympathetic "angels." A substantial part of such loans or donations finds its way into the Party's funds. A
cruder way, if the front organization is thoroughly controlled by the Party,
is to have the secretary-treasurer hand over the amount required and then
cover it as an expenditure incurred by the union or front in the course
of its legitimate activities. The members of a union, even if they suspect
such practice, would find it very difficult to do anything about it in an
organization where the secretary-treasurer, the bookkeeper, and even the
auditor are all party members or fellow travelers. Union treasuries are
thus pilfered to contribute to the Party. Also used are the organizations
captured by the Party through infiltration. Since the fronts and the captives actually operate the short-range program of the Party, the Party's
funds can be used for its long-range strategic designs.

In the United States all of these organizations are tax exempt as non-
profit organizations and much of the activity is voluntary. Hence, each
dollar that falls into communist hands goes a long way in making capitalism pay for its own downfall.

Communist operational techniques and organizational approaches are
far from static. The fronts are merely the outer shell. The core and the
co-ordinator behind them is the fraction system of the communist parties,
imbedded in all their fronts, ultimately controlled by the international
party apparatus in Moscow. Without that hard core on the inside, the local
parties and their fronts would be apt to wander off in all directions instead
of following the line of "the integral World Communist Movement."

CHAPTER IV

THE SCOPE OF COMMUNIST POLITICAL WARFARE

MODERN MEANS OF COMMUNICATION AND INCREASING POLITICAL awareness have made it possible to reach the minds of men far more rapidly and persuasively than in previous centuries. This, in turn, makes it possible to organize interest groups effectively along economic, social, and political lines.

The days when the Church and the state were the only organizations of social consequence have long since passed. The political parties which evolved with the development of representative government are no longer the only large political-influence organizations in the social panorama. Today's individual is increasingly an "organization man" who belongs to numerous pressure groups, ranging in the United States from the National Association of Manufacturers on the one hand to labor unions on the other.

In Western countries, the leaders of special-interest organizations—representing labor, farmers, merchants, manufacturers, and other groups—seek constantly to obtain for their members an ever larger slice of the profits of production. Their competing claims create a pattern of continued social conflict conducted in the name of divergent ideologies. This conflict can easily be held within bounds in times of prosperity, but it can become explosive in times of political or economic crisis.

The Communist Party was designed to exploit the turmoil of continuous ideological and social conflict in modern societies. It offers a *total* solution of the conflict, ostensibly in favor of those most aggrieved: the proletariat. In every country in which it exists, it seeks to aggravate rather than harmonize conflict; to pit the contending segments of society against each other; to penetrate the existing organizations and use them for its own purposes; to promote crises as means of seizing power.

All totalitarian parties, whether communist or fascist, have certain essensential characteristics: (1) they use hostility to make their propaganda tangible, practical, and forceful; (2) they are monolithic and highly centralized; and (3) once in power, they suppress and liquidate all opposition. The total party then becomes the total state; with all internal conflicts suppressed, the nation becomes militarized and inner hostilities are diverted toward the outside.

On a tactical level, however, there are considerable differences between communist and fascist parties. Communist hate propaganda is primarily social and is aimed at stirring up class hatred and exploiting class animosities, while fascist—or nazi—propaganda is primarily nationalistic and racial. Communists do, however, use "nationalism" when it serves their purposes, just as Fascists will make use of class hatred.

Similar differences exist in their methods of organization. The Fascists have generally given more emphasis to direct use of military power, employing political warfare merely as a supplement, while the Communists, even in this age of ICBMs, consider all warfare, whatever the instrument, as political.

Political warfare as conceived by Lenin and Stalin is far more than agitation and propaganda to "sell" communism as an idea. It involves, above all, the systematic organizational penetration of a country—the infiltration of strategic unions, associations, communications, and government agencies for the purpose of utilizing such organizations for communist ends.

Communist Opportunism

The Communists' shift from a one-class to a multiple-class base has facilitated their operations greatly. A major part of these operations is carried out by psychological warfare, which consists of two main categories: propaganda and agitation. Propaganda deals with long-term indoctrination undertaken to recruit and sustain the intellectual leaders of the movement. It is the mental food (or poison) for the thousands, while agitation, which simplifies the objectives of propaganda, is the diluted feed for the millions, the masses. The latter is the more deceptive of the two.

Propaganda, as conceived in such political-warfare colleges as the Lenin School, does not deal only with the universal objectives of communism— the abolition of all forms of private property and the replacement of capitalism by socialism or "communism"—but also embraces subsidiary objectives which either lead directly to the ultimate goal or are of aid in the disruption of the "old" society. Communists, for instance, will often pose as fanatical advocates of nationalism ("national liberation"), not because they believe in it, but because it helps to weaken and fragment their enemies. Once in power they will advocate just the opposite, dialectically justifying their conduct on the ground that in the new society, communism, there is no room for historical nationalism. In the same category is communist anti-imperialism, whereby the builders of a world empire blandly pose as anti-imperialists.

A vast theoretical literature has been produced by the communist movement to fan emotion-ridden demands. Thus Communists rationalize themselves as champions of peace while engaging in permanent war or as saviors of the poor peasants while aiming at their subjugation. The Communists' propaganda thus includes (1) advocacy of their over-all doctrines; (2) propagation of their long-range demands; and (3) immediate demands (e.g., "ban the bomb today").

Agitation popularizes the objectives of propaganda. In the twenties, and even before, the Soviet regime was popularized at home and abroad through claims that the workers, acting through factory committees, were in control of the factories; that exploitation of man by man had been abolished in Soviet Russia; that unemployment—a basic evil of capitalism—was no more; and that women had not only equal rights but also maternity pay, with their children cared for in factory kindergartens while they and their husbands worked. The peasants were told that they were the lords of the countryside through membership in village soviets; that the land was being equitably distributed; that they were insured against natural calamities; that modern agricultural machinery and advice would be supplied to them; and that the Soviet government guaranteed a fair price for their product. The promises for the future were even better. Everyone was to be a comrade and Soviet society would achieve genuine equality. Setting the tone for these glittering promises was a catching phrase from the *Communist Manifesto:* "From each according to his ability, to each according to his needs."

By the mid-thirties the Kremlin masters of agit-prop tired of their own mendacity. The false agitation slogans, which sounded increasingly hollow in the face of the obvious realities, were repeated only on such ceremonial occasions as the anniversary of Lenin's death or the anniversary of the communist seizure of power. But outside Russia, the extravagant slogans continued to be repeated and believed by many. And each time the Communists seized another country after World War II, they repeated their slogans to the as yet inexperienced masses who wanted to believe.

In Russia and to a large extent in the satellites, communist propaganda and agitation have been discredited for a long time. In the non-communist countries, especially those least experienced in political warfare, they are still quite effective, particularly when centered around long-range demands. As a rule, the demands are built around latent grievances exacerbated by well-organized propaganda and agitation. The striving for national independence is a prime example. Such a demand, with its strong anti-imperialist coloration, is capable of uniting the active nationalist elements in the colonies with large sympathetic segments of the population in the home country.

A long-range demand of this sort, reduced to the level of mass agitation, would read something like this: All social ills, real or imaginary, in the colonized country are the result of imperialist exploitation by the home country. As a result, the indigenous bourgeoisie (businessmen, big and small) will be induced to believe that after the "imperialists" are expelled, they, the native bourgeoisie, will have the field for themselves, including the profits and enterprises of the "imperialists." The native intelligentsia in particular will anticipate a great future inside and outside the new government in the form of more jobs, promotions, prestige, and power. The workers will be encouraged to strike against the imperialist enterprises in the hope of receiving great benefits after liberation from the foreign yoke. The worker activists will be told that the native bourgeoisie can be fought more effectively if separated from the imperialist bourgeoisie of the home country. The peasants will be promised major reforms, expropriation of "imperialist" landlords, abolition of usury, government aid and credit, and democracy and organization to protect their interests.

If in the course of the development of such a national liberation movement the Communists succeed in gaining hegemony over the campaign, the coloring of the immediate demands will be changed to include land for the peasants (expropriated from all landlords) and nationalization of industry (expropriated from the more well-to-do native bourgeoisie).

The orderly, calculated communist methodology can be summarized: (1) the over-all goal (seizure of power); (2) long-range demands, which comprise the general social strategy for reaching this goal; and (3) immediate demands, the tactical implementation of strategy. The first two elements are propaganda, and the third is a form of agitation, the retail version of the second element. The agitation process is quite detailed, adjusting itself to each segment of the population and the ever changing situation.

We shall now deal with the Communists' strategy of demands. Communist demands are divided into socialist demands and bourgeois democratic demands. Socialist demands require only brief treatment because they are better known and understood. The bourgeois democratic demands are more deceptive.

As an irresponsible opposition which aims not to improve, but to destroy, existing democratic or non-communist forms of society, the Communists have produced wagonloads of demands. To an untutored observer, the profusion of these demands seems chaotic—but there is order and purpose in this seeming confusion.

In Karl Marx's time almost all demands were socialist, as were most demands in the early stages of the communist movement. Lenin introduced the concept of bourgeois democratic demands, a concept which on a tactical level was developed much further by Stalin and which now predominates in communist political warfare outside the Iron Curtain. Socialist demands, however, have not been abandoned, especially in those industrialized countries where socialist parties are also competing for the workers.

A socialist demand is one that aims at undermining the foundations of capitalism. Nationalization is one such long-range demand. By calling for government ownership of the factories, mines, subsoil resources, and principal means of communication, it aims eventually to eliminate the big bourgeoisie, thus creating a breach in the bourgeois front.

Nationalization is not a demand of the Communists alone; it is a demand of the Socialists as well. The Socialists used it first. Experience has shown that if the demand for nationalization is confined to the big industrial enterprises, it is possible to line up on its behalf not only large sections of the intelligentsia but also the small farmers, especially in the more backward countries. The fact that farmers rarely like big industrial finance and marketing corporations is exploited in this maneuvering.

The Communists are not interested in nationalization as a socialist reform; they are interested in it as a means to an end. To the Communists, the elimination of the big bourgeoisie through nationalization can be the start of a total overturn. Nationalization of the big enterprises can end with the total nationalization of everything and everybody.

The strategic long-term communist demand pattern has been to weaken the bourgeois democratic world structure by splitting the colonial and metropolitan bourgeoisie under the anti-imperialism slogan while simultaneously seeking the elimination of the big bourgeoisie in both the colonial and metropolitan countries under the slogan of nationalization. Even though the Communists fail to reach the end goal of such a movement, the minimum objective of wounding or softening up the social structure of the enemy will at least be realized.

Generally, the demand for nationalization becomes potent during periods of economic or political crisis, when the existing system is weakened. Post–World War II Britain provided a good example. The success of that demand will depend on objective factors, as well as the duration and effectiveness of the preceding propaganda and agitation.

The tactical orchestration which accompanies a nationalization drive includes the discrediting of private ownership as a social institution. Insistent demands are made for more government control; class hatred is generated and fanned to a point where production morale goes down, while demands for wage increases, shorter working hours, and other benefits go up. At the same time, communist-oriented unions and factory committees gradually edge in on the functions of management. By this process all is made ready, ideologically and organizationally, for the owners to be pushed aside. Nationalization then becomes a reality.

The Socialists and Communists may be found working together (directly or indirectly) up to the point of the nationalization of the big bourgeois interests. If the Communists do not gain hegemony and thus become the agents of nationalization, they will continue the fight against the new bosses, the socialist state managers of industry, even more viciously than before. New demands, even more exorbitant, will be pressed against the new socialist state, and if the Communists have enough influence, strikes and stoppages will continue and production morale will be lowered. The new system will be denounced as state capitalism and the socialists as traitors to the working class. The fight for hegemony will continue, even at the expense of the national economy.

While such disruptive operations are carried on in the enemy camp, the opposite tack is pursued in the Soviet Union. There, tight labor discipline is the order of the day. Typical is this excerpt from a January, 1960 Soviet ideological directive:

The instilling of a communist attitude toward labor, the struggle for practical implementation under present conditions of the principle "He who does not work does not eat," and the struggle against loafers and the vestiges of parasitic elements which wish to live off society while giving nothing to it, have not occupied a proper place in propaganda work.

The communist strategic and tactical approach to the masses of democratic countries is rarely made through communist theory but through seemingly practical and desirable long-range and immediate demands. The Socialists, who often originated such demands in the first place, undercut this approach. Thus in many countries, such as Germany, Austria, and Sweden, where the Socialists have established themselves, they have blocked the Communists effectively. The persistent bitterness of the Communists against genuine Socialists is understandable.

It is significant that the Socialists believe in the reforms they advocate. With the Communists, reforms are merely a means to an end, a trick of warfare, of "revolutionary opportunism" as Lenin called it. The Socialists' belief in their reforms or demands stems from the fact that they aim to transform capitalism more gradually, by parliamentary and semiparliamentary methods—reform it away, as it were—and take over an intact government. Socialism seeks control, in the main, by persuasion plus political and economic pressures. Communism seeks power with persuasion backed by force.

A companion demand to nationalization, also originating with the Socialists at the outset of the twentieth century, is progressive taxation. Within reasonable limits progressive taxation can be a socially constructive way of raising revenues. It is generally forgotten, however, that schemes for progressive taxation were originally devised to place the burden of armament, as well as of reforms demanded by the Socialists, upon the upper classes. The Fascists, under Mussolini (himself a former socialist leader), found more extensive uses for the idea of progressive taxation. Mussolini conceived of taxation as a substitute for nationalization. In short, taxes were to take the earnings while letting the owners keep their property. The squeeze could be put on gradually. The upper classes would be permitted to retain enough of the profits to keep them relatively content, and the government, thus strengthened, would rule the country's economy.

The communist high command in Moscow at first showed little interest in using progressive taxation as a demand. They were, however, keen observers of the political-warfare methods of their direct competitors, the Socialists and Fascists. They observed in particular that the Fascists and Nazis, while engaging in a direct frontal attack against the Communists and the Socialists, took over the bourgeois democratic state under the cover of legality, i.e., by infiltration. They did not destroy the bourgeois state there, as Lenin advocated, but took it over semi-legally and then destroyed it, step by step.

Borrowing from their enemies the tactic of political infiltration, the Communists adopted the so-called Trojan-horse tactic in 1935 at the Seventh Congress of the Communist International. In asking Communists to infiltrate the democratic organizations of the West, Bulgarian Georgi Dmitrov, Stalin's front man in the Comintern, called it the method of getting "into the heart of the enemy" in preparation for the "second round of battles, for the proletarian revolution."

The new tactic became known in the West as the "Democratic Popular Front." Everyone the Communists had denounced before (except the Nazis and the Fascists) was invited to join. The maneuver was a greater success than Moscow had expected. It is to be doubted, however, that Stalin, who shared Hitler's contempt for bourgeois politicians, anticipated the impact of the new tactic upon the politically unsophisticated United States. By 1936, united fronts had mushroomed all over the American social landscape and were advocating a myriad of reforms. To pay for the reforms, taxes were to climb progressively higher and higher and cut deeper into earnings—to the point of becoming confiscatory. Capital accumulation was thus to be shifted from its former private base into the hands of the government.

There were other groups advocating progressive taxation in the United States for legitimate reasons. But the Communists were the most energetic. The depression created a favorable climate for these ideas and World War II made higher taxes mandatory.

History teaches that the handling of a crisis situation, such as a depression, may be resolved in several ways. The Communists, posing as friendly partners of the democratic front, were interested in solving it in ways which, if carried to extremes, would ultimately weaken the basic structure of the system.

Progressive taxation, like political unionism, became a tool of communist economic-political warfare because it could be aimed at certain strata of bourgeois democratic society: the managerial groups, whose incentive and energy are so important to production. To the Communists, progressive taxation is not based on a principle but is merely a tactic that might serve a communist purpose.

The long-range aim of communist demands in the major Western nations remains the same, namely to weaken capitalism's base of private enterprise and property by making these institutions insecure. Once the sense of security and stability is gone, there remains a condition of fluidity propitious for the various forms of communist political warfare.

Using the "Unfinished Tasks" of the Bourgeois Democratic Revolution

The Communists' use of bourgeois democratic demands began with Lenin's theory of "the bourgeois democratic revolution carried out by the proletariat." Lenin developed several theses. First, the bourgeoisie had failed in a number of countries to carry through its own bourgeois democratic program. This was particularly true in the backward colonial and semi-colonial countries which came under the political domination of industrialized nations. Second, during the nineteenth century the bourgeoisie, according to Lenin, had become politically moribund. Third, since the bourgeoisie had become decadent, only the proletariat could carry out the unfulfilled tasks of the bourgeois democratic revolution and in the process transmute liberal democracy into the socialist revolution.

The bourgeois democratic revolutions of France, England, and the United States established individual liberty, abolished servitude and slavery, established equality and fraternity among men, and by the free market released the productive forces of industrialization. In seeking to exploit the revolutionary impulse, Lenin added a few demands which were not necessarily inconsistent with the purposes of the bourgeois democratic revolution, such as the breakup of the big landed estates, the right to a job, and the right to free education. In Stalin's time, the tactic of advocating bourgeois democratic demands was expanded.

Since the late thirties the Communists have been using both long-range and immediate bourgeois democratic demands and long-range and immediate socialist demands. It is this combination which makes possible a communist penetration of the Western and Western-trained intelligentsia and the lower middle class.

The socialist-type demands are more readily recognizable because, as a rule, they strike at proprietary relationships, which are the bedrock of capitalism. Bourgeois democratic demands, on the other hand, are not directly aimed at the fundamentals of the system; they are designed, instead, to strain and overstrain the system, softening it up for the more direct socialist demands. Taxes, per se, are not a socialist demand, but when taxation becomes confiscatory, it becomes anti-property. Capitalism, the most flexible of all social systems, can also absorb a certain level of nationalization. However, when nationalization invades production and commerce, restricting the fields in which competition increases the chances for efficiency, it strikes at the roots of the system.

It may well be that necessity was the father of Lenin's political invention. The proletariat in 1917 was such a small segment of the population in Russia that Lenin had to win the support of sections of the bourgeoisie, as well as the peasants, in order to win and stay in power. By posing as a proponent of the bourgeois democratic revolution, he was able to gain these essential converts. This scheme was later applied in China with refinements added by Stalin and Mao Tse-tung. It was further perfected in Fidel Castro's takeover of Cuba. The idea of a party based on the proletarian class, pretending to carry out the revolutionary tasks of the bourgeoisie while actually intending to abolish it as a class, shows the scope and the daring of the political thinking of Lenin and his associates. It reflected their confidence in their capacity to outmaneuver not only the bourgeoisie but also their socialist competitors.

Posing as agents for the bourgeois revolution would have been anathema to nineteenth-century Marxism, but Lenin defended his thesis as the Marxism of the twentieth century. According to Marx and Lenin, capitalism is both a constructive and destructive force. It is constructive in that it liberated the forces of production from the chains of feudalism and thus made possible modern productivity. Communists regard capitalism as self-destructive because as it grows it tends to liquidate small private enterprise in favor of big corporations. In thus "proletarizing" the former small property owners, as well as allegedly reducing the workers to a below-subsistence level of living, it creates the conditions for its own destruction. Actually, the failure of the poor to become poorer in the industrialized nations of the West has proved one of the fundamental errors of the Marxian analysis. From a political-warfare strategy point of view, nevertheless, the communist problem is how to take advantage of these assumed contradictory processes in order to accelerate the destruction of the system.

Lenin contributed the thesis, discussed in his book entitled *Imperialism, the Last Stage of Capitalism,* that the initial progressive course of the bourgeoisie in advanced countries was terminated by their exploitation of their colonies. At the same time, according to Lenin, this exploitation checked the otherwise inevitable decline of the factory proletariat into abject poverty; but aside from this short-term gain, capitalism ossified because of its bigness within the advanced countries and its alliance with landed feudalism in the colonies. When capitalism reached this stage, Lenin contended that the unfulfilled objectives of the bourgeois democratic revolution could be carried forward only by the new progressive class, the proletariat.

Major Demands

With this theoretical framework in mind, let us review the chief bourgeois democratic demands pressed by the Communists, always keeping in mind their "double think" on the subject, namely, "Don't do as I do; do as I say."

(1) *National liberation.* This demand, if fully realized, would double the number of nations in Europe and Asia. But this, of course, is not the true goal of the Communists, since the Soviet Union itself could be divided into at least a dozen nations and China into several distinct countries. Obviously, the strategic objective behind this democratic demand is the splintering of the non-communist camp into numerous weak units.

(2) *Division of the land* in favor of the small farmers or peasants, without compensation to present owners. This demand (with limited compensation) was carried out in Japan by the American occupation authorities under General Douglas MacArthur. It, too, is a double-edged sword capable of strengthening democratic capitalism in some countries and hence is used by the Communists only in such areas and at such times as may serve their purpose.

(3) *Abolition of slavery and involuntary servitude and all its impediments.* Since this demand had been carried out in most areas before the Communists came on the scene, their emphasis is on the resulting problems. They may press for the end of the system of sharecropping, racial discrimination, caste discrimination, indebtedness through usury, "feudal class justice," and other remnants of "feudalism." These demands, too, are pressed only where and when it suits Moscow. Wherever Moscow finds it expedient to deal with tribal and feudal lords, for example in the Middle East, such demands are held in abeyance.

Each of these long-range demands of international significance can be social dynamite, given a favorable situation and at least an embryonic communist organization. Given sufficient ineptitude in the governing circles, they can shatter political stability.

Still pursuing the theme of bourgeois democratic demands, let us look at some less obvious ones: a guaranteed living wage, old age pensions at full pay, and unemployment insurance at full pay. These democratic demands are advanced in the more developed industrial countries, and the Com-

munists always have ample arguments to justify them. Each demand is
designed to meet the aspirations of a particular group in mass society. As a
rule, the Communists tailor the more moderate demands to give them the
aggressive character necessary for communist purposes. They thus attract
to themselves the more "militant" or extremist elements in each pressure
group.

The traditionally conservative small farmer in the more developed
country often finds himself in a tight squeeze for reasons beyond his control. He has to buy at high prices and sell at cost or even below. This offers
the Communists an opportunity to move in and gain a "beachhead" by
pushing such democratic demands as:

(1) One hundred per cent price parity—to give the farmers an income
commensurate with that of industrial workers (the base calculation is taken
to be a ten-year period when farm income was the highest);
(2) Free fire, hail, flood, and natural-calamity insurance—to protect the
farmer against loss of income due to causes beyond his control;
(3) Tax exemption for low-income farms and farm co-operatives; and
(4) Divisions of the land in share-cropping (plantation) areas.

Among the theories set forth to justify these and similar demands is the
one that the nation is a boarder eating at the table of the farmer and hence
must pay for its board. The demands can be met by price-fixing—abolition
of the free market—by various types of government subsidies paid from
taxes, or both. That the family farmer often is in need of help is obvious,
but the medicine prescribed by the Communists is the one most destructive
to the basic tenets of the capitalist system. Their medicine is concocted to
weaken individual ownership.

From the few examples cited, it should be clear that communist political
warfare is built largely around demands of a social nature which the Communists exaggerate so as to make them potentially destructive of society
itself. A list of all the demands of the Communists, coined or redesigned,
socialist or democratic, would fill a book.

Demands to be of most value, however, must eventually be translated into
governmental action. To effect this, the communists seek to elect legislators
to the parliaments of democratic countries. Communist operational doctrine requires that each party member elected to a legislative office work
as an agitator in the enemy's camp. The communist parliamentarian either
disrupts the legislative machinery; prevents it from working smoothly; or
backs legislation designed to hobble the government's ability to deal with

pressing problems. The Czechoslovakian coup was a prime example of a revolution achieved mainly through "Revolutionary Parliamentarianism."[1]

The Strategic Aim

When the capitalist system is healthy, many communist sponsored demands are realizable with only a small amount of friction. But the Communists are interested in the generation of continuing friction, not the realization of demands. Therefore, the sharper the formulation of the more extreme demands, the more friction created. The weaker the system gets, the more utopian become the demands and the bitterer the struggle.

It should also be observed that, theoretically, most of these demands seem realizable under capitalism. In other words, they are not a direct attack upon the system, as socialist demands generally are, but an indirect attack. They are designed to admit the communist Trojan horse into the bourgeois camp and to induce elements of that camp to side with the Communists.

Capitalism, midwife of representative government and of democracy, has had many a crisis in its relatively young and vigorous life. It has met these crises and has continued to develop. It never had to fight for its life as a social system because there was no better system to challenge it. It never met an antagonist ready, willing, and able to take advantage of its faults and crises, aggravating them, and seeking to use them for the kill. Rarely has a political force representing an inferior social vision—communism— been so well organized for the destruction of a superior society.

1. For a full exposé of how the communists use bourgeois legislatures in political warfare see "How Parliament Can Play a Revolutionary Part in the Transition to Socialism and the Role of the Popular Masses," by Jan Kozak, published by the Independent Information Centre, 4, Holland Road, London, W. 14 (G.B.). In his introduction to this work the Right Hon. Lord Morrison of Lambeth, C.M. wrote:

"The technique of Communist [Parliamentarian] revolution (if expedient and possible without war) has been attempted with varying degrees of success in several countries since the Communists gained power in Prague. It is continually being improved and adjusted, as envisaged in the document, to local conditions in new target territories. These targets are to be found nowadays largely in Latin America, Southern Asia, the Middle East and Africa, especially among the newly-independent nations, and in all these areas we may be sure that the Communists are busy passing on the lesson of Prague. The purpose of this translation is that it may be a warning and an indication of what to expect from those who work in their own countries on behalf of the international Communist conspiracy against Parliamentary Democracy.

"It will be seen that Communist totalitarianism and imperialism are closely similar to fascism. Even the "dictatorship of the proletariat" is a fraud, for it is the dictatorship of the Communist Secretariat."

CHAPTER V

THE IDEOLOGICAL ATTACK

A FAVORED METHOD OF ATTACK AGAINST "BOURGEOIS MENTAL-ity" is the corruption of non-Marxist ideological symbols. Naturally enough, the Communists regard all non-Marxist ideas as being obsolete or anti-Marxist and therefore fascist.

Certain key concepts provide us with shorthand descriptions of complex relationships and make it easy for us to understand one another. In the Western world, words like "liberalism," "democracy," "religion," and "justice" have for us stable meanings which assist us in forming political judgments. The Communists have sought to undermine these semantic pillars in order to hobble our political process.

Lenin first tested the technique of semantic erosion against the Social-ists, rather than against the bourgeoisie, by revising Marx and claiming that his own interpretation was authentic Marxian socialism as applied to the twentieth century. By this device he sought to capture the socialist movement in Czarist Russia from within. Even when repudiated, by the major socialist intellectuals of Europe and forced to label his own follow-ing the "Communist" Party, Lenin still claimed that his communism was authentic socialism and called his new state the "Union of Soviet Socialist Republics." Lenin's persistence in wearing the label of socialism was no mere caprice. At the time of World War I, the socialist movement had a following of millions throughout the globe. By claiming to be part of it, albeit uninvited, he improved his chances of recruiting from or neutraliz-ing large parts of the international socialist movement. To European work-ers and many European intellectuals, the symbolic word "socialism" is of an importance comparable to that of "liberalism" among Americans. The German and French Communist parties would have remained small sects had Lenin not entered the European socialist movement and demoralized it. Other communist parties, such as the one in the United States, might never have been formed if communism had not worn the "socialist" trademark.

After the proletariat inside Russia was crushed in a series of steps, from suppression of the Kronstadt revolt of 1921 to the great purge of 1935-38, political power in the Soviet Union was based on the new managerial upper class led by a political bureaucracy. The shift in class relations inside Soviet Russia amounted to a veiled counterrevolution carried out under the semantic cloak of Leninism. The reorientation was noticed outside Russia only by dissident Communists. The Communist Party now became the vanguard of the managerial class, and communist politics, both inside and outside Russia, reflected the new relationship. The drive for absolute dominion and universal empire remained, but in all other respects the change was considerable.

With the Kremlin's political warfare now cut from its working-class anchor, the internal contradictions of capitalism were reassessed from the viewpoint of their maximum exploitation for political gains. This does not mean, of course, that what the Kremlin calls the "central contradiction" in capitalist countries—between employers and workers—will not remain the principal ideological target, but it does mean an expansion of divisive tactics to other strata in order to utilize the central contradiction more effectively.

The problem was no longer only how to get at the socialist mind, but also how to get at the bourgeois mind. That could scarcely be done by infiltration of the conservatives, who were invariably dubbed "reactionaries" by the Communists. Progressives or liberals appeared better prospects. The Communists concentrated on the intelligentsia: professors, teachers, writers, ministers, scientists, politicians—in short, those who shape or act upon public opinion.

To facilitate this new attack, much of the old communist and socialist phraseology had to be dropped and replaced by democratic bourgeois symbols. In the United States, the Communists posed as *avant-garde* liberals. The Party even stopped running its own candidates during elections in the United States and supported the liberal-progressive bourgeois democratic parties in many other countries. This new-found liberalism was a political-warfare sham. The blood purges of the thirties were proceeding within the Soviet Union, while the liberal reorientation of communist politics was taking place outside.

Even if the Communists had been dolts, they could not easily have avoided the opportunities which history forced upon them. The post-1929 disenchantments in the West with the existing economic order drove many sensitive, intelligent people to the left. The horrors of fascist and nazi brutality in Italy and Germany, the aggression of Japan in Manchuria and China, and the battle for Spain during its agonizing civil war—these drove many people toward the communist camp. The Communists met them, joined them, and undid them in the very process of alliance. George Orwell's *Homage to Catalonia* and Ernest Hemingway's *For Whom the Bell Tolls* are records of disenchantment. Others did not have time to be disenchanted; they were sent to their deaths by the Communists or killed behind the front. Still others remained allies to the Communists. Whenever the Communists made an error, Hitler or the Japanese retrieved it for them by some act of aggression or bestiality which drove the "united front" of Communists and honest leftists together again. The alliance was one of expediency, but not all of the expediency was contrived by the Communists; part of it was real.

Furthermore, the communist parade under modern liberal banners would not have been as effective had there not been some confluence of ideas. The Communists are totalitarian superstatists; the Socialists are democratic statists; many liberals, particularly in the United States, tend to see the solution of many political and social problems through more, rather than less, direct government involvement. Because these groups are agreed that the state must play a major role in modern industrial societies, there are at least some parallels in economic philosophy, however much they disagree with regard to methods. The Communists, the most energetic group, have continually sought to push others farther and farther along the path of big government. In such an alliance, the Communists represent the maximum goal, namely, an unqualified totalitarian government, a goal temporarily concealed for tactical reasons. The Socialists represent the longe-range demands: more and more power for the central government, delegated to it by the masses, including partial nationalization. The liberals, who are pragmatists, advocate immediate demands, that is, immediate government answers to such pressing problems as slums and schools.[1]

1. The social changes represented by the New Deal included many reforms which were long overdue and which, in part, have stood the test of time. The Communists did not believe in the New Deal program: they were against effective "reformism," even though

Let us now examine the type of social targets at which the Communists aim their sustained and varied ideological attack.

Literary Piracy

In communist political warfare, hard targets—e.g., ultra-conservatives who refuse to adjust to changing conditions—are just as important as penetrable ones. A hard social target helps to amass political opposition, in the midst of which a purposeful group like the Communist Party can operate effectively. A hard target is used as a whipping boy on whom everything is blamed, and this, in turn, facilitates the penetration of the softer targets. While socially static targets have their place in this type of warfare, the real organization is built out of the penetrable targets.

Posing as progressives and friends of progressives, the Communists interpret liberal theories loosely and expediently in order to gain the maximum benefit. A keystone among these is the theory that social discontent arises exclusively out of economic ills. Communism, according to this popular view, is but the expression of a widespread economic malaise, and the function of progressive policy must be to strengthen and supplement political democracy—here and abroad—with economic democracy. If the Western nations create economic well-being the world over, the problem of communism will solve itself. The Soviet system, say some supporters of this line, is a new democracy, superior to ours since its emphasis is on the economic aspect of democracy. The tyrannical practices in Russia are a temporary necessity in order to accelerate the creation of a superior, genuine economic democracy. If the United States could use its industrial superiority to help bring about economic democracy throughout the world, economic and political democracy could merge into a new synthesis, and communism and democracy would become friends. Some of that ideological chimera passed into the working credo of the American people; repetitions of it can be found in our political literature, articles, and speeches of the past and present. Bits and pieces of it, in fact, became United States

---

they tried to capture reform movements. An entire volume could be written about the "fronts" created and the uses made of "captive" organizations and infiltrated agencies at that time. At a particular time, any movement of protest can serve communist purposes. Lenin did not believe in "land to the peasants," but he adopted the program of the Peasant Party (Social Revolutionaries), thus taking the wind out of its sails. The Communists contaminated the American left of the thirties for parallel reasons. To pretend to be liberal, as the Communists did and do, does not mean that the pretender *is* liberal.

government policy. Eric Sevareid commented on this type of liberal thinking with refreshing candor:

And they [the Kremlin gamesmen] must love the large school of American liberals who assume that any given country, however barren and illiter-
ate, however profound its background of violence and chieftanship, is capable not only of economic modernization but of parliamentary democracy.

They must love the liberals with social-worker mentalities who do not
grasp that illiteracy, low wages, concentrated landownership, and so on are
not "social problems" but integral parts of a system of life and therefore
enormously resistant to quick change by anything less than the "totalitarian disciplines" the same liberals abhor. They must love the liberals
who assume that because a Marshall Plan worked in modern Europe, a
similar plan can work among those regimes of Latin America where statis-
tics are wild guesses, where trained economists hardly exist, where economic planning is finger painting, where, as between countries, there is
very little background of communications, normal trade, or even intellectual interest in one another.

The gamesmen in the Kremlin must smile in their sleep as they realize
how deeply ingrained is the American illusion that a ton of wheat can offset
a ton of Communist artillery shells, that a squad of Peace Corpsmen is a
match for a squad of guerrilla fighters.[2]

During the thirties, many well-meaning liberals were so mesmerized by
the clouds emanating from the communist psychological-warfare factory
that they did not want to hear or see evil in connection with Soviet Russia,
or if it had to be seen, they were disposed to explain it away. The Communists in the United States assisted their progressive partners by cloak-
ing themselves in the garb of modern American liberalism. They muted
discreetly the theme of penultimate fulfillment: communist dictatorship.
Even such long-range demands as nationalization or the creation of
a separatist Negro republic in the South were dropped or modified. Smearing of the Founding Fathers stopped, and the Communists' very training
centers were named the Thomas Jefferson School, the John Adams School,
or the George Washington School. In 1936, when they recruited Americans
for combat in the Spanish Civil War, they called the volunteer group the
Abraham Lincoln Brigade.

Outstanding among the semantic perversions which took place—and
which continue to this day—was their reinterpretation of the word "democracy." Until the thirties, the word used to designate their social goals was
either "socialism" or "communism." In their own political family litera-

2. Eric Sevareid, "The Facts of Life," *The Reporter* (July 6, 1961) , p. 13.

ture they continue to use these words, of course, but in their public activity, they now pose as "democrats" or "progressives."

Under our interpretation of democracy, the growing participation of the great mass of the people in self-government is a key feature. The powers of the state are limited, for men have certain basic, inalienable rights which are the foundation of the system. These rights are secured by such measures as the division of power between the executive, legislative, and judicial branches of the federal government and between the federal government, the states, and the people. These rights, including the right to individual property, cannot be voted away by a majority; they are held by the individual as such. The stability of the system, political and economic, is based on the concepts of individual rights and the sanctity of contractual relations among men. Were these concepts to be annulled the whole social and political fabric would be rent.

According to the Communists in their new "progressive" pose, *their* democracy is also the rule of the majority because a self-appointed minority party presumably acts in the real interests of the masses. *Their* democracy is allegedly superior because it is not hampered by socially irresponsible and selfish private-property relationships. The centuries-old socialist fable that what the government owns the people own was refurbished with progressive-democratic phraseology. The fact that under Soviet communism the government itself is owned by the Communist Party, in which the people have no voice, is discreetly omitted.

The Communists assert that majority rule is ingrained in their system. The Communist Party in Russia has never been in the numerical majority —but it has always *represented* the majority of the ruling class.[3] In short, the Soviet definition is that the ruling faction is the "majority," no matter what its numerical strength, and hence "the majority rules." In the curious communist juggling of logic, the minorities have no rights whatsoever. This explains many ramifications of Soviet action which are otherwise unintelligible to the Western mind. This explains why the Soviets have no opposition parties; why any would-be opposition has been, "for the common good," bundled off to Siberia; why anyone who disagreed with Stalin

---

3. The communist theory of representation has been that anyone who has a correct (i.e., communist) view of the future becomes entitled to represent all the workers who may be affected by that future when it comes to pass. Representation is a mystical (the Communists call it "historical") process, not a legal or political one. With this theory, the Communists can either claim the majority of today or—at their own whim—appeal to the infinite unborn majorities of all the tomorrows.

had to expiate his sins publicly—and disappear. In Russia, Stalin *was* the majority, and Khrushchev, too, has demonstrated that even a numerical majority within the Presidium can become a scapegoat minority, with all loss of rights.

With strange arithmetic to back them, the Communists favor any immediate demand leading in the direction of the alleged new democracy and helping to uproot the political and economic relationships of bourgeois democracy. Many of these demands, as already indicated, are contrived in their own psychological-warfare factory.

On another front, John Dewey's concept of liberal progressive education was also reinterpreted to facilitate communist penetration of American colleges and schools[4] through infiltration of the teaching staffs and teachers' unions. How much this has damaged the American social structure cannot yet be assessed. In a number of "progressive schools," the emphasis continues to be placed on relieving the young of inhibitions. Call your father Willy and your teacher Suzy. Do not disturb the child if he tears up a book or two or dirties the floor, or he will develop a complex. Many of our schools are now "progressive." Who is to stand up and say, "I am against progress; I want my child to be inhibited"?

It should be obvious that within the territories they control the Communists do not tolerate "progressive" education. A moving and beautiful Soviet film entitled "A Summer to Remember," shown to American audiences in 1961, depicted an idealized Soviet family in which there was both affection between members of the family and unquestioned submission by the children to parental authority of the kind which generally characterized American society not too many decades ago.

Progress in itself is a desirable goal, but only a small percentage of what is new represents real progress. An important leader may have only one or two great ideas in his lifetime. Only one invention in hundreds receives a patent, and of these only a few come into actual use. Nevertheless, a handful of doctrinaire progressives plead, "Off with the old and on with the new," discarding at least nine tried and true methods for each useful new one they apply.

Such people have been useful to the Communists. Without the progressive-democratic cover the communists, small as they are in numbers, could not have penetrated our social fabric as deeply as they have. They are most

4. For a more detailed explanation of this point, see Louis F. Budenz, *The Techniques of Communism*, p. 216.

dangerous in a politically unsophisticated country when they pose as "friends" and are accepted as such. The average American takes for granted the foundations and basic values of our system; he knows too little about the explicit legal and philosophical components of his own structure of freedom. Until he knows more, he will be putty in the hands of skilled political manipulators.

There was a time when the communist psychological-warfare slogan was "class against class." The Communists are still in the business of inciting class strife, of course, but behind the shield of progressivism, they aim at a broader objective. Noticing the incipient polarization of society into progressives and conservatives, they want more than a haven in the progressive camp. They want to do more than to exploit progressives ideologically for their purposes. Ultimately they wish to obtain hegemony over the progressive movement by whatever subterfuge. To achieve a platform of this sort in American society requires additional perversions of bourgeois ideology. "Class against class," an essentially socialist slogan, is too narrow for that purpose.

Stalin, extending Lenin's concepts about the bourgeois democratic revolution to encompass forces of discontent even in bourgeois democratic countries, swung the Communists around to pursue a path which they had originally condemned as crass opportunism. The first fruit of that strategy was Stalin's profitable alliance with the democracies; later on came success with the federation of "people's democracies" within the Sino-Soviet orbit. Up to the time of Stalin's democratic reorientation, democracy was symbolic only of the social system of the West. All else was either socialism, communism, or fascism. After the Communists' grand assault on "democracy," confusion reigned in many minds and many countries, as it still does.

The initial defeat of the communist drive to capture the Western world's key thought symbol—the most concentrated and prolonged drive of that sort ever undertaken by the Communists—came about not as a result of a conscious counterdrive by the Western democracies but by the workings of history itself. It came with the repeated revelations of the vast slave-labor camp system inside Russia, the horrors of the war against the peasants, the wide-sweeping blood purges, the revelations about Stalin's secret political murders and tortures, and last but not least, the crushing of the Hungarian uprising. In short, the communist "animal" was behaving contrary to its preachments. It took a long time for these facts to sink into the Western mind, drugged for years with deceptive pro-communist propaganda. But facts are impressive, and genuine liberals now find it hard to believe that any democracy exists under communism, not even "superior" democracy.

If the communist campaign of demoralization against democracy had succeeded, the West would have been ideologically weakened. The communist defeat on this psychological front is far from conclusive, partially because victories achieved unconsciously are seldom adequately followed up. The planning and initiative in this type of struggle are still almost entirely in Moscow's hands.

The victory is inconclusive for other reasons. The drive on bourgeois ideological values via the progressives was a multipronged drive, with the main prong aimed at the West's key symbol: democracy. Events helped us to defeat the main drive. The drive on American labor, too, suffered a severe setback, credit for this going to labor and its leaders. Communist attempts to create a network among the Negroes was also unsuccessful. But the communist penetration of U. S. and other Western colleges and schools is far from ended. The communist beachhead among certain farmers' organizations is still held, as is that among the scientists, the holders of the highest status symbols in the modern world. On any one of these fronts a relatively quick communist recovery is possible and from there on, a new advance. Statism, so assiduously fostered during communism's honeymoon with the liberals, has receded but slightly on a number of critical fronts.

The role of government in the United States has grown as a necessary response to internal evolution and external pressures. It is more likely to grow than to diminish. Relative degrees of governmental involvement must be a matter of judgment with respect to specific issues. But we need not become enamored with big government per se. Statism and tyranny are first cousins. The question of America's evolving into a more satisfactory society in an era of increased governmental influence depends upon our ability to keep totalitarians out of the bureaucracy. In particular, we must never forget that the Communists thrive within the intellectual climate of statism.

A Look at the Record

Let us review some specific communist efforts to apply the principles discussed in this chapter. A limited summation of Communist Party activities in the United States over the past twenty years, based on the testimony of defectors before various Congressional committees and the legislatures of several states well illustrates this type of warfare.[5] The following activities were planned and carried out by and at the behest of the Communist Party:

(1) The utilization of Hollywood for the production of demoralization films. This was carried out by directors, script writers, and actors who were secret party members and fellow travelers in the various studios.

(2) The use of secret party members inside the Newspaper Guild to influence the press to work discreetly for goals of the Party and for a favorable slanting of the news of Soviet Russia or the Communist Chinese.

(3) The creation of an anti-militarist committee to organize and direct the infiltration of the armed services.

(4) Promotion of strikes and stoppages in defense plants (so-called soft sabotage). This was carried out by union officers who were secret party members and by secret groups inside these plants.

(5) Co-ordination of activities facilitating the communist conquest of China. The co-ordination involved secret groups inside the United States government, the Chinese "fronts" of the Party, and the secret party groups inside the Newspaper Guild and in the Institute of Pacific Relations.

(6) Concentration on strategic activities in communication services, in public opinion–forming media (press, radio, etc.), and among scientific and engineering personnel in nuclear laboratories.

(7) Development of secret infiltration activities in the railroad brotherhoods, in view of the role transportation might play in the event of war against the Soviet Union.

(8) Reorientation of Communist Party youth activities toward infiltration of existing large youth organizations and a more effective utilization of infiltrated teachers' unions and teaching staffs in influencing youth.

(9) Concentrated use of the party women's organization for the infiltration of existing large non-communist women's organizations.

(10) Utilization of the Treasury Department for communist purposes.[6]

(11) The creation of a special committee to conduct a "bring the boys home" propaganda campaign at the termination of World War II in order to induce a quick demobilization of American armed forces, thus leaving the Soviet armed forces in military predominance in both Asia and Europe. (The hurried demobilization originated because of spontaneous popular pressure, but the communist apparatus, including "fronts" and captive organizations, gave it maximum support. Secret cells in the armed services

5. The Committee on Government Operations; the Tydings Committee of the United States Senate; the Senate Internal Security Sub-committee; the House Committee on Un-American Activities; and the state committees on un-American activities of the states of California, Washington, Ohio, and others.

6. Harry Dexter White, Under Secretary of the Treasury, and other important officials were members of a secret communist cell. Under cover of the initial UNRRA program of foreign aid, hundreds of millions of dollars in cash and supplies were diverted to Soviet Russia and its satellites and the financial system of Nationalist China was manipulated adversely.

helped stage demobilization riots in Manila and Frankfurt.) This campaign proved to be more effective than even the Politburo expected. The boys came home so quickly that there was no space on board ships for their equipment—tanks, guns, and planes—nor were there enough men left overseas to maintain it there. Tanks were driven off coral atolls to make breakwaters and clear the land area. Planes, all usable, were heaped onto burning pyres. In a few months, our victorious armed forces had little more than rifles with which to resume any conflict.

(12) Greater emphasis on the development of sports clubs and physical-fitness activity (strong-arm squads) in the unions. Sports clubs or sports associations are the usual cover for training communist riot squads, who then "practice" breaking up anti-communist meetings, beating up opponents, leading in rioting on picket lines, etc. At a later stage, from these "sport" formations are recruited insurrectionary squads and guerrilla units. Mention has been made of this type of organization participating in the Peekskill, New York, riots.

(13) Promotion of books dealing with problems of American foreign policy. (The books are authored by "progressives" working with the Party. Party followers on the staffs of large newspapers assure favorable reviews for such "correct" books.

(14) Infiltration of the Secretariat of the United Nations and its special agencies by communist-oriented American personnel.

(15) The creation of a special "front," suitable for operation among the intelligentsia, with these characteristics: (a) it was to be respectable enough to attract sympathizers, and progressives in general; (b) its board of directors was to be composed of "progressives" who had worked with the Party or were tolerant of its immediate objectives; and (c) no known party members were to be on any of its leading committees. The front became known as the Federation of Arts, Sciences and Professions. It operated for a number of years and at its start was headed, unwittingly, by the late Secretary of the Interior Harold Ickes.

(16) Infiltration into organizations, associations, or agencies dealing with United States foreign policy.

It should be noted that the number of card-bearing party members involved in the creation and operation of communist fronts is extremely small. The Communists prefer to work with sympathizers whose formal organizational tie-in with the Party either does not exist or could never be established.

The Communists are aware of the fact that somebody who sympathizes with them is generally more valuable than a dozen militant communists. A professor who—without being a communist party member—stands up for the interests of the Soviet Union is more valuable than a hundred men with a membership-book. The writer who—being no party member—stands up for the Soviet Union, the trade union leader who defends the international politics of the Soviet Union, is more valuable than a thousand party members. Those who are not considered as party members and are not known as communists have more freedom of activity.

Strategic Purpose

The reader should note that the strategic orientation of many of these operations served to influence United States foreign policy in a direction favorable to the aims and purposes of the Soviet Union in a particular part of the world and at a particular time. The Communists engineered the setting up of suitable foreign-policy "fronts" and infiltrated non-communist organizations which were active or could be activated on matters of foreign policy. A count of communist "fronts" between 1932 and 1952 shows that most of them were either expressly created to influence United States foreign affairs or concentrated on that objective. The concentration was particularly heavy after 1936, reaching its apogee during the war and its aftermath. By using the "infiltrators," the Kremlin keeps posted on what the United States is doing and is planning to do and influences this country to act sometimes contrary to its own best interests.

From the listings of these pre- and post-war activities, it can be seen that the penetration was carried out simultaneously in many segments of society. Each segment is considered a "fort" to be conquered, whether it is a union, a professional organization, an office, a studio, or a government agency. In each of these, starting with one party member, the Communists will scheme and plot until there is a functioning party cell. Once entrenched—and then depending on their over-all growth of strength—they proceed more boldly.

We have listed these varied activities in capsule form to illustrate the workings of the communist organization. During much of the period from which these illustrations were drawn, the Soviet Union was our ally and self-delusion was easy.

At the height of the operations the American Communist Party did not exceed eighty thousand members. Its membership is considerably smaller in 1962. But its basic general operational pattern remains the same. The operational skills of the Communist Party have, of course, increased as a result of many years of practice. The American people, too, have become more alert to this type of penetration. It is unlikely that communist-inspired attacks can be launched again as freely upon our institutions and our government.

The astounding performance of a small, hard-core communist party, slicing into our social fabric and government, undoubtedly represents a unique phase of American history. It could happen only in a country as unsophisticated in the arts of political warfare as ours was. But let us not rejoice prematurely at our awakening. The Communists are still far ahead in this type of combat. All we are aware of is that an enemy whose power is growing throughout the globe is also in our midst. His machinations are infinitely varied: we can expect them to continue because the Communists' hostility toward our system is an inherent characteristic of their own.

CHAPTER VI

SOCIAL TARGETS

WE HAVE EXAMINED THE EVOLUTION OF COMMUNIST POLITICAL
warfare and its various methods of ideological attack, particularly the
displacement or the capture of middle-class symbols. In this chapter we
will examine certain specialized applications of these methods before exploring their techniques for destroying a democracy by invoking democracy's most cherished rights.

The Pattern of Social Conquest

With the Communists, thought always precedes action. "Without correct
theory there can be no correct practice," was a concept stressed again and
again in the Lenin School. All great social movements of history were built
on dynamic patterns of thought, magnetic thought, which by rousing and
engaging man's spirit helped to destroy old societies and created new ones.

The twentieth century has produced short-lived movements of considerable scope based on what one may call "quack theories." Most important
were the nazi concept of the superiority of Aryan whites and Mussolini's
fascist theory, which combined "Roman" supernationalism with state socialism. Both were thin covers for aggressive expansion.

The communist program is far superior to its most recent competitors
because it calls not only for a total conquest of the earth—the ultimate
empire—but also for a total internal and social upheaval. The Communists,
in short, are ultratotalitarians.

Contrary to the highly touted communist theory that communist totalitarianism is "progressive" and therefore represents a new form of democracy, the fact is that under communism all former classes are debased or
eliminated while a new political "aristocracy" (the hard-core Communist

Party) rises to the top. The political bureaucracy organized into *one* party in total control of the state then becomes an absolute ruling caste. Essentially, communist political warfare aims at the disintegration of existing democratic society and the development and consolidation of totalitarian power.

Communist disruptive strategy tries to concentrate primarily on the most vulnerable and exasperated sections of the social strata. The order of strategic concentration has not always been constant. In backward nations, the stress is primarily on the peasants and the intelligentsia (students included), while in countries like Italy and France, the "proletariat" is the chosen instrument. In areas where opportunities for concealed infiltration are or have been unusually favorable, the strategic concentration may be on the intelligentsia. This has generally been the case in technologically backward countries. In industrialized countries, the strategy is generally based on the workers because "the factory is," according to Lenin, "the key arch of capitalism."

A secondary aim is the neutralization of sections of society which the Communists feel cannot easily be won over to their cause. Among those are: (1) the mass of middle-class farmers in the technologically advanced countries or the upper strata of peasants in backward countries; (2) the petty bourgeoisie (shopkeepers) in the cities and towns; (3) sectors of the upper intelligentsia; and (4) the "white-collar" workers.

To Demoralize Is to Conquer

In pursuing its strategy, communist psychological warfare seeks to raise the morale of its own combatant force and demolish that of the enemy. This is also the general aim of Western psychological warfare in wartime. The Communists, however, are at war continuously, using political warfare in "peace" time and both political and military weapons in wartime.

The key planners in Moscow believe that the best time to demoralize a bourgeois nation is in peacetime, for during periods of hostilities, democracies are on the alert for all threats to their national security. Demoralization work will be effective in wartime only to the extent that the preceding peacetime penetration has been effective. If it has, the enemy nation may collapse at the first blow; or if circumstances are most favorable and an internal crisis has been induced, it may even be taken by infiltration.

Morale in a combat force demands that its men know what they are fighting for and feel that the stakes are high enough to justify risking their lives. Most important, they must *believe* in and have faith in their leadership. The essence of psychological warfare is to build that belief on one's own side and destroy it on the other.

The communist goal, as proclaimed by all communist parties, is a universal brotherhood to be established by the overthrow, expropriation, and liquidation of the wealthy classes. Claiming to be the party of the underdog, the Communists say their aim is the abolition of exploitation of man by man.

There are three types of communist propaganda: (1) propaganda to build up party morale and to combat deviations from the Moscow line; (2) propaganda and agitation highly camouflaged as "democratic" criticism, "democratic" demands, to lower our morale; and (3) demoralization agitation as such. The first type is easily recognized. The second, often appearing under bourgeois "liberal" or "progressive" auspices, is more difficult to identify. The most illusive of the three categories, however, is the last.

Demoralization propaganda and agitation has as its objects the discrediting of the social system and its institutions, the discrediting of leaders, and the smearing of organizations and individuals who are consciously and actively fighting communism. The over-all aim is the weakening of the enemy's will to fight.

Democratic capitalism is by its very nature pluralistic. Large and small conflicts of interests and views exist openly all the time. Like all social systems, capitalism has its unpleasant sides. The communist political-warfare machine concentrates on these conflicts, not to remedy the faults but to make use of them.

If one were to examine and believe the communist propaganda and agitation produced in any year, the conclusion would be that everything outside the communist realm is rotten, cruel, and corrupt and that behind the Iron Curtain perfection reigns in tranquility. A Communist finds it psychologically impossible to limit himself to the truth. The truth, for him, is the most persuasive statement of opinion that he can voice at the moment; it is truth because it will advance his cause. It therefore need not be justified.

Through demoralization propaganda and agitation the Communists seek to weaken the roots of our beliefs and question the origin and validity of our social institutions and basic thought patterns, pervert these thought patterns by means of reinterpretation favorable to the Communists, weaken our will to act on matters of vital interest, and disorient our policy to bring it into consonance with Soviet policy or make it helpful to the purposes of Soviet policy.

Communist demoralization work is not necessarily related to either long-range or immediate demands, but it is related to our thought patterns. It seeks to enter those thoughts and influence them from within: to do by propaganda what cannot be done by force. If the thought patterns which place value on individual freedom, democracy, and the right to property could be washed out of our minds, the alternate communist concepts of state ownership and domination, one-party monopoly, and regimentation of the individual could more easily replace them.

With that aim in mind, the Communists try to rewrite our history. According to them, the War of Independence was fought to determine who should exploit this land and how it should be exploited. George Washington was a slaveholder; John Adams, a buccaneering merchant; Thomas Jefferson, a demagogue put forward to attract the masses; and Thomas Paine, the only unquestionable patriot. Abraham Lincoln was, according to the communist interpretation of the Civil War, an opportunist who declared against slavery only when he was about to lose the war. The Communists call such literature the "class interpretation of history," according to which "history is a history of class struggles" or "exploited against exploiter." Hence the Civil War was a conflict to decide whether the Northern or the Southern type of exploitation—wage slavery or chattel slavery—should prevail in the United States.

According to the Communists, the American West was developed by colonists who, finding the exploitation in the eastern states intolerable, were willing to risk the unknown. With them went the degenerate flotsam and jetsam—crooks, thugs, fakers, and humbugs of every sort—who became the leaders of the West. In brief, the Communists depict America's stage of industrial growth, whether in the East or West, in the darkest colors while contraposing Soviet Russia as a social paradise.

During the communist decade in Hollywood (1937–1948), much of this sort of interpretation of our history found its way into motion pictures and thence into the minds of our youth. America's past was pictured as consisting of political corruption, amorality, soulless exploitation, class injustice, and clerical humbuggery.

Much communist literature appears under "progressive" labels and is often published by non-communist but communist-infiltrated publishing houses. In fact, communist demoralization propaganda or agitation usually appears under non-communist auspices; it would be much less effective otherwise. If one picks up a book, particularly a historical novel, which appears objective, one absorbs the distorted communication unsuspectingly.

In choosing illustrations to explain the demoralization phase of communist activity, we have confined ourselves to the United States, but the same operation goes on in all capitalist countries. "Debunking bourgeois history," according to Nicolai Bukharin, "is an important phase of communist activity." The most formidable progress along this line was made in France and Italy. Without it the growth of the communist parties there could hardly be explained. The process originated with the Socialists and anarcho-syndicalists of these countries, but with them it was a companion piece to their philosophy. It took the Communists to pursue this effort as a calculated part of their psychological-warfare strategy.

Communist smearing of bourgeois history and tradition is addressed to that part of man's mind predisposed to suspect, hear, and see evil, especially if it relates to others or the past. Big lies, which are difficult to check, are most effective, for they are remembered unconsciously long after they are denied. On a political level, vilification of the historic past plays the same role as describing one's parents, grandparents, and great-grandparents as soulless, amoral scoundrels. It knocks out the base of tradition, faith, and trust in the society in which we live.

The Two-Pronged War on Religion

Communist operations in the field of religion provide a classic illustration of demoralization. Since Communists are atheists, religion is complete anathema to them. One of their first steps after seizing power in Rusia in 1917 was to launch a direct frontal attack on religious ideas and organization. All church property was "nationalized"; thousands of priests and active laymen were arrested and executed. A special organization called the Anti-God Society, was created to carry on the drive. The smear campaign carried on against the Russian Orthodox Church exceeded in virulence even that against the landlords or capitalists.

The Church was put in the same position as a man who, tied hand and foot, is insulted, spat on, and manhandled, with execution or slow death staring him in the face. If any priest, high or low, attempted to answer the smears, he was arrested, charged with counterrevolutionary propaganda, and executed or sent to one of the nameless camps of the secret police.

The war against the Church proved to be a bigger problem than the Communists had anticipated. The direct attack succeeded fairly well in the cities, where the organized force of the Party proved adequate to carry it through. The peasants, however, could not think or live without religion. Religion in the villages could be liquidated only by liquidating the peasants themselves, and that was impossible. The irresistible fury of the direct attack thus met an immovable object. Although well versed in social manipulations, the Communists met for the first time—and on a grand scale—an obstruction which was entirely *ideological* and not amenable to materialistic pressure.

This conflict produced a vast contradiction within the Soviet system. When the war against religion was at its height, the Communists actually controlled only the big cities and thirty-mile strips of land on each side of the railway lines. Beyond these places, especially after sundown, it was not safe for a Communist to venture. Under such circumstances, something had to give. The Communists yielded on the ideological front by giving up the direct attack against religion. Had they not done so, the regime would have collapsed for lack of food supplies in the cities.

The Communists, however, could not really abandon their attack on religion and remain Communists. What they did was to relax the direct attack in favor of an indirect one. They undertook the prostitution of the Russian Orthodox Church from within.

To date, the Communists have not reverted to their direct attack on religion. During World War II, the Kremlin appeased the Church—or what was left of it—and eventually recognized it by putting it under a state-controlled commission, a political police operation. However, recognition did not mean giving the Church the status it occupies in the West; it simply meant that the manhunt ceased. Church property still remains nationalized. Teaching religion to the young and engaging in any social activities beyond formal church services are still forbidden. Even within these restricted limits the Church is not autonomous; its internal affairs are under the control of the State Church Commission, composed of Communists. The Anti-God Society has been abolished, but beyond that, atheistic propaganda has free rein. In short, the Church is still attacked and can reply only in a whisper.

The fate of religion in Soviet Russia is important because this is where the methods of combatting religion originated. The Communists in this case retreated a step, as Lenin said, in order to prepare for a better advance.

Another factor which prevented the Communists from returning to the direct attack was the influence of religion in the colonial and semicolonial countries of Asia (especially India) and the Middle East. In those countries a direct attack on religion would practically cancel the communist operation; it would be political suicide. But these were the countries (the "soft underbelly" of capitalism) which became the Kremlin's special target after Stalin abandoned the Marxian orientation toward the proletariat. In many, religion had to be either bypassed or penetrated. Infiltration, wherever possible, was the new form of attack decided upon, and its first tryout was in Russia herself.

Stalin, who in his youth spent several years in a theological seminary in Tiflis studying for the priesthood, conceived of the indirect attack under cover of religious reform. Russia was to be given a badly needed and long-delayed "reformation," inspired and directed—behind the scenes—by Stalin. The Russian Orthodox Church was "reformed" through the police, who gave the surviving clergy in the cities the choice of joining the reformation or else. The new "patriarchate" thus set up was aimed at the village clergy, to influence them for Soviet purposes. Religion and the Bible were reinterpreted toward that end. The reformation was delayed for a time (1929–1935) by the war on the peasants, which put the reformed clergy to a test. All of those who resisted, clergy included, were either liquidated or left to perish in slave-labor camps. The survivors comprise the reformed Soviet Church of today, the creation of an atheistic state.

To a Communist, religion is but bourgeois philosophy with feudalistic connotations and background or bourgeois philosophy anchored to deism. According to Marx, it is "the opiate of the people." Lenin added that it "darkens" the minds of men with "superstitions." But Communists are not merely atheists; they plan to conquer the minds of men, and in so doing they must deal with reality. The reality is that millions are still in the "dark" embrace of religion; consequently, that stronghold must be bypassed or penetrated if Lenin's advice that "the communists must be where the masses are" is to be followed. So, from their own experience in Russia and the dictates of their program of world conquest, the Communists knew they had to attempt to enter this ideological fortress—if not to conquer it, at least to neutralize it.

Infiltrating religion ideologically and organizationally involved an *ideological solid* alien to bolshevism. How to reach the inside of organized religion and to influence it was the problem. The gap between bolshevism and religion was such that many Communists who, as political strategists, were accustomed to advocating things they did not believe felt ill at ease in this new posture. In fact, in the beginning this special operation was carried out by the Politburo, unknown to the mass of party members. Even in Russia, where the Communists had total control of the state, the new venture was at first carried out haltingly and experimentally. Only in proportion to its success did similar operations become possible outside Russia.

The first test of the new tact in a major country outside the Soviet Union was made in the United States. Many Protestant ministers had sympathized with the Anti-Czarist Revolution in Russia; some of them transferred their sympathies to the new Soviet regime. The main group that initially lent itself to the communist purpose was "The Methodist Federation for Social Service," a semi-official church group later repudiated by the parent body. The communists gained entry into that group through the personality of Harry F. Ward, then its secretary and most prolific writer.

By the late thirties and the early forties, the social panorama of the United States was studded by a number of communist fronts burrowing into every phase of American society. Gracing the letterheads of these fronts were the names of hundreds of Churchmen, most of whom were unwittingly supporting communist aims. Many of these fronts were designed as instruments to forward the Soviet's foreign policy in our midst.

Wherever the communists burrow into a large organization, their primary objective is the public opinion forming media—in this particular case, the church publications, journals, books, booklets, and tracts, official or unofficial. By the early forties, they had, through their infiltrated publication of a few denominations. On behalf of most of the clergy and the few idealists who were unwittingly misled, it must be said that the communist operation against religion was most cunning and deceptive.

Operation religion was not aimed at converting believers away from God, but merely from the capitalist system. Once the limits of "operation religion" were clearly fixed, the tactical pattern of infiltration emerged: Capitalism was to be condemned in the name of God. Christ's teachings were interpreted to suit the purpose. For example, because "Christ chased the money changers out of the Temple," he was anti-capitalist. The early Christians lived in communes, hence the pattern of communist social organization is the ideal. Christ believed in the brotherhood of man and worth of the individual in the face of God, hence he opposed Roman slavery. If He were alive today, consequently He would also oppose capitalist wage slavery. Reverend Claude Williams, who headed a religious front known as "The Peoples Institute of Applied Religion," and wrote numerous pamphlets, put it this way: "Why condemn religion in the name of Marx when religion can be interpreted to uphold Marx?"

The success of this maneuver has had important consequences. Hitherto the Communists had concentrated almost exclusively on penetrating the labor movement. The penetration of a bourgeois bastion like religion opened up new vistas. It revealed the possibility of penetrating other realms of bourgeois thought and twisting bourgeois ideology to communist purpose.

Fragmenting a Democracy

Additional communist propaganda and agitation techniques of disintegration have been used in the armed forces of capitalist nations. Communist "anti-militarist" activity is modeled largely upon the methods used to disorganize the Czarist armies in World War I and the Chinese Nationalist armies in the Chinese Civil War.

Anti-militarism has long-range as well as immediate objectives. Its long-range goal is the "democratization" of the capitalist armed forces; its immediate demands may be better food, higher pay, degradation of officers and noncoms, election of mess-hall committees by the men, or modification of the system of military justice. "Democratization" may involve the election of officers or their approval by the men before taking command, equalitarianism between men and officers, or reduction of the officers' privileges and status.

A "democratized" army would be little better than an armed mob. If the Communist Party, through its secret cells within an army, succeeded in emasculating the authority of command, the party cells would be the only disciplined forces and could use the residual armed mob for their purposes. That, of course, is the hidden aim.

Whereas the disintegrating effect of actions such as these is obvious when applied to an organization as cohesive as an army, it is not nearly so obvious when applied to a *laissez faire* democratic system as a whole. Yet a similar idea lies behind the Communists' everlasting crusade for irresponsible democracy. Thus we have the phenomenon of the most rigid totalitarians on earth acting as the most energetic advocates of the very democracy which they aim to destroy.

According to communist dialectic, there are two simultaneous processes

at work in modern societies. One is the process toward centralization (monopoly); the other is the resistance of the masses to centralization.

For the Communists to operate effectively in a Western country, the
more democratic freedom the better, not only for themselves, but also for
those whose latent dissatisfaction they want to incite and use. To hurl the
masses against the existing foundations of society, one needs all the freedom
possible. For the flood to run freely, one must destroy the dikes.

Breaking down the dikes is one of the preoccupations of the Communist
Party. The Party labors constantly toward reinterpreting civil rights in
order to allow it to operate freely. In the name of the right to assemble and
to organize, the Party argues for an unlimited right to overthrow the
government, an unlimited right to use the streets for picketing and demonstrating, an unlimited right for its unions to strike anywhere and at any
time, regardless of contracts. The right to strike is interpreted as the right
to sit down inside the factory and to use force to keep *all* personnel out.
The Party interprets the right to picket as including mass picketing anywhere at any time; mass rioting at factory gates; picketing courtrooms or
the homes of judges, hostile legislators, or government executives; and the
denouncing of any of its opponents by picketing homes.

In the name of the right to free speech, the Communist Party, its fronts,
and its captive organizations want not only an unlimited right to advocate
the Party's civil-disturbance program but also the right to lie, pervert,
fabricate, slander, and smear their opponents. At the same time—still in
the name of free speech—the Party wants Congressional investigating committees which seek to reveal the Party's subversive machinations either
abolished or reduced to impotence. In fact, the Party wants all efforts of
the government to defend itself declared unconstitutional. It wants its
party-controlled unions to have utmost freedom to slander and misrepre-
sent, while the manufacturers and other "reactionaries" are accused of
interfering with the right of free speech and organization.

In short, the Communists are to remain free no matter what they do,
while their opponents—dubbed as reactionaries and fascists—are to be suppressed, all in the name of progressive freedom and democracy. The strategic aim is to loosen the discipline of bourgeois democratic society while
increasing the free play of communist subversion. In the ideal state of
transition sought by the Communists, every individual in bourgeois society
(except the "reactionaries") would have the right to do as he pleased, anywhere and at any time. Thus any union or subdivision thereof could call

a wildcat strike or slowdown, regardless of the "reactionaries"[1] in control of the national union. Government employees (police included) could go on strike or debate whether or not to carry out an order from their superiors. If a state of democratic disintegration and paralysis is reached, the Communist Party and its allied organizations can operate to the greatest advantage. This condition is the ultimate goal of the Party's fight *for,* but actually *against,* democracy.

To weaken or destroy bourgeois social discipline, the Party must fight and discredit the leadership elite that assures social discipline, particularly the most conscious and aggressive anti-communist element. This elite must be replaced, gradually, either by Communists or by their ideological sympathizers. By destroying or weakening the respect and prestige of its leadership, the Communists can subvert bourgeois society, paralyze its defenses and social mobility, and annul its discipline.

This does not mean that *all* of the bourgeois elite must be fought with the same intensity all the time. On the contrary, it is necessary to take advantage of every crack and division, to align oneself with some against others and thus atomize the elite itself. If a labor leader, a politician, or a church leader, supports the Communists on one or more issues of importance or even joins some fronts, he may be temporarily treated as a progressive or the next-best thing, a liberal. If he is, however, a real liberal and fights the Communists, then he is declared a false liberal, hence more dangerous than a reactionary.

The advocacy of "extended democracy," is a vital function of every communist-party front or captive organization. The tactical specialists in this field are the organized communist lawyers and their sympathizers in the profession, who are welded into special fronts such as the International Juridical Association, the Lawyers Guild, or the Civil Rights Congress. The representatives of these fronts have penetrated government agencies, legislative staffs, the legal staffs of labor unions, and other organizations. Communists in trouble are not merely defended; they are shielded by attorneys who have the same aims and who are specializing in this phase of subversion. Every loophole in the law, every procedural flaw in the trial itself, and every pressure, direct and indirect, is used to secure acquittals.

Running legal interference on behalf of Communists in trouble is, however, the smaller contribution that communist lawyers make to the cause

1. George Meany, President of the AFL-CIO, is consistently called a renegade reactionary in the communist press. See *Worker,* November 12, 1961, p. 60.

of "extended" democracy. More important is their role in obtaining the liberal interpretation of existing laws and their influence on the creation of new laws. They create systematically the legal framework for the communist drive for extended democracy and block the laws or legal procedures that run contrary to communist purposes. Nor do the Communists state their objectives so frankly; to do so would be self-defeating. On the contrary, all of these objectives are stressed as being essential to the welfare of the common man. The Communists are at their deceptive best in psychological dissimulation, the manipulation of semantics used in the presentation of their extended-democracy program. The inner intent under the cover of this program is the disintegration and paralysis of bourgeois society and the building up of the communist totalitarian machine.

The reader must not assume that the communist leadership actually believes in any of the freedoms urged. While in opposition to bourgeois society and advocating all kinds of freedom to destroy it, the Party maintains rigid discipline. Without such discipline the Party could not maneuver. No matter how confused the middle-class social elite and how low the discipline in the "demoralized" army, the mob ("masses" in party language) can be hurled against the existing social order only by a solidly organized force.

The Communist Party in the United States had at its height in 1946 about eighty thousand members. Organized around it into fronts were about six hundred thousand sympathizers, and around them were approximately two million members of captive organizations such as labor unions, fraternal societies, and other groups. The ensemble works like a system of wheels within wheels moved by the innermost wheel, the Communist Party. The party members are organized into special units, called fractions, within each of these controlled mass organizations, their pattern of operations simulating the spokes of a wheel. Thus a relatively small organization of eighty thousand moves an ensemble of several million. The force behind that mechanism is the discipline of the center wheel. If that discipline were to break down, then the spokes would fly apart and each would be inoperable alone.

Such an assemblage of satellite organizations led and united by the Party can wield considerable power. It is more mobile than any of the bourgeois political parties, and its weight in the total picture increases in proportion to the loosening of social discipline among its adversaries. In the event of an economic crisis, that process can be accelerated; in the case of national defeat in war or a combination of economic and political crises, it proceeds much faster. According to the Communists, bourgeois democratic society tends to disintegrate by itself. The function of the Communist Party is to accelerate that disintegration consciously and systematically and to exploit it.

Not a few of the planks in the communist extended-democracy program or revolutionary opportunism, as Lenin calls it, have been taken from the reformists. The goal is to undercut the reformists' influence and use, for communist purposes, the masses thus weaned away. In general, reforms are a double-edged sword. The urging of reforms may have revolutionary impact in a country unable to grant them, but they may work in the very opposite direction—ameliorating the lot of the masses—in countries better situated. In the United States, a country of perpetual reform and high standard of living, the Communists can hardly expect to change the system by merely setting forth exaggerated reform demands.

In the political field, however, the Communists have scored heavily. They have destroyed almost entirely the once-virile Socialist Party, wiped out the erstwhile militant syndicalist movement represented by the I.W.W., and made considerable inroad among the liberals, all of which would hardly have been possible without the ruse of an extended-democracy program. Thus in regard to genuine American radicalism, the Communists have almost taken over the field, to the detriment of legitimate protest movements.

Genuine reform movements should play a dynamic role in an effective democracy. Consequently, the destructive impact of "Operation Disintegration" should not be underestimated. Or as one astute student of the Soviet Union expressed it:

> I can think of only one way in which the Kremlin may still conquer us, and that without war. It is by so frightening us (but it is we who allow ourselves to be frightened) that for fear of the enemy within we transform our own society imperceptibly into . . . a system in which the bully and the corrupt may not be denounced or the underdog uplifted because nobody will dare risk being called a Red.[2]

2. Edward Crankshaw, *Cracks in the Kremlin Wall*, p. 279.

CHAPTER VII

THE COMMUNIST STATE IN
POLITICAL WARFARE

ONLY ON THE SURFACE IS THE COMMUNIST STATE LIKE OTHER states; in essence it is an instrument of the protracted communist conflict against the Free World. It is an engine created to destroy the "hostile outside world," at the service of the all-powerful Communist Party.[1] Lenin conceived of the communist state as an instrument of force designed not to guarantee rights to any individual but to "crush all antagonists."[2] After the seizure of power in 1917, Lenin said that the Bolshevik Revolution was "merely one phase through which we must pass on the way to a world revolution." The Soviet Union was a stage in the process of creating a universal communist state.

All political power in the Soviet Union is in the hands of the communist-party apparatus. The Party rules the government. Nevertheless, the Soviet Union contains all the trappings of a state: elections, the bicameral Soviet parliament (Supreme Soviet), premiers, presidents, ministers, judges, *et al.* Since these trappings are entirely subservient to the Communist Party, it would be the height of naïveté to come to think that they resemble exactly or approximately ordinary governmental institutions such as those functioning in the Free World. As Leonard Schapiro reported in 1960:

1. "The goal is to consolidate the dictatorship of the proletariat in one country, using it as a base for the overthrow of imperialism in all countries. Revolution spreads beyond the limits of one country; the epoch of world revolution has begun." See Historicus, "Stalin on Revolution," *Foreign Affairs,* Vol. XXVII, No. 2 (January, 1949) , pp. 198-99.

2. On November 6, 1920, Lenin reaffirmed his conviction that the reason for the existence of Soviet Russia was to assist in spreading the revolution to other countries: "We have always known, and shall never forget, that our task is an international one, and that our victory is only half a victory, perhaps less, until an upheaval takes place in all the states, including the wealthiest and the most civilized." *Collected Works,* Vol. XXXI, p. 371.

Whatever material concessions have been made since 1953 by the communist leaders, they have repeatedly made it plain that they will not tolerate any kind of basic relaxation of the grip of the party apparatus on the whole life of the country. The constant attacks on "revisionism" which have been so noticeable since the Hungarian revolt bear witness to the fact that the right of the party machine to control all institutions within the state, the state itself and all creative activity of the individual has been asserted as forcibly as before. . . . The party apparatus has, since 1953, extended and consolidated its hold over the country to a greater extent than ever before. Our familiarity today with this form of one-party dictatorship should not be allowed to obscure the fact that when it was first devised by Lenin, after the Bolsheviks seized power in 1917, it was brilliantly original. . . . The institutions which he created were from the start fake institutions, in the sense that they were . . . party-controlled, and not the freely elected bodies which they purported to be—soviets, trade-unions councils, law courts and the like. This made it possible for the Party to preserve the semblance of popular democratic activity, and indeed in the course of time to destroy all memories of the real nature of free institutions, without in any way endangering executive control over all aspects of life. It is small wonder that the preservation intact of this powerful new device of control should be the first aim of those who stand to lose most by its disappearance.[3]

A Communist state has all the paraphernalia of popular government—separate from but parallel to the party machinery. It may at times ignore or bypass the government, but the basic formula of acting on matters of state through or in the name of the government instead of in the name of the party remains the *modus operandi*. The point to bear in mind is that any communist unit of government, at whatever level, is the corresponding organ of the Communist Party:

[In the U.S.S.R.] the Party remains as strictly disciplined and as centralized as before. True, the central apparatus, the Secretariat, has adapted its pattern to correspond to the increased functions of the republican governments, by splitting its main departments into two—one for the Union as a whole, one for the union republics. But this in no way impairs the supreme authority of the First Secretary and his powerful subordinates. Again, whatever new freedom to speak his mind may have been cautiously asserted by the ordinary citizen, few signs of real democracy are discernible in the Party.[4]

An understanding of party-state relationship is necessary to comprehend the communist state's role in political warfare. Relations with non-com-

3. Leonard Schapiro, "Has Russia Changed?" *Foreign Affairs*, Vol. XXXVIII, No. 3 (April, 1960), p. 392.

4. *Ibid.*, p. 394.

munist countries (government-to-government relations) must, of course, be carried on in the customary manner through diplomatic ministries, legations, and consulates abroad, but that is not the only reason why the Soviet state strives for the appearance of legitimacy. To the outside world, the Communists seek to appear as a modern—nay, *supermodern*—genuine, representative government elected by the people, a government with allegedly superior political, economic, and social systems. They want to be considered a mass democracy in which everything is owned and managed by the people under the benevolent guidance of the Party. This charade is played for the purpose of propaganda, which is designed to gain politically unsophisticated supporters outside the Iron Curtain. The Kremlin leaders know, better than anyone else, that if the real fate of human freedom under their regime became known on the outside, the appeals of the Soviet Union as a "democratic country" would fade. To infiltrate politically into the outside world with moral appeals, desirable political goods must be sold, and if the goods are not there, they must be faked.

The Cold War

On the foundation of wartime collaboration, preparations were made for the round of battles between the Soviet bloc and the Western world which began after World War II. The intermittent conflict which then ensued was aptly dubbed "the Cold War" by Bernard Baruch and Walter Lippmann. The peculiar character of the Cold War is that it combines political subversion carried on by the communist parties as "private" organizations with aggressive operations carried on by the Soviet state (subsequently aided by Communist China). The two are intertwined, although the state plays the leading role.

Soviet military maturity has stretched the limits of communist political warfare.[5] The Communists are no longer limited to minute penetration activities here and there, but can aim to undermine and subvert countries and continents politically and psychologically.

5. The Soviet communist leaders have always made it abundantly clear that a strict calculation of what is called "the relation of forces" is the basic scientific analysis which guides the formulation of foreign policy toward the outside world, i.e., permitting maneuvering, tacking, the transition from certain methods of struggle (pressure) to others (conciliation), alternate attacks, and retreats. The calculation of the relation of forces takes into account ideological and psychological factors, as well as economic and military factors, which, though ever present, are always changing and dynamic in development, and fundamental to the calculation are hardheaded estimates of relative military capabilities. For a detailed discussion, see Raymond L. Garthoff, "The Concept of the Balance of Power in Soviet Policy Making," *World Politics*, Vol. VI, No. 1 (October, 1951), pp. 85-111.

The popular term "Cold War" describes the present state of affairs far more accurately than the terms previously used, e.g., "psychological warfare," "subversion," "infiltration," and "brainwashing." Such terms merely describe certain manifestations of the Cold War. Moscow's master propagandists sensed the dangerous implications of this descriptive slogan: if the West once understood its confrontation with a new type of war, it would wake up and act accordingly. Moscow therefore ignored the new slogan, counting on its being but a casual phrase likely to lose vividness in time. But this accurate two-word description of reality did not fade. Potent slogans (the supreme art in propagandistic agitation) are hard to beat, as the Kremlin well knows, and this was one of them. Moscow then resorted to the old stratagem of tossing its guilt back at us by claiming that the West initiated and was engaging in cold warfare.

Slogans, no matter how descriptive of things actual or potential, can be only as effective as the efforts put behind them. Furthermore, even the best slogan can be beaten or neutralized by an effective counter-slogan. Moscow eventually countered, at least in part, by projecting the slogan of "peaceful coexistence," or peace based on competitive coexistence.[6] The high command in Moscow has, of course, no more intention of coexisting permanently with capitalism than the wolf with the sheep, but in its perpetual quest for deception, the propaganda of "peaceful coexistence" serves its purpose. The propaganda slogans projected by Moscow have the sustained weight of the Soviet government and of the communist parties abroad behind them, whereas Western slogans are very often mere journalistic inventions which come and go.[7]

"Cold War" is not a mere slogan; it is a state of affairs, just as the term

6. There exists a basic difference in thinking between the communist bloc and the Free World with regard to the term "peaceful coexistence." For details, see N. S. Khrushchev, "On Peaceful Co-existence," *Foreign Affairs,* Vol. XXXVIII, No. 1 (October, 1959) , pp. 1-18, "The 1960 Moscow Statement," reprinted in *The China Quarterly,* No. 5 (January/March, 1961), pp. 25-52, and *For Victory in Peaceful Competition with Capitalism,* pp. 1-784; Harry A. and Bonaro Overstreet, *The War Called Peace;* Wladyslaw W. Kulski, *Peaceful Co-Existence*; George F. Kennan, "Peaceful Co-existence: A Western View," *Foreign Affairs,* Vol. XXXVIII, No. 2 (January, 1960) , pp. 171-90; and the Twelfth Report of the Commission to Study the Organization of Peace, Research Affiliate of the American Association for the United Nations, *Peaceful Co-existence: A New Challenge to the United Nations* (New York, June, 1960), pp. 4-46.

7. For authoritative understandings of the manner in which the Communists use words, slogans, and language as weapons, see "Words That Divide the World," by Stefan T. Possony, in *The Saturday Evening Post* series "Adventures of the Mind," *The Saturday Evening Post* (July 9, 1960) , p. 42, and "Language as a Communist Weapon," Consultation with Dr. Stefan T. Possony, Committee on Un-American Activities, House of Representatives, (86th Cong., 1st Sess.,) March 2, 1959.

"imperialism" was in the nineteenth century. It is the method by which the neo-imperialism of the Kremlin advances. The Socialists[8] understand its significance better than any other organized force in the West. They know the difference between a political offensive and defensive and the slogans used for both purposes.

In the early fifties, the West tended to develop some effective counter-slogans, such as "liberation," aimed at the communist satellites in Eastern Europe, or "peace in freedom," which could exert a powerful influence on the freedom-craving Soviet peoples themselves. But influential forces within the West blocked this effort in favor of peaceful coexistence based on the *status quo*.[9]

Conflict Diplomacy

While the Soviet Union carries on and supports many covert activities abroad, Soviet diplomacy is of necessity an openly avowed responsibility of the state. In considering the role of diplomacy as a leading instrument of Soviet political warfare, it is essential to recognize that Communists always act as Communists. They must adjust themselves tactically to the organization through which they work, be it a union, a peasants' league, or an embassy. If in an embassy or consulate, they conform to the protocol of diplomacy and use it as a cover for their conspiratorial operations. This fact has been corroborated by the testimony and documentation supplied by defectors from the Soviet diplomatic corps.

Before World War II, when the Soviet state was mainly on the defensive, it hid its role in political warfare. It often went out of its way in pretending to abide by diplomatic protocol. The only outward manifestations of its participation in political warfare were its leading role in the Soviet peace campaigns and its maneuvering to line up the democracies against the Axis powers after the rise of Hitler. In short, its diplomacy sought to make use of, and was dependent upon, the policies of other powers. After

8. In communist jargon, "socialism" actually means Soviet-Chinese communism. However, the term "socialists" in this context is used in a Western sense.

9. Walter Lippmann, who interviewed Mr. Khrushchev on the meaning of the *status quo*, wrote later: "In his [Khrushchev's] mind, the social and economic revolution now in progress in Russia, China, and elsewhere in Asia and Africa is the status quo, and he wants us [the West] to recognize it as such. In his mind, opposition to this revolution is an attempt to change the status quo. Whereas we [of the West] think of the status quo as the situation as it exists at the moment, he thinks of it as the process of revolutionary change which is in progress. He wants us to recognize the revolution not only as it is but [as] it is going to be." *The Communist World and Ours*, p. 13.

the war, with the capitalist world weakened and the United States almost disarmed, the Kremlin turned sharply toward aggression. The international class struggle, called off during the war, started again on a larger scale,[10] spearheaded by the communist take-over of countries in Eastern Europe and Asia.

Soviet diplomacy became a conflict diplomacy in the full sense only after the war. In the take-over[11] of the satellite nations, Soviet embassy personnel provided the political leadership. Communist parties in the satellite countries, with the exception of Czechoslovakia, were very small. They had to be built up in a hurry by manipulating and forcing the larger socialist and petty-bourgeois peasant parties into a united front with the Communists and then absorbing them completely. Those who resisted fled, or else disappeared.[12] The activities of these embassies, operating unhindered, revealed the nature of Soviet diplomacy as an instrument of conquest.

A July, 1961 report of the Assembly of Captive European Nations presents in capsule form the process by which Soviet-communist rule was established over the nations of Central and Eastern Europe. The report tells, with adequate documentation, how the Soviets came to power, not by ballot but by intrigue and coercion:

They imposed their system by direct and indirect aggression, by use or threat of force. That system is now protected by the barbed wire and mine-fields of the Iron Curtain from the outside, and is maintained by Soviet bayonets inside. Exhibiting all the trappings of police states and denying the basic human rights to the people they rule, the Communist regimes in Eastern and Central Europe represent nobody except their Soviet masters.[13]

10. For example, the new international communist organization—Cominform—was formed in September, 1947, by the Soviet Union. The Cominform reaffirmed international class struggle against "the capitalist countries,"—namely, the West. See *Facts on Communism* (by David Dallin) , Vol. II, *The Soviet Union: From Lenin to Khrushchev*, Committee on Un-American Activities, House of Representatives, 86th Cong., 2nd Sess., December, 1960, pp. 255-57.

11. For details on the steps leading to the bolshevization of Eastern Europe, see D. Tomasic, "The Structure of Soviet Power and Expansion," *Annals* of the American Academy of Political and Social Science, Vol. CCLXXI (September, 1950), pp. 32-42, and B. Radista, "The Sovietization of the Satellites," *ibid.*, pp. 122-34.

12. *Fighting Warsaw: The Story of the Polish Underground State, 1939–45*, by Stefan Korbonski, last chief of the Polish wartime underground, graphically describes the process of communist take-over.

13. ACEN *Documents* 236-44 (VII).

Communist State Diplomacy

It is common to confuse the role of the Soviet Union in political warfare with the warfare carried on by the communist parties in non-communist countries or to minimize the difference as inconsequential. For instance, the Soviet Union, as a state, cannot be expected to preoccupy itself with what goes on inside a local union or a farmers' organization in Timbuktu, but the Communist Party can. The Communist Party, on the other hand, cannot offer peace because that is a function of states.

Diplomacy reflects the nature of the government it serves. Conventional diplomacy serves the purposes of facilitating trade and other relations between nations. If frictions occur, it provides a means of smoothing them out by give and take. If it fails, critical differences may be decided by a showdown known as war. Until the advent of totalitarian powers, wars were limited to certain concrete objectives; after these were reached, former relations were resumed.

The Soviet government not only aims at world conquest under Soviet communism—an unlimited objective—but also at the destruction of the social pattern within each nation. It aims at a universal state and a universal social system in which the conventional state relationships, whether diplomatic or otherwise, would be abolished. Soviet diplomacy is used as an instrument in the attainment of these long-range objectives.

With the post-war rise of the Soviets to a first-class military power, the Soviet Union not only dominates the international communist movement far more effectively than it did originally but also, as a state, intervenes more actively through political warfare. Although the Comintern was formally "dissolved" in May, 1943, the various communist parties were still directed by the Communist Party of the Soviet Union, though not overtly.[14] What little autonomy the national parties still had was whittled down and the Moscow apparatus built up, both as to number of operatives and the degree of its authority over the national communist parties. Soviet embassy and consular staffs expanded, and so did the secret Soviet political-police apparatus in the "capitalist" countries. The trading apparatus, too, was much larger than the volume of trade with the Soviets warranted. The

14. Actually, the Comintern was never really dissolved. It merely functioned in secret. See Wolfgang Leonhard, *Child of the Revolution,* pp. 1-447. In this personal account of life as a professional communist-party functionary, the author tells of his assignment to the German section of the Comintern in Moscow after its "dissolution" in May, 1943. There he was trained for future political tasks in Germany. The Comintern apparatus was kept intact; the Soviet merely moved its headquarters to another section of Moscow.

friendlier a "capitalist" country became toward the Soviets, the faster the growth of the Soviet apparatus in that country. If the country was considered ripe for wholesale subversion, the Soviet apparatus would be doubled and tripled. The satellites, whose foreign policy is directed from Moscow, would also move in and establish their embassies and consulates, co-ordinated and directed by the Soviet apparatus.

A government whose objectives are unlimited and which engages in political warfare to soften up the world for conquest is in need of considerably more information—strategic and tactical—than other governments. If one is in command of large armies of subversion, one needs competent staffs to direct such operations. The best-trained and most-experienced political workers for that purpose are, as a rule, in the Soviet embassies and consulates. The experts in secret and underground organizations of various kinds are in the political-police apparatus, some of which are attached to the embassies and consulates.

The Kremlin does not believe in the sanctity of international treaties.[15] Communist strategy lulls the bourgeois to sleep by a treaty while the Kremlin prepares its undoing. If the Kremlin takes a country by subversion, it will insist, in the name of the national sovereignty of the country involved, that the Western powers keep their hands off, but if a Soviet satellite (Hungary) rebels, its display of sovereignty will be crushed. The Kremlin thus serves notice on the West that in the name of peace it must tolerate subversive incursions into the Western areas but that no countersubversion will be tolerated within the Soviet empire. It means to keep what it has conquered and take more—all in the name of peace.

Some Operations of the Soviet State

The difference between what the communist state does and what the communist parties do is not only qualitative but also quantitative. Take, for instance, the question of guerrilla warfare. The Communist Party is essential in that operation, and it can by itself organize such warfare on a small scale. But only when aid from a communist state provides arms, funds and trained personnel does guerrilla warfare assume real significance.

Another key feature of the Soviet Union's political warfare is its exten-

15. See the U.S. Senate staff study "Soviet Political Agreements and Results," prepared for a subcommittee of the Senate Committee on the Judiciary, 86th Cong., 1st Sess., *Senate Document* 125, pp. 1-107.

sive system of training colleges, already mentioned. While the Soviet Union was on the defensive, these colleges concentrated mainly on political-war-fare organizers, tacticians, propagandists, and agitators. Since World War II, this system has been vastly expanded, with greater emphasis on special military training, with colleges in Russia, China, and the satellites.

Moscow propaganda also contributes to the total communist political-warfare campaign. Radio Moscow and its co-ordinated stations in the satel-lites broadcast around the clock in all languages. Moscow's broadcasts are of the variety that other nations use only in wartime, breeding hate, sus-picion, and confusion. Moscow's radio propaganda is attuned to the long-range political objectives of the Soviet Union and to the Soviets' special or immediate objectives in the various areas of the globe. Moscow and Peking radios are also utilized to transmit secret coded instructions to agents and to party leaders throughout the world.

The Soviet Union, in accordance with its expanding political-warfare role, has taken over many of the functions formerly performed by or in the name of the Comintern. As a state, it can perform these functions in a different way and on a broader scale. It can use Nasser's or Sukarno's nationalism as the Comintern could not, and it can use Soviet diplomacy in a way which the Comintern, as a limited, presumably unofficial organi-zation, could not.

The same can be said about the Soviet state publishers and their branches in the various non-communist countries. This complex is a huge enterprise publishing communist propaganda literature in many languages, all paid for by the Soviet Union and given free to the communist parties. The state publisher is a factory which turns out learned and theoretical inter-pretations in justification of the Soviets' policies in any field of Soviet or communist activity. A vast staff of theorists, writers, and researchers is employed for that purpose. It thus provides the intelligentsia in the non-communist world and its own Communists or fellow travelers with plausible, prefabricated theories, suitable facts, and interpretations for ready use in any field. Vast as the state publisher is as an enterprise, little is known about its role in the non-communist world. Its function, how-ever, as a molder of thought in areas of social ferment can hardly be exaggerated. No other nation owns a comparable brainwashing enterprise.

Potemkinism

Among the most deceptive of Soviet activities on the political-warfare front are the so-called cultural relations with the non-Soviet world. Cultural relations include a wide range of activities centralized under a Soviet governmental agency which arranges tours for foreign diplomats and visitors through the Soviet Union, publishes literature about the accomplishments of the Soviet regime, produces movies for non-Soviet audiences, organizes Soviet displays in international fairs, arranges for visits of Soviet cultural and amity delegations through foreign countries, and organizes pro-Soviet amity societies, such as the Council of American-Soviet Friendship, in foreign countries. The cost of all this activity is defrayed from the Soviet treasury, except for such collections as the semi-official Soviet amity societies obtain in the various countries. Comparable organizations operate under various names in Red China and in the European satellites.

The average American, by reading the newspapers or listening to radio or television, concludes that Soviet cultural relations are simply a pro-Soviet advertising job. This is not the intention of the Kremlin, to whom cultural relations are an operation of the highest political importance.[16] If the Soviet Union can be presented to the outside world as a country where the underdog has come into his own, the attitude of the outside world will be favorably swayed. The psychological softening of critical attitudes could paralyze any hostile actions against the Soviet Union and also generate a climate of quasi-friendly co-operation.

One of the subjects taught in the political-warfare colleges in Moscow is how to sell the Soviet Union to the outside world. Quality goods simply do not exist for legitimate advertising. One can, however, sell imaginary goods or samples created for that purpose and, through propaganda, create the impression that the goods actually exist.

It is a difficult task to sell the amalgam of communist totalitarianism to the more advanced outside world as the society of the future. The mere showing of model structures, factories, and collectives to a normally skeptical world would not be convincing alone, no matter how cleverly managed. However, since there is little free entry into the Soviet Union, no really free travel within it, and the viewers can be selected, a comprehensive deception becomes possible. A politically calculated control of the entry-visa system makes that feasible.

All the world's news media of any consequence are represented in Moscow. Newspapermen accredited to Moscow are, for the most part, involun-

16. For a detailed study of what is called "cultural relations" of the Soviet Union toward the outside world, see Frederick C. Barghoorn, "Cultural Relations and Soviet Foreign Policy," *World Politics,* Vol. VIII (1956), pp. 322-31, and *The Soviet Cultural Offensive,* pp. 1-353.

tary witnesses. Since they can report freely about Soviet affairs only after they have left the Soviet Union for good, the difficulties connected with getting the facts about Russia cannot be overlooked. Western newsmen in Moscow cannot freely visit places or interview people as they can in open countries or, in a limited way, in semiclosed ones. They must obtain their news from controlled sources. To make sure that they interpret this news "correctly," there is censorship on wired or cabled dispatches. The foreign-mail postal division of the secret police, the M.V.D., censors all dispatches. If correspondents leave the country to transmit adverse news, they may not be able to return or may be expelled.

News, like everything else in a free society, is a competitive business: the public wants to know. Even lies are news, whether they are recognized as such or not; thus comes the temptation to keep accommodating representatives in Moscow. With all sources of information thoroughly controlled, the newsmen get their news either from official handouts or from the Soviet press or radio, doctored to serve the Kremlin's purposes. It does not matter how many words a correspondent sends or how much of it the editor at home prints or broadcasts. If it is based on Moscow, it is derived from Soviet-concocted news. If relations with the Kremlin are good, much of it will get into the bourgeois press and radio. If not, less of it will be in the home newspapers. Either way, it is still Soviet propaganda. Thus the West's news media in Moscow are made use of as instruments of the Kremlin's ideological penetration.

If the correspondents in Moscow and the editors at home are impressed by some of the Soviet releases or accept them as true (like those on planned economy), they will publish more. Most newsmen consider it good business to print some, for what use is a foreign correspondent who has never had a by-line? If there are sympathizers among the correspondents, or some who are willing to collaborate with Soviet authorities, they may be favored with scoops or leaks.

In addition to using the bourgeois news media represented in Moscow, the Kremlin has its own news service, Tass, operating in all countries with which it has diplomatic relations. Tass is well endowed and able to dispense material at cheap rates. It specializes in transforming propaganda into news—ready to print. It is not a news service in the conventional sense, but a political-warfare agency operating in the news field.

Tass propaganda stresses the dominant Soviet role in world affairs. The Japanese, for example, surrendered not to the United States but to the mighty Red Army; the Germans, too, were defeated by the Red Army, led by Stalin, with the Americans and British playing, at best, only a secondary role.

Soviet achievements in the realm of nuclear weapons, ICBMs, and space exploration, significant as they have been, are the result of a one-sided emphasis on military-technological development. They have been used by the Kremlin, however, to convey the picture of all-around Soviet ascendancy over the United States. Khrushchev, in his important Moscow speech of January 14, 1960, put it this way:

The high pace of economic development of the Soviet Union is no longer doubted by anyone abroad. Disputes concern only how much more rapidly we are forging ahead than the United States and about when we shall catch up with it. A large number of eminent economists, representatives of business groups, and statesmen are actively participating in the discussion of these questions in the United States.

Despite the boasting and calculated misinformation about the five-year plans, over-all Russian economy is many years behind that of the United States. The steel-producing capacity of the Soviet Union is far below that of the United States, after forty years of communist rule. Most of Russia's steel goes into military hardware to create military strength—to the detriment of the individual consumer. After forty years, Soviet Russia is to the average citizen still a horse-drawn civilization, and the horses, like the men, work for the state.

Colin Clark, Oxford University economist and research director of the Econometrica Institute, analyzed Soviet economic achievement in a book, published in 1960, entitled *The Real Productivity of Soviet Russia*. In this study the British economist comes to this conclusion:

Governed by fanatical materialists, the Russian people have been called upon to sacrifice their personal liberties, their national traditions, and their religion for the sake of material progress; and all that they have received in return is a rate of material progress far below that of most other countries. . . . It should be made clear how very mediocre the economic results of communism have, in fact, been.

Despite flaws in his data base, Clark's observations are generally valid with regard to the consumer section of the Soviet economy. In other areas, particularly military hardware, heavy industry, and research and development, the Soviet economy has scored some notable gains since the death of Stalin. These have resulted in a high rate of over-all economic growth, although in terms of food, clothing and shelter the Soviets lag far behind the West.

The period since Stalin's death has seen the Soviet economic planners abandon many Marxist prejudices in search of more flexibility and more effective planning. The weaknesses of the institutions and operations of the Soviet economic system over a period of thirty years are fairly well known. Detailed control resulted in wrong decisions—which could not be avoided—by people on the spot, who lacked authority. Many relatively small questions were settled only by those at the top of the pyramid of decision-makers, and the freedom of managers at lower levels to find solutions was limited by the rigidities of raw-material allocation and by arbitrary directives from above.

The picture is changing. The Russian economy is now very much bigger, more complex, and more decentralized. The weaknesses of old institutions having made clear the need for new approaches, Soviet leaders are now permitting more initiative on the part of planners, administrators, and managers. One can envisage many other improvements such as a better understanding of the usefulness of the price system and some effort to make Soviet prices a better tool for economic calculation.

The Soviet leaders have also examined the inequities and irrationalities in their system which eroded morale and were economically wasteful. Steps to eliminate some of the most glaring of these weaknesses have already been taken.

As a result of increased flexibility, greater capital resources, and far more trained personnel, the Soviet economy is growing rapidly.[17] The economy remains basically oriented toward heavy industry and military preparations. The draft program of the Communist Party of the Soviet Union, published at the end of July, 1961, made few changes in the basic Soviet economic allocation between guns and butter:

In general, the scantiness of concrete economic goals in what had been earlier advertised as a twenty-year economic program surprised observers. This also encouraged speculation about possible changes designed to make

17. For a more detailed exposé of Soviet economic potential, including the aspects just treated, see Francis P. Hoeber and Robert W. Campbell, "Soviet Economic Potential, 1960–1970," *SRI* (May, 1961).This report was prepared for: Office of the Chief Research and Development, U. S. Army.

the program more vague than originally intended. In this way the Soviet leaders would have more maneuverability for future economic planning.

The greatest surprise was the failure of the new program to announce a replacement of the historic Communist policy of increasing heavy industrial production more rapidly than consumer goods output by raising both types of production at an equal tempo.[18]

18. Harry Schwartz, "New Soviet Policy Represents a Shift in Khrushchev's Goals," *New York Times,* July 31, 1961, p. 2C.

CHAPTER VIII

COMMUNIST OPERATIONS IN THE FREE WORLD

BEARING IN MIND THE INCREASED ROLE OF THE SOVIET STATE in communist political-warfare operations, we now turn to a few of the specific ways in which the Soviet Union exploits popular trends and aspirations in the areas outside its domain.

The Use of Nationalism as a Trojan Horse

Soviet cold warfare has been exploiting increasingly nationalism, particularly in the underdeveloped countries of Asia, Africa, and the Middle East.[1] The Soviets' concept of nationalism, as developed for export, aims at the fragmentation of the capitalist world: let every nation stand alone to be dealt with or picked off individually, and let there be as many nations born as possible. The Soviets want the maximum of unity on their side and the maximum of division on the side of the enemy. Nationalist ambitions and suspicion of the West must be roused to the utmost. Anyone entering into a political-military combination with the United States, be it through NATO, SEATO, or the Organization of American States, must be opposed and denounced as a "flunky" of American "imperialism." On the other hand, so-called neutralist combinations in opposition to the United States must be encouraged as the first step towards drawing them into the orbit of Soviet conflict strategy.

What are the implications of communist policy vis-à-vis nationalism? Soviet state power, or communism, is based on a social concept, namely, the presumed rule of certain classes of society and the elimination of

1. The antecedents of this development lie, of course, in Stalin's modification of nationalism to a system of thought aimed directly at exploitation of emergent political situations in Asia.

others. Nationalism, on the other hand, is a unifying political concept based on history, territory, language, and other characteristics common to all people inhabiting a given area. The two concepts of political organization are basically antagonistic.

The contradiction in this case cannot be truly reconciled. In exploiting nationalism, the Soviet state deals with nations as they are, whether feudal, semifeudal, or bourgeois. Soviet power penetrates other states and manipulates all elements within them, regardless of sociological considerations. The Soviets justify this on the grounds that the social part of their program will be carried out after the take-over, after the elimination of the propertied classes and other hostile elements. Under this formula, the expansionist role of the Soviet is considered a superior form of the class struggle in which any and all means and methods may be used (under proper supervision), provided they serve the cause.

Let us keep in mind that the original *raison d'être* of the Soviet state was (1) to elevate the working class to a supreme status in society, a status allegedly promised to the working class by irreversible history; (2) to free the peasantry from servitude and penury to the landlords; (3) to raise the material and cultural level of the masses in general; and (4) to erase from society all those classes and institutions which might obstruct the realization of these objectives. In the Soviet Union the regime has, in practice, long departed from the principles proclaimed at its birth and has devoted its energies, not to the improvement of the lot of the masses, but to building the power of the Soviet state.

The departure of the Soviet state from strict class politics into the exploitation of nationalism is rooted in some of Lenin's strategic theories. But prior to World War II, nationalist aspirations were linked with class politics, as was the case during the "popular front" period of the mid-thirties. During World War II, Stalin dealt with nations as war enemies or allies and called off the class struggle.

Nationalism, according to Marx and Lenin, is a bourgeois philosophy of state and society. If it is permissible to consort with bourgeois nationalism wherever it is in opposition to the dominant major nations of the Free World, then one can utilize all dissidents in the Free World, regardless of class and ideology, provided their divergence is amenable to Soviet purposes.

That, precisely, has been the practice of Soviet diplomacy and its underground apparatus in recent years, particularly in countries where the communist parties are weak. The operating center of the conspiracy in those countries is not in the national headquarters of the communist parties but in the Soviet embassies. It functions through the underground and subsidiary Soviet organizations, such as the trade missions, official cultural delegations, and news services (Tass). In many of these countries, the national communist parties have become secondary forces in the total complex of the Soviet's political warfare.

The manner in which the Communists maneuver in the Middle East is illustrative of their manipulation of nationalism as a battering ram against what seemed only fifteen years ago an impregnable Western position. Soviet collaboration with Great Britain and the United States in the creation of Israel in 1947 paved the way for subsequent excursions into the Middle East. Communist arms sent to Egypt shortly after the 1955 summit meeting in Geneva marked the arrival of the Soviet Union as a power to be reckoned with in the Middle East. Backing Pan-Arab nationalism by itself would not suffice because the communist parties in the Arab countries were not strong enough. Arms, diplomatic support, technical aid, and credits were used to establish the Soviet Union politically in the Middle East and, ultimately, strengthen the Arab communist parties.

The primary motive for the Kremlin's alliance with Pan-Arab nationalism is, as Khrushchev says, "to oust the West from the area." That process is well under way but, as yet, far from completed; hence he continues the alliance with Nasser while building strength in Iraq. He even offers to tolerate Nasser's suppression of communism in his domain if it is not done "in a noisy manner." Khrushchev also assures the Arabs that "the developments in the Iraqi Republic have nothing in common with Socialism" and that Soviet policy toward the Arab countries "was never based on that principle." But if a nationalist leader will not cooperate, Khrushchev resorts to the gloved threat of invoking the "democratic demands of the people." All of this is in good Stalinist style, conformable to the game played in China in the years preceding seizure of power.

The trump card held in reserve by Moscow (but likely to be played at a propitious time in the Middle East) is the appeal to the masses. This will not be a mere psychological appeal to nationalism, which by then will be threadbare, but a social appeal for the division of the possessions of the wealthy. The masses of the Middle East have been starving for centuries. Their accumulated hatreds can be aroused and organized by a communist jinni. Hatreds do not reason; they explode if afforded the opportunity, and if ably guided they can be a potent force. Such a force can obliterate a Nasser and even a Kassem and enthrone an Arab Mao Tse-tung. The fact that such a revolution can later be derailed into state slavery is kept hidden from the masses, who, as Marx said, are incapable of much foresight.

In the Middle East, as elsewhere, the communist game is played in stages. The present stage, in the underdeveloped countries, is not socialism but nationalism. But the end result sought is socialism, communist style. The Communists will of course promote the demand for Arab socialism when Nasser and other Arab leaders of the nationalist phase of the revolution are unable to deliver on their promises to the masses.

Nasser, at least, seems to be getting ready for this next revolutionary phase by propounding his own theory of Arab socialism. The men around Nasser have begun to speak about the failure of the "old cadre," the "old elite," and the "old intelligentsia," who had identified themselves with the old ruling classes and remained isolated from the popular will.[2]

The Question of National Communism

Moscow does not tolerate organized dissension within the Communist Party of the U.S.S.R. or in any affiliate in another country. If such dissension occurs, it must be liquidated. If dissenters have a majority in any part of the movement, they must be expelled and the party reorganized. If the Party is in power in a country, then the dissenters may also be arrested; formerly they were carried off to slave-labor camps or executed in a purge.

The purging of communist dissenters is a long-established practice.

2. In a series of articles, President Nasser's unofficial spokesman, Mohamed Hassanein Heikal, editor of *Al Ahram*, explained what happened on July 23, 1952, was merely a coup removing a king. Apart from that and the beginnings of land reform, he says, most things remained as they were. But the coup paved the way for the revolution that took place much later. The daring young army officers who carried out the coup, Mr. Heikal declared, had plenty of "revolutionary driving force," but initially lacked a theory of revolutionary action. Little by little, this "missing link" has crystallized around an economic development plan. "It was deemed essential to depart completely from the traditional slow process to a new one marked by greatly increased productivity," Mr. Heikal wrote. "A development plan embodying a constant increase in the national income and equity of distribution could be described as the pivotal point." See "Nasser Now Hero in Economic Role," by Dana Adams Schmidt, *New York Times*, August 13, 1961, p. 13.

Tito's expulsion in 1948 was the first case of a party leader in power, with outside assistance, being able to survive such an action. The inability of Stalin to liquidate Tito thus attracted world-wide attention.

The purge as developed by Stalin is the key to the final development of a police state. Stalin did not wait until an opposition developed; he anticipated and provoked it. He designed the preventive purge. It took fourteen years (1924–1938) of these methods to transform the Russian Communist Party, in effect, into a fascist or national-socialist party. When it came to the satellites, Stalin wanted to impose his fascist version of bolshevism at once. The non-Russian communist parties had been accustomed to considering the Russian Communist Party as being first, but first among equals. This concept was particularly strong among those parties which had attained state power in Eastern Europe through Soviet aid. They were not ready to become direct instruments of Moscow. Stalin, sensing the situation, began to apply his preventive purge. Heads began to fall. Tito was provoked into opposition and expelled. After Tito's defiance, national communism became a deviation, and the purge in the other satellites rolled on.

Lenin, practical revolutionist, considered it permissible to use nationalism as an ally for his purposes. He was willing to work with it in order to kill it. Tito's concept differed little. With his back to the wall, he had to play up to nationalism, but no sooner was Stalin dead than he began to veer back to the communist center. There was no other choice.[3]

If one were a "National Communist," one would let a particular nation prescribe the essential conditions under which that nation should live. This is precisely what Tito or Titoists do not wish to do, for there can be little democracy and no authentic national self-determination under communism. Communists are willing to fool the West with pretensions of "national communism." They are even willing to bolster this deception by relaxing forced collectivization and easing up on some other fringe items; but they do not yield on essentials.

Western acceptance of Tito's "national communism" cannot be explained on the grounds of appeasement. Tito was not important enough for that. The willingness of many Western opinion-makers to accept

3. Tito, as a Communist, knows that if the Soviet empire crumbles, his own coexistence beside it would also come to an end; hence he is like a particle drawn to a magnet: Moscow. As the 1961 Belgrade Conference should demonstrate, Tito's basic orientation toward the communist bloc remains, despite occasional tactical flurries of pseudo-independence.

"agrarian reform" or "national communism" in order to justify toleration
of the Communists was born of both ignorance and sympathy. The latter
was aroused during the crucial period when a false image regarding communism was widely spread throughout the West.

The sympathy, of course, was never for Stalin's fascist bolshevism, but
for the pretty pictures painted for us of social progress within the U.S.S.R.
When, after the war, much of its horror became known, a gradual shift
began to take place. But deep convictions do not change overnight. Gradually, those attracted to communism before World War II separated themselves from Stalin but would not admit that they had been altogether
wrong.

Stalin's break with Tito gave sympathizers a diversionary chance: they
could climb on the anti-Stalin bandwagon—without repudiating their
ideological sympathies—by sponsoring the "national communist" Tito,
who might reform world communism. Some who had been lured by communism in the thirties even claimed that the break in the solid communist
front was the result of their clever and positive policies against it. They
could thus convert their failure to recognize the totalitarian nature of
communism into an image of success. At the same time, some communist
apologists continued a pro-Mao policy regarding China, inventing alleged
differences between Mao and Stalin. When the pro-Mao policy failed as a
utopian escape, Tito offered a substitute symbolic of moderate communism.

Tito has tried to maintain the benign image of the moderate national
communist leader by pursuing certain domestic policies at variance with
those practiced inside the Soviet Union. He has also tried, unsuccessfully,
to develop a theoretical rationale for national communism since a communist operating without a plausible theoretical base is always insecure.

Thus national communism, which was no more real than Mao's "agrarian communism," was invented to cover past failures. That does not mean
that nationalism, which in this case was synonymous with the craving for
freedom, does not exist in Yugoslavia or behind the Iron Curtain. On the
contrary, it does exist, but no communist party or sympathizers can be its
champions. If any proof was needed that communism and nationalism are
antithetical concepts, the insurrections behind the Iron Curtain, and more
particularly the Hungarian revolt, supplied it.

If we wish to advance the national liberation of peoples by dealing with
communist leaders in trouble, we can do so only by forcing them to relax
their oppressive grip over their people. We would thus be demonstrating

our friendship for the people and not for their communist masters. If we go along with the rulers, it should be only to the extent that they yield essential liberties to their people. Unfortunately, we have helped Tito to stay in power on *his* terms—and have invested more than a billion dollars in this effort. The limited results of this policy justify questioning and reappraisal.

On the international front, Tito has never failed to support the Kremlin. Tito, like Khrushchev, advocates the "end of colonialism, disarmament and a total ban on nuclear weapons." He contends that West Germany, "armed nearly to the teeth," is a "danger to peace."[4]

Following the July, 1961 visit of Yugoslav Foreign Minister Popovic to Moscow, a joint communiqué, expressing satisfaction that relations between the two countries "are developing normally and their positions are similar or coincide on the major international questions," was issued. "They expressed the hope," the communiqué continued, "that co-operation between the two countries in the questions of the struggle for peace and the reduction of international tension will go on developing successfully."[5] The United States has paid quite a price for this kind of independent "national communism."

The Soviet Underground

The Soviet secret service depended entirely upon the various native communist parties when it was established in the early twenties. In subsequent years, intelligence activities became specialized and were detached from the communist parties, but were still dependent upon them for personnel. In assigning or transferring such personnel a liaison was established between the native communist party and the Soviet secret service in each country. The direction of these networks was established through the Soviet diplomatic service or its trade agencies and, in its most critical elements, through resident undercover agents operating outside official Soviet agencies.

By now, each Soviet network operates through many separate groups of agents, not known to each other, so that the total operation is not endangered if one network is discovered. If contact is lost, it can always be reestablished through the liaison apparatus of the Party. A party member assigned to the Soviet underground is detached from all other communist-party

4. *New York Times,* July 4, 1961.
5. *Ibid.,* July 13, 1961, p. 1.

activity or contact and transferred to the jurisdiction of the underground. He "quits" the Party for the more discreet activity of the hidden apparatus.

A Communist is never an intelligence agent in the narrow sense; no matter where he operates, he is a trained, politically sensitive person, always ready to engage in any sort of conspiratorial activity. He may be a mere secret agent today, but he is ready to be a rebel leader tomorrow. As a rule, he does not like to be a professional spy, but if he is, it is for the larger cause he serves. The Soviet underground is highly responsive and hostile to any ideological disturbances in the movement. Most defections from communism are the product of such disturbances. A Communist is a Jack-of-all-trades in the field of subversion. Thus the specialized Soviet intelligence agent of today, operating in liaison with the Communist Party, may become the highly skilled cadre of a revolution tomorrow.

To understand the Soviet underground and its political division, one must cast out of one's mind any idea that it is bound by principles. The Soviet underground is a no-holds-barred organization in which anything is acceptable if and when it serves the designated purpose. The underground is not obligated to advocate communism; on the contrary, it is supposed to disavow it. The political division of the Soviet underground has been known to buy into businesses through native intermediaries or to use the business of party members and sympathizers for smuggling and other purposes. It has been known to buy into radio stations, newspapers, and publishing houses in order to support subversive activities. It has engaged in schemes to launch hostile and defeatist news analysts and radio commentators in its effort to influence the foreign policy of a nation in a direction favorable to the Kremlin. The political division is the specialist in organizing sabotage, assassinations, guerrilla warfare, and arms smuggling. In the political division, there is concentrated the organizing genius behind much that is happening in the Middle East, Latin America, Africa, and other disturbed areas.

There are four over-all differences between our intelligence agencies and those of the Soviet state. First, our intelligence units are highly technical and pragmatic, whereas the Soviets' are highly political. Second, their intelligence services aim to undermine and subvert our social system, whereas ours usually aim merely at the gathering of information. Third, the political division of Soviet intelligence is allied with the various Communist Parties and plays a primary role in their underground operations; we have nothing comparable. And fourth, the political sector of their intelligence not only stores up information but acts upon it from the bottom up and the top down. In short, it exploits dissension, unrest, and discontent and, in liaison with the Party, even creates these things. Our intelligence agencies do not fish in these murky waters.

The political division of the Soviet underground directs the more sensitive underground maneuvering and organization. The record indicates that the activities (under its direction) of secret cells in United States government departments dealing with America's policy toward China were not even known to the Politburo of the Communist Party, U.S.A. They were known only to those directly involved and only to the extent that they, as participants, had to know. Only Moscow knew the total pattern of operation. The Soviet underground's function is to guide non-communist elements down the wrong path. The function is one of diversion, of leading non-communists toward self-inducted paralysis, unpreparedness, demoralization, and defeatism.

The Soviet underground is the ultimate refinement in conspiratorial political organization. It does not work through communist-party fronts; it leaves that phase of the operation to the Party. It works through key individuals whose political identity is obscure or unknown and uses them to move other individuals or organizations who often do not suspect that they are being used. Naturally, the most amenable to this purpose are those who genuinely believe in statism, unconditional pacifism, or other theories that lend themselves to Soviet plans.

Much has been said about the deceptiveness of communist-party fronts pushing communist-inspired reforms. But these operate in the open. At least their outward purposes are known and can be tied in with the general scheme of communist operations. The Soviet underground is entirely anonymous. It can be felt, but not seen. It took forty years of experience in political warfare to perfect its techniques. Forty years ago even the communist leaders in Moscow found it difficult to conceive of such an operation. The Soviet underground operates in the political realm like the buccaneers of old, who had the permission, and even the support, of their respective governments but were officially disavowed.

Growth of the Soviet Underground

The control of political warfare by the soviet state rather than the communist parties began with the abolition of the Comintern in 1943 and has been increasing ever since. Theoretically, the role of the communist parties as leading organizations remains the same, but the weight of the Soviet state has become more and more important. This has expressed itself not only in the growing staffs of Soviet embassies and trading agencies but also in the growth of the Soviets' political secret-service organizations and operations. The precise rate of that growth is not known, but the public records, as shown in hearings and investigations in the United States and elsewhere, indicate that it has been considerable. Nor is that growth confined to the usual secret services of a government, such as military intelligence. The revelations in Canada, Australia, and elsewhere show that the main work is done through the Soviet embassies. The same can be said about the secret infiltration groups in the United Nations and in its specialized agencies.

The West has not learned to make a clear differentiation between the Soviet state and the indigenous communist-party undergrounds.[6] It is true that their objectives are related, if not identical. Some hard-core Soviet-underground personnel are apparently still recruited from the Party. But otherwise the difference is considerable. The Soviet underground is qualitatively superior and as an arm of the Soviet government has superior means at its disposal. It concentrates only on the most strategic spots in the enemy's structure, whether in government, communications, transport, or industry, leaving secondary targets to the Party. It has no ideological limitations and hence can employ any and all personnel suitable to its immediate or long-range purposes. It uses unknown Communists and fellow travelers, as well as non-communist dissidents, if and when that serves its purpose.

Pro-Soviet apologists will allege that other governments also engage in secret intelligence operations. But the Soviet underground is not primarily an intelligence operation; intelligence is only part of it. The Soviet underground is primarily a political operation, inciting and co-ordinating internal strife and engaging and specializing in internal demoralization, paralysis, and disintegration.

From among the divergencies existing in every free country, the Soviet underground operators select those most useful to their purposes. They need not reveal their true political identity. On the contrary, they are under instructions to conceal it. In special cases they may even be permitted to pose as anti-communists. This is not possible for an avowed Communist,

6. It should be kept in mind that the Soviet government is itself an arm of the Communist Party of the Soviet Union.

but is is for a covert one, especially if he did not formally join the movement or any of its known fronts. Being politically non-identifiable is
particularly important in infiltrating sensitive spots in government, the
news media, and other strategic forces in the Free World.

Susceptible Targets

In its endeavors to penetrate the West, the Kremlin high command is
constantly preoccupied with strategems designed to exploit the contradictions in Western society. This requires the utilization of elements which,
although non-communist, are ideologically at odds with the open society.
These include the more doctrinaire Socialists, statist liberals, pacifists,
extreme right-wing conservatives, and some of the nationalists in the underdeveloped countries. Moscow is fully aware that these elements are
generally wary of any open alliance with Soviet communism or with communist parties in capitalist countries.

Such people are not necessarily disloyal to their country, but have an
ambivalent disloyalty or a lukewarm attitude toward part or all of the
system upon which it rests. Moscow considers people with such views as
potential part-way partners in its undermining activities. In the name of
peace, a Socialist will be suspicious of the foreign policy of his nation on
the ground that it is capitalist-inspired. Motivated by this hostile ideology,
a Socialist may favor measures which undermine free enterprise and morale
or divert the nation's resources from military preparedness. Frequently,
the western Socialist is still battling capitalism and not communism. There
are also capitalists who, for the sake of profit, are willing to trade with the
Soviet empire—and paradoxically, many Socialists are in favor of such trade
in the name of peace. We are not apportioning blame; we are merely
indicating a situation used to advantage by the enemy.

The following elements are considered ideologically accessible and perhaps can be utilized in a variety of operations:

(1) Fellow travelers and sympathizers;

(2) Anti-capitalist Marxists and syndicalists;

(3) Opponents of private capitalism other than Marxists (statists), including Fascists;

(4) Radical nationalists in underdeveloped and dependent nations (such
as the Mau Mau in Kenya);

(5) Corrupt elements (non-ideological) known for greed and pilfering,
including racketeers; and

(6) Politically naïve businessmen and extreme conservatives who concentrate on internal subversion and almost ignore the external power squeeze.

Not that all of these elements (except in the first category) are on the communist side. (Most of them, in fact, are slated for liquidation if and when the Communist Party comes to power.) Few of these would knowingly cooperate with communist efforts. Even in the first category, the most vulnerable, many will refuse to become Soviet spies. But wittingly or unwittingly they can be induced to serve communist tactical ends.

Interdiction

Soviet diplomacy first entered the field of political warfare with the defensive formula of "peace," and then reinterpreted that slogan to serve its aggressive purposes after World War II. In recent years it has added nationalism to its political armory for conquest and penetration. More recently, Soviet diplomacy has branched out into the area, hitherto pre-empted by the communist parties, of using propaganda to prevent the enemy from working in his own interest or from acting in time. We shall call this campaign of frustrating Western counteraction *interdiction*. The Communists call it "diversionism" or disorientation. It is a method which aims, through psychological means and maneuvers, to prevent the enemy from adopting or following a course of policy inimical to Soviet interests.

The Communists never falter on the proposition of doing away with capitalism while the West wavers between resistance and coexistence. Western policies, grounded in *laissez faire*, worked well enough before the advent of totalitarianism, but continued aherence to ad hoc decisions based on divergent assumptions may lead to defeat. Soviet diplomacy's role is to exploit this inconsistency, hence the relative impotence of our diplomacy in comparison with theirs. In Soviet diplomacy, interdiction seeks to tie our hands behind our backs while their military designers sharpen weapons of conquest.

Soviet interdiction is aided by the contradictions inherent in free society, expressed in the form of a struggle for supremacy by the contending parties or groups and resulting in many paralyzing compromises or in errors of leadershp. Moscow is well aware of the antagonistic forces operating in capitalist society and seeks to utilize and accentuate them. Ways of doing this are perennial subjects in Moscow's political-warfare colleges. If a Supreme Court decision paralyzes the government's internal-security program, that is a victory which the Communists are sure to appreciate. If, through their agitation and "humanitarian" propaganda, they can inhibit the testing and manufacture of A and H weapons, that, too, will be a successful utilization of the self-paralysis factor. Another major victory will be achieved if they can eliminate anti-communist agitation (or aid) addressed to their own freedom-craving peoples while they subvert at will on our side.

Soviet Trade in Political Warfare

A primary justification for large Soviet embassies in many countries of the Free World is the alleged possibility of Soviet trade. The possibilities could be immense if trade with the Soviets were not conducted by a government monopoly and determined largely by political considerations. The Kremlin does not buy what the people need or want, but rather what is essential from the point of view of building its power machine—mostly industrial capital goods and essential raw materials. As these needs are satisfied trade declines. Thus we have the phenomenon that as the Soviet empire grows, the area under its jurisdiction is increasingly withdrawn from existing world trade.

That does not prevent Moscow's propaganda machine from dangling the alleged possibility of big profits from Soviet trade before bourgeois noses. These profits are proffered with particular energy for the purpose of obtaining diplomatic recognition or other diplomatic gain. Trade, of course, is possible without diplomatic recognition. But with respect to vulnerable small countries trade is hardly a major consideration. The intention is to move in Soviet experts on subversion. Thus the Trojan horse in striped pants combines with, reinforces, and takes over the direction of the local communist party.[7] Disproportionately large Soviet Embassy staffs are located in small countries, such as Uruguay or Thailand, an indication that Moscow considers them politically vulnerable. In return for the crumb of trade offered, the country sends its newsmen and other communications people to Moscow, and these are used by the Kremlin to broadcast propaganda back to the country. The trade, even if not essential to Soviet purposes, is used to finance subversion.

According to the *Great Soviet Encyclopedia* "The Foreign Trade Policy of the U.S.S.R. is part of the over-all foreign policy of the U.S.S.R." Soviet

7. The metaphor is no more mixed than the fantastic realities which such combinations often require.

foreign trade is conducted, not for trade's sake, as is Western trade in peace-time, but as a means to attain Soviet political aims. We come closest to understanding it if we compare it to Western trade methods and policies in wartime.

Like all activities behind the Iron Curtain, foreign trade is centralized into a state monopoly which does all the buying and selling. Its policy is not decided by the needs of the people but by the needs of the state as viewed by those in command of the Communist Party. The over-all trade needs of the state call for the acquisition of capital goods (tools, processes, and machines) for the building up of those industries essential to the creation of military power and using trade to penetrate the West. They also import equipment such as textile plants which enables them to pro-duce essential consumer goods without diverting resources from military production.

Communists in general are not traders; they are revolutionaries with whom trade is but an additional means of conquest. When necessity dic-tated trade with the capitalist world while they were preparing new revo-lutionary incursions into it, the problem was how to exploit trade most effectively. Trade was a new weapon for the Bolsheviks. Since they had no precedents for its use, they had to accept initially the bourgeois rules of the game. They had to give an adequate equivalent for what they bought or, as they said, "submit for the time being to exploitation by international capital." In the beginning, Soviet trading agencies were largely staffed by old-time Czarist traders who had survived the revolution, supervised by whatever party members had some slight experience in this field.

Soviet trading began with the creation of the foreign-trade monopoly. Next appeared the Soviet-staffed governmental foreign-trade agencies in the large capitalist countries. This was the basic apparatus which eventually spread to all countries having relations with the Soviet Union. During the twenties and thirties, a great effort was made through the foreign-trade agencies and the communist parties in foreign countries to recruit foreign technicians and engineers to help develop Soviet industry. The recruiting also called for skilled workers, who were paid and treated as second-grade engineers. Recruiting on a large scale was supervised by the Soviet trade agencies through "societies for technical aid to Soviet Russia," organized in the highly developed industrial countries. Thousands of technicians were thus enlisted from Western Europe and the United States. It was the first successful effort on the part of the Bolsheviks to tap Western industrial knowledge. Foreign technicians and industrial espionage became keys to the absorption of Western industrial efficiency.

World War II and the vast industrial aid received as a result of it became another milestone in the industrial development of Soviet Russia. But the significant breakthrough came after the war, when in the name of reparations the Soviets seized vast booty from Continental Europe, especially areas under their occupation. Their winnings included not only vast stores of industrial equipment but technicians as well, who were either hired or shanghaied.

Industrial espionage has always played an important role in the Soviet appropriation of industrial knowledge. The Kremlin has found the West an easy mark, not only because of its anxiety to trade, but also because of its free and easy habits. In most Western countries there are no laws or precautions against industrial espionage, or if there are any, they can be by-passed with relative ease by communist organization. Since a Communist considers it perfectly moral to use any subterfuge to fool a capitalist or steal from him, the Soviet government considers it legitimate to ignore patent rights and to copy and reproduce tools and machinery it buys as samples. Through its industrial-espionage system it seeks to obtain advance information on new devices and processes, particularly those with military value, even while they are in the making. Its so-called trading and purchasing agencies are loaded with industrial-espionage experts who roam through our facilities, learning much and buying little. Even its so-called visiting and cultural delegations are filled with personnel bent on learning all they can about industry, not as friends, but as enemies. This appears to be one of the key motivating objectives of the relatively large-scale exchange of scientists and technicians between this country and the Soviet Union.

Paying the Bill

Soviet expenditures for political warfare are sizable. Since Soviet money or currency is not accepted on the international market, Soviet imports must be paid for by actual exports or in gold. All political-warfare expenditures outside the Iron Curtain must ultimately be settled in foreign currencies, which are obtained through trade. The large subsidies to the communist parties come from foreign trade, as do the expenditures for the large staffs of Soviet embassies, consulates, trading agencies, and news services.

Another Soviet method, scarcely known because of the extreme secrecy involved, is using third parties to buy up or into capitalist export and import firms to bypass the customary surveillance. These transactions are usually entrusted to businessmen who are secret party members or sympathizers. Covertly controlled companies can operate more freely in the business world and can buy up goods for transshipment, first to similar firms in neutral countries and eventually into the Soviet Union. Firms whose communist ownership was concealed played a considerable role in the early penetration of Nationalist China (the late twenties), and the practice has since spread to other countries. The motive for this device was originally political. It was used for espionage purposes, to transmit money for communist operations, to equip communist agents with business credentials enabling them to travel freely in and out of Nationalist China, and to engage in arms smuggling. Such activity has been expanding since World War II, in both its political and its commercial aspects.

The control of presumably non-communist companies can be used politically and for black-market purposes. Even if they are used merely as a supplement to Soviet trade practices, their profits can be used to sustain and finance the communist movement as was the case in Italy after World War II.

The Soviet Economic Offensive

For a nation suffering from an acute shortage of consumer goods to take the economic offensive against the economically far superior capitalist nations is, to say the least, unusual. The Soviet economic offensive must be considered as both an effort to bolster its political offensive, which began during the fifties, against the capitalist world and a response to our extensive foreign-aid program. The Soviets fear that the former colonial and underdeveloped nations may remain with the West, thus blighting all of their hopes for further expansion. Their economic offensive is not a natural product of their economic growth, but a by-product of their aggressive foreign policy.

Soviet methods of economic warfare fall into three main categories: (1) dumping goods at low prices; (2) withholding trade as a reprisal or withholding it where such deprivation will help local communist parties; and (3) credits, trade, technical aid, and armaments to countries which pursue policies amenable to Soviet objective and might eventually be swung into the Soviet orbit.

Let us examine a few examples of this strategy. The dumping of Soviet tin in 1959 reduced the price by two hundred dollars per ton on the international market, causing a major economic crisis in such tin-producing countries as Malaya and Bolivia. The dumping in this case had an economic motive—the procurement of foreign cash—since it would not immediately strengthen the communist cause in these countries. But memories are short. Of course, the Communists in Bolivia and Malaya blame the crisis on American "imperialism."

In 1955, Nasser bartered the Egyptian long-staple cotton crop for several years to come in exchange for Soviet tanks, warplanes, and other aid, only to discover that Khrushchev was not using it for textiles at home. The latter re-exported it for cash and thus hurt Egypt's normal cotton markets. Egypt depends upon cotton as its chief revenue crop. Khrushchev thus hurt Nasser economically and made him more dependent on the U.S.S.R.

Monoculture countries, and that includes most of South America, are particularly vulnerable to manipulated pressures of this sort. To Brazil, the Soviets have offered a barter trade of 200,000 tons of crude oil for her coffee crop, most of which would find its way into the international market (the Russians drink tea, not coffee). By bartering products of their own cheap labor and selling them for foreign currency on the international market, the Soviets can depress world markets and at the same time obtain the currency necessary to pay for their political-warfare operations. Khrushchev has already managed to resell rubber from Indonesia and Ceylon, rice from Burma, wool from Uruguay, and cotton from Egypt, all obtained by barter. Red China has been doing its dumping by underselling all other countries, including India, in tea, coal, textiles, and jute. Red exports to Hong Kong, Singapore, Malaya, Thailand, and Burma have steadily increased since 1958. Communist trade on the international market thus far is less than 10 per cent of world trade, but it is a sizable beginning; manipulated, as it is, from two centers, its impact is far in excess of the amounts involved. The ruthlessness of the communist trade policies can perhaps be illustrated best by Mao Tse-tung's huge trade in narcotics—grown, processed, and exported from Red China—an illegal trade in cash estimated to bring in many millions of dollars yearly.[8] It is strictly forbidden inside the

8. Harry Anslinger, head of the anti-narcotics operations of the U.S. Treasury, knows both drugs and finance. He has repeatedly pointed out that the opium-based drugs, chiefly morphine and heroin, are an ideal international currency for criminal and quasi-criminal purposes.

Red empire but is deemed useful to undermine the morale and health of the world outside that empire.

Another method likely to be practiced on an increasing scale, particularly against small or weak nations, is the use of Soviet trade as a political club. Finland, having to pay huge war reparations in kind to the Soviet Union, had geared much of its economy to that purpose. When the reparations terminated, a new trade agreement had to be negotiated. That was the moment when Khrushchev stopped all trade, chiefly as a club to displace the conservative government in favor of one friendly to the Soviets. The crisis thus produced was taken advantage of by the Communist Party of Finland for large-scale infiltration and for demanding representation (cabinet posts) in government.

When Australia gave asylum to a defector (Petrov) from the Soviet Embassy, Moscow's trade boss, Mikoyan, stopped purchases of Australian wheat as a punishment for that government's grant of political asylum. Needless to say, the Communist Party of Australia sided with Moscow—all of which does not inhibit Moscow from alleging that there are "no strings attached" to its trade.

Soviet Technical Aid

To an outsider, technical aid seems the most non-political of all operations, but not in the eyes of the Kremlin leaders. No one leaves the Soviet Union without being thoroughly screened and instructed regarding his role and how to serve the purpose for which he (or she) is sent.

Technical aid is part of the effort of penetrating the underdeveloped countries. Exporting technicians is new for a country like the Soviet Union. The Soviets are just beginning to afford such a luxury, and they engage in it only for political reasons. Soviet technical aid goes to countries on which the Kremlin concentrates for strategic reasons and is used to build up Soviet influence there. Soviet influence and communist penetration are synonymous. In some cases, as in Egypt, technical aid is both military and industrial; but the chief purpose is infiltration.

Soviet technicians speak the language of the country to which they are sent, not because they have learned it in expectation of being sent there, but because they are drawn from a pool of individuals taught to speak the language of a target country. All they have to do is to brush up on it. The Kremlin, in line with its ambitions for world conquest, has promoted the extensive learning of foreign languages. Since the early thirties, every Soviet Communist undergoing advanced education has had to learn at least *one* language in addition to his own. The result is that the Soviet Union has a reservoir of linguists on which to draw for use in foreign operations. There is generally less of a linguistic barrier between the Soviet technicians and the natives of the country to which they are sent than is the case in analogous American endeavors.

If we keep in mind that technical aid presupposes friendly relations between the country receiving it and the Soviet Union—that the technicians come as "Greeks bearing gifts"—then we can guage the atmosphere in which the operation takes place. Technicians are never sent as outright communist agitators; they come as good-will messengers and work to maintain that pose. Their mere presence advertises their own country. They also know that secret-service police representatives are in their midst and that when they return home their political conduct will be subject to scrutiny.

Keeping these considerations in mind, let us see how Soviet technical aid works out in practice. The leftist and pro-Soviet press in the host country takes advantage of the presence of Soviet technicians, who are interviewed and invited to social gatherings in the name of friendship. That is the public or respectable part of their role. A part of technical aid is the training of the native personnel who are to operate the plant, installation, or facility which is receiving the aid. The personal contact with the natives thus afforded is another factor to be utilized. If there is a worth-while communist party in the country, members and sympathizers will be among those recruited for additional training. When the aid project is completed, the Communist Party will possess a sizable nucleus among the workers and other personnel operating the new facility.

Another part of technical aid is the training of native technicians who are to operate not only the facility put up through Soviet aid but also others, either on hand or to be created. This involves supervisory personnel, be they engineers, managers, or even army officers, handling the new Soviet equipment. The Kremlin prefers to give this training behind the Iron Curtain in the various colleges and facilities available for the purpose. Once there, the trainees are indoctrinated politically, and many of them become sympathizers, if not party members, upon their return.

Soviet technical aid is thus cleverly interwoven into the political scheme of conquest. Teaching local people to operate Soviet instruments, to install Soviet technical devices, and, in general, to lean on Soviet logistics in these fields insures a long-term continuity of effort. This is one of the foremost objectives of Soviet technical aid—and political warfare.

Youth, Violence, and Riots

Rioting Japanese students prevented President Eisenhower from paying a good-will visit to Japan in 1960 and scored a signal victory of communist political warfare. J. Edgar Hoover called:

The successful communist exploitation and manipulation of youth and student groups throughout the world today . . . a major challenge which free world forces must meet and defeat. Recent world events clearly reveal that world communism has launched a massive campaign to capture and maneuver youth and student groups.

Communists have become experts at using this force to create chaos. In Japan, for example, Communists carefully nurtured and developed a growing body of students over a 10-year period, using them periodically in protest demonstrations. The culmination of this training was reached this year, when the highly organized and tightly disciplined rioters shocked the world with their uproarious displays.

The seeds for future large-scale demonstrations of this type have been planted by communists in other countries. The small demonstrations staged by Communist-oriented students in Uruguay earlier this year—demonstrations which marred an otherwise cordial welcome extended to the President of the United States on the last stop of the Latin American tour—were reminiscent of Communist-instigated actvities of student groups in Japan 10 years ago. Communists are hopeful that the seeds in Uruguay and other countries will sprout as they did in Japan, leading eventually to demonstrations of the type that rocked Japan.[9]

Mass demonstration is a long-standing technique of Marxism. The Socialists used street demonstrations, and the syndicalists resorted to it in the form of short-lived general strikes. The Communists combined the two, using them either together or alternately. Mass demonstrations, the most dramatized form of psychopolitical warfare short of actual attempts at the seizure of power, were used by the Socialists as an extraparliamentary method to compel radical reform. The Communists incorporated them into their total methodology of conflict.

Lenin conceived of mass demonstrations as a proving operation to test both the responsiveness of the masses and the staying power of the government. If the government proved weak, then a third element might be employed, namely, the revolutionary goon squads, or "revolutionary detach-

9. *Communist Target—Youth,* a report published by the House Committee on Un-American Activities.

ments." While government forces were busy with the demonstrators, these groups would try to seize such designated strategic places as communication centers, government offices, and police stations; if the government forces were demoralized or infiltrated, the revolution would be on. In that case, the pivotal elements would be the "detachments," and the demonstrators would become auxiliaries acting as a covering force. If a communist-led mass demonstration takes place without participation of the "detachments," the situation is considered unripe for seizure of power. There were, however, several instances in the early twenties in Germany, in the Baltic States, and in China when, pressing the element of surprise, the "detachments" attempted to seize power without the concurrent mass mobilization through demonstrations. These failed and were later criticized as "putschism."

In subsequent years, other functions were devised for the "detachments." They brawled with organized anti-communist forces, raided headquarters of anti-communist organizations, and added "punch" to communist-led demonstrations and picket lines in the guise of "protecting" them. In recent years they were used as the key element in mass demonstrations, such as the violent demonstrations against Vice-President Nixon in Latin America and those against Kishi in Japan.

Mass demonstrations as a tool of the Kremlin's foreign policy had fallen into disuse during the "popular front" period (1935–1939) and the war alliance which followed. They were revived as part of the Cold War under Stalin, but never were they used on the scale now practiced under Khrushchev. They are part of the new aggressiveness of the Soviet state. Pro-Soviet demonstrations now accompany Khrushchev's state visits to foreign countries, and, conversely, anti-American demonstrations frequently accompany visits of American heads of state, reflecting the concentration of the Moscow-Peking axis on political warfare and its focus upon the United States. In other words, Khrushchev, as head of state, is not engaging in "personal diplomacy" but in the stimulation and mobilization of his political-warfare armies with "diplomacy" as the cover.

The techniques of communist-led mass demonstrations, given the existence of an adequate and experienced party, are relatively simple. Communist-controlled and allied organizations are assigned their proper places in the line-up, with the Communists not marching separately but spread out among the others. The ideologically most fanatic element, whether students, youth, or others, will be placed in the key sectors of the demonstration, with the goon "detachments" mixed among them as shock troops. If violence is intended, the "detachments" will have the leading role in the fighting. They may be armed with primitive weapons or with firearms and incendiaries, depending upon the violence desired. If violence is not intended, they will merely march along with the rest or patrol among the spectators to ward off any attack from that quarter.

The big communist demonstrations of the twenties and thirties usually took the form of parades, the Communists marching as Communists under hammer-and-sickle emblems and slogans. In time, they learned to hide under the cover of "fronts" or captive organizations. A further development of this type of opportunism under Khrushchev is the stressing of nationalist demands and grievances skillfully serving the objectives of Soviet foreign policy. The appeal to students and other nationalist elements is thus broadened. In Japan, the regular Marxist Socialists did not participate in the June, 1960 riots; the infiltrated splinter Socialists acted as the major group. Communists hiding under the flag of nationalism roused and exploited national animosities against the United States.

The techniques used in the student demonstrations in Korea and Turkey, particularly the former, also indicated knowledge of communist methods, though they were not communist dominated as in Japan. In general, when students turn out in large numbers with such spontaneity, it is indicative of much unrest among the middle classes. In such a situation even a small underground party can play a considerable role if it has the necessary contacts. Dissident elements, of course, can use communist techniques with or without the presence of Communists. The fact that the 1960 student demonstrations in Korea and Turkey were not turned against the United States shows that communist influence was either slight or absent. In the student riots against Vice-President Nixon in Latin America, on the other hand, communist presence and direction was obvious, as it was in Japan. However, these riots revealed, not a preponderance of influence among the students, but the power of well-organized minorities.

In the absence of spontaneity, large demonstrations require the existence of sizable organizations under communist control and influence. These are costly and they require a great deal of preparation. On the other hand, with spontaneity, even a small party can arrange a big demonstration, as a page from the American depression of 1929–35 will illustrate. A national demonstration under the auspices of the Unemployed Councils had been called by the Party for March 6, 1930. The party then had less than 15,000 members. It sensed spontaneity in the air, however, and speculated on a turnout of about 300,000 nationally. In New York City, it anticipated about 50,000. When March 6 came, the national turnout was over 2,000,000, with 300,000 in New York alone. In the fifteen years that followed, the Party grew more than sixfold in size and influence but it was never again able to mount a demonstration of comparable size. The conditions which prompted spontaneous participation had passed.

Not all communist-led demonstrations are violent; on the contrary, physical violence is often absent or held to a minimum. The average Communist or sympathizer considers participation in such demonstrations enough of a risk without challenging an armed riot-trained police force. It is the "detachments" who provide the violence, and they do so only when instructed. Trigger-happy police may also provide violence but whoever is responsible for the provocation, the Communists always blame the police.

Whether or not there is to be planned violence is decided on the highest level. If the Soviet state is conducting an aggressive phase of the Cold War, all types of violence in and out of mass demonstrations, small or big, should be expected—especially against weak or demoralized governments—on the local or national level. In that case, violence is a probing operation, and if it is successful, there will be more of it. Such violence is a form of guerrilla warfare adjusted to urban environment. If violence-ridden mass demonstrations are successful, as they were in preventing President Eisenhower's planned visit to Japan, the psychopolitical impact is much greater than that of a peaceful parade; success dramatizes communist power. The same result can be achieved with more difficulty by innumerable small hit-and-run actions over a period of time if the Party is capable of mounting them and if the government's response is inept or absent.

Using the United Nations

Pursuing a policy aimed at world conquest, Soviet aims are in contradiction to the basic purposes stated in the United Nations Charter. The U.S.S.R. participates in that body because the United Nations is an incomparable medium for Soviet splinter operations among the free nations. The United Nations is also a forum of world-wide dimensions for the spreading of Soviet propaganda.

The Kremlin does not permit the United Nations or any of its specialized agencies, such as UNESCO, to operate behind the Iron Curtain, although it influences the decisions of that body. The Kremlin does not permit the

United Nations to intervene in any dispute behind the Iron Curtain, such as that in Hungary, but it intervenes through the United Nations in all the disputes among the free countries: Suez, Korea, the Middle East, Taiwan, the Congo, Laos and South Vietnam. It goes to war, by proxy, against the United Nations, as it did in Korea, and still sits in the United Nations with full membership rights. In short, the Kremlin insists that the West abide by the mutually agreed-to rules and treaties which established the United Nations, but does so itself only when convenient. Rarely has a power bent on conquest and political subversion been afforded such opportunities.

Soviet tactics for using the United Nations have the same range and flexibility as those associated with the communist "front" concept. The Kremlin has always believed that its best security would either come from establishing control of border states through communist governments or from influencing them through politically active communist parties. When it could not pervert the United Nations into an instrument to assist communist subversion of free governments, it sought at least to prevent it from thwarting these projects. Hence a prime Soviet aim in the United Nations was to minimize the mobilization of anti-Soviet sentiments within it.

Basic diplomatic objectives have conditioned Soviet attitudes toward the United Nations. Since subscribing to the United Nations Charter—and while giving lip service to it and its principles—the Soviet Union has followed an aggressive foreign policy constrained only by its estimate of what would be imprudent at any given time. While creating and expanding spheres of control and influence, it has sought to limit its diplomatic commitments in the United Nations and elsewhere to vague generalities permitting maximum evasion.

An examination of Soviet pronouncements and actions in the United Nations clearly reveals the guiding principle of Soviet conduct there: to make Soviet participation in the United Nations contribute to the advantage of international communism. If anyone has any doubt concerning the true nature of Soviet diplomacy, he need only read the speeches of Soviet representatives before the United Nations, speeches which if delivered in Moscow would command little attention but when delivered before the United Nations in New York reach far beyond the confines of the communist propaganda machine. The speeches are always loaded with communist propaganda clichés, fabrications, and distortions. Only inferentially are they related to the problem at hand. Actually, they seek to create and deepen dissension in the Free World and are aimed over the heads of the assembled delegates at the masses. This procedure accords with the well-known Leninist method of using a bourgeois parliament as a sounding board for communist activity and propaganda, not as a means to solve problems. The tools of democracy are thus utilized to frustrate democracy.

By now the Western nations are no longer particularly susceptible to Soviet rhetoric at the United Nations. The newer members from Asia and Africa provide a far more promising audience, one readily accessible through the world organization.

Soviet representatives in the UN's various bodies are competent individuals specializing in UN activities in the Free World. These men work tirelessly to convince the novitiate diplomats that the "socialist camp" wants only to liquidate tensions by ending colonialism and the arms race that prevents the rapid development of their countries. Thus they try to exploit the hopes and aspirations of the underprivileged of the world for equality, dignity, and, most important, economic and cultural progress.

The Soviets dwell on subjects of concern to the new nations, particularly those countries inclined toward neutralism. Every Soviet word is designed to make it appear that the "socialist camp," rather than the West, is the best friend of and sole model for the underdeveloped nations. If through such tactics the bloc and its allies could win a sustained majority in the United Nations, the Communists would then move to strengthen the world organization and turn it against America and her remaining allies.

The Communist Forgery Circuit

The Soviet Union, as a state, and the Communist Party frequently combine their operations. A particularly sinister combination is the systematic perpetration of forgeries and their propagation. The Soviet state masterminds the operations, prepares the documents, and uses Communists or crypto-communist affiliates in the Free World to spread the word.

This operation was spotlighted in the spring of 1961 in a hearing before the Senate Subcommittee to Investigate the Administration of the Internal Security Act. Information furnished by the CIA gave a comprehensive picture of how the communist forgery circuit operates. From the testimony of Mr. Richard Helms, Assistant Director of the CIA, we learn that the Communists are as skillful as the Nazis were in the production and exploitation of forgeries. In 1957 they began to aim them frequently against American targets, to turn them out in volume, and to exploit them through a wide-flung international network. Each Soviet forgery is manufactured and spread according to a plan. Each is devised and timed to mesh with other techniques of psychological warfare in support of Soviet strategy.

These forgeries have three main purposes. The first is to discredit the West generally, and the United States and its government specifically, in the eyes of the rest of the world. Bloc audiences are often presented with forgeries seemingly validated by a West-to-East replay technique. The second purpose is to sow suspicion and discord among the Western Allies, especially between this country and our friends. The third purpose is to drive a wedge between Free World peoples and their governments by fostering the line that these governments do not represent their citizens because they are puppets of the United States.

Campaigns to sell these three themes to the world are planned by the leaders of the Communist Party of the Soviet Union. Staff units of the Central Committee work out the details. If the plan includes forgeries, they are prepared by a Soviet or satellite intelligence service.

One of the devices used by the Communists is the documentary fraud. Of these there are several kinds: the false news article, the forgery, the fabricated intelligence report, the distortion of a genuine document, and the false or true account attributed to a non-existent organization. Mr. Helms tells us how these are used by the Communists.[10]

In recent days we have seen an excellent example of how the Communists use the false news story. In late April rumors began to circulate in Europe, rumors charging that the Algerian-based generals who had plotted the overthrow of President De Gaulle had enjoyed support from NATO, the Pentagon, or CIA. Although this fable could have been started by supporters of General Challe, it bears all the earmarks of having been invented within the bloc.

In Western Europe this lie was first printed on the 23d of April by a Rome daily called *Il Paese.*

The story charged—"It is not by chance that some people in Paris are accusing the American secret service headed by Allen Dulles of having participated in the plot of the four 'ultra' generals. . . . Franco, Salazar, Allen Dulles are the figures who hide themselves behind the pronunciamentos of the 'ultras'; they are the pillars of an international conspiracy that, basing itself on the Iberian dictatorships, on the residue of the most fierce and blind colonalism, on the intrigues of the CIA . . . reacts furiously to the advance of progress and democracy. . . ."

We found it interesting that *Il Paese* was the starting point for a lie

10. "Communist Forgeries," Hearing before the Subcommittee to Investigate the Administration of the Internal Security Act and Other Internal Security Laws of the Committee on the Judiciary, United States Senate. Testimony of Richard Helms, Assistant Director, CIA, June 2, 1961, pp. 5-6.

that the Soviets spread around the world. This paper and its evening edition, *Paese Sera,* belong to a small group of journals published in the free world but used as outlets for disguised Soviet propaganda. These newspapers consistently release and replay anti-American, anti-Western, pro-Soviet bloc stories, distorted or wholly false. Mario Malloni, director of both *Il Paese* and *Paese Sera,* has been a member of the World Peace Council since 1958. The World Peace Council is a bloc-directed Communist front.

On the next day *Pravda* published in Moscow a long article about the generals' revolt.

These quotations are taken from the Soviet version:

"Taking part in the war against the Algerian people is not only the France of arms manufacturers. . . . The war in Algeria is a war of NATO. This was openly and cynically stated by American General Norstad, Commander in Chief of the Armed Forces of the Atlantic Bloc. US reactionary quarters are helping the French colonists. . . . The traces of the plotters lead to Madrid and Lisbon, these hotbeds of fascism preserved intact with the money of American reactionaries and with direct assistance of top NATO circles. The traces from Spain and Portugal lead across the ocean to the Pentagon and the Central Intelligence Agency of the US. . . ."

The Popular Front Revived

The communist forgeries seeking to discredit the Central Intelligence Agency were part of a broad and persistent pattern of subversion. According to Marx, Engels, and Lenin, the first commandment for revolutionary victory is: smash the military and internal security structure of the target government. Lenin concluded in 1901, after watching his bands of discontented workers, peasants and revolutionaries clash ineffectively with police, that such loosely organized groups could never compete with trained security agencies. He came up with a typical bolshevik solution: tear down the enemy by infiltration and subversion.

Lenin and his followers developed this tactic into the Soviet science of "revolutionary anti-militarism," and used it during World War I to demoralize and win over the Russian military forces. Without this "softening up" process, the bolsheviks could never have won the 1917 revolution. In 1920, when he promulgated his famous "21 demands," listing the duties foreign communists must perform to be acceptable to Moscow, Lenin made persistent and systematic efforts to infiltrate, subvert, and destroy "capitalist" military and security forces one of the primary tasks. Ever since, a prime duty of communist agitators around the world has been to try to hamstring the military and security efforts of a government from without and from within.

For example, communist attacks on the Central Intelligence Agency have grown in both volume and cunning since the 1960 U-2 incident. The communist campaign follows the familiar theme; implant suspicion in the public mind, destroy confidence and reinforce fears of the super-secret.

The Helms testimony previously quoted illustrates how the communists took advantage of this situation. When the Algerian generals' revolt flared, they planted a story in an Italian Red controlled newspaper that C.I.A. promoted the revolt. It appeared on Sunday, April 23, 1961. The next day, *Pravda* printed it in Moscow, quoting "Italian sources." On Tuesday, TASS, the official Soviet news agency, carried it to Europe and on Wednesday, Radio Moscow relayed it to the Middle East. On Thursday, the London *Daily Worker* ran the story and it began to appear in the non-communist press in Paris. By the next week, the "rumors" had reached the proportion of an international incident and were poisoning Franco-American relations. The American ambassador in Paris was asked point blank about C.I.A.'s role in Algeria, and French government officials indicated dissatisfaction with a direct statement from Allen W. Dulles, C.I.A. director, branding the charges false. Even the American press discussed the story at great length, without pointing to its source. Not until C.I.A.'s own assistant director, Richard Helms, was called before the Senate Internal Security Subcommittee was the full story of Soviet forgery and manipulation of the Western press revealed.

The communist strategy followed a general pattern: C.I.A. was said to have become a reactionary state-within-a-state in the United States Government. It usurps policy-making functions from the President and State Department. The U-2 episode was really caused by faceless bureaucrats usurping presidential authority; C.I.A.'s officials are fanatical anti-communists and often commit grave blunders by zealously betting on weak, unpopular anti-communist factions abroad, as for instance in Laos.

The communist's experts in psychological warfare have decided the Western fear of accidental nuclear war provides a perfect "target of opportunity." They use this fear to play on the ingrained American suspicion of any secret agency and secret government operations. The communists and their fronts lose no opportunity to depict C.I.A. as a secretive and free-wheeling giant involving itself in everybody's business, usurping powers that do not belong to it, taking over the conduct of U. S. foreign policy and conspiring to drag us into war.

This kind of assault on free societies are based on the highly sophisticated and subtle Soviet science of mental subversion. The Central Intelligence Agency recently revealed in Congressional testimony that campaigns to sell communist propaganda themes to the world are planned by the leaders of the Soviet party. Special staff units of the party's central committee work out the details. These units include experts in the politics and psychology of non-communist parties and factions.

In the United States a major campaign was launched during 1961 to show that American military leaders were ideologically susceptible to fascist, ultra-rightist and reactionary tendencies. In a series of magazines and newspaper articles and editorials the military link with the "rightwing" was presumably established.

The Worker claimed credit for having started it all: "During the past several years *The Worker* has regularly spotlighted the insidious alliance between the military leaders—active and retired—and rightwing groups in the United States," the communist newspaper stated in its July 23, 1961 issue.

The Fulbright memorandum[11] questioning the propriety of the armed services to sponsor seminars designed to inform the public about communism, was not published until August 2, 1961. But note the similarity between its wording and that of Gus Hall's article in *The Worker* that was printed July 13, 1961, before the existence of the Fulbright memorandum was even publicly known:

It is now known that a secret directive, issued by the National Security Council in 1958, instructed commanding officers here and abroad to "enlighten" both the armed forces and civilians in their areas on the cold war policy. It was followed by additional guides and materials still classified as secret issued by the Joint Chiefs of Staff on the basis of which seminars and meetings were organized by the military commands often in cooperation with local business groups. Complaints have been pouring into the Pentagon against the political activities of the military staffs, especially their wide dissemination of Birchite propaganda and the obnoxious films "Operation Abolition" and "Communism on the Map." The entire line of policy, coupled with C.I.A. and similar training in subversive and putschist activities, cannot help but create our own "French Generals," who feel at home in fascist circles, and are ready to lend themselves to their objectives. It is an outgrowth of 20 years of militarization.

11. The Fulbright memorandum was transmitted by Senator William Fulbright, chairman of the Senate Committee on Foreign Relations, to the Secretary of Defense in June, 1961. It was published in the Congressional Record on August 2, 1961. The purpose of this memorandum was, according to Senator Fulbright, ". . . to give some indication of the dangers involved in education and propaganda activities by the military, directed at the public, and to suggest steps for dealing with the underlying problem."

This was the head of the U.S. Communist Party writing. Note how carefully he followed Lenin's advice to "use wording of such a kind as to provoke the worst notions, the worst suspicions about the adversary."

Now compare an observation made in the memorandum of the Chairman of the United States Senate Foreign Relations Committee:

... Perhaps it is farfetched to call forth the revolt of the French Generals as an example of the ultimate danger. Nevertheless, military officers, French and American, have some common characteristics arising from their profession and there are numerous military "fingers on the trigger" throughout the world.

We are seeing something analogous to what happened to France in the 1935-40 period. The current communist campaign to discredit the United States military is patterned after the communist drive to discredit and demoralize the French armed forces that contributed to the fall of France in 1940. A 1958 study at Georgetown University prepared by Robert E. Beerstecher, stated:

The communists made fascism the most important political factor in France. The communists portrayed fascism as existing in many forms and places in France, but place primary emphasis in their propaganda and agitation on fascism in the armed forces. Marcel Cachin the mentor of French communists claimed that the whole fascist offensive in France was led by high military officers on the retired list who worked closely with their brother officers still on active duty.... The French Communist Party issued calls to "purify" the armed forces, and proposed establishment of soldiers' committees "for the defense of the Constitution and the Republic" whose job would be to "check the subversive activities of the fascist officers and organizations within the armed forces.

The Georgetown study, after reviewing the full course of communist tactics applied to the French armed forces in the 1935-40 period, concluded: "The fall of France was celebrated in both Moscow and Berlin, for France was as much a victim of communist anti-militarism as of German militarism."

There is one major difference, however, between the popular front of the thirties and its growing revival, particularly in the United States, in the early sixties. In the first instance, Hitler and the nazis provided the enemy against which liberal and democratic forces were marshalled. In today's world the communists are seeking to identify the United States, and particularly its armed forces and security agencies with incipient fascism. With this maneuver they hope to enlist the democratic and liberal forces of the world in a campaign to destroy the chief bulwark that blocks a communist victory.

Conclusion

This cursory roundup of Soviet operations in the Free World has traced the Soviet use of nationalism, characteristics of the Soviet underground, Soviet interdiction campaigns, Soviet exploitation of trade, the UN, the systematic use of forgery and the revival of the popular front strategy in the United States. We next turn to the significance of raw military power to communist political warfare.

CHAPTER IX

WAR, PEACE, AND COEXISTENCE

THE CONCRETE FORCES POSSESSED BY BOTH SIDES DETERMINE THE judgment by which communist political warfare is waged. In this array, the significance of military power is clearly summarized in the following quotations from Mao Tse-tung:

Every communist must grasp the truth that political power grows out of the barrel of a gun.

With the help of guns, the Russian communists brought about social-ism. . . . Experience in the class struggle in the era of imperialism teaches us that the working class and the toiling masses cannot defeat the armed bourgeoisie and landlords, except by the power of the gun; in this sense we can even say that the whole world can be remolded only with the gun.

The central task and the supreme form of revolution is the seizure of political power by force of arms and the solution of problems by war.[1]

The relation of Soviet military power and communist conduct of polit-ical warfare was clearly revealed by Khrushchev's early handling of the 1961 Berlin crisis. His appeal for a "peaceful" settlement of the Berlin question was reinforced by dramatic steps in Soviet military preparations. A spectacular air display in Moscow was quickly followed by a three-bil-lion-ruble increase in the Soviet military budget.[2] The 1961 Soviet testing of a 50-megaton nuclear weapon, an even cruder demonstration of military

1. See Mao Tse-tung, *Selected Works* (New York: International Publishers, 1954) Vol. 21, p. 272.

2. According to the official but inaccurate exchange rates, this was estimated to be three and one-half billion dollars. In actuality it is believed to be closer to eight billion U.S. dollars.

strength, strikingly reminiscent of Hitler, reflected the increased use of military power in communist political warfare.

Military Political Warfare

From now on, threats of war followed by appeals for peace on communist terms are likely to alternate with increasing frequency. The aim of the peace or coexistence cycles will be to induce a state of mind in the West in which accommodation to communist designs will seem preferable to the defense of vital interests—particularly if the defense carries the risk of nuclear war. War threats will reinforce this goal. The over-all aim of this strategy is to prepare for the climax of the decisive battle or to render that battle altogether superfluous. The nuclear age introduces major uncertainties. Unless the American will to use its most powerful weapons, if need be, is eroded, a communist victory could be sabotaged at any stage of the game. Khrushchev is well aware of this. If one could be permitted to speculate on his views on this vital issue, they would read something like this:

The policy of co-existence guarantees the way toward communist victory. The latter cannot be stopped if events develop peacefully. A violent acceleration by means of great world revolutionary actions is risky, as long as there is the danger of an armed Western counterattack, which—in view of the present power equilibrium and the development of new arms—could even deprive a victorious Soviet Union of the fruits of her victory.

We shall do better to deprive the capitalist countries of the resources of the developing countries by political and economic means. The communist countries must not shrink from importing Western goods in peaceful trade exchange and using them for their own development. After the Socialist camp has once achieved superiority over the West—an end already in sight —the West will be forced to surrender, without being able to play with the idea of delaying or reversing this revolutionary development by means of weapons. Over this final goal there is complete agreement with the Chinese too. Except, they believed for a long time that the final goal would be achieved more rapidly by world revolutionary attacks. However, the method of "a big step forward" is too risky on the international field, *as long as certain Western warmongers are not 100 per cent convinced that a resort to weapons would mean their total destruction.*

Contrary to "revisionist" theories—refuted and attacked by both Moscow and Peking—cessation of hostilities between communism and capitalism (in Lenin's language called "competitive coexistence") should merely be an exception. Thus "coexistence" is only a tactical intermezzo to weakening the will and power of the West. This also gives the Soviets time to improve their military position, further reducing the risk of Western counterattack.

Both Lenin and Stalin, as well as Mao Tse-tung, have derided the notion that any war must be total. They assert, contrary to certain experts, that limited conflict, particularly guerrilla struggle, represents the type of war in which politics and military means can most easily combine all psychological and physical components against the weakest point of the adversary. Mao considers the following conditions as necessary for a communist victory:

(1) To fight firmly in every conflict or battle in which the victory is certain;

(2) To avoid a final decision in every conflict or battle in which the victory is doubtful; and

(3) To avoid—at any price—a strategic decision if the existence of the communist system is at stake.

Mao has defined the communist strategy as a "long, limited war." The developments after World War II indicate clearly that limited actions, in which there is always a way open for retreat, will be an important part of communist strategy in the future. Nevertheless, the Soviets will take maximum advantage of their nuclear, ICBM, and space achievements. Khrushchev has frequently extolled his "beloved" rockets. Anne Jonas, former Rand researcher, wrote:

Khrushchev has modernized, but not abandoned, Communist doctrine on the need for a mixed-force structure, the combination of all arms, and the continuous variation and modernization of the weapons of conflict. He is adapting his force structure to permit all-out surprise attack. In addition, he is retaining a spectrum of capabilities to wage all types of warfare. At the two extremes of his force structure are nuclear-delivery systems and proxy guerrillas. His views that no single weapons system is decisive under all conditions conforms to traditional guidelines of Communist strategy. New in the Communist operational lexicon is the realization that nuclear weapons must figure, in one way or another, in any attempt to defeat the United States and its major allies.[3]

3. Anne M. Jonas, "Changes in Soviet Conflict," in Walter F. Hahn and John C. Neff, *American Strategy for the Nuclear Age*, p. 156.

The present phase of communist strategy is to avoid thermonoculear war,[4] play down sizable conventional wars of the Korean scale, and concentrate on guerrilla wars—the so-called wars of national liberation. In his speech of January 6, 1961, Khrushchev asked rhetorically, "What is the attitude of the Marxists toward such uprisings?" To this he replied, "A most positive one. These uprisings must not be identified with wars among states, with local wars, since in these uprisings the people are fighting for implementation of their right for self-determination, for independent social and national development. These are uprisings against rotten reactionary regimes, against the colonizers. The communists fully support such just wars and march in the front rank with the peoples waging liberation struggles." With the growth of military power, new political warfare weapons became available. The new means called for new methods, supplementing and in part even displacing the old ones.

Political warfare is not static; it adjusts to means, opportunities, and environment. As in military warfare, the means and methods of yesterday may become obsolete. The communist parties of Eastern Europe and China, for instance, did not come to power by their own effort, as the communist script required, but with military and political assistance, direct and indirect, from the Soviet Union.

Formerly, Moscow's political warfare was based almost entirely upon stirring up the masses in capitalist countries; now it plays a new double game. As a state, it supports and encourages new dictators and would-be dictators in newly independent countries, at the same time using the communist parties in those countries to woo the masses. Preferably the Communists seek to infiltrate a legitimate revolution that someone else has started. This combination places revolutionary leaders operating under precarious conditions in weak countries in a difficult position. They become dependent upon the Soviet state and, fearful of their own masses,

---

4. Dr. Stefan Possony postulates that "it is self-evident that Khrushchev fears a global thermonuclear war among states. I do not think that Khrushchev fears this war badly enough so that he will never wage it, nor that his successors will be bound by his fears. I believe above all, that he is doing all he can in order to get the Soviet Union into a position where such a war could be waged under optimal conditions for communism. In my judgment, this is one of the main reasons why the Soviets have been pushing the nuclear test ban and are suggesting fraudulent agreements to stop nuclear production. At any rate Khrushchev's objection to global war, taken by itself, as well as to thermonuclear weapons within a nonglobal war, or to global nuclear war between hostile 'social systems,' would be considerably less acute than those to a global thermonuclear war among states. . . .

are held in check by the Soviet-controlled communist parties. If the first communist-front man loses his grip, the men who succeed him will be ideologically closer to communism and may pave the way to an eventual communist take-over.

Twenty-five years ago the Soviets could neither afford nor risk the expanded new form of warfare. They had to confine themselves to the propaganda and subversion upon which the communist parties were originally founded, except for relatively minor guerrilla operations in the interior of China. The communist parties are still based, in the main, on political warfare, but a change has occurred in turbulent areas, even those distant from the Soviet empire. There, a creeping but limited guerrilla war has become an intermediary form of conquest in which political and physical warfare are meshed into one. If one were to count the number of trained communist-party members who, in the last fifteen years, had participated in guerrilla warfare in Asia, Europe, the Middle East, North Africa, and Latin America, the number would go into six figures. Even so, the potentialities of "wars of national liberation" are still in the process of being developed. Modern methods of supply and communication are likely to assist this type of communist strategy.

Soviet Military Doctrine

Soviet military doctrine is governed by over-all communist doctrine as it has evolved from Marx to Khrushchev. The political thrust of current Soviet military doctrine can be properly understood only within this perspective. Marxist-Leninist operational doctrine therefore furnishes insight on how the Soviets apply armed might to the pursuit of their objectives.[5]

Soviet military writing shows that fundamental political objectives determine military strategy. "The objective of military strategy," states a

---

"This emphasis on uprisings, to which we have already alluded, is a reversal to Communist 19th century doctrine. Yet there are significant changes. First, as we have deducted before, such uprisings are to be undertaken as proper and major military operations and second, military operations of this type henceforth will be provided with the strategic cover—and possibly support—of nuclear missile forces and other modern weapon systems." Quoted from "Analysis of the Khrushchev Speech of January 6, 1961," Hearing before the Subcommittee to Investigate the Administration of the Internal Security Act and Internal Security Laws of the Committee on the Judiciary, United States Senate, 87th Cong., 1st Sess. Testimony of Dr. Stefan T. Possony, June 16, 1961, p. 29.

5. For the contemporary military doctrine of the Soviet Union in the nuclear age, see H. S. Dinerstein, *War and the Soviet Union*, pp. 1-257, and Raymond L. Garthoff, *The Soviet Image of Future War*, pp. 1-137.

Soviet colonel, "is the creation by military means of those conditions under which politics is in a position to achieve the aims which it sets for itself." Clausewitz's conception that war is but a continuation of diplomacy by other means has been carried to its logical conclusion by the Soviets; to them, peace is a continuation of conflict, but by other means.

According to Raymond Garthoff, "political and military strategy are integral in the sense of identity of purpose: to further the basic objectives of Soviet policy. They are, in another sense, complementary: they co-exist with one another at all times, the one dominant in peacetime, the other in war. Each is planned in a number of variants, to fit various conceivable contingencies." It is fundamental to an understanding of communist doctrine to recognize that they regard conflict as an "organic whole."[6]

There is no arbitrary division between civil and military authority in the Soviet Union. Both the political and the military arms of the Soviet state report to the same integrated command post in the Kremlin.

It is the Kremlin alone which decides on the structure, proportion, quantity, quality, aim, finance, strategy, tactics, organization, and education of all Soviet armed forces. The time, manner, and direction of Soviet military operations will be decided solely by the few persons standing at the head of the Kremlin oligarchy, uncontrolled and unhindered by any independent body.

In carrying out the fusion of political warfare with armed force, the communist spectrum of weapons and techniques is all embracing. It ranges from political action through nuclear missiles and bombers to jungle fighters, terrorists, infiltrators, and finally to a group of skillful semanticists. In short, the Soviets have never accepted the view that the outcome of war can be decided by any single weapon. Yet the advent of nuclear weapons and missiles has broadened to this spectrum:

6. "The communists have a firm and an all-encompassing strategy. They wage conflict along an entire spectrum of techniques and they are constantly learning new techniques. The management of the world conflict is the central core of the Soviet or communist power structure. They have central direction—sometimes they get into a little argument with a theater commander—but fundamentally, central direction is giving real cutting strength to their strategy. At home, in all spheres of life, they are organized for this unceasing struggle. They are not interested in increasing standards of living, except to the point of keeping people alive and not too dissatisfied. Fundamentally, theirs is a militant or combat society which is organized in order to produce military power, power in its totality, and broad superiority of power. The entire organization is linked to this one overriding objective. Organizations abroad, outside the Soviet Bloc, some *openly* communist, are used to further the objectives of the communist states and notably, to reduce the power of all hostile states." From a speech, "The Challenge of Communist Strategy," given by Stefan T. Possony in Atlanta, Georgia, on March 10, 1961.

For the first time in the history of the communist movement, the possibility has emerged to combine non-military conflict methods of international scope with military weapons of global range. In a Marxian sense, this constitutes a "qualitative leap" of fundamental importance—the kind that can be expected to usher in a new epoch of history.[7]

Communist conflict doctrine requires that they use any and all means of conflict, use them in larger quantities than their opponents, "according to the suitability and utility of these means at a given place, at a given time, and whenever the risk is acceptable."[8]

Within this over-all system there are no master weapons or master techniques. Soviet strategic concept and military doctrine are comprehensive, designed as they are to meet the requirements for all possible types of wars. One remarkable fact in the history of the Soviet military as a political factor is the unanimity of military strategic thought, particularly with regard to the flexible forces required by an opportunistic political strategy.

Recently, the attitude toward violence and the employment of force for communist advance has changed slightly. Communist doctrine once clearly contended that communist seizures of power are feasible only by the application of force and violence. At the Twentieth Party Congress it was suggested that the possibility of peaceful transition to socialism could be possible. This does not mean that the chances of peace have improved but, rather, that the possibility of "peaceful transition" to socialism—a semantic term for revolution or seizure of power—has improved.

Nuclear weapons have introduced a series of innovations into communist strategy. The choices open to Soviet policy-makers will become more numerous as the Soviet Union builds more nuclear weapons and sophisticated delivery systems.

Nuclear weapons could conceivably offer the Soviet Union the possibility of crushing the United States, the only major obstacle in the path of its avowed goal of world revolution. The Kremlin might be tempted to seek to capitalize on the immense advantage of a surprise nuclear attack. But since it is also a cardinal principle of communist operational doctrine that the Soviet Union, the base of the world revolution, must not be recklessly risked in the pursuit of any one objective,[9] the Kremlin may be just as willing as the United States to prevent a full exchange of nuclear stockpiles.

7. Colonel Thomas Wolfe, lecture at Defense Strategy Seminar, July, 1960.

8. Stefan T. Possony, lecture at Defense Strategy Seminar, July, 1960.

9. For a detailed study of the operational code of the Bolsheviks, see Nathan Leites, *A Study of Bolshevism*, pp. 1-538.

Yet if this should be the case, is it conceivable that the United States and the Soviet Union could subscribe to a nuclear *modus vivendi* that would mean the same thing to both?

At any time during the last decade, while the Soviets were developing their own nuclear capability, it would have been folly for the Kremlin deliberately to provoke a major war. A perfect stalemate, under which each side remains within the confines of the *status quo,* is equally unthinkable. The problem, then, for the communist strategists was and remains this: How can the greatest freedom of limited maneuver be maintained, so that power and space might be gradually amassed without the accompanying risk of an unacceptable American nuclear response?

The Soviet Union believes it has found the answer in combining the threat of nuclear war with a systematic strategy of attrition. On one end of the scale, it maintains a powerful missile force and leads in the race for space. Yet, despite communist infatuation with surprise nuclear attack, the Sino-Soviet bloc still maintains the largest conventional-atomic forces in the world.

No matter how long a particular peace offensive continues, there is no reason to believe that the Soviet system can continue to grow or even to hold what it now has unless it employs force or presents the specter of force to cow its opponents. The communists are well aware of the dangers inherent in prolonging a given period of "relaxation of tensions." Party discipline always suffers from any prolonged pose of peaceful coexistence, since the psychology of the communist movement is essentially aggressive.

It is conceivable that the passage of many years in which there were no striking successes for the movement might result in the internal erosion of the communist bloc. It is inconceivable, however, that the communist empire will choose a genuine *status quo* policy. The dynamics of the mid–twentieth century militate against a static equilibrium. What is more, the geographical, economic, political, and ideological factors of the global revolutionary conflict permit the Communists to maximize their pressure against the West at a minimum cost to themselves and at a minimum risk of overextending themselves.

Despite publicized rejection of limited war,[10] in the communist planning files one will certainly find plans for initiating a wide range of wars. The

10. In his celebrated speech of January 6, 1961, Khrushchev asserted: "A small-scale imperialist war . . . may develop into a world thermonuclear and missile war. We *must,* therefore, fight against both world war and against local wars."

possibility of limited war cannot be discounted, since Moscow may under certain circumstances deem it profitable to ignore the sensitivities of the neutralists and add another conquest in order to keep up the momentum of communist advance—especially if the United States might be paralyzed by fear of thermonuclear war and unprepared to deliver a riposte by other means.

Peace: The Universal Slogan

The advent of nuclear weapons has made peace the most important single demand of communist political warfare. It is the thread which ties together the nuclear rockets, Khrushchev's scheme for general disarmament, and communist support of wars of national "liberation for the purpose of freeing" peoples from the "imperialists."

Up to World War II and shortly thereafter, Moscow's chief universal slogan was "anti-imperialism," with "peace" a close second. The aim of "anti-imperialism" was to liquidate the British, French, Dutch, and Japanese empires, to ally the colonial peoples to Moscow and in the process to demoralize the colonizers. The Communists interpret as imperialism any influence—military, economic, or cultural—exercised by the industrially advanced nations upon colonial peoples. Similar influences emanating from the Kremlin, however, are termed "liberation." World War II culminated in the disintegration or transformation of the Japanese and most of the European empires. The anti-imperialist slogan consequently lost much of its force, and, in fact, the Kremlin has come increasingly under attack as the largest and most ruthless imperialist power. Consequently, it became imperative to shift the main emphasis to peace as the sustaining universal slogan.

From its birth, the Soviet Union has nurtured the myth of hostile encirclement. Except during rare periods of "thaw," a few months spent inside the Soviet empire gave one the impression of living in a nation surrounded by frenzied militarists. The Soviet press, the movies, the radio, the measures of the government—all the arts of propaganda have been synchronized to create that impact upon the mind. A war provoked by the "imperialists" is always just over the horizon.

To justify the "guns and no butter" policy guiding the first five-year plans and to intensify the beleaguered-fortress psychosis, the Soviet government periodically made propagandistic peace proposals to the outside world and then reported their alleged rejection. If the Soviet people heard at all about the Kremlin's peaceful intentions and peace drives, it was only to condition them to the militarization of Soviet life. So effectively was obsession with the war danger implanted that even when there was a purge inside the Soviet Communist Party those purged were accused of being agents of a foreign power and shot as traitors.

It is not new in history for aggressor governments to dissimulate their real intentions by professing love of peace. It is new, however, for a government to engage in *permanent* peace drives. Such permanent peace drives make sense only if the government considers itself permanently at war—covert or overt—with the world around it and uses the peace drive as a means of covert warfare to undermine the enemy and justify militarization at home. It is consistent with communist dialectics to pretend to seek peace on the one hand and on the other to prepare for war or even wage war in the name of peace.

The Kremlin owes a major debt to war. The U.S.S.R. was born in the First World War, and the Second World War spread communist power "in a number of countries of Central and Southeastern Europe and to the victory of the great Chinese people." Looking towards tomorrow, Kremlin spokesmen assert that if the imperialists unleash a third world war, it will mean the death not only of individual capitalist states but of the whole world of capitalism.

In 1935, Soviet Ambassador to France Potemkin asked: "Why should war frighten us? The Russia of the Soviets emerged from the last war, the Europe of the Soviets will emerge from the next." Peace-loving Stalin encouraged rather than restrained Hitler's invasion of Poland, aware that he would pick up the pieces of a world shattered by a major war.

Communist export propaganda, however, tries to create the impression that every act of aggression committed by the U.S.S.R. is undertaken solely in self-defense. Defense of peace combined with vicious attacks on the intentions of potential victims is a typical example of Soviet practice. One of the reasons for communist successes has been the failure of many military men to understand the Communist Party's pattern of unconventional conquest. There has been an equal failure of democratic civil leaders to understand the military threat of communism. The popular but superficial cliché "You can't fight an idea [communism] with force" ignores the record. Communism has liquidated many opposing ideas with force. "It is impossible," according to the *History of the Communist Party of the Soviet Union,* "to defeat the enemy without knowing how to attack properly."

The Kremlin's plan for expansion derives from the realization that communism will not develop spontaneously. Therefore, as Lenin confessed, "victory over the bourgeoisie is impossible without a long, obstinate and desperate war for life or death—a war demanding steadfastness, discipline, firmness and singleness of will." In the light of these teachings, the hope that the Soviet Union will never employ aggresive strategy against other countries is wishful thinking—even in the nuclear age. Communist "peace propaganda" is no more genuine today than it used to be, although the tactic of "peace" rather than armed conflict may better serve the U.S.S.R.

The Soviets wish us to believe that the Kremlin may have changed its basic attitude toward global conquest because of nuclear weapons. Yet the U.S.S.R. has become more aggressive as its nuclear power has grown.

Soviet propaganda tactics regarding the atomic bomb were far different when the United States enjoyed an atomic monopoly from those used during the uneasy nuclear stalemate of the sixties. The initial Soviet campaign was to prevent the United States from exploiting its atomic monopoly during the period when the U.S.S.R. was developing its own nuclear capabilities. When information obtained by Stalin's espionage activities regarding United States atomic secrets was confirmed at the 1945 Potsdam meeting, Stalin faced a choice. He could end all aggressiveness toward his wartime allies and gain the necessary time to become an atomic power, but he would then lose the opportunities offered by the post-war disorganization and war weariness of the non-communist world. On the other hand, he could continue that aggressiveness cautiously, being ready to pull back if necessary. The extent of his aggressiveness would depend largely on America's willingness to fight and use her atomic superiority.

To prevent our use of the atomic bomb, this was the problem. Since, before the mid-fifties, the Soviets had only conventional weapons in any quantity, the neutralization of American nuclear power had to be accomplished by political means. The Kremlin chose to continue its post–World War II aggression, counting on the unwillingness of the United States to fight.

Always suspicious that we might awaken to its scheme, the Kremlin did not depend entirely on passivity and opportunism but went to work politically to keep us asleep. Dangling peace in front of us, the Soviet propaganda machine tried to scare us with our own atomic bomb. In the name of humanitarianism, the bomb must be outlawed. By spreading such ideas among our scientists, it tried to prevent and slow down the development of the more powerful hydrogen bomb. (The results are recorded in the Oppenheimer hearings.)[11]

The Soviet peace campaign, planned around the prohibition of the A and H bombs and carried out under the flag of humanitarianism, was a colossal propaganda and agitation effort. The lead throughout that campaign was taken by Soviet diplomacy, which by its propagandistic proposals at all levels, including the United Nations, dramatized its efforts against the use of A and H bombs for military purposes. Behind the campaign was the full Soviet apparatus, the communist parties and their fronts, and millions of innocent dupes who joined the drive.

The anti-A and H bomb campaign helped to prevent the American use of the atom bomb in Korea even after the Red Chinese entered the war. A few A bombs dropped on massed Chinese "volunteers" could have changed the complexion of the Korean War. We reserved the use of the A bomb for the unlikely eventuality of outright Soviet intervention. Our highly intimidated and propagandized allies in Europe unwittingly assisted in the Soviet campaign.

11. It is impossible to summarize the entire statement of J. Robert Oppenheimer to the Personnel Security Board of the Atomic Energy Commission, concerning his role in the development of the H bomb. He and some of his associates had been accused of delaying the production of the bomb for supposed technical and moral reasons. The following excerpt from his statement is most pertinent:

"As to the super (bomb) itself, the General Advisory Committee stated its unanimous opposition to the initiation by the United States of a crash program of the kind we had been asked to advise on. The report of that meeting, and the Secretary's notes, reflect the reasons which moved us to this conclusion. The annexes, in particular, which dealt more with political and policy considerations–the report proper was essentially technical in character—indicated differences in the views of the members of the committee. There were two annexes, one signed by Rabi and Fermi, the other by Conant, DuBridge, Smith, Rowe, Buckley and myself. (The ninth member of the committee, Seaborg, was abroad at the time.)

"It would have been surprising if eight men considering a problem of extreme difficulty had each had precisely the same reasons for the conclusion in which we joined. But I think I am correct in asserting that the unanimous opposition we expressed to the crash program was based on the conviction, to which technical considerations as well as others contributed, that because of our overall situation at that time such a program might weaken rather than strengthen the position of the United States." Cited in *In the Matter of J. Robert Oppenheimer,* Transcript of Hearing before Personnel Security Board, Washington, D.C., April 12, 1954 through May 6, 1954, Atomic Energy Commission, Washington, D.C.: U.S. Government Printing Office, 1954, p. 19.

According to Stefan T. Possony "an artificial debate delayed the U.S. fusion program for almost a year. The Soviets, who had been developing H-weapons since 1946, exploded their first fusion device *before* the United States. If the Fabians [those who advocated stoppage or delay in this and other nuclear developments] had won, the U.S.S.R. would have achieved fusion monopoly by 1953." For a full exposition of the issues involved see *ASC Washington Report,* "Nuclear Fabianism," WR 62-1, January 8, 1962.

By the mid-fifties, Washington veered toward prohibition of nuclear weapons if there could be foolproof inspection and a reduction of conventional arms based on a parity in military strength between the Soviet bloc and the West. But the Soviets would not agree to this. The Kremlin wanted to disarm the West in the name of peace but not disarm itself.

The offer to accept the prohibition under the above safeguards represented a Western compromise. It amounted to recognition of all the Soviet conquests hitherto achieved, a *status quo* peace based on "coexistence."

The Soviets could have accepted the Western offer, built up their newly acquired empire with the help of the West, and left the liquidation of the capitalist world to a future generation of Communists. This would have confined the present generation to subversive political warfare carried out by proxies (the communist parties) on a more limited scale. For a brief period after the death of Stalin (1953–56), Malenkov appeared tempted to experiment with the communist coexistence. The rise of Khrushchev marked a rejection. The Kremlin still talks about coexistence and general and complete universal disarmament, but only to deceive the West.

In the combined political-military warfare pursued by the Soviet Union, the intimidation value of a powerful nuclear striking force can be heightened by adroit appeals for peace and disarmament. In propaganda there are two basic types of appeal. One uses motivating ideas and the other paralyzing ideas. It is a difficult task to motivate people positively; it is easy to spread paralyzing ideas.

The propaganda of peace also aims at influencing the decision-making processes—not necessarily by opposing directly decisions that are being made, but by so influencing decisions (such as the issue of nuclear tests) that they will be made too late and result in too little. The purpose is to neutralize the development or use of armaments by strong anti-communist powers and to create conflict among non-communists. Communist propaganda is abetted by the West's illusion that communism is no longer aggressive but wants genuine peace; that peaceful coexistence is possible on a lasting basis; that war must and can be avoided by means of settlements and nuclear disarmaments; and that, if war breaks out, it will be the non-communist world that will be blown up.

Beginning with the Soviet notes at the time of the Suez crisis, Khrushchev has written into recent world history a new chapter on ballistic blackmail, culminating in the threat to back Castro with a direct missile attack on the United States. The gains the Soviets have got thus far out of a small quantity of missiles and sputniks should give the West warning of what to expect when and if the Soviets ever believe that they have forged their ICBM's into a decisive weapons system.

One aspect of Soviet infatuation with missile potentialities deserves special mention in connection with their calls for disarmament and nuclear-test bans. The ICBM, which reinforces the Soviet bid for world domination, owes its utility entirely to the nuclear warhead it carries. The further perfection of ICBM's will be tied to major advances in nuclear technology, which will almost inevitably require continued nuclear testing.

The Soviets callously demonstrated in their 1961 Arctic tests that they will not jeopardize the future growth of their new-found globe-shaker by adherence to any negotiated standstill in nuclear development. Soviet power and the might of the communist bloc have made their biggest increase since ICBM's joined their arsenal. The fear of war in the Free World has increased and the resolution of the Free World has declined as Soviet missiles have advanced. These developments are the measure of the success of nuclear blackmail.

Disarmament propaganda is not a device to keep both peace and the *status quo*—that is, to keep the peace and at the same time keep the Soviets behind their Iron Curtain and the Americans and the West on this side of the Iron Curtain. The disarmament issue is clouded by Bertrand Russell, who argues that the West should surrender in order to save the human race. However, there is no evidence that our surrender would guarantee lasting peace. The Communists are bellicose. Infighting is their main preoccupation in life. After our capitulation, there would be uprisings and other disorders in the communist paradise, and eventually they would go to war against each other. Such a war would have all the pitiless bitterness of the fraternal struggles of the past. It is an illusion, therefore, to think that our surrender would end the prospects of nuclear war.

Despite its horrors, the Soviets contend that a nuclear campaign could mean ultimate victory for them. Their official doctrine for nuclear war puts an unprecedented emphasis on the importance of a surprise first strike. Since periods of tension alert the West, the midst of a peace campaign might provide a more suitable atmosphere for a surprise attack. Consequently, Khrushchev's advocacy of "peaceful coexistence," and "disarmament," may be familiar communist deception tactics as well as elements in a psychological campaign to weaken the Western will.

If the Soviet government actually meant to coexist peacefully, it could recognize the Red Cross, permit UN agencies to operate in its territory, join the other treaties regulating normal international relations, and agree to arms control with effective inspection. It could also—and would—dismantle its network of subversive organizations and behave like a normal government. It would not merely talk peace at its convenience but would actually practice it. If the Soviet government continues to use peace as a propaganda weapon, the reason must be sought, not in alleged peaceful intentions, but in the hostile nature of that government. Only thus can we grasp the significance of permanent peace drives.

The Communist Party, whether in or out of government, is fundamentally a war party. In the twenties it preached its warlike aims—class against class—quite openly. It championed peace only when the revolution in Europe (after World War I) failed to materialize and it had to retreat to prepare for a new advance.

At the same time, the non-Russian communist parties were organizationally very weak and inexperienced. Time was also needed for the building up of the Soviet Communist Party as an international party of subversion. The Soviet Union, as a state, consequently ceased to be warlike and transferred militancy into the field of psychological-political warfare waged by the communist parties. This complex of factors triggered the Kremlin's initial peace drive.

Despite subsequent peace drives and in spite of the excruciating poverty of the Russian people, the Soviet Union concentrated on heavy industry and military hardware. The Soviets held to this course even during the period when pre-Hitler Germany had only a nucleus of an army and when the rest of the capitalist world, with the exception of Japan, neglected its military establishment. Soviet Russia became and remains the most militarized country in the world, exceeding even Hitler's in the years that followed his triumph of 1933.

The aim of the Kremlin's continuous peace drive is the destruction of the enemy's will to fight, a concept hitherto used only in the military sense. Lenin, Trotsky, Stalin, and all the Bolshevik leaders were assiduous readers of military literature. They were particularly impressed by the thoughts on strategy of Karl von Clausewitz, a Prussian staff officer of the nineteenth century, whose writings were required readings in communistic military-staff colleges. They regarded themselves as political generals.

In the West, a military man was among the first to see the significance of political warfare in the wars of conquest of our day. In 1920 General J. F. Fuller, the British tank expert, in a book called *Tanks and the Great*

War wrote, "Mechanical and chemical weapons may disappear and be replaced by others more terrible. This method of imposing the will of one man on another may, in turn, be replaced by purely psychological warfare wherein weapons are not even used." The General saw far beyond our time. Today, the Kremlin, while using the ideological weapon fully, is ready to consider the military one as well. The General failed to see that the communist type of political warfare causes the biggest loss of life—comparable to that anticipated in modern atomic warfare—in the liquidations that take place after the conquest of power.

If the West accepts the Kremlin's alleged peaceful intentions even though it remains armed, its masses, influenced by communist-inspired peace propaganda, can become ideologically disarmed. Consequently, our will to fight could be neutralized or destroyed.

The difference between the past and present peace drives is that the latter are no longer defensive. They are designed to gain time to digest the East European satellites, harass the West through aggressive political warfare to keep it off balance, allow Red China to rise as an industrial and military power, and gain technological-military supremacy for the Soviet Union over the United States. The time is also needed to adjust the post-Stalin Soviet internal situation and increase food production. We live in a twilight period between peace and war, an undeclared armistice. This armistice, which the West may mistake as peace, could last a decade or even longer, depending on (1) the situation behind the European and Asian "curtains"; (2) the possible splits among the Western powers; and (3) the progress of internal subversion directed by Moscow behind our lines.

It will be seen from the above that military preparedness, important as it may be, is not the only decisive factor. Moscow is working methodically and aggressively to shift the world power balance in its favor, while its opponents merely arm and wait.

Khrushchev's personal bid for general and complete disarmament at the 1960 meeting of the United Nations General Assembly was the most notable example of communist "peacemanship." The follow-up to such overtures is, as a rule, thoroughly organized. The foreign-correspondent press corps in Moscow and through its press corps and radio facilities, the United Nations are used as sounding boards. The Moscow and satellite radio and press services publicize the peace drive in foreign countries. The communist parties outside the Soviet empire organize specialized peace fronts to link up professional pacifists and take advantage of pacifist sentiment in each country.[12] The horrors of a future war, which Moscow claims it is aiming to avoid through its peace overtures, are painted in lurid colors. National conferences to demand peace are organized in each country (outside the Soviet empire), and summit conferences of the statesmen of the major powers are proposed.

All of this "waging of peace" is carried on exclusively outside the Soviet empire. Nothing comparable is permitted on the inside.[13] A special characteristic of Soviet peace drives is the method of linking other issues or demands with the ideas of peace. Behind this lies the theory that wars initiated or sanctioned by the Kremlin are just wars and all other wars are either imperialist wars or wars waged in the interests of capitalist exploitation—Wall Street wars. To be for peace, therefore, means to be against the merchants of death, the munitions profiteers and business leaders. All Soviet wars are painted as defensive wars, just wars—people's wars—in defense of the best interests of the people.

On the basis of that ideological formula, the workers are told not to support imperialist war but to sabotage it, through strikes and exorbitant demands, and to transform the imperialist war into a civil war. The colored peoples are told not to support it because only through the defeat of the white imperialists can they attain their liberation. Thus the universal slogan of peace is linked to the immediate and long-range demands the Communists have formulated for every stratum of society. All of these, according to communist claims, could be realized by helping to defeat one's own—

12. For example, a British pacifist organization published a guide to Great Britain: "The map appeared in a publication called *Sanity,* the monthly news sheet of the Campaign for Nuclear Disarmament.

"Marked on a map were nineteen places listed as sites for the American Thor missile—the 1,500-mile rocket now in operational readiness here. Also shown were sixteen bomber bases manned by United States crews, four rocket-control centers and three hydrogen-bomb depots.

"Sir Edmund Huddleston, Chief of Air Staff, said: 'Nobody should publish this. It certainly does not help this country.' " *New York Times,* July 24, 1961, p. 6.

13. Joseph Z. Kornfeder relates how he asked Molotov in 1929 why there was no discussion of peace inside the Soviet Union. The latter's answer, after overcoming surprise at such a question, was quite blunt: "Obviously, we are not going to cut our own throats," he said.

A study sponsored by the Brookings Institution, called "Post-War Negotiations for Arms Control," concluded that the aim of the Soviet Union in disarmament negotiations apparently was to disarm only the West or to achieve a disarmament agreement without effective controls. The study said that the record of fifteen years of disarmament negotiations demonstrated that the Soviet Union had "not yet shown a desire to sacrifice" its system of secrecy to obtain disarmament. The study was prepared by Bernhard G. Bechhoefer, a State Department expert on disarmament questions from 1946 to 1958. *New York Times,* July 24, 1961, p. 3.

capitalist—government. Thus the goal of defeating the opposing government is combined with the tempting bait of victory for the masses in alliance with the Soviet Union. Lest there be any doubt as to this interpretation, the December, 1960 report adopted by the Moscow Congress of 81 Communist Parties stated the concept with disarming frankness:

> Peaceful Coexistence . . . does not imply renunciation of the class struggle. . . . The *coexistence* of states with different social systems *is a form of class struggle between socialism* [communism] *and capitalism.*
>
> *In conditions of peaceful coexistence favorable opportunities are provided for the development of the class struggle in* these capitalist countries and [in] the national liberation movement of the peoples of the colonial and dependent countries. In their turn the successes of the revolutionary class and national liberation struggle promote peaceful coexistence. . . .
>
> The Communists . . . will do their utmost . . . to *weaken imperialism* and *limit its sphere of action* by an active struggle for peace, democracy and national liberation.
>
> *Peaceful coexistence . . . does not mean conciliation* of the socialist [communist] and bourgeois ideologies. On the contrary, *it implies intensification of the struggle* of the working class, of all communist parties for the triumph of socialist [communist] ideas. . . .
>
> Through an active determined struggle by the socialist [communist] and other peace loving countries, by the . . . broad masses in *all* countries, it is possible to isolate the aggressive circles [i.e., the United States and its allies], foil the arms race and *force* the imperialists into an agreement on general disarmament.[14]

Implications for the United States

As long as the Communists rule the U.S.S.R., the dangers of nuclear, limited, and guerrilla wars with the United States will remain. We must distinguish between communist doctrine, communist intentions, and communist capabilities in order to reach an accurate appraisal of communist behavior. We must understand communist military doctrine and interpret it realistically, without being taken in by communist deceptions or carried away by superficial and cursory readings of a vast and complex literature.

Our strategic problems and those of the Communists are not symmetrical. Simply put, our objective could be reached if over the years we frustrate communist purposes. In order to achieve their objective, the Communists must not only bring about our military defeat, they must also occupy and communize our country. The accomplishment of this objective in terms of technology, firepower, and political seizure will remain—unless we fall down on the job ourselves—beyond Soviet capability.

14. Italics and clarification of terms added.

Developing an adequate concept and structure of military deterrence and giving it substance with the proper global and regional force levels cannot be the final answer to the problems confronting the West. But these steps would provide the military framework in which the communist world and the Free World could be pitted against each other at the broader level of political strategy.

The West cannot win, or even survive, without a political counteroffensive. The posture of "survival" and "deterrence" spells the failure of such a counteroffensive from the start. We must take risks comparable to those the Kremlin is willing to take in the prosecution of such a political offensive. We must strive for our own kind of peace in order to avoid ending up with the Kremlin's kind. American and Free World political counterwarfare is the only road to this end. It is a basic question which cannot be bypassed, lest we shall end facing surrender or a war of desperation.

CHAPTER X

THE EXPANDING CONFLICT
OF SYSTEMS

CHANGES HAVE OCCURRED INSIDE THE SOVIET UNION SINCE
Stalin's death, but they have not altered the totalitarian character of the
Soviet state or downgraded political warfare as a prime instrument of
Soviet policy.

Khrushchev, who consolidated his power by denouncing the nightmarish
regime of his late chief, Stalin, has tried to give communism a new look by
reinvigorating and reforming it from the top. He has purged and reorganized Stalin's political police and has dramatized this action by eliminating
the old Stalinist leadership represented by Beria, Molotov, Kaganovich,
Bulganin and Malenkov, purging their followers in the process. The new
regime has released from slave-labor camps hundreds of thousands, perhaps millions, of minor political offenders and has rehabilitated posthumously some of the major ones. It is seeking to remedy the food shortage,
inherited from Stalin's rigid policies toward the peasants, by opening new
lands to cultivation. There has been some reversal of Stalin's policy of
supercentralization of industry; there has been more attention to consumer
needs. These measures, taken together, have created speculations and illusions, both within the U.S.S.R. and in the outside world, about the possibilities of a new style and gradual reformation of communism.

New Sophistication

The *Brave New World* which emerges from the announced 1961 program[1] for the Communist Party of the Soviet Union serves to emphasize

1. "Draft Program of the Soviet Communist Party," presented to its twenty-second
congress in October, 1961, translated into English by Tass, the official Soviet press agency,
and published in the *New York Times*, August 1, 1961, pp. 13ff.

the general lack of awareness among Western thinkers and analysts about present-day communist theory and practice and the true nature of Soviet long-range objectives, strategy, and tactics.

The irony of this failure to recognize the realities is that, far from keeping their plans and intentions hidden, the communist leaders make unceasing attempts, through every known medium of communication, to set forth explicitly their program for achieving a universal communist order in their own image and for the creation of "World Communist Man." But even supposedly expert Western observers, including many of the more sophisticated scholars of Marxism-Leninism and of "Kremlinology," have too often refused to take the Soviet declarations of intent seriously. Skepticism and incredulity based on traditional and outworn images of communism have led to a series of dangerously mistaken evaluations of the dynamism inherent in the communism of the sixties and of the real Soviet potential for conducting the "world conflict of systems" (one Soviet equivalent of the Western term "Cold War"). On a much more encompassing scale, the Soviet explicitness is compatible to that of Hitler's *Mein Kampf,* which, available for everybody to read, was met with general disbelief and ridicule by the very people who ultimately fell victim to the Nazis. The fact that much of the Communists' expressed intentions, just as those of the Nazis, are often fanatical and utopian, tends to blind moderate, rational Western men to the fact that the irrational exerts great motivational strength. When emotional drives are backed by the hardheaded and scientifically planned organization of modern communism, their psychological and political momentum becomes formidable.

The vision projected by the 1961 Soviet party program of an opulent communist society in which a great many personal needs will be satisfied and the conception of a "classless" communist world are certainly at first glance utopian and at second glance Orwellian. This should not distract the reader, however, from recognizing that they are part of an extended restatement of the major goals in the Soviets' campaign to make appealing the "transition from socialism to communism." The importance of the concept and the program for this "transition" are insufficiently comprehended in the non-communist world, partly because the terms in which they are couched are typical of the communist jargon used to express their mystique of the future. *Transition* explicitly implies completion of the world revolution and the conflict attendant thereto. The realities underlying the "transition to communism" involve strategies and tactics of tremendous importance to the rest of the world. These include not only major Soviet internal or domestic goals but political- and economic-conflict objectives, as well as sweeping developments in the organization and integration of the entire bloc of "socialist" states. The "transition," in fact, becomes the over-all cover for a grand-scale strategy unparalleled in history.

Khrushchev's statement of the new party program, which is designed to extend over the next twenty years, thus stands as a résumé of what has been a series of announcements and declarations issuing from the Kremlin since 1956. Out of this mass of words emerges the brave new world of communism and the futuristic strategy of the Soviet Union.

The year 1956 was a milestone for the Soviets and world communism. This was the year of the loosening of the iron grip of Stalinism, of the assumption of full power by Khrushchev, of the Hungarian revolt, of tremors within the communist bloc and then restabilization, of cracks in the Kremlin wall hurriedly recemented. It was the year, less noticed, of a relatively new freedom for Soviet scientists and academicians and of the revitalization of the Soviet Academy of Sciences as a more dynamic arm of both state and party. Likewise, the Academy of the Social Sciences was constituted as a party organ out of the remains of the defunct, Stalin-suppressed League (Academy) of Red Professors. It was also the year in which Soviet mathematicians, physiologists, psychologists, economists, and engineers officially and ardently embraced the science of cybernetics ("the science of control of man, machine and society"). Cybernetics had previously been disdainfully denounced as a capitalist device for the further exploitation of workers through automation.

Since 1956, a steadily mounting tempo of new developments in methodology and organization for co-ordinating and applying the newer sciences and other knowledges has been in evidence in the Soviet Union. On the basis of these and many other developments, the meaning of the term "transition" has become increasingly clarified. The "holistic,"[2] all-encompassing nature of the domestic and international program it envisages is now delineable, both in general and in fairly specific terms.

The General Bases and Pattern of the "Transition" Program

The transition to the "higher" stage of development regarded by the Party as true "communism" will rest upon the transformation of the three

2. A term, mostly used in psychology, meaning to take a *whole* rather than fragmented approach to major social problems. The term is attributed to Jan Smuts of South Africa.

great "bases" of the development of Soviet society. These are (1) the "material-technical" base, i.e., economic and technological progress; (2) the socio-cultural base, i.e., the political and social "education" of the people, including the application of the newest psychological and propaganda techniques to the shaping of "Soviet Man" and his environment; and (3) the "ideological" base, or the refinement and adaptation of Marxist-Leninist doctrine and dogma to suit the needs of the new age.

The transition is regarded in its entirety as a social and conflict process requiring the adaptation and use of the latest physical- and social-science methods and techniques. These will be applied not only to the solution of internal Soviet problems but also on a world scale for the achievement of global communist political, social, and economic ends. Thus what in the past was mere hypothetical "science" in Marxist-Leninist terms is advanced as the universally applied technology of the atomic and space age. Marx's so-called "scientific socialism"[3] (as opposed to "utopian" socialism) becomes an infinitely more advanced "scientific communism."

Some of the More Specific Portents of Soviet Plans and Strategies

From analysis of the new program for the future, the following major goals to be pursued by the Kremlin leadership within the next two decades emerge into view:

(1) The creation of a "model" Soviet society of "demonstrable excellence" (a phrase borrowed from Plato by the Communists) for the rest of the world to emulate. This is the most long-range goal—if ever to be achieved. It is the familiar strategy of influencing the non-communist world "by example," whether or not the "example" ever becomes reality.

(2) Co-ordinated application of all sciences and technology to the totality of society, economy, and conflict.

(3) The shaping of a new "Soviet Man" who will become the model for "World Communist Man."[4]

(4) Within their own admitted definition of "peaceful coexistence," to

3. It should be noted that the 1961 draft program of the Soviet Communist Party reiterated that "Marxism-Leninism discussed the objective laws of social development—and of the transition of society to communism." Many of the utopian concepts in the 1961 program have been part of the party's "pie-in-the-sky" from the beginning. Promises without delivery can be effective so long as no one keeps the record straight. The idea of using science to breathe life into moribund Marxist ideology is being advocated by some left-wing deviationists. It is doubtful, however, that the orthodox party officials now in the driver's seat have really bought the concept, except as a tactical façade.

4. The arrival of the new "Soviet Man" is far behind schedule, yet his noble, socially constructive characteristics will be available for export long before his most unlikely appearance.

mobilize the masses and step up the "relentless struggle" in the "conflict of systems" for the victory of communism throughout the world. This struggle is to include all forms of political, psychological, ideological, economic, and military warfare.

(5) Surpass the United States in both industrial production and technology (the current target date is 1970, but it can always be moved ahead).

(6) Perfect new organizations and common administrations for the bloc, both political and economic, leading to a "commonwealth of socialist states."[5]

(7) Support and direct the communist parties of other countries to take over the reins of power in the "decaying" societies, whether "capitalist-imperialist" or "underdeveloped."

(8) Accompany the political- and psychological-conflict measures with economic measures in the uncommitted areas and the penetration of markets customarily served by the "capitalist countries."

(9) Maintain a powerful military structure centered around systems capable of delivering firepower at all ranges, as a psychological threat, as a strategic cover for limited operations, and as a usable force in major conflict.

This systems conflict will, as in the internal measures, call for the discovery and application of modern science and the best devisable techniques for influencing the minds of men and manipulating groups and individuals in other countries in the interest of communist purposes.[6] To this end, the social and physiological sciences (including the many applications of cybernetics) will be called upon as conflict weapons. (Greater sophistication in Soviet propaganda approaches are already evident. For instance, the current communist appeal is not merely to the "proletariat" or to the underprivileged of other countries along the familiar lines of the past; it, as was the *Communist Manifesto,* is directed to "all humanity," with the old, old motif of the "New Humanism.")

5. The Kremlin has given currency to a relatively new Aesopian term, "The Commonwealth of Socialist Nations"—*sodruzhestvo sotsialisticheskikh stran* (or States") *gosudarstv.* The English term "commonwealth," implying voluntary association of states, gives the wrong connotation. For a full development of the operational significance of this concept, see Kurt L. London, *The Emerging Socialist Commonwealth.* As a logical development of Marxism-Leninism applied to organization, the *sodruzhestvo* concept must be regarded by the Kremlin as an eminently practical instrumentality. It can be made to serve the broad purposes of foreign policy, such as the promotion of "peaceful coexistence." It can be propagated as a global united-front tactic. Most of all, it offers an organizational framework for the era of communism, which is the avowed goal of the transitory period of socialism. It depends upon the tempo of the "transition to communism."

6. Again, we are stating their operational dreams. This last ambition requires more intellectual flexibility than communists have thus far demonstrated.

Party declarations, as well as articles in *Kommunist,* have stressed the role of the Party, not alone as the "vanguard of the proletariat," but also as the "vanguard of humanity." Thus the philosophical ancestors of modern communism include not only Marx, Engels, and Lenin but also Plato, Sophocles, the Greco-Roman tradition generally, and the "great utopians," including Campanella the Dominican (author of *City of the Sun*), St. Simon and Fourier, Sir Thomas More, and others. In essence, much of what we have considered the "culture of the West" has been adopted by the Communists as their own.[7]

Another striking ideological bombshell was the declaration that "cybernetics will replace historical materialism as the guide to social processes" (Arab-Ogley, 1959) and that "cybernetics is completely in harmony with dialectical materialism" (Nesmeyanov, 1960).[8]

The Emerging Pattern of Future Soviet Organization for Conflict Management

A pattern of organization for the combined purposes of engineering the "transition to communism" internally and of using more sophisticated means for conducting the global conflict of systems has been emerging for some time. Stalin, prior to his death, recognized the need for greater organizational and tactical flexibility. Many of the stratagems for splintering the Free World now identified with Khrushchev were embodied in the program of the Nineteenth Congress of the Communist Party of the Soviet Union convoked by Stalin in the fall of 1952. Communist machinery for

7. This is reminiscent of the days just after World War II when huge lettering on the banks of the Arno River proclaimed the communist slogan "Christ was the first Communist."

8. Although most Soviet leaders don't believe they need to find a new scientific rationale for the moss-covered dogmas of Marxism, the fact that some of the more daring communist thinkers recognize the problem is indicative of serious philosophical deficiencies in modern communism. The views expressed by Arab-Ogley and Nesmeyanov (later demoted) are in fact heresies. Fundamentally, cybernetics as a tool of analysis is no more compatible with dialectical materialism than it is with spiritualism. Nevertheless, the December 1961 issue of *Soviet Review* has an article, "The Human Element in Automation Systems," by D. A. Oshanin and D. Y. Panov, which throws interesting light on Soviet work in cybernetics: "We are convinced however that our polytechnical schools, in training specialists for the future, must look ahead and give serious attention to fostering in the students those psycho-physiological functions, faculties and qualities which are decisive in many promising fields of work and necessary for man's participation in highly automated, highly exacting production processes. . . . Research work on psychology and physiology is being conducted by a number of establishments in Moscow, Leningrad, Kiev, Tbilisi, Kazan and other cities. This work is assuming particular significance for us."

global co-ordination has been steadily evolving since the World War II dissolution of the Comintern.

The formal abolition of the Comintern in 1943 was accompanied by the liquidation of the Young Communist International (YCI), the communist trade-union front known as the Red International of Labor Unions, and other global communist fronts. These had outlived their usefulness because they had become too narrow. They stood in the way of the communist opportunism which blossomed after World War II. Subsequently, the global fronts were reconstituted on a much broader basis, and the system of persuasive fronts with innocent-sounding names was increased and expanded. Thus the YCI was reconstituted, with the word "communist" eliminated from its title, and henceforth became known as the World Federation of Democratic Youth.

The Red International of Labor Unions reappeared as the World Federation of Trade Unions, with the word "red" eliminated from its name. It aimed to attract and to accept as affiliates all labor unions, whether or not controlled on a local level by Communists or their sympathizers.

During the last decade, the Communists have been concentrating upon the intelligentsia. Several global fronts have been set up specifically for them. These include the World Federation of Teachers Unions, the International Organization of Journalists, and the World Federation of Scientific Workers. These intelligentsia fronts are actually political instruments designed for co-ordination and infiltration on a broad scale. There is also a new global front for the co-ordination of activities amongst women known as the Women's International Democratic Federation.

There have been some innovations in the Communists' use of their universal slogans. The old global front known as the Anti-Imperialist League has been abolished. In its stead *anti-imperialism* is being pushed through other organizations in regions where it pays off politically, as in the Middle East, Asia, Africa, and Latin America. Furthermore, anti-imperialism, in line with the new opportunism, is now being used not merely to incite extreme nationalism but to incite racial antagonism as well.

These organizational trends set in motion by Stalin have been greatly accelerated by Khrushchev. The discernible characteristics of the Khrushchev pattern are: (1) party and state organizations within the U.S.S.R. are better co-ordinated than ever before; (2) the governmental administrative apparatus is being overhauled, and in several instances new "super" integrating bodies are being created; and (3) the international organizations of both state and party are being modernized.

The new (April, 1961) State Committee for the Coordination of Scientific Research Work is a prime example of the creation of a "super" agency designed to provide over-all direction of an area of major importance. It is also an example of the Soviet tightening up of administrative control in order to co-ordinate "peacetime" and military programs. The State Committee was headed at first by a lieutenant general of the Soviet air force and former head of the Soviet atomic industry, M. V. Khrunichev. When General Khrunichev died, soon after his appointment, he was replaced by Konstantin Nikolayevich Rudner, former Minister of Defense Technology of the U.S.S.R. As the "czar" of all scientific research and development, it is Rudner's mission to improve co-ordination among the academic, industrial, and military "R & D" throughout the Soviet Union.

The new and more sophisticated efforts being made in the direction of improving Soviet plans and programs for influencing and penetrating foreign areas are exemplified in the creation of the new Council for Coordination of Scientific Work on Africa. This relatively innocuous-sounding title cannot hide the Council's true purpose, for the first priority given members is to conduct "profound and comprehensive study of the modern political and economic problems of the African continent." This is further specified as the study of "socio-economic processes in the emergence of new social forces opposing colonialism in Africa, disintegration of the colonial system of imperialism, the national liberation struggle of enslaved peoples, the workers and peasants movement in African countries, [and] contradictions between imperial powers." Nothing could, of course, be more explicit in restating the familiar and precise communist objectives in Africa. It may be conjectured that the council on Africa will be followed by similar new co-ordinating organizations to assist Soviet policy-makers and planners in programming Soviet propaganda and infiltration for other areas, such as Latin America, the Middle East, and the Far East.

Despite these grandiose plans, there is no doubt that communism is confronted with a series of problems, old and new. Khrushchev's new program recognizes that today's problems can be solved neither with the tools of Stalin's police methods nor on the basis of non-existing formulae found in the scriptures of Karl Marx or Nicolai Lenin.

Among the pressing internal problems are the rise of a new bureaucratic ruling class, a phenomenon not anticipated by either Marx or Lenin; the problem of agriculture under communism, apparently insoluble under the communist system of "collective" farming; the loss of individual rights and hence the *de facto* lawlessness of the state; and the vampire-like growth of militarism, which impedes the solution of other problems. All of these are contradictions far deeper than any existing in the West, contradictions which are occasionally ventilated by purges, but never solved. Without drastic changes in the system, they are in fact, insoluble.

When Stalin, in 1936, proclaimed his "Constitution for the Soviet Union," many reforms were promised, including free speech and free assembly. The document resembled superficially the American Constitution. There were profound differences, however. The government itself was a tool of the Communist Party, and there were no inalienable rights reserved to the people. Even the semblance of freedom was negated by the fact that only one political party was recognized: the Communist Party. This "liberal" constitution did not prevent Stalin from carrying out the bloodiest purge in Soviet history shortly after it was proclaimed. Those who were supposed to be enjoying the freedoms guaranteed by the constitution ended up before the executioner or in concentration camps.

Mao Tse-tung, Red China's Stalin, carried out a similar maneuver in a speech in 1958 when he proclaimed freedom of discussion, "letting a hundred different flowers bloom." A few months later, those that "bloomed" were arrested. How many of them are still talking, only Mao and his political police know. Observation suggests that when political reforms are proclaimed behind the Iron Curtain, they are largely deceptive in nature. One reason for them is likely to be the smoking out of the opposition. Only in the technical and management spheres is reform likely to be real.

Experience thus far indicates that totalitarian regimes, especially of the communist variety, tend to move toward greater totalitarianism. The pressure can be relaxed from time to time, but the over-all tendency toward control is constant. In Lenin's time there was limited discussion *inside the Party* for some months prior to a party congress. It was also possible for non-party members in party-controlled unions and other organizations to voice some minor criticisms or complaints. Lenin's formula of democratic centralism within the Party represented the apogee of democracy in practice inside the Soviet Union.

Presumably, the proposed 1961 program of the Communist Party of the Soviet Union is to create the Khrushchev epoch of a reformed and reinvigorated communism. It proposes a more democratic system for both the government and the Party. The program proposes but does not define socialistic democracy, in which the people of the Soviet Union would play a more active role. Other provisions are presumably designed to curb the self-perpetuating bureaucracy. Yet despite the eventual goal of "inner party" democracy, the Communists are admonished to "behave and act in all matters in full accordance with the principles of the party and its lofty aims."

The real essence of reform in the political arena, which Khrushchev will not concede, is the redistribution of power. If the labor unions had their collective-bargaining rights fully restored, including the right to strike and to elect as leaders people other than candidates supported by the Communist Party, that would be a reform. If the farmers were granted basic property rights over the collective farms, plus the right to an independent organization to protect these rights, that, too, would be a reform. If genuine political debate took place within the Communist Party, that would be a reform. If the kangaroo-court system of justice were to be rearranged so that the individual were endowed with rights, even within the system of collective property, that, too, would be a reform.

The above suggestions are but an indication of what, at least theoretically, should be feasible even under the Soviet system. The Communists pretend to the outside world that those things, except for the right of the farmers to organize independently and the right to strike, already exist. In reality, these things do not exist; nor are they feasible without reforming (democratizing) the Party's control system.

We are in accord with Leonard Schapiro's conclusion that "despite all the important developments which have taken place in the Soviet Union since 1953, there has been no basic change. At home the supremacy of party rule remains not only unchallenged, but by reason of its broader base and greater benevolence, more firmly established than ever before; abroad, the conduct of foreign policy remains a bold game of political warfare, aimed not at compromise, agreement, equilibrium and relaxation of tension, but at gaining, more skillfully than ever before, a succession of points on the long road to 'World Communism.' "[9]

As long as the supremacy of party rule remains, reforms can be snuffed out at any time. Nor are the present leaders of the Soviet Communist Party, judging by their actions in Hungary and Berlin, likely to initiate real reforms, which they condemn as "revisionism." On the contrary, they blame the Hungarian events on the inadequate extermination (purges) by the political police of the freedom-seeking opposition. In Hungary, they applied the remedy of all reactionary regimes of the past—force.

There is confusion in the West regarding the meaning of Soviet admin-

9. Leonard Schapiro, "Has Russia Changed?" *Foreign Affairs*, Vol. XXXVIII, No. 3 (April, 1960), p. 400.

istrative reforms, such as the turning over of the tractor and agricultural-implement stations to the collectives, making the latter responsible for maintenance. These represent increased efficiency in the implementation of communist totalitarianism. Back in the early thirties, when the peasants were forced into the collectives, that, too, was applauded by many Western leftist liberals as a reform. Actually, it was the very opposite; it represented the spread of communist-party totalitarianism to the countryside.

If one speaks of reform in the sense that the Communists do, reform goes on all the time. After all, the atheist, totalitarian party-state is a new phenomenon in society, one with little, if any, precedent. Many innovations and improvisations are adopted which, in view of its rulers, strengthen the party-state. Even during the stagnant period of Stalinism, when the political scenery was enlivened mainly by purges, there were always some innovations, methods either of enslavement and exploitation or of management and police control. Only when the death of Stalin removed some of the paralyzing fears did the country return to what may be called normalcy under totalitarianism. After the nightmarish reign of Stalin, even a normal purge can look like a reform.

The extreme purge carried out in Hungary after the revolt, Khrushchev's increased provocations in foreign affairs, and his own proclivities toward purges as shown by his performance at the 1961 Twenty-second Party Congress[10] negate the introduction of real democracy inside the Soviet Union.

Communism's pattern of development, to the extent that it may be perceived after more than forty years of communist rule, is based on the negation of individual property rights, regimented labor, and state-controlled trade. Its economic structure reflects political regimentation expressed in the total monopoly of one party, a party which exercises complete sover-

10. "History is sure to list the 15 days of Moscow's 22nd Party Congress as among the most momentous in the annals of Communism, even though no wars were declared and, so far as anyone knows, no blood was shed. Out of it all, Nikita Khrushchev emerged as indisputably the biggest tiger in the Red jungle. A few of the things he did: He threatened to read Albania out of the Communist brotherhood for its 'Stalinist' tactics. He stared down the Red Chinese when the delegates from Peking rose to Albania's defense. He lowered the boom on old-line Stalinists Georgi Malenkov and Vyacheslav Molotov. He literally buried Josef Stalin, greatest Stalinist of them all, who had been enshrined since death in a public memorial. He sent Finland a chilling note asking for talks on 'mutual security' to scare the rest of Scandinavia. He boosted his secret police chief, Aleksandr Shelepin, to a spot in the party secretariat. And punctuating his whole performance, he more than made good a boast that Russia would test a 50-megaton hydrogen bomb, with political and physical reverberations felt around the world." *Life*, November 13, 1961, p. 31.

eignty over the state and all social, economic, and other affairs within it.

Communism has shown no capacity for social reform. Of course the Communists contend that the advent of communism itself is the greatest reform and the total embodiment of all reforms; hence all that need be done is efficiently to administrate communism through the Communist Party. With all basic rights and freedoms, the vehicles of reform, abolished, "reforming" is confined to the bureaucratic adjustments and manipulations of the high command in the party-state.

This does not mean that a regimented party-state cannot be an efficient state, particularly from the point of view of war-making capabilities. On the contrary, for that purpose it has many advantages. Nor does it mean that the party-state may not progress technologically. After all, it can draw upon the resources and knowledge of others and develop them further for its own purposes. But problems which the party-state can never solve are those stemming from the desire for freedom.

The aspiration toward freedom among the peoples could be overcome at least temporarily by: (1) ameliorating reforms; (2) internal force, which was Stalin's method; (3) a combined effort to conquer the capitalist world; or (4) a combination of the three with emphasis on conquest. This combination is what Khrushchev, in concurrence with Mao, strives toward.

To the communist leaders, universal domination must appear to be the most durable, if not the only, solution. If communism wins its conflict with the West, the problem of freedom may be postponed into the distant future. Meanwhile, the Communists work ceaselessly to eliminate the vestiges of bourgeois thinking which center around individual freedom:

The party considers it an integral part of its Communist education work to combat manifestations of bourgeois ideology and morality, and the remnants of private-owner psychology, superstitions and prejudices.

It is necessary to explain patiently the untenability of religious beliefs, which were engendered in the past when people were overawed by the elemental forces and social oppression and did not know the real causes of natural and social phenomena. This can be done by making use of the achievements of modern science, which steadily solves the mysteries of the universe and extends man's power over nature, leaving no room for religious inventions about supernatural forces.[11]

Perhaps the U-2 incident and the subsequent torpedoing of the May, 1960 Paris talks, the 1961 Berlin crisis and the Soviet resumption of nuclear

11. The *New York Times*, August 1, 1961, "Text of Soviet Party's Draft Program," p. C19.

tests have restored a more objective view of Soviet realities. The clash is between the free, open societies of the West and the closed areas dominated by the communist power elite. "It was in order to prevent the emergence of free institutions," Leonard Schapiro argues, "that the whole Leninist system of party rule was devised and has hitherto been preserved."[12]

12. Leonard Schapiro, "Has Russia Changed?" *loc. cit.*, p. 397. Contradicting the Schapiro thesis, at least in part, and showing the two-world conflict in relatively optimistic terms is the recent anthology edited by James C. Charlesworth, "Is International Communism Winning?" which appeared as Volume 336 (July, 1961) of *The Annals of the American Academy of Political and Social Science,* Philadelphia, Penna.

PART TWO

The Battleground

THE BATTLEGROUND

PART TWO WILL EXAMINE THE RECORD OF COMMUNIST EXPAN-
sionist activities since the end of World War II. The survey cannot be
complete. The take-over of Eastern Europe by the Soviet Red Army will
not be discussed. Enough of the total pattern will be examined, however,
to show the methods, strengths, and weaknesses of communist political
warfare.

It will be evident from this survey that the Communists are more often
successful in preparing and capturing someone else's revolution than in
making one of their own from start to finish. There are many ways in which
the Communists can make any revolution their own:

They can spoil a barely completed revolution by displacing the new-
born state and replacing it with a monstrosity of their own. The chief examples of this can be found in Russia following the democratic revolution
of 1917, and in China following the adoption of the open multiparty constitution of 1947–1948.

The Communists can capture a revolt already underway as exemplified
in the case of the Cuban revolution, the Foochow Revolt of the 1930's, or
Tongking before 1945. From certain aspects their dominance in the Spanish Republic can be regarded as a manifestation of this phenomenon.

The Communists can initiate a revolt under the banner or subject to the
conditions of some other person's or group's possessing a revolutionary
cause which can be carried out.

The Communists can penetrate a revolution which is planned, but not
yet launched, as in the case of the Anti-Fascist People's Freedom League
of Burma.[1]

It is not easy to launch a revolution. It is difficult to anticipate the exact
conditions, particularly the ideal timing of the attack. Once the hard work
of revolution has been done, whether by support of international public
opinion or by the collapse of authority (domestic or external), the Com-

1. Suggested by Dr. Paul M. A. Linebarger.

munists can attempt the capture of the movement. The Communists often find that it is cheaper, easier, and quicker to take over a revolt which is already under way than it is to initiate a new revolt themselves.

Initiation, in 1961, of a revolt in Angola by Holden Roberto demonstrated this point. It is significant that many of the heroes in the communist pantheon are *titular non-communists.* The Communists are fond of seeking major charismatic figures and elevating them into national and international heroes without the specific label of communism. They do not always have communist cadremen to match Sun Yat-sen in China, Patrice Lumumba in The Congo, or the many other figures whom they have adopted. It can be expected that again and again the Communists will help someone to initiate a revolution from which they, the Communists, subsequently expect to profit.

The communists' reliance on the automatic unfolding of history through the "dialectic process" means that they must remain alert to the appearance of potential allies in societies governed by ideas other than their own. They never know when the one perfect ally may come along, but they do not count on his appearance. They must therefore gamble on a variety of leaders whom they may snatch from history and attempt to make their own.

Certain conclusions may be drawn from the survey of communist political-warfare operations. The first is that communist methods and the supporting structure can be identified fairly easily. The tactics are primarily political and psychological, reinforced by the military power of the Soviet Union and Communist China. The technological development of the Soviet Union makes its military forces politically formidable in the world today. Nevertheless, this visible power does not reach directly into that part of human affairs controlled by unconventional warfare or by the dynamics of revolution.

In subsequent chapters, we do not cover all past or future trouble spots. Iran, North Africa, and Africa south of the Sahara are omitted altogether.[2]

2. Any comprehensive analysis of communist prospects in Africa must be preceded by an examination in depth of the sociological terrain of that area. Both at present and in the future the turbulent character of the unfolding African scene will dictate the major Soviet efforts there toward the exploitation and the maximization of conflict. The Soviets will seek to heighten the tensions within Africa and between Africa and the West.

Thus far, communism as a doctrine has not made many converts in Africa. The patterns of African culture and life, the African personality itself, and the feeling on the part of many Africans that they should cull features of each competing system and adapt them to their own cultural environment are limiting elements. The disciplinary and doctrinaire aspects of communism are incompatible with the African way of life

But the story of the communist take-over of China and the subsequent transformation of that country into a political-warfare base cannot be ignored. In a limited fashion—for a thorough sociological-political survey of each area would require a book in itself—we also survey the communist record in Southeast Asia. Finally, we close this section with a more detailed analysis of communist operations in Latin America.

---

and help dampen communism's appeal. At the moment, communist-party membership in Africa is negligible. There are few communist parties in sub-Saharan Africa. An exception is the Union of South Africa, which has a small party, dating back to the early twenties, which is illegal and is forced to operate underground.

The new African nations and some of the territories about to achieve their independence attach great importance to a position of neutrality in the East-West struggle. They are generally inclined to seek and accept aid from either bloc. Some nations have already received it from both East and West. The Soviet Union is rapidly attaining influence through aid and technical advice to the African governments and is opening economic as well as diplomatic missions in many of the newly independent states.

A favored technique of the Communists is infiltration through existing African political organizations, and there will undoubtedly be further attempts to march with the Pan-African movement—as long as it operates against the presence of the West. The advocates of positive neutralism, such as Kwame Nkrumah, find it more congenial to support the communist bloc than the West. Nkrumah, for example, congratulated Castro on his success at repelling the April, 1961 invasion of Cuban refugees—which he dubbed a triumph of the anti-imperialists. Likewise, Nkrumah extolled the anti-imperialist theme in the communiqué following his five-day visit to Peking in August, 1961. The communiqué, signed by Chairman Liu Shao-ch'i, Chinese Prime Minister, and President Kwame Nkrumah of Ghana, expressed the "opinion of the Chinese and Ghanian leaders that imperialism and colonialism were the 'plague of humanity.' "

In Africa, as the post-independence-history of the Congo indicates, the Soviet Union faces serious obstacles in communist penetration. The basic geography of the continent is itself a deterrent. The diversified tribes, cultures, religions, languages, and level of education mitigate against a continuity of effort on the part of the Soviets. This is the first primitive continent with which the forces of communism have had to cope. There is not a class system as such, but merely a stratification of society. Religion, the tribe, and the family play important roles in the loyalties and life of the African. His loyalty to these institutions will make it harder to win him away from them.

The ambitions of individual African leaders will not always serve the Communists, for most will jealously guard their powers and prerogatives. They are unwilling even to subordinate themselves to another African in federation, to say nothing of allowing communist whites, or for that matter even blacks, to dominate them.

Many African intellectuals, however, are ignorant of the true nature of communism and see in contemporary Soviet propaganda a catalog of their grievances against colonial rule and a panacea for the present problems. The West has failed to provide for Africa an alternative ideology of sufficient strength to supplant the appeals of communism. To some educated Africans, the vision of the future appears to be more in accordance with the Soviet and Chinese Communist societies, whose true outlines they have not seen, rather than with the West, from whose influence they feel themselves to have been delivered. In this sense the geographical remoteness of the Soviet Union is an asset to communist activities.

Regardless of whether the Communists are ever able to impose their system on any part of Africa, their disruptive hand will feed the fires of chaos that will continue to plague the emerging continent.

CHAPTER XI

COMMUNIST CHINA IN POLITICAL WARFARE: PAST, PRESENT, AND FUTURE

THE PROCESS BY WHICH THE COMMUNISTS GAINED CONTROL OF China has so many ramifications that research and debate concerning the factors involved will continue for many years to come. It is our intention, however, to examine certain political-warfare aspects in this process, with particular emphasis on the support given to the Chinese Communists by the Kremlin and communist efforts to influence American policy toward China in a direction favorable to communism.

The Setting of the Stage

Although the groundwork for the communist take-over of China was laid with the 1921 formation of the Communist Party in China, many developments were to transpire before the seizure of power could become a realistic objective. These included strange episodes, such as the early communist alliance with Dr. Sun Yat-sen within the Kuomintang, the "Long March" of the Communists from Southern China (Kiangsi and Fukien) to Northwestern China (Shensi), the kidnaping of Chiang Kai-shek, all interspersed with Nationalist efforts to halt repeated Japanese invasions.

The Role of Comrade Mao

Mao Tse-tung did not dominate the Chinese Communist Party until 1935. On July 1, 1921, the Chinese Communist Party (CCP) convened its first congress and formally established itself, with Ch'en Tu-hsiu as Secretary General.[1] At its second congress, held in 1922, the Party took a formal step in affiliating itself with the Comintern.[2]

The Sixth Congress of the Chinese Communist Party, held at Moscow in July, 1928, emphasized peasant organization and guerrilla warfare but also insisted that the main task of the Chinese Communist Party was to recapture leadership of the urban labor movement. The Congress also confirmed the downfall of Chu Ch'iu-pai, who had succeeded Ch'en Tu-hsiu as Secretary General but had been purged after the failure of the uprising of 1927. Until Mao Tse-tung came to power in 1935, there had been an internal power struggle within the Chinese Communist Party between Mao Tse-tung and the returned students from the Soviet Union. Among the "returned students clique" were Li Li-san, Secretary General from 1928 to 1930, Wang Ming (Ch'en Shao-yu), Secretary General from 1931 to 1932, and Pa Ku (Ch'in Pang-hsien), Secretary General from 1932 to 1934 and also the principal representative of the Chinese Communist Party to the Comintern from 1932 to 1937. Mao Tse-tung seized control of the Central Committee and the Party's military machinery at a crucial conference held at Tsunyi, in Kweichow, in December, 1934, to January, 1935, after the now-famous "Long March" was under way. Mao's ascendance to the actual leadership of the Chinese Communist Party was the *fait accompli* which Moscow and the Comintern accepted later in 1935.

Despite the internal disputes over leadership, Moscow, throughout the gestation period, gave guidance, support, and training to its communist allies in China. The present communist rulers of China recognize the value of the support which Moscow gave to the Chinese Communists. An authoritative study, *Stalin and the Chinese Revolution*, written by Ch'en Po-ta, Vice-President of Academia Sinica, and published in Peking in 1953 had this to say:

Under the leadership of Comrade Mao Tse-tung, our Party, by advancing along a devious path, finally overcame both the objective difficulties

1. For a detailed study of the establishment of the Chinese Communist Party and the Chinese Communist movement in China in the early 1920's, see Ch'en Kung-po, *The Communist Movement in China* (edited and with an introduction by C. Martin Wilbur). This master's thesis, written in 1924 at Columbia University, was recently produced for private distribution by the East Asian Institute of Columbia University (Series No. 7, September, 1960, pp. 1-146). Mr. Ch'en actually and directly participated in the First Congress of the Chinese Communist Party and was a member of the Founding Congress in July, 1921.

2. See "The Communist and Minor Parties" in Paul M. A. Linebarger, *The China of Chiang Kai-shek*, pp. 159-175; a convenient short summary of this period is provided in Peter S. H. Tang's *Communist China Today*, pp. 26-70.

and subjective errors and carried the revolution to victory. This is because Comrade Mao Tse-tung's views on the nature and tactics of the Chinese revolution were based on the teachings of Stalin and were identical with the views of Stalin. Furthermore, he has developed in the concrete practice of the Chinese revolution Stalin's teachings regarding the Chinese revolution. . . .[3]

As everyone knows, Comrade Mao Tse-tung in his *A New Democracy* made clear what an important enlightenment Stalin's works had been to him. Comrade Mao Tse-tung explained that the correct thesis that the Chinese revolution is part of the world Socialist revolution, as advanced by the Chinese Communists, was based on Stalin's theory. It was on the basis of this theory of Stalin's that Comrade Mao Tse-tung elaborated on the idea of the leadership of the proletariat.[4]

Comrade Mao Tse-tung is Stalin's disciple and comrade-in-arms. He is Stalin's outstanding disciple and has been able to lead China's revolution to victory because his method of work and his way of reasoning are those of Stalin's. He uses Stalin's methods to learn from Stalin. These are the methods of creative Marxists which Stalin referred to in his famous article written to commemorate Lenin's fiftieth birthday.[5]

The Communists, of course, have a penchant for rewriting history after the fact. It is generally recognized that Moscow's policy toward China during the period from 1921 to 1927 was a failure, for Chiang Kai-shek outwitted Moscow in 1927 by destroying the Chinese Communists within and without the Kuomintang. Moscow's directive to the Chinese Communist Party through the Comintern during the period was to assist the Kuomintang in the nationalist revolution through subtle Trojan Horse tactics until the opportunity was ripe for communist take-over.

It is not our intention to retrace the tortuous paths which brought Mao to power[6] or all of the pre–World War II shifts in Kremlin policy toward

3. Ch'en Po-ta, *Stalin and the Chinese Revolution*, p. 23.

4. *Ibid.*, p. 25.

5. *Ibid.*, p. 28.

6. There is an interesting and important controversy over whether a communist power strategy based on essentially armed peasant support, which Mao Tse-tung employed in China from the winter of 1927–28 to 1947, can be traced back to the basic principles of orthodox Marxist-Leninist communism. One group, led by Professor Karl A. Wittfogel, contends that Mao's strategy can be traced to Marx and Lenin, whereas the other group, led by Professor Benjamin Schwartz, contends that the Chinese communist revolution was indigenous in concept. For the details of this controversy see *The China Quarterly*, No. 1 (January/March, 1960), pp. 72-86; Karl A. Wittfogel, "Part II, The Legend of 'Maoism'," *ibid.*, No. 2 (April/June, 1960), pp. 16-34; and Benjamin Schwartz, "The Legend of the 'Legend of Maoism,'" *ibid.*, pp. 35-42. This controversy over the legend of Maoism bears importantly on the post–VJ Day communist take-over of China and the role of communist political warfare in this development. Wittfogel's position on this controversy seems persuasive.

China in the twenties. Our concern in the first half of this chapter is with the post–VJ Day communist take-over of China (which evolved in the context of political warfare). The assault preparations for the communist conquest of Nationalist China were completed during World War II while the Soviets were posing as an ally of the West. The strategist of the operation was Stalin, who had the able local leadership of Mao Tse-tung, the present top leader of Red China, to assist him.

During the time the United States was at war with Japan, Stalin adhered to a non-aggression pact with that country. Until the last ten days of the war, Stalin was at war only against the European part of the Axis. Japan, its hands tied by the war against the United States, did not attack Stalin's empire in East Asia.

Stalin wanted the defeat of Japan because without the destruction of this hostile power, his main aim in Asia—the engulfment of China—would never be accomplished. Yet to pursue his larger goal he had to play a double game—humor the United States on one hand and pose as a friendly neutral toward the Japanese on the other. How could one play friends to both sides of the controversy, double-cross each, and then choose the right time to stab both in the back and walk away with the prize—China? That was the problem.

Stalin was an expert in dealing with this kind of issue.[7] In his struggle for supreme power inside the Soviet Comunist Party, he had practiced and tried out the art of playing with various factions, liquidating them one at a time, and coming out as the dominant personality. The last act of the communist play for China was Stalin's masterpiece, although his China policy in the twenties was a failure.

In order to understand what took place in China, one should remember that in Stalin's mind and in the minds of the Communists all non-Soviet contenders in the Second World War were considered enemies. Mao, for example, faithfully adhered to the Soviet position after the signing of the Nazi-Soviet Pact by declaring that certain of the Western democracies were worse than Nazi Germany. Chou-En-lai, former Foreign Minister and now Prime Minister of Communist China, wrote an article for the April, 1940

---

7. Stalin was the master of "double-deals" ("divide and rule"): to divide his political opponents, to provoke them to hostile action against each other, to cause them to waste their strength in this way while he conserved his. For an excellent description of this technique, see George F. Kennan, *Russia and the West Under Lenin and Stalin*, pp. 241-59. For the layman, an excellent summary of the rise of communism in China can be found in the appropriate chapters of Franz H. Michael and George E. Taylor, *The Far East in the Modern World.*

Communist International in which he attacked England, France, and the United States as warmongers and instigators of the new world war.

Infiltration Through Alliance

The fact that after June 21, 1941, a *de facto* alliance was concluded between the Communists and the West against the Nazis changed nothing in that basic thesis. It did mean a change in the tactical play. If by necessity one had to ally oneself with one side of the bourgeoisie against the other, this did not mean that the goal of defeating all of them should be forgotten. On the contrary, it was an opportunity to use one side to knock down the other and, thus strengthened, to proceed against the former ally. In this sort of fight, it was anticipated that the United States, at the beginning, would be a very strong factor and would have to be treated respectfully.

The active contest to take over China had started long before World War II. The principal contestants were Japan and the Soviet Union. Japan used the conventional methods of economic penetration, military invasion, and political intrigue, while the Soviets supported internal subversion and guerrilla warfare. The United States, Great Britain, and, to a lesser degree, France, were interested but were not direct participants in the struggle.

During the thirties, Nationalist China, led by Chiang Kai-shek, was facing two fronts at the same time, one directed from Tokyo, the other from Moscow. The Communist Party of China, supported by Moscow, survived the Long March as an armed party in control of eighteen *hsien* (counties) in Northwestern China. Its operations center was Yenan, and it had affiliated guerrilla units and secret party cells and fronts inside both Nationalist China and the Japanese-controlled territories. The Japanese, after their attack in 1932, occupied Northeast China (Manchuria) and the treaty ports and cities in the east, compelling Chiang Kai-shek to move his capital to Chungking.

The advent of the Sino-Japanese conflict presented Stalin with a dilemma regarding the struggle for China. If the Communist Chinese were to continue active warfare against Chiang Kai-shek, they would help the Japanese conquest. This would be a very unpopular course and could discredit the Communists and antagonize Stalin's Western allies. Or, in spite of his neutrality treaty with the Japanese, Stalin could reverse the party line in China and Asia and support Chiang against the Japanese through his communist proxies. Since Tokyo was the greater menace to Stalin's plans in Asia, he decided upon the latter course.[8] Thus came about the alliance between Chiang and the Chinese Communists against the Japanese. It was not a genuine alliance, as certain elements in the West assumed, but merely a marriage of convenience.

Consummation of the alliance may have been rational, but the precipitating factors were melodrama of the highest sort. Chiang Kai-shek went to the city of Sian just before Christmas in 1936 to find out why the troops of Marshal Chang Hsueh-liang were not more active against the communist enclave. The Chinese (actually Manchurian) troops under Marshal Chang were, perhaps, the most vulnerable to communist propaganda, and what is more important, they did not favor the idea of fighting in northern Shensi against other Chinese—the Chinese Communists—when their own country was occupied by foreign invaders—the Japanese.

While he was in Sian, Chiang Kai-shek was kidnaped by Marshal Chang and his troops. The Chinese Communists came to a swift decision. They had a chance to urge—perhaps to obtain—the immediate shooting of Chiang Kai-shek because they believed that he had determined to avoid war with Japan, at least before he completed the elimination of the Chinese Communists. The Communists (especially Chou En-lai) pleaded for his life instead, asking only that he agree to an internal truce and to a common front against Japan. Chiang Kai-shek agreed to abandon his plans for an "extermination campaign" against the Chinese Communists, and to fight Japan under the scheme of the united front, assisted by the Chinese Communists, although some of his followers were willing to risk their chief's life by resisting the kidnaping and blackmail plot.[9] It seems highly probable that the decision of the Chinese Communists to wage war with Chiang Kai-shek against Japan after having saved Chiang's life was arrived at through consultation with Moscow because the war between China and Japan served well the Soviet Union's strategic interests in the Far East.

8. Stalin actually *had little choice* but to advocate an uneasy collaboration between the Chinese Communists and the Kuomintang in the 1930's. The growing threat from Germany and Italy in Europe and the threat from Japan in the Far East caused a drastic shift in Soviet foreign policy and its communist party line. To counteract the Japanese threat in the Far East, the Soviet leaders (especially Stalin) realized that support of the Chinese Nationalist government was a *sine qua non* of effective resistance to Japan. Diplomatic relations, broken off by China in 1927, were resumed in 1932. The Sino-Soviet *rapprochement* was later followed by a Sino-Soviet non-aggression pact concluded on August 21, 1937.

9. For details of the Sian episode, see John Gunther, *Inside Asia* (1942 war edition), pp. 245-55, and James M. Bertram, *First Act in China: Story of the Sian Munity*, pp. 1-284.

The Sian episode[10] produced a war between China and Japan. The Chinese Communist strategy of a common front with Chiang Kai-shek against Japan was not entirely designed to liberate China from the Japanese aggression. The Chinese Communists also hoped to use the Japanese invaders "as a sword of revolution to beat down the Nationalist armies."[11]

During the early period of the Japanese invasion of Nationalist China, the Communists confined themselves to relatively overt and covert infiltration inside the Nationalist areas and refrained from using their armed forces to attack Chiang's forces. In the main, they conserved their strength and built it up for the day when the internal war against Chiang's government could be resumed.[12] In short, they let their enemies bleed each other, giving but limited support to the national government and asking much in return.

According to one widespread report, the military allocation of the Communists "was to devote 10 per cent of their strength to resisting Japan, 20 per cent to dealing with the Kuomintang and the remaining 70 per cent to expanding and consolidating their own areas. . . . Whatever the relative distribution of their effort, the communists certainly gave first priority to the development of their own strength and last to the prosecution of the anti-Japanese effort."[13]

While they were ostensibly teamed with Chiang, they flattered the Gen-

10. Marshal Chang was later arrested by Chiang Kai-shek and sentenced to ten years in prison and ended up serving twenty-four years instead. Too dangerous to Chiang to be turned loose, he was transported to Formasa in 1948, along with the gold stock of the treasury and the cream of the palace museum. He was finally released in September, 1961, when the "Sian episode" had passed into history.

11. Quoted from Stephan T. Possony, *A Century of Conflict*, p. 302.

12. Mao Tse-tung is the master of the communist doctrine of protracted conflict. For a study of it, see Robert Strausz-Hupé, William R. Kintner, *et al.*, *Protracted Conflict*, pp. 1-203, and Henry A. Kissinger, *Nuclear Weapons and Foreign Policy*, pp. 316-61. Mao Tse-tung once said: "Thirdly, the principle of truce. After we have repulsed the attack of the die-hards and before they launch a new one, we should stop at the proper moment and bring that particular fight to a close. In the period that follows, we should make a truce with them. Then on our own initiative seek unity [i.e., peace] with the die-hards, and, upon their consent, conclude a peace agreement with them. We must on no account fight on daily and hourly without stopping, nor become dizzy with success. In other words, the three principles are 'justifiability,' 'expediency' and 'restraint.' Persisting in such justifiable, expedient and restrained struggles, we can develop the progressive force, win over the middle-of-the-road forces, isolate or heedlessly starting a large-scale civil war. And we can in this way win a favorable turn in the situation." See Mao Tse-tung, *Selected Works*, Vol. III, p. 198.

13. See Peter S. H. Tang, *Communist China Today*, p. 61. See also House Committee on Foreign Affairs, *The Strategy and Tactics of World Communism*, Supplement III, "Communism in China," 81st Cong., 1st Sess., p. 24.

eralissimo as the most outstanding statesman of Asia, the George Washington of China, the Iron Man of Principle, the only man who could unite China. Mao Tse-tung remained discreetly in the background. Communist criticism was confined to minor leaders and minor faults. Their proposals for reform were always in the name of improving the morale and creating more perfect unity against the common enemy.

In 1943, after the Battle of Stalingrad, the need for the superficial co-operation between the Chinese Communists and the Kuomintang had passed. Not only was the Soviet Union safe, but an American victory over Japan also seemed assured. Sino-American and Sino-British treaties of equality (January, 1943) had greatly strengthened Chiang Kai-shek's internal position. International Communists branded this move as a "policy of appeasing China's ruling class." Meanwhile, Mao Tse-tung was already in the midst of a "rectification" movement in Yenan designed to purge his followers of either liberal or nationalist inclinations and to pave the way for the era of "Maoism"—the Chinese version of Stalinism.

A Widening Rupture

As it became clear that the Japanese were losing the war, the Chinese party line changed. It was not the customary abrupt change but a gradual withdrawal which only a disciplined political army such as the Communist Party could carry out. An abrupt change would have alerted not only the Kuomintang, but, more important, it would have alerted Stalin's Western allies, the United States in particular. A major reason why the stiffening in the communist line was unnoticed was the May, 1943 dissolution of the Comintern. Chiang Kai-shek admitted that he "mistook it to be an expression of Russia's sincere desire for co-operation with the United States."

The changed party line meant that tactical priorities had been changed. Chiang and his Kuomintang were once again the avowed arch-enemy, and Chiang became the object of mounting criticism of the alleged undemocratic character of the Kuomintang, a loosely organized one-party regime composed of varied elements. American Communists helped spread the word in the United States that the Kuomintang was corrupt, incompetent, and reactionary. Nevertheless, the Chinese Communists did not formally withdraw from the united front but pretended to strive for its strengthening through certain reforms of a social and political character, including their participation in Chiang's government. They wanted to keep and expand what they already had and move into the enemy's government apparatus.

There are those who allege that the Chinese Communist seizure of power was made inevitable by the widespread corruption that came to characterize the Kuomintang during its last years of rule. While it should be borne in mind that Chiang Kai-shek never had a chance to carry through a positive program in periods of comparative internal tranquility, the self-seeking conduct of some high Nationalist officials helped demoralize the Chinese military and governmental structure. These tendencies were not fully comprehended in time to save the regime in the face of the single-minded communist effort to unseat it. On the other hand, the communist picture of the Nationalists—as unsalvageable and beyond reform—contributed to the indifference with which many foreign officials viewed their departure from the Chinese scene.

Whenever Chiang's government yielded to their demands, the Communists demanded more. Chiang was pressured by Washington to maintain the united front policy (which, in turn, was influenced by such groups as the Institute of Pacific Relations).[14] Chiang, however, refused to yield on any of those points which would facilitate take-over by the Communists. Still pretending to favor the united front, the Communists went all out in their psychological warfare and stepped up their guerrilla warfare as well, thus diverting a considerable part of the Nationalist government's forces from fighting the Japanese. Chiang Kai-shek was no longer the

14. The activities of the Institute of Pacific Relations over the years 1925 to 1950 were examined in detail at hearings held from July 25, 1951, to June 20, 1952, by the Internal Security Subcommittee of the Senate's Committee on the Judiciary. The Institute was in the forties generally an instrument of communist propaganda and misinformation, as well as a tool by which Soviet military intelligence obtained, via America, data on Japan, China, and Great Britain. The Institute was used by the Communists "to influence United States public opinion," "to promote the interests of the Soviet Union in the United States," and "to orientate American Far Eastern policies toward Communist objectives." Many organizations were linked with the Institute of Pacific Relations, including *Allied Labor News, Amerasia,* American Committee in Aid of Chinese Industrial Cooperatives, American Friends of the Chinese People and its official publication, *China Today,* American-Russian Institute, China Aid Council, Committee for a Democratic Far Eastern Policy and its official publication, *Far East Spotlight,* Japanese-American Committee for Democracy, Russian War Relief, etc. See Natalie Grant, "Disinformation," *National Review,* Supplement (November 5, 1960), pp. 43-44. For additional insight see *Guide to Subversive Organizations and Publications,* Committee on Un-American Activities, U.S. House of Representatives, (Revised and Published as of January 2, 1957, to supersede Guide published on May 14, 1951), 85th Congress, 1st Session, House Doc. No. 226, Washington, D. C., pp. 5-142. The Institute of Pacific Relations has since purged itself of this influence and regained its tax-exempt status in April, 1960.

"George Washington of China" but was described as an unscrupulous feudalistic dictator presiding over the most corrupt regime on earth. The Kuomintang was now a party of feudal landlords, usurers, thieves, and criminals. In contrast, the Communists were pictured as the sole champions of the peasants and liberators of the oppressed, the true unifiers of China. The civil war was on again. But for the benefit of wishful thinkers in Washington, Moscow pretended to recognize and support the Nationalist government only, covering its real aims by occasionally disparaging the Chinese Reds in public statements.[15]

Mao Tse-tung co-operated in this deception by pretending to uphold the united front with Chiang. Deprecatory statements made by the Soviet leaders were deliberately calculated to mislead the United States. Prior to the assurance of Allied victory in World War II, they might also have reflected a certain lack of confidence on the part of the Kremlin leaders in the capability of the Chinese Communists to play a decisive role in the war with Japan, as well as the feeling that Chinese Communist interests had to be subordinated to Soviet policy for unified anti-Japanese war efforts in China under Chiang Kai-shek and the Kuomintang.

Once Stalin decided that the time was ripe (in 1944), for the resumption of the communist take-over of China, the problem was how to do it without alerting Washington. The communist disengagement from Chiang had to be cautious and gradual, leaving an opening for retreat if Washington should wake up to realities. Moscow's diplomatic relations with Chi-

15. In June, 1944, for instance, Stalin told W. Averell Harriman, then American Ambassador to Moscow, that "the Chinese Communists are not real communists. They are margarine communists." See Herbert Feis, *The China Tangle*, p. 140. In talks with Harry Hopkins, Stalin followed an identical line. A similar statement was also given to Secretary of State James Byrnes at Potsdam in July, 1945 (see James F. Byrnes, *Speaking Frankly*, p. 228). Other Soviet leaders (among them Molotov), expressed this identical view in talks with various Americans (e.g., Patrick J. Hurley, Donald M. Nelson). Molotov presented the situation as follows: "The Soviet government could bear no responsibility for internal affairs of developments in China for which at times it had been unjustifiably held responsible. . . . In part of that country the people were half starved and miserable; and thus they called themselves 'Communists,' but they had no relation to communism; they used the name as a way of expressing their discontent over their condition; but if these were improved, they would forget that they were 'Communists'; and so, if the United States helped these unfortunate people, there would be fewer 'Communists' in China. . . . The Soviet people would be very glad if the United States helped China." See Herbert Feis, *Churchill, Roosevelt, Stalin: The War They Waged and the Peace They Sought*, pp. 408-409. Meanwhile, for a number of years an idea had circulated among some foreign observers in China that the so-called Communists under Mao Tse-tung were in reality "agrarian reformers," which implied that their allegiance to Moscow was tenuous. This concept of the Chinese Communists had been advanced in the United States as early as 1932. See Nathaniel Peffer, "The Chinese Idea of Communism," *Current History* (July, 1932), pp. 400-404, and J. O. P. Bland, *China: The Pity of It*, pp. 273-84.

ang's Nationalist government, as part of the war alliance, remained correct until almost the day of communist victory, and the Moscow press co-operated in the deception.[16]

The greatest concrete contribution that Stalin was able to make to the communist cause in China flowed from a secret clause in the agreement reached between Stalin, Roosevelt, and Churchill at Yalta in February, 1945. American military authorities pressed Roosevelt for Russian participation in the final stages of the Japanese war, particularly against the large Japanese army stationed in Manchuria. In return for this participation, the Soviets were promised, among other things, the restoration of the lease of Port Arthur as a Soviet naval base and joint Soviet and Chinese operation of the South Manchurian Railway. Nationalist China was to retain full sovereignty in Manchuria, although specific Soviet rights were to be safeguarded. The agreement also contained an expression of Russian readiness to enter into a treaty of alliance with China with the object of helping the latter to defeat the Japanese.

On August 14, 1945, a Sino-Soviet treaty of friendship and alliance was signed between the Nationalist government and the Soviet Union. Some contend that the Soviets signed this treaty under the assumption that the United States would maintain considerable armed forces intact once the war against Japan was over and would back Chiang Kai-shek's efforts to retain control of his country. As will be explained subsequently, many United States officials meanwhile took the existence of this alliance as *prima facie* evidence that the Kremlin was pursuing a hands-off policy toward the Nationalist-Communist conflict.

Stalin-Mao Relations

The reader should, of course, be aware that much of the literature on the communist take-over of China presents the view that Mao Tse-tung pursued an independent line and was often hostile to Stalin's publicly

16. There is some argument about whether or not Stalin completely called the tune. Top-ranking Yugoslav Communists have claimed that there was a basic disagreement between Moscow and the Chinese Communists on strategy in China in the immediate post-war period. In his authorized biography of Tito, Vladimir Dedijer asserts that in 1948 Stalin told a Yugoslav delegation that after the war, "we told them [the Chinese Communists] bluntly that we considered the development of the uprising in China had no prospect and that the Chinese comrades should seek a modus vivendi with Chiang Kai-shek, that they should join the Chiang Kai-shek's government and dissolve their army." Reportedly, Stalin added that "the Chinese comrades agreed here with the views of the Soviet comrades but went back to China and acted quite otherwise." See Vladimir Dedijer, *Tito*, p. 322. Of course the Yugoslav Communists may also have been deceived by Stalin.

avowed policy of neutralism toward the outcome in China. Stalin went out of his way to convince the world that the Soviet Union had no political connection with the Chinese Communists. He repeatedly assured Chiang Kai-shek that the Soviet Union's moral and material help to China would be extended only to the Chinese government and not to the Chinese Communists. He did, however, hope that the Chinese government would make more concessions to meet the communist demands that they might "engage in peaceful competition."

These are the facts regarding Mao Tse-tung's presumed independence:

(1) The Chinese Communist Party was an affiliate of the Comintern until the latter was formally—but not really—dissolved by Stalin in 1943. All parties so affiliated had to follow the Comintern line.

(2) Sun Yat-sen University was established in Moscow in 1925, and from then on, it and other colleges training Chinese Communists turned out at least one thousand graduates per year. By 1941, at least sixteen thousand were so trained—the decisive part of the cadres of the Chinese Communist Party.[17]

(3) Though there had been little direct military aid from Russia to the Chinese Communists in the Yenan period, Mao Tse-tung's guerrilla and other combat forces became heavily dependent on supplies released by the Soviet military authorities in Manchuria after 1945.[18] The amount of this aid, in dollar replacement cost, has been put as high as four thousand million American dollars. It is difficult to imagine that Stalin would supply a dissident force. The ideological and physical dependence of Mao Tse-tung was so overwhelming that Stalin had no need to temporize with, let alone tolerate, a dissident Chinese Communist movement.[19]

17. As of 1945, 57 per cent of the Central Committee of the Chinese Communist Party was Moscow trained. See Robert C. North, *Kuomintang and Chinese Communist Elites*, p. 72.

18. The Soviet Union turned over to the Chinese Communists large quantities of Japanese arms, which had been surrendered to her in Manchuria, as well as a considerable amount of Russian equipment. See Cheng Tien-fong, *History of Sino-Russian Relations*, pp. 274-75.

19. In this connection, it is worth remembering Mao Tse-tung's celebrated "lean-to-one-side" doctrine. Mao said in 1949: " 'You (the Chinese Communists) lean to one side.' Precisely so. The forty years' experiences of Sun Yat-sen and the twenty-eight years' experiences of the Chinese Communist Party have taught us to believe that in order to win and to consolidate the victory we must lean to one side. The experiences of forty years and twenty-eight years, respectively, show that, without exception, the Chinese people either lean to the side of imperialism or to the side of socialism. To sit on the fence is impossible; a third road does not exist. We oppose the Chiang Kai-shek reactionary clique who lean to the side of imperialism; we also oppose the illusion of a third road. Not only in China but also in the world, without exception, one either leans to the side of imperialism or to the side of socialism. Neutrality is mere camouflage and a third road does not exist." Mao Tse-tung, "On the Dictatorship of the People's Democracy," statement of July 1, 1949, (in commemoration of the Twenty-eighth Anni-

Interestingly enough, the Chinese Communists, after their victory over Chiang, have always been willing to recognize the contribution of Stalin and the Soviet Union to their success. According to Ch'en Po-ta, a member of the Central Committee of the Communist Party of China, "the great Chinese people, under the leadership of the Communist Party of China and its brilliant leader Comrade Mao Tse-tung, *and with support of the mighty camp of Socialism and democracy,* finally vanquished the Chiang Kai-shek bandits, smashed the fantastic plan of U.S. imperialism to colonize China, and founded the People's Republic of China led by the working class. That is to say, it was the second path, pointed out by Comrade Stalin in his brilliant work *Problems of the Chinese Revolution,* published in 1927, that the Chinese Revolution took."[20]

Nevertheless, it was tactically expedient for several crucial years that the appearance of independence between Mao Tse-tung and Stalin be created and sustained. This demanded skillful deception—particularly of the United States government.[21] The main role of deceiving the American government fell upon a group of China experts operating within the Institute of Pacific Relations. This was originally a legitimate organization, but the American Communists moved into it and, by infiltration, gradually converted it to serve their own ends. The experts on China, in turn, became

---

versary of the Chinese Communist Party), reproduced in *Pravda,* July 16, 1949. For an English translation see Brandt, Schwartz, and Fairbank, *A Documentary History of Chinese Communism,* (Cambridge: Harvard University Press, 1952) , pp. 453-54.

20. *Stalin and the Chinese Revolution,* p. 46; italics supplied. As is now well-known, there is a dispute between Moscow and Peking over the policy of *de-Stalinization* which was launched by Khrushchev at the Twentieth Congress of the Soviet Union Communist Party in 1956 and later intensified openly at the Twenty-Second Party Congress of 1961. The Chinese Communist leaders strongly resent Moscow's policy of de-Stalinization and have manifestly tried, ever since 1956, to avoid undue public attention at home (in China) to the repudiation of Stalin.

The following reasons seem plausible in explaining Peking's objection toward Moscow's policy of de-Stalinization: (a) Peking asserts that such an important issue as downgrading the Stalin myth is clearly a concern of the whole international communist movement and not of the Soviet Communist Party alone. That is to say, Peking believes itself entitled to more voice in the international communist movement and policy; (b) Peking still needs a Stalinist policy and external tensions for the purpose of justifying continued sacrifices from the Chinese people. Communist China is at a much more difficult stage in the development of communism than the relatively more highly industrialized Soviet Union.

21. On the widespread illusion in the United States, especially the U.S. government circles that the Chinese Communists were agrarian reformers independent of Moscow, see *Military Situations in the Far East,* Hearings before the Senate Committee on the Armed Services, 82nd Cong., 1st Sess., Part I, pp. 292 and 509; Part III, pp. 2401 and 2543; Part IV, pp. 2905, 2913, 2914, and 2928; and Part V, p. 3219.

influential advisers to the American government. The details of how the Institute helped shape United States policy in the Far East came to light in 1952 in a thoroughgoing investigation of its activities by the Senate Internal Security Subcommittee.[22]

The Institute of Pacific Relations group did not actively support the Chinese Communists against a legally constituted Allied government. This would have been distasteful to the American public, and it might have canceled the Institute's influence on American officials. Therefore, a myth was invented: the Chinese Communists were not really Communists, but merely "agrarian reformers"—oriental Tom Paines fighting to make China a truly democratic country. They were said to be dedicated idealists bent on carrying out the bourgeois democratic revolution, people who merited our sympathy and support. Chiang Kai-shek and his party, on the other hand, were painted as greedy die-hards resisting progress—ultrareactionaries out for nothing but loot and pilferage.

The planned misinformation fed into American public-opinion channels reached its crescendo after 1945. By then Chiang was entirely black, a despicable personality who, for the sake of a successful prosecution of the war in the East, and for the good of China, should be made a mere figurehead or removed. Communist-inspired anti-Chiang and anti-Kuomintang propaganda began to have an impact on the United States' China policy. By 1945, some were advocating that the United States force Chiang to admit the Communists into his government on terms agreeable to the Communists or recognize the existence of the Yenan (communist) government and arm and aid its forces, all for the sake of unity and a successful prosecution of war.[23]

Washington was vacillating, and, although still officially recognizing Chiang's government as the only lawful government, it began to act more than ever as a peacemaker and umpire between the disputants. In 1944,

22. See Note 14 of this chapter.
23. The Chinese Communists were being made popular in the United States at the same time that China was being supported in its fight against Japan. In 1942, the American Communists put pressure on the State Department and extracted from it a pledge that the United States would not oppose the Chinese Communists, that it would not support Chiang in civil war, and that it would work for unity in China. This pledge was given, in written form, by Under Secretary of State Sumner Welles to Earl Browder, General Secretary of the American Communist Party, after Browder had attacked the State Department. It was published by the *Daily Worker* on October 16, 1942. See "The Institute of Pacific Relations," Hearings before the Subcommittee to Investigate the Administration of the Internal Security Act and Other Internal Security Laws of the Committee on the Judiciary, 82nd Cong., 1st Sess., Part II, pp. 594-601.

Chiang Kai-shek complained that "much pressure has been brought to bear by the United States Government to have the Chinese Government reach a settlement with the Chinese Communists, but the United States Government had exerted no pressure upon the [Chinese] Communists."[24]

The Closing Chapter

After VJ Day, the picture changed—not so much in substance as in tactics. With the Japanese defeated but still existing as a nation, there arose the question of who was to take over from them and how. In Moscow's calculations, a beaten enemy is an asset. Not only can the troops, as prisoners, be used for reconstruction, but, more important, they can be brainwashed and then shipped home as a communist fifth column. The recalcitrants can be done away with as "war criminals"—a term of communist origin.

At the end of the war, there were hordes of Chinese Communists organized and ready to use captured Japanese arms. The Japanese surrender was thus to be the occasion for consolidating the Chinese Communist position in North China.

The Generalissimo's Nationalist government, at last freed from the Japanese enemy, was now ready to cope with the internal enemy in a decisive way. Its armies, moreover, were deployed against the Communists before the latter could avail themselves of all the new armament. The civil war moved from a political into a military phase. In the first few months, all indications pointed to a containment of the Chinese Communists because the armed strength of the Nationalists was superior, but then the diplomatic wand began to paralyze the effectiveness of the Chinese Nationalist armies.

In 1945, the American armed forces in the Pacific, by supporting the Nationalists, even indirectly, could probably have helped Chiang Kai-shek decisively. Moscow's problem was how to get rid of these American forces and how to drive a deeper wedge between Washington and the Nationalists in order to isolate Chiang's government from American support. Chiang's troops, as wartime allies, were armed with American equipment and hence dependent upon the United States for replacements, spare parts, and suitable munitions. Wrecked by many years of war, the Nationalist economy was also greatly dependent upon American aid.

The Soviet armed forces entered the war in the Far East on August 7,

24. *U.S. Relations with China, with Special Reference to the Period 1944–1949,* Department of State Publication 3573, pp. 553-55.

1945, one week before the Japanese surrendered. The Soviets quickly seized control over Manchuria and delayed the landings of Nationalist forces in Manchuria until the Communists were practically in control of that pivotal area. In addition, they turned over to the Communist forces the equipment they had captured from the Japanese Kwantung (Manchurian) Army, as well as the enormous quantities of supplies of the puppet Chinese army in Manchuria, the so-called Imperial Manchukuo Army. Up to that time, the Communists were not militarily strong enough to contest Chiang Kai-shek in open battle. But as a result of this gift and the subsequent American-sponsored truce—during which the United States refrained from giving any military aid to the Nationalists—communist military ascendancy was more or less assured.[25]

Whenever Soviet excursions into China became too blatant, Moscow made offers which appeared to Washington to re-establish good intent. After violating the Sino-Soviet treaty of friendship and alliance, the Kremlin would reiterate on paper its support and exclusive recognition of the Nationalist government, including Nationalist control of Manchuria. It appeared superficially that Moscow was willing to throw the Chinese Communists to the wolves. At any rate, even if the Chinese Communists were to lose, the Kremlin had assured its own victory. The Manchurian settlement provided that this key area of China was to be returned to the jurisdiction of Nationalist China but was to remain under economic control

----

25. On November 27, 1945, Secretary of State James F. Byrnes made the American decision with respect to China as follows: "The wise course would be to try to force the Chinese Government and the Chinese Communists to get together on a compromise basis, perhaps telling Generalissimo Chiang Kai-shek that we will stop the aid to his government unless he goes along with this." See Walter Millis (ed.), *The Forrestal Diaries*, p. 123. General George Marshall ordered an embargo on military equipment from the United States to the Nationalists. This embargo, in which Britain and most arms-producing countries participated, was enforced from early August, 1946, to the end of May, 1947, but, with the exception of one ammunition shipment and a transfer of equipment from the United States Marines, no military supplies were sent to Chiang until the beginning of 1948. See *Military Situations in the Far East, op. cit.*, Part IV, pp. 2579 and 2593. In 1948, the Congress of the United States passed the China Aid Act, approved on April 3, which included an allocation of $125,000,000 for military assistance to China (*ibid.*, Part II, p. 1888). During 1948, a total of $60,700,000 was spent under this program, and during 1949, an additional $55,000,000 was made available, for a total of $115,700,000 worth of military equipment under this grant (*ibid.*, p. 1869). Thus the military help which the Nationalists received between the summer of 1946 and their expulsion from the mainland was $115,700,000 (to which, perhaps, may be added minor amounts of abandoned material and military purchases in various countries). The bulk of this help came after the military situation of the Nationalists had degenerated to the point of no return, i.e., after mid-1948.

from Moscow through the control of its ports and joint control of its railway. The Soviets pretended to give but stayed in a position to take.

In the United States, the Communist-inspired campaign to alienate Washington's support from Chiang's government reached its peak. Rarely before had so many persuasive lies and fabrications been piled up to influence a country's foreign policy. Admittedly, the Communists struck at Free World weakness in China, not at strength, but rarely had an ally been so psychologically crucified.

Many Americans, including Generals MacArthur and Wedemeyer, refused to come out for support of the Nationalists until it was too late. The China story is the century's most formidable illustration of the power of psychological-political warfare. It is the only one that presents the gamut of Communist political warfare, starting with a crusading minority movement and evolving into adroit psychological warfare and finally into a military organization. There was an interplay of double-faced Soviet diplomacy, co-ordinating the Chinese, the American, and other communist parties and finally using armed assault upon the Chinese Nationalist government.

Outside China proper, communist influence on the United States government was probably most important. Washington policy-makers had not learned at that time how to read the Kremlin's real intentions and were themselves confused by psychological-political warfare illusions created by the Communists.[26] In short, they were predisposed to accept at face value the Kremlin's deceptive agitation and propaganda on the subject of China.

The Communist Party of the United States was itself much stronger in 1945 than it is now. It controlled thirteen of the national unions of the C.I.O., each of which possessed a formidable propaganda machine. It also controlled and co-ordinated hundreds of fronts. Altogether, the network

26. On July 5, 1945, the Military Intelligence Division of the Army General Staff produced an estimate of the situation in China. According to this estimate, the Chinese Communists were not a democratic group but part of an international communist movement "sponsored and guided by Moscow." This estimate warned that the Soviets probably planned "to create Russian-dominated areas in Manchuria, Korea, and probably North China," but that China could not exist without the natural resources of Manchuria and North China. The report pointed out, quite correctly, that the Communists were the "best-led and most vigorous of present-day organizations in China," with a "high morale, sharply defined policies, and fanatical devotion to their cause." See IPR Hearings, Part I, pp. 169 and 213ff. *This warning was ignored* by the United States government; its circulation was totally prohibited within the Pentagon, and more than two years elapsed before the paper was allowed to circulate, even within the U.S. government. These two years were precious.

reached several million people, among them influential intellectuals. The Communist Party of the United States controlled unions of newspapermen and teachers, unions which, from a psychological-political warfare point of view, were particularly effective. In addition, the Party had its specialized China fronts, such as the Committee for a Democratic China Policy, feeding the other fronts with Communist-designed information and propaganda. Most important was the captive Institute of Pacific Relations already mentioned. The communist control over this group was not generally suspected, and its propaganda was utilized indirectly by the government itself.[27]

Through the Institute of Pacific Relations, the Communists had a virtual monopoly over the available United States China experts, both in Washington and in China. Thus at the very source from which information was disseminated and policy was shaped, the Communists had their way. This was the psychological-political warfare machine that made Chiang Kai-Shek a hero—and then a villain.

After Japan's surrender, when the military phase of the communist conquest of China became uppermost, sabotage of United States military and economic aid to Nationalist China began. Congress authorized the aid, but orders, manipulated by Lauchlin Currie, Executive Assistant to the President, commanded the destruction of surplus stocks of arms and munitions located in the Pacific which might have kept Chiang's armies operating. Harry Dexter White, Under Secretary of the Treasury, torpedoed the Nationalist financial structure and economic aid. The "bring the boys home" campaign, alluded to previously, hastened the demobilization of our armed forces. It was sparked in the various theaters of operation by secret communist cells in the armed forces. In a matter of months, America's huge military machine in Asia, with the exception of forces in Japan, had disintegrated. Stalin's communist armies remained intact.

At this juncture the formation of a coalition government between the Communists and the Nationalists became the chief goal of American diplomacy toward China. Under pressure from Washington, Chiang Kai-shek invited Mao Tse-tung to Chungking to negotiate an agreement. By October 10, 1945, an agreement was actually signed, calling for a "Political

27. IPR infiltration of General MacArthur's staff in Japan was particularly notable. IPR personnel were used to man the government agencies dealing with Far Eastern affairs. The IPR publications were used as orientation material for government officials having to do with application of policy, and IPR materials were bought by the government and used as orientation material for our troops.

Consultative Conference." Meanwhile, sporadic fighting between the two forces continued. The Communists were still not strong enough to withstand a concerted Nationalist military campaign. At this critical stage, President Truman, on December 15, 1945, sent General Marshall to China to mediate a settlement.

The Marshall Mission

The final chapter in this crisis in American foreign policy came with the Marshall mission to China. Marshall's instructions reflected the hostility created in the United States toward Chiang's Kuomintang government. He sought to compel Chiang to unite with the Communists. The latter, although still pretending to favor such unity and utilizing the various "cease fires" imposed upon Chiang by Marshall, were merely playing for time to arm themselves. Chiang could have surrendered to them under the cover of uniting China, and the Communists would have agreed, but that was the only kind of unity they would have accepted then. Chiang, although in every way humoring General Marshall as the representative of the United States, would not agree. So, after months of frustration, months well utilized by the Communists, Marshall returned to the United States and made a report that was essentially hostile toward Chiang Kai-shek.[28] Shortly afterward, George C. Marshall became Secretary of State.

In China, also, preparations for the closing phase were complete:

There is no blinking the fact that a considerable and active proportion of Chinese students in Peking in 1948, were working for the entrance of the Chinese Communists into that city. Some were honest idealists. Some were

28. By January, 1947, General Marshall had reached the conclusion that his mission could not be successful. As he explained in a public statement, both the Nationalists and the Communists had been responsible for his failure. He was more severe, however, with the Kuomintang than with the Chinese Communists. He said: "There is a dominant group of reactionaries who have been opposed, in my opinion, to almost every effort I have made to influence the formation of a genuine coalition government. . . . They were quite frank in publicly stating their belief that cooperation by the Chinese Communist Party in the government was inconceivable, and that only a policy of force could definitely settle the issue. . . . Between this dominant reactionary group in the government and the irreconcilable Communists . . . lies the problem of how peace and well-being are to be brought to the long-suffering and presently inarticulate mass of the people of China. The reactionaries in the government have evidently counted on substantial American support regardless of their actions. The Communists by their unwillingness to compromise in the national interest are evidently counting on an economic collapse to bring about the fall of the government, accelerated by extensive guerrilla action against the long lines of rail communications—regardless of the cost in suffering to the Chinese people." U.S. Relations with China, pp. 687f.

opportunists with a realistic understanding of coming political events. Some, we discovered later, were trained agitators planted among us by the Communist Party . . .

The other side was more frightened of us—or rather of the Communist underground which gave us leadership—than we were of them. Our agitation and propaganda, the slogans we painted on walls, the illegal newspapers we posted at night, and our other "acts of rebellion," provoked the fear as well as the anger of the authorities.[29]

From then on the Communists capped by military force what they had started by maneuver, subversion, and deceit. Moscow, which had helped arm the Chinese Communists and make the conquest possible, was still pretending friendship with Chiang's government on the basis of the Sino-Soviet treaty. Deceptive maneuvering and propaganda had played a big role in breaking up the country internally and externally for final Communist conquest. But, alas, the non-communists did not help each other but, rather, helped the Communists through omission, confusion, ignorance, and inaction.

There were, of course, other factors besides political warfare involved in the communist take-over of China. According to Stefan T. Possony the following factors contributed chiefly to the conquest of China in 1949: "the effectiveness of communist strategy, antimilitarist techniques, and combat tactics; the ineffectiveness, demoralization, and military ineptness of the nationalists, accentuated by communist infiltration; the foreign assistance given to the communists; and the lack of adequate assistance from abroad to the nationalists."[30]

Toward Wider Influence

The seizure of power in China by the Chinese Communists under Mao Tse-tung was largely successful because of the Soviet Union's skillful conduct of political warfare which paralyzed the will of the West, especially the United States,[31] to help its ally, Nationalist China, and because of opportunities offered by the collapse of Japanese power in Asia.[32]

29. Maria Yen, *The Umbrella Garden*, pp. 6-7.

30. See Stefan T. Possony, *A Century of Conflict*, p. 350.

31. It is interesting to note that President Kennedy said at his news conference of November 29, 1961 that he still believed, as he did in 1949, that the United States should have done more to keep China from falling under Red control. See *New York Times*, November 30, 1961, p. 14.

32. According to Mao Tse-tung, the following external factors were significant: the strength of the Soviet Union; the defeat of Germany and Japan; the sovietization of

The primary concern of the Chinese Communists after 1949 has been the protection and simultaneous expansion of their home base in what Mao Tse-tung has termed "protracted conflict"[33] against the non-communist world. In the process, China was transformed into a major Asian power with Draconian efforts to accelerate its political, economic, military, and industrial development.

In China today the Chinese Communist Party, not the government, formulates national as well as revolutionary policies. Under a Soviet-type party-government combination, the role of the Chinese government is to draw up and execute detailed national plans consistent with the policy guide-lines prescribed by the all-powerful Party.

While Mao Tse-tung has bound his regime firmly to the Soviet Union, he has avoided Soviet control over the essential instruments of Chinese Communist power and has developed a vigorous foreign policy linking predominantly Chinese imperialistic elements of historical tradition with new, aggressive, and radical elements predominantly communist in origin.

The foreign policy of Communist China has two basic motivations: the ultimate communization of the world in cooperation with the Kremlin; and the immediate national interests of Communist China both as a state and as a major political power in Asia. The immediate national interests are specifically: normalization of "friendly" relations with other Asian nations, especially Japan; reduction of American and Western influence in Asia; diminution and elimination of the rival Chinese regime on Taiwan; full international acceptance as a major power;[34] and the preservation of "buffer zones" as well as the shaping of political forces and regimes hospitable to Chinese Communist influence in neighboring Asian regions. Chinese Communist interests, however, have now expanded beyond Asia. The tentacles of expansion recently moved into Africa and Latin America.

Eastern Europe; the nationalist struggle of the Asiatic peoples; and the "struggle inside the United States, Great Britain, France, Germany, Italy, Japan and other capitalist countries between the popular masses and the reactionaries who rule over them." If there had been no such external assistance, Mao finally asserted, the Chinese Communists could not have been victorious. See Mao Tse-tung, *People's Democratic Dictatorship*, p. 13.

33. The concept of "protracted conflict" was given classic formulation by Mao Tse-tung in the 1930's when he wrote his essay on the subject before the beginning of the war against Japan. See Mao Tse-tung, *Selected Works*, Vol. I, pp. 175-234.

34. For example, Premier Chou En-lai said in 1959 that "Communist China must have the right to participate in any important international issue that concerns her own interests or interests of the world peace." *New York Times*, October 7, 1959, p. 17.

Chinese Communist leaders, encouraged by their success in mainland China, claimed that Communist China was uniquely qualified to lead the underdeveloped countries of Asia[35] and, by extension, all the underdeveloped countries of the world in the pattern of "socialist construction."[36] This grandiose claim was accompanied by the subtle and implicit assertion that Mao Tse-tung, as the foremost living Marxist-Leninist theoretician, is uniquely qualified to provide ideological and policy guidance to the revolutionary movement throughout the underdeveloped world.[37]

While the foreign policy of Communist China blends many elements,

35. At the Trade Union Conference of Asian and Australasian Countries held at Peking in November, 1949, under the auspices of the World Federation of Trade Unions, Liu Shao-ch'i said: "The path taken by the Chinese people in defeating imperialism and its lackeys and in founding the People's Republic of China is the path that should be taken by the peoples of the various colonial and semi-colonial countries in their fight for national independence and people's democracy." *New China News Agency,* November 23, 1949.

36. It is pertinent to note that there has been Sino-Soviet friction in respect to the underdeveloped areas for the past three years, which still remains unsolved. It has manifested itself in three forms: (1) a dispute over strategy and tactics with regard to the so-called "national liberation movements" in "colonial or semi-colonial" areas; (2) vigorous competition for favor and influence among the newly emerging and independent nations of Asia, Africa, and the Middle East, as well as the nations of Latin America; and (3) a rivalry for control of the local communist parties in all of the areas above mentioned. For details, see Donald S. Zagoria, "Soviet-Chinese Friction in Underdeveloped Areas," *Problems of Communism,* Vol. X, No. 2 (March/April, 1961), pp. 1-13.

37. In August, 1946, Liu Shao-ch'i told an American correspondent: "Mao Tse-tung has created a Chinese or Asiatic form of Marxism. His great accomplishment has been to change Marxism from its European to its Asiatic form. He is the first who has succeeded in doing so." See Anna Louise Strong, *Dawn Out of China,* p. 29. In his *On New Democracy* (1940), Mao Tse-tung elaborated the formula of a revolutionary struggle for the transitional period prior to "socialist construction," claiming it to be valid for all underdeveloped countries of the world. Mao's formula envisaged a new revolutionary struggle which embraces all classes willing to take part in the "anti-imperial and anti-feudal struggle," including a part of the capitalist class (i.e., the "national bourgeoisie"). This new formula was the theoretical origin of the "four-class strategy" applied by the Chinese Communists in their struggle for power in China in the postwar period, and, as has already been mentioned, Liu Shao-ch'i proclaimed in November, 1949, that this strategy was the most suitable model for "colonial and semi-colonial" areas. Dormant since 1949, the claim of ideological pre-eminence for Mao Tse-tung reappeared in *Jen-min Jih-pao (People's Daily)* on September 13, 1958. The Soviet Union, however, has been consistently reluctant to endorse Mao's new formula or Chinese experience as models for the underdeveloped countries. As early as 1952, Y. Zhukov, a leading Soviet commentator on the communist movement in underdeveloped areas, stated: ". . . It would be risky to regard the Chinese revolution as some kind of 'sterotype' for people's democratic revolution in other countries of Asia. In particular, it is difficult to presuppose that other countries of the Orient following the path of a people's democracy could necessarily calculate on acquiring the vitally important advantage of the Chinese revolution—a revolutionary army such as there is in China." See *The Current Digest of the Soviet Press,* published by the Joint Committee on Slavic Studies, New York, June 28, 1952, p. 3.

e.g., the imperial Chinese tradition, modern Chinese nationalism, and contemporary Chinese communism, it is, for all intents and purposes, Cold War diplomacy which develops in a two-pronged fashion—the official (conventional) policies and the unofficial (unconventional) policies.

The conventional instrument of diplomacy (government-to-government relations) has the purpose of winning allies, or at least wooing and neutralizing "uncommitted" nations against alignment with the enemy (primarily the United States). But the Mao regime conducts its foreign relations by many special means—unconventional policies which the Chinese Communists euphemistically call "people's diplomacy." In essence, Communist China's "people's diplomacy" comprises an amalgamation of political, economic, cultural, and psychological warfare. "People's diplomacy" often bypasses governmental channels and is aimed at the development of direct contacts and relations between official or state-controlled agencies at home and unofficial groups and organizations abroad. Through these unconventional contacts and relations, Peking is able to derive political benefits which it would not gain via conventional diplomatic relations. Therefore, formal diplomatic exchange at the government level is often the least important aspect of Communist China's foreign relations within the framework of "people's diplomacy." And the various strands in her foreign relations, in turn, are not isolated from one another but, rather, are interwoven, interacting, and complementary.

Communist China's foreign policy has undergone tactical changes during the past decade. In the period from 1949 to 1952, Mao Tse-tung and his regime enthusiastically embraced the then current Soviet picture of a world sharply divided into two antagonistic camps—the two-camp thesis adopted by the Comintern in September, 1947.[38] Accordingly, the Peking regime branded all non-communist countries, regardless of their political

38. For details of the adoption of the two-camp thesis by the Comintern see *New York Times*, October 6, 1947, p. 3; David Dallin, *Facts on Communism: The Soviet Union from Lenin to Khrushchev*, Vol. II, pp. 255-57, published by the Committee on Un-American Activities, House of Representatives, 86th Cong., 2nd Sess., December, 1960.

Liu Shao-ch'i wrote in 1948: "The world today has been divided into two mutually antagonistic camps: on the one hand, the world imperialist camp, composed of American imperialists and their accomplices, the reactionaries of all countries of the world; on the other hand, the world anti-imperialist camp, composed of the Soviet Union and the New Democracies of Eastern Europe, and the national liberation movements in China, Southeast Asia and Greece, plus the people's democratic forces of the world. American imperialism has become the bastion of all the reactionary forces in the world; while the Soviet Union has become the bastion of all progressive forces. . . . These two camps include all the peoples of the world—of all countries, classes, sections of the population, parties and groups." Liu Shao-ch'i, *Internationalism and Nationalism*, p. 32.

orientation, as "hostile." Peking's approach to the non-communist world was rigid and antagonistic and, by and large, dominated by blunt aggressiveness that looked to the rapid spread of communist revolutions throughout Asia.

A major change occurred in 1954 when Communist China signed an agreement with India on Tibet and, at the same time, accepted the so-called "five principles of peaceful co-existence" (Panch Shila).[39] This appeared to parallel a shift to a less militant policy by the Soviet Union.[40] Following Stalin's death in March, 1953, Communist China's trend toward more flexible political warfare vis-à-vis the non-communist world was accelerated. At the Twentieth Congress of the Soviet Communist Party of 1956 Khrushchev endorsed the doctrine of "peaceful co-existence" and also recognized the existence of a neutral belt of nations, which he called the "zone of peace," to be accepted as an ally against the Western powers led by the United States.[41]

A new concept of the role of the "uncommitted" or "nonaligned" countries standing between the two antagonistic blocs had emerged in Soviet-

39. Peking's "soft" approach to the non-communist world actually began in April, 1954, when the agreement with India on Tibet was signed. Acknowledging Communist China's sovereignty over Tibet, this Sino-Indian agreement also set forth the first statement of the so-called "five principles of peaceful co-existence" (Panch Shila). Later, Communist China and India co-sponsored the "five principles of co-existence," which were widely endorsed at the Bandung Conference of 1955. For details see *(Indian) White Paper*, Indian Ministry of External Affairs, September, 1959, pp. 98-104; and Royal Institute of International Affairs, *Collective Defense in South East Asia*, (London, 1956), pp. 105-170.

40. In the spring of 1952, wide publicity was given to a statement by Stalin to the effect that "peaceful co-existence of capitalism and communism is fully possible." See Richard P. Stebbins, *The United States in World Affairs*, p. 43. Stalin's treatise on "Economic Problems of Socialism in the U. S. S. R.," written in early 1952 and published in October of that year on the eve of the Nineteenth Party Congress, set the keynote for the Congress and pointed to an important shift of Soviet communist strategy. See extensive excerpts from this work in Alvin Z. Rubinstein, (ed.), *The Foreign Policy of the Soviet Union*, pp. 25-29.

41. See excerpts from Khrushchev's speech at the Twentieth Party Congress of 1956 in Rubinstein, *op. cit.*, pp. 25-29. It is important to note the operational differences between the Free World and the Sino-Soviet bloc in respect to the issue of "peaceful co-existence." For details see Nikita S. Khrushchev, "On Peaceful Co-existence," *Foreign Affairs*, Vol. XXXVIII, No. 1 (October 1959), pp. 1-18; "The 1960 Moscow Statement," reprinted in *The China Quarterly*, No. 5 (January/March, 1961), pp. 25-52; Nikita S. Khrushchev, *For Victory in Peaceful Competition with Capitalism*, pp. 1-784; George F. Kennan, "Peaceful Co-existence," *Foreign Affairs*, Vol. XXXVIII, No. 2 (January 1960), pp. 171-190; Wladyslaw W. Kulski, *Peaceful Co-existence*, pp. 1-572; *Peaceful Co-existence: A New Challenge to the United Nations*, 12th Report of the Commission to Study the Organization of Peace, Research Affiliate of the American Association for the United Nations, New York, June 1960, pp. 4-46.

Chinese strategy. In this new conception the contemporary world is divided into three groups, two of which are the Sino-Soviet orbit and the newly emerging and independent "uncommitted" bloc which Moscow and Peking seek to align together against the third, the Free World led by the United States.

Communist China (and the Soviet Union) came to realize that not all of the countries outside the Sino-Soviet bloc, especially the so-called "uncommitted" underdeveloped countries, were necessarily enemies. India is a case in point.[42] Communist China observed during the Korean War that neutralized or "uncommitted" nations could be used tactically to her political advantage.

The aggressive and revolutionary policy of the bloc toward the non-communist countries, adopted at the Comintern meeting of 1947 under Stalin's direction, stimulated the Western powers to build up their defensive military posture in both Europe and Asia (NATO and SEATO) and strengthened Western determination to resist communist aggression. It also antagonized many "uncommitted" underdeveloped countries in Asia which were otherwise well-disposed toward Communist China. The Korean War had been costly, and the strains on the Chinese economy were severe.[43] At the same time, Communist China was preparing to launch its ambitious first five-year plan at the start of 1953. In this painful and stubborn conflict between domestic and costly external commitments, a decision to push ahead with ambitious economic goals inevitably compelled the Peking regime to adopt a more cautious and "soft" foreign policy.

42. Since India became independent in 1947, she has been favorably disposed toward Communist China. In fact, India was the second country in the non-communist world (the first was Burma—another "uncommitted" country) to extend China diplomatic recognition. During the Korean War, Indian leaders (especially Nehru) actively opposed Western policies toward Communist China, and made every effort to mediate between the Western powers and Communist China. Although India endorsed the original United Nations police action in Korea in June 1950, she warned the Western powers, especially the United States, that any advance beyond the 38th Parallel would bring Communist China into the war. When China finally intervened, the Indians opposed the Uniting for Peace Resolution and also United Nations' efforts to brand Communist China as aggressor. India also opposed the United States' "neutralization" of Taiwan in 1950 and endorsed Peking's claim to the island. She strongly criticized the peace treaty with Japan, which was sponsored by the United States, partly because it had been negotiated without the participation of Communist China and the Soviet Union. In 1952, India played the role of a mediator in the complicated efforts to end war in Korea through a truce.

43. See A. Doak Barnett, *Communist Economic Strategy: The Rise of Mainland China*, pp. 5-6. For detailed study of Chinese Communist participation in the Korean War, see Allen S. Whiting, *China Crosses the Yalu*, pp. 1-207.

Bid to the Uncommitted

Communist China's "soft" approach to the non-communist world portrayed her as the good neighbor, the Asian patriot sympathizing with all the aspirations of the "uncommitted" underdeveloped countries for national independence and economic progress. But the switch did not involve the abandonment of long-range communist revolutionary goals by either Peking or Moscow. The Chinese Communists give short-run tactical priority to "friendly" relations with "national bourgeois" regimes in the "uncommitted" world, while soft-pedaling the long-range policy to encourage and support communist-led revolutions against them.

The tactic of the "united front," which played an important role in the communist take-over of China, is often employed by the Peking regime in its foreign policy, both in official relations with other governments and in revolutionary relations with the peoples of the non-communist world to mobilize present and potential followers under the banner of communism. Its objective is to achieve the broadest possible alignment of both national and "class" forces, to bring them under communist guidance and influence, and to harness them in struggling for the common goal: the elimination of Western influence and power.

The composition of the "united front" has varied, depending on the Chinese Communists' assessment of current political needs and opportunities as well as the changing political conditions of the world. The Soviet-Chinese Communist leaders are still bedeviled by the lack of adequate answers to the important questions of whether, when, and how cooperation of the Communists with specific "national bourgeois movements" in the backward countries is possible and desirable.[44]

Following the Polish and Hungarian crises of 1956 the foreign policy

44. There is possible Soviet-Chinese friction over this problem. Moscow takes an optimistic view that further communist gains could be made through collaboration with nationalist movements in the underdeveloped countries and that the "national bourgeois" leaderships in the newly independent countries can continue to play "progressive" roles for the cause of communism. On the other hand, the Chinese Communists take the more pessimistic view that the "national bourgeois" leaderships in the newly emerging and independent underdeveloped countries have exhausted their usefulness and that collaboration with these leaderships for further communist gains will involve grave risk of imperialist restoration. They advocate more revolutionary help to communist parties in Asia, Africa, the Middle East, and Latin America. See Zagoria, "Soviet-Chinese Friction . . . ," *op. cit.*, pp. 1-13; Richard Lowenthal, "Diplomacy and Revolution," *The China Quarterly*, No. 5 (January/March, 1961), pp. 1-24; *The Sino-Soviet Dispute*, (paperback) , (Documented and analyzed by G. F. Hudson, Richard Lowenthal and Roderick MacFarquhar), pp. 1-8.

of Communist China displayed much more militant and "hard" tendencies. After 1957 the Chinese Communists reverted to militant pressure not only against the United States, as in the case of the Quemoy-Matsu offshore islands crisis of late 1958, but also against several Asian nations, as in the brutal suppression of the Tibetan revolt of 1959, the Sino-Indian border controversies of 1959, and the recent Laotian crises. Communist China combines both "soft" and "hard" tactics at the same time in her recent approach toward the non-communist world. As of 1962, there is scant indication, however, that the Chinese Communists have decided to revert to a general policy of long-range military aggression. The militant pressure which they have been exerting on their Asian neighbors has been localized and for limited political purposes.

Communist China uses all the instruments of her foreign policy—military pressure and threat, political warfare, conventional diplomacy, psychological warfare, economic offensive, cultural exchanges, and revolutionary subversion—to promote her long-range political objectives. Although the Chinese Communists employed military pressure and threat against Tibet and India, as well as South Vietnam, Communist China *still* emphasizes conventional diplomacy, psychological warfare, economic offensive, and "cultural diplomacy" within the wider framework of political warfare. She has manifested much more interest in developing "friendly" relations with the neutralized and "uncommitted" underdeveloped countries and much less with the developed countries of the West.[45]

In the sphere of conventional (formal) diplomacy, Communist China has now been accorded *de jure* recognition by thirty-nine countries of the world. These include the entire communist bloc (twelve countries including Yugoslavia), as well as twenty non-communist countries of Asia, Africa, and the Middle East, and seven in Western Europe.[46] While she has made

45. As a matter of fact, seven nations in Western Europe extended *de jure* recognition to Communist China: Denmark, Finland, Netherlands, Norway, Sweden, Switzerland, and United Kingdom. Many other countries of the West have also developed trade or other relations with Communist China, for example Canada.

46. The nations with which Communist China has established official diplomatic relations are: Afghanistan, Albania, Bulgaria, Burma, Cambodia, Ceylon, Cuba, Czechoslovakia, Denmark, East Germany, Ghana, Guinea, Hungary, India, Indonesia, Iraq, North Korea, Mali, Outer Mongolia, Morocco, Nepal, The Netherlands, Norway, Pakistan, Poland, Romania, Somali Republic, Sudan, Sweden, Switzerland, the Soviet Union, Egypt, United Kingdom, North Vietnam, Yemen, and Yugoslavia. For political reasons, Israel's recognition of Communist China on January 1950 has not been reciprocated by the Peking regime. The Chinese Communists also maintain diplomatic relations of a sort with the "Provisional Government of the Algerian Republic" as they did with the

consistent efforts to participate in international conferences and to gain
membership in international organizations, especially the United Nations,
her policy of refusing to participate in any international conferences and
organizations which include representatives of her rival regime on Taiwan,
Nationalist China, has virtually excluded her from non-communist international organizations and meetings.

Communist China has also developed an informal but active program
of political liaison with many of the non-communist countries of the world,
excluding the United States. Her growing posture in the communist bloc
has also provided increasing opportunities to influence communist parties
inside and outside the bloc.[47] And her quest in the non-communist countries for legitimacy and status in contemporary world affairs has been
conducted through a broad program of political liaison with foreign political leaders and legislators. For example, countries having formal and informal diplomatic relations with Communist China have frequently sent
parliamentary and other delegations to mainland China, and Communist
China, in turn, has dispatched groups representing her National People's
Congress[48] abroad.[49] Her political liaison has now been extended to nation-

---

short-lived Stanleyville regime in the Congo under Antoine Gizenga. Communist China
granted the Provisional Government of Algeria a formal diplomatic recognition on
September 22, 1958. Moscow did not concur although Peking strongly urged the Soviets
to do so. Algeria is now the focus of the controversy between Moscow and Peking. For
details see Isaac Deutscher, "Uneasy Allies in Algeria," *The Reporter,* November 10,
1960, pp. 21-24.

47. For example, Albania appears to be an ally of Communist China in the latter's
frictions with the Soviet Union. See William F. Griffith, "An International Communism?,"
East Europe, Vol. X, No. 7 (July 1961) , pp. 3-9 and 41-42. Potentially the most significant
aspect of Sino-Soviet conflict in the underdeveloped regions is the incipient struggle for
power between pro-Soviet and pro-Chinese factions in the communist parties of Asia,
Africa, and Latin America. For details see *Christian Science Monitor,* September 10, 1960;
"Indian Communists Divided," *The (London) Times,* December 6, 1960; *Times of India,*
August 18, 1960; *The Hindustan Times,* September 2 and 5, 1960.

48. Constitutionally, the National People's Congress is a legislative organ, but actually
it is a rubber-stamp which approves policy decisions already formulated by the Chinese
Communist Party (especially its Politburo).

49. The visit of the British Labor Party mission (August 1954) was noteworthy. Leading French politicians—Edgar Faure (May 1957) and Pierre Mendes-France (August
1958)—have been Peking's guests. Eager to increase her political support in world
affairs, Communist China has also invited Latin America legislators to come to China
as government guests; more ominous have been the sojourns of Nepal's K. I. Singh and
Thailand's Nai Pridi Phanomyong in Communist China, for this suggests the way in
which Communist China's diplomatic hospitality may be extended to include political
asylum. The significance of this program of political liaison, always well advertised,
may be noted in the variety of foreign dignitaries who visited Communist China in late
1957 alone: Vice-President Radhakrishnan of India; former Vice-President Hatta and

alist revolutionary groups struggling for independence from the Western powers.[50]

Communist China also used economic weapons in the implementation of her "people's diplomacy," and her economic offensive since 1953 has in many cases strengthened Chinese Communist influence where her political and diplomatic position has been poor. The Peking regime has employed foreign economic aid and trade as instruments competing with the West in support of her "people's diplomacy." Since 1953, the Chinese Communists have entered the field of foreign economic aid to the communist bloc, as well as to the "uncommitted" underdeveloped countries of the world,[51] despite the heavy demands of their domestic industrialization drive. The loans and grants offered by Communist China to non-communist countries of the world, especially the "uncommitted" underdeveloped countries, since 1956 represent an increasingly important element in her foreign economic aid policies. As of 1961, this aid has not been very large compared to that of either the United States or the Soviet Union, but it has

Speaker of Parliament Sartono of Indonesia; Chief Justice U Myint Thein, Deputy Prime Ministers U Ba Swe and U Kywa Nyein, and a parliamentary delegation of Burma; and Deputy Prime Minister Crown Prince Mohammed El-Badr of Yemen—the first from an Arab state. Leftist President of Brazil Joao Goulart visited Communist China at the end of 1961, as did K. Nkrumah of Ghana. For details see Shen-yu Dai, "Peking's International Position and the Cold War," *The Annals* of the American Academy of Political and Social Sciences, Vol. CCCXXI (January, 1959), pp. 116-17; Morgan Phillips, *East and West*, (London: Lincolns-Praeger Publishers, 1954) , pp. 9-54.

50. Abba, former Premier of the Algerian Provisional Government, was given a lavish treatment by the Peking regime and received political and economic support from Communist China in his struggle against France. According to some press reports, the Chinese Communists have granted between four and five million dollars in credit to the Algerian rebels and are said to be providing military instructors to help train the FLN army. See *Washington Post and Times Herald*, September 4, 1960. In May, 1960, Communist China played host to Odhiambo Okello from Kenya, whose militancy led him to an open break with the more responsible nationalist leaders in that British colony. See *The London Daily Telegraph*, November 12, 1960. The "African Revolutionary Front of Struggle for National Independence of Portugese Colonies" was established in Conakry, the capital of Guinea, where Chinese Communist aid and advice were readily forthcoming. See Denis Warner, "Proxies for Communism," *The Reporter*, June 6, 1961, p. 28. Early in May, 1961, Angolans representing the African Revolutionary Front of Struggle arrived in Peking from Casablanca. On May 8, a mass rally was held in Peking "in support of the struggle by the people of Angola." *Ibid.*

51. For details see *Intelligence Information Brief* (Unclassified), Bureau of Intelligence and Research, Department of State, No. 375 (February 20, 1961) ; "Soviet Bloc Foreign Aid to the Various Underdeveloped Countries," *United Asia*, Vol. XII, No. 5 (1960) , p. 452; *Far Eastern Economic Review*, Vol. XXIV, No. 19 (May 8, 1958), p. 580; A. Doak Barnett, Communist Economic Strategy. . . . , *op. cit.*, pp. 61-77; the *New York Times*, March 22, 1960, p. 5E; and American Consulate General, Hong Kong, *Survey of China Mainland Press (SCMP)*, No. 1691 (January 16, 1958) , pp. 21-23.

gone entirely to small, neutralist-inclined countries of Asia, Africa, and the Middle East, and has reinforced Communist China's influence in these areas.

Since the beginning of her foreign aid program in 1953, Communist China has extended approximately $1.3 billion in grants and credits, about 75 per cent having gone to other members of the communist bloc and the remainder to nine "underdeveloped" countries of Asia, Africa, and the Middle East.[52] Despite serious internal economic difficulties, 1960 set a record for new Chinese commitments. Grants predominated in the earlier years of Communist China's foreign economic aid program, but the trend in recent years has been toward long-term, interest-free credits.

While frantic efforts are being made by underdeveloped nations to rid themselves of exclusive economic relations with the Western powers at any cost, they are compelled to look for aid from all available sources. This makes them psychologically vulnerable to Chinese Communist propaganda preached in the names of "anti-imperialism," "anti-colonialism," "national democratic independence movements," and "assistance for development." As a result, they have a tendency to fall unconsciously into the traps set for them.

A broad program of trade expansion is another key element in Communist China's foreign economic program. The total volume of Communist China's trade with the non-communist world (excluding the United States) in 1950, 1952, 1956, and 1958 was, respectively, $987 million, $638 million, $1.05 billion, and $1.47 billion.[53] Communist China claimed in 1958 that she had established trade relations with more than ninety nations and territories;[54] with more than half of these she had concluded formal commercial treaties, or contracts with unofficial trade organizations.[55] Communist China now regularly takes part in international fairs in both Asia and Europe and sends trade representatives and delegations abroad. At the same time, she sponsors export-commodities fairs and invites foreign industrialists, businessmen, and bankers to visit Communist China.

52. *Ibid.*
53. See A. Doak Barnett, *Communist Economic Strategy. . .* , *op. cit.*, p. 62.
54. *Ibid.*
55. These include: North Korea, North Vietnam, Outer Mongolia, Afghanistan, Malaya, Singapore, Burma, Ceylon, India, Indonesia, Cambodia, Nepal, Pakistan, Japan, Lebanon, The Sudan, Egypt, Syria, Yemen, Jordan, Saudi Arabia, the Soviet Union, all East European communist countries, Great Britain, France, Finland, Sweden, Denmark, Switzerland, Belgium, Italy, West Germany, Netherlands, Austria, Argentina, Chile, Cuba, and Uruguay.

Through these channels, she attempts to overcome the handicaps of her partial diplomatic isolation and also to increase her prestige and influence by paving the way for closer political relations.[56]

A program of "cultural diplomacy" or "cultural exchange" has also added a significant dimension to Communist China's "people's diplomacy." This program is operated not only by obvious government agencies but also by nearly two dozen major "people's organizations" in Communist China, e.g., the Overseas Cultural Association and the Overseas Cultural Liaison Committee. Through this active program of "cultural diplomacy," a steady stream of individuals and "visiting delegations" composed of political leaders, parliamentary members, party representatives, individuals, workers, youth, cultural, scientific, literary, and religious bodies flows to and from Peking.[57]

The main objectives of "cultural diplomacy" toward the non-communist countries are an intensification of the anti-Western (especially anti-American) propaganda with "anti-colonialism" and "anti-imperialism" slogans and a strengthening of the cultural interflow between Communist China and non-communist countries. It is through this program of "cultural exchange" that Communist China carries on subversive activities of political, ideological, and economic infiltration in various parts of the world, particularly in the "uncommitted" underdeveloped regions. Here, too, she pushes forward her "united front" tactics tinged with "anti-colonial" and "anti-imperialist" movements, and attempts to export the "advanced experience" of Communist China. She has recently revealed her great interest in "cultural diplomacy" in Africa and Latin America, aided by economic assistance, with ultimate political breakthrough as the objective.[58]

56. For instance, Cambodia had concluded trade agreements with and received aid from Communist China well before July, 1958, when she recognized Communist China. Communist China attempted to use trade not only as a wedge in her efforts to obtain recognition and establish diplomatic relations but also as a crude weapon to influence domestic Japanese politics. See Harold S. Quigley, "The Chinese-Japanese Courtship," Current History, Vol. 33, No. 196 (December, 1957), pp. 353-357; Paul M. A. Linebarger, "China's Failure in Japan," ibid., Vol. 37, No. 220 (December, 1959) , pp. 350-353.

57. See Richard Walker, "Guided Tourism in China," Problems of Communism, (September/October, 1957), pp. 31-36. Communist China claimed that through such channels of "cultural exchange" she had developed contacts with sixty-three countries in 1955 and seventy-five (including sixty-three non-communist) countries in 1956. See Jen-min Jih-pao (People's Daily), January 21, 1957.

58. In the last five years ending in November, 1960, the Chinese Communists sent to the African countries more than 50 visiting delegations composed of over 400 members representing government and civic bodies—culture, science, education, arts, youths, students, economy, trade, friendship association, agriculture, military, and congress. At the

Closely related to Communist China's cultural offensive is a constantly expanding program of propaganda designed to portray Communist China

---

same time, about 150 African delegations numbering over 700 persons of the same description were invited to visit inland China.

Particularly in the last year, a large number of Africans—young students, teachers, cultural workers, lawyers, and party representatives—came to visit Communist China at the invitation of the Chinese Communists. On August 18, 1960, Chou En-lai gave a reception in honor of the youth and student delegations from Congo, Dahomey, Ghana, Guinea, Upper Volta, Somaliland, The Sudan, Tanganyika, Chad, Uganda, Kenya, etc. The speech Chou En-lai made at the reception used the theme "Common Fate Requires a Common Struggle."

On August 20, 1960, the Chinese Committee of the Afro-Asian People's Solidarity Council and the China-Africa People's Friendship Association held a big rally to welcome the Zanzibar Nationalist Party Delegation, the Sierra Leone Delegation, the Angola People's Liberation Movement Delegation, the Guinean Independence Party Delegation, the South-West African People's Federation Delegation, etc. See *Communist China in Africa,* published by the Asian People's Anti-Communist League, Republic of China, April, 1961, pp. 20-22.

The Central Committee of the Chinese Communist Party has set up an Institute for South American Affairs and an Association for Sino-Latin-American Friendship. Many Associations for Sino-Latin American Friendship have been established in such major cities of Latin America as Mexico City, Buenos Aires, La Paz, Santiago, Bogota, Montevideo, and Caracas.

From January, 1959, to the end of 1960, the Chinese Communists sent out no less than nine sizable missions to Brazil, Cuba, Uruguay, Venezuela, and Colombia. The nine missions were: Chinese Communist journalists, headed by Yao Chung; a trade-union delegation headed by Liu Chang-sheng; communist women's delegation headed by Lu Shu-chang; a New China News Agency mission headed by Teng Kang; a youth delegation headed by Chang Chao; another youth delegation headed by Chen Li-jen; a General Confederation of Labor delegation headed by Soh Tsai-wen; an artist delegation headed by Chen Chung-ching; and an economic mission headed by Lu Hsu-chang. During the same period, more than 137 missions and representatives from 18 Latin American countries were invited to visit Communist China. They came from Cuba, Brazil, Chile, Peru, Haiti, Panama, Argentina, Uruguay, Mexico, Nicaragua, Honduras, Venezuela, Ecuador, the Dominican Republic, Bolivia, Guatemala, and Costa Rica.

In the last five years, an increasingly large number of visiting exchange groups crisscrossed between Communist China and Latin America. Peking has been inviting more and larger missions from the Latin American countries. A survey shows that from January, 1956, to the end of 1960, the Chinese Communists sent 14 journalist, cultural, art, and education groups, totaling 300 persons; one medical and public-health mission, three economic and trade delegations, five trade-union missions, one women's group, two youth and student groups, and one communist-party delegation, altogether totaling 27 missions to Latin America. The number of people involved was close to 400. Invited to Communist China were 96 governmental, parliamentary, and party groups and individuals; 65 bar, journalist, educational, cultural, and art missions; four economic and trade delegations numbering 20 persons; nine medical and public-health missions of 61 persons; 30 women, youth, and student missions of 248 persons. The total number of visits amounted to 231, and the number of visitors was over 1,300. For details see *Latin America's Red Peril,* published by Asian People's Anti-Communist League, Republic of China, April, 1961, pp. 17-18; Victor Alba, "The Chinese in Latin America," *The China Quarterly,* No. 5, (January/March, 1961), pp. 53-61.

in the most favorable light. The Chinese Communists make use of all available media. Radio Peking now broadcasts daily in Mandarin, as well as several other Chinese dialects, and in more than a dozen foreign languages besides English—including Arabic, Burmese, Cambodian, French, Indonesian, Japanese, Korean, Laotian, Persian, Portuguese, Spanish, Thai, Turkish, and Vietnamese. A recent Western report indicates that Communist China was broadcasting abroad 680 hours per week as of June, 1961.[59] Special radio programs are beamed toward crucial areas of the world as world events require; for instance, toward Latin America at the time of the zenith of the American-Cuban crisis and toward Africa in anticipation of the Afro-Asian Solidarity Conference in Conakry in April, 1960.[60] The official New China News Agency (NCNA), Hsin Hua, has twenty-one offices abroad.[61] as well as thirty in Communist China proper, and it is reported that NCNA's daily news file averages some ten thousand words in English alone.

Communist China's propaganda program also emphasizes publication. She produces a mass of propaganda material in the Chinese language depicting the progress of "socialist construction" in Communist China for the Overseas Chinese. The Foreign Language Press in Peking prints and publishes books and periodicals for distribution abroad in English, Russian, French, German, Spanish, Japanese, Indonesian, Vietnamese, Burmese, and other foreign languages and publishes several important journals for the Western world, such as *People's China, China Pictorial, China Literature, China Reconstructs,* and *Peking Review.* The Chinese Communists also make a broad use of movies abroad in order to make effective propaganda for their country in many parts of the world and at international film festivals.

59. See the *New York Times,* June 25, 1961, p. 3E. The same report indicates that the Soviet Union was broadcasting abroad 1,000 hours per week and the United States (through the Voice of America) 660 hours per week in thirty-five foreign languages.

60. Peking radio broadcasts more extensively to sub-Saharan Africa than Moscow. At the Afro-Asian Solidarity Conference, held in Conakry in April, 1960, the Chinese delegation was the largest and most active, overshadowing the delegation of the Soviet Union. Particularly worthy of note here is the fact that the Chinese Communist propaganda expenditures in the African countries rose from 65 billion (old) francs in 1959 to 100 billion (old) francs in 1960. See *Communist China in Africa, op. cit.,* p. 42.

61. A new office of the New China News Agency was established in Havana at the end of 1959, and is now a center for the news releases and distribution of Chinese newspapers and magazines to Latin America. Its news service is distributed by Prensa Latina, run by Fidel Castro's government.

Conclusions

Through this comprehensive program of "people's diplomacy," the Chinese Communists have constructed an imposing engine of political warfare which aims at the exploitation and aggravation of domestic unrest in the non-communist world; the sowing of distrust between the West, Asia, Africa, the Middle East, and Latin America. Art, scientific exhibitions, movies, sports teams, military threats and economic-technological breakthroughs are synchronized to propagate the Marxist-Leninist-Maoist myth.

The prospect facing humanity, short of the outbreak of World War III, is a continuation and intensification of the Cold War. In the foreseeable future the Chinese Communists will continue, while rapidly building up their economic and military capabilities, to depend primarily on the use of political warfare rather than military means to expand their political influence abroad. They will probably continue to use "soft" tactics toward the non-communist countries while standing ready to exploit revolutionary changes in any of these countries if and when they should occur. At the same time the Chinese Communists will apply military pressure, as in the recent cases of India, Laos, and South Vietnam, in order to achieve their objectives. The Chinese Communists hope that in the long run internal revolutions of the non-communist countries, especially the "uncommitted" underdeveloped regions, will bring communist regimes to power in these countries, and they can be expected to work persistently toward this purpose.

Even if the chosen tactics of the Chinese Communists be primarily political at this phase of the Cold War, they will be reinforced by Chinese Communist military power which casts a shadow over all of East Asia. Mao Tse-tung and his communist colleagues still believe, as they did in 1938, that "politics are made out of the barrel of a gun."[62] Fundamental to policy calculations of the Chinese Communists under all contingencies is a hard-headed estimate of relative military capabilities of their own military power as well as their enemy's.

Given a "balance of terror" at the present moment, the most conspicuous threat of Communist China today is political; certainly it is on the psycho-political battleground that the Chinese Communists, backed by military powers of their own and those of the Soviet Union, will attempt to advance at the expense of the Free World.

62. This statement was made by Mao Tse-tung in 1938. See Mao Tse-tung, *Selectel Works*, (New York: International Publishers, 1954), Vol. 2, p. 272.

The traditional Chinese talents for guile and trickery, celebrated in the sanctification of the strategist Chu-ko Liang (third century A.D.) and by generations of story-telling and popular opera, as well as by the weight of the written classics, can be applied to political warfare as readily as any talents on earth.

Bewildered and hurt by their sudden arrival into a modern world, a world they had no part in making, the Chinese have been cut off from their own past by the literary revolution which followed the language change in 1915. Russians, as long as they are Russians, will read Tolstoi, Turgenev, Dostoevski, and Gogol; the Russians have their own past to neutralize the fanaticism of their communist present. With the Chinese, this is not the case. Almost all serious writing published in the Chinese language before 1915 has become unintelligible, since the scholarly style (*wên li*) has lapsed, except for archeological purposes.[63] The Chinese—more, perhaps, than any other people in the world—have become the victims of this frenzied present epoch. This means that they can throw all their energies into trickery, power politics, propaganda and political crusading. For them, the past is no restraint; they are wholly committed to winning a place for themselves as the world's dominant power of the future.

63. Among students of China there are two schools of thought concerning the relationship of Communist China to its Confucianist predecessor. The more pro-Nationalist group holds that modern China was evolving toward democracy, that the communist take-over was one of the great accidents of world history, and that there is nothing inevitable about communism in China. Writers in this group include George Cressey, Richard Walker, George E. Taylor, Paul M. A. Linebarger, Djang Chu, Peter S. H. Tang, and Stanley K. Hornbeck. Another group feels that communism is a fairly direct continuation of the Confucianist tradition in modern dress and that the arrival of a party-line state was inherent in the structure of Chinese culture. In this group belong writers such as C. P. Fitzgerald, Helmut Callis, John K. Fairbank, Mary Wright, and Joseph Levenson, the last-named having presented the most eloquent argument for this particular point of view in his *Confucian China and Its Modern Fate*. It is interesting that the Chinese scholars living on the mainland of China agree with Professor Levenson and his colleagues that China would have turned communist anyhow, even if there had been no Europe and no Russia. [See also Albert Feuerwerker and S. Chang, *Chinese Communist Studies of Modern Chinese History* (Cambridge: Harvard University Press for the East Asian Research Center, 1961), pp. 21 ff. and 181 ff.] But if they escape, as did Chow Ching-wen, they immediately disagree and consider communism merely one of the many great disasters which the Chinese people have suffered.

CHAPTER XII

SOUTHEAST ASIA: CONFUSED BATTLEGROUND

THE NATIONS OF SOUTH AND SOUTHEAST ASIA WILL BE PRIME targets of communist political subversion and guerrilla action during the next decade. The Communists, riding the forces of nationalism,[1] "anti-colonialism," and internal discord, will exploit the chaos and volatility of poverty-stricken nations ruled by weak, frequently strife-torn, and inexperienced governments. The pattern of attack will vary from country to country. The political campaign will be reinforced through the pressure exerted by massive Chinese Communist military power and both Chinese and Soviet trade and aid forays designed to dislocate the economies of the region.

When the Communists began their operations in Asia, they tried to apply the Marxist-Leninist doctrine as it had developed in Europe and the Soviet Union. They started in the big cities, where there was the beginning of a small bourgeois class, a small group of Westernized intelligentsia, and a small number of factory workers. Their operations were based on an imperfect sociological analysis of the peoples in the area. They overlooked the

1. The identification of nationalism with communism as a variant of nationalism is a consummation devoutly wished by communist programmers and policy-makers. They themselves would like to ride the nationalist tide as long as they conveniently can before standing forth as rulers in their own right. The distinguished Australian statesman and scholar, W. Macmahon Ball, makes it plain in his *Nationalism and Communism in East Asia* that he regards the Chinese and Vietnamese Communists as nationalists. This does not make Professor Ball a Communist, but it does show the ideological ground in which the issues have been muddled. Much the same point of view is shown in John Kerry King, *Southeast Asia in Perspective*. Dr. King's approval of neutralism and his doubts about pacts were not in vogue when his book was published. Within five years of publication, the official climate in the West had come closer to his point of view. Political-warfare problems, on the Free World side, are complicated by the different views of men, all of good will, who disagree on something as simple as modern Asian nationalism.

fact that variants of capitalism, feudalism, and a wide range of concepts of property had often made their appearance in the thousands of years of Asian history.[2]

There is immense variety in the area we call Asia. In some countries the peasants who tilled the land were abused and exploited by absentee landlords. In other areas the peoples were subject to authoritarian political or even religious systems, as in Tibet. But in some countries the number of freeholders or rich villages without landlord control was much greater and far more dynamic than the orthodox Marxist analysis was willing to admit. The Malayan cities were founded by merchants, not by kings or princes. Shipping around the Malayan Peninsula goes back to the time of Christ or earlier, and the use of speculative capital was well known to the great Indian and Arab trading combines which existed while Europe was passing through the Middle Ages. Even after Western influence began to make itself felt in India and China the picture of Asia as reacting solely to outside forces is an inaccurate one. Around 1830, for example, there were more than one hundred millionaires living in Canton, each possessing a personal fortune of more than one million silver dollars. There were far fewer men of equivalent wealth then living in the United States.

There was, of course, no exact parallel between Asian society and that of the West. In general, the former consisted of three main classes. First, there were those who maintained the governments and who comprised the political bureaucracy as typified by the mandarins of China. Next were the tradesmen and handicraftsmen, who approximated the guilds of medieval Europe. The last and by far the largest group was composed of the peasants.

In the mid-twenties, when the Soviets, through their communist parties, started to work on Asia, Europe's capitalistic penetration into that continent was not deep. Most Asians still made their living from agriculture and handcraft. The modern capitalistic class stratification upon which Communists are accustomed to base their operational methods simply did not exist or was present to an insufficient degree.

By 1925, it had become clear to the Kremlin that thorough reappraisal of the Asian social complex was necessary. There was no point in basing operations upon the proletariat in an area where none existed or where it was weaker than required for even a beachhead. The discussion concern-

2. An interesting review of the transition period is provided by Amry Vandenbosch and Richard Butwell, *Southeast Asia Among the World Powers.*

ing the strategy to be pursued in Asia raged in the upper levels of the
Soviet Communist Party and the Comintern up to 1928. Meanwhile, in
China, between 1925 and 1927, the proletariat had been replaced by the
alliance with the bourgeoisie (working agreement with the Kuomintang),
and after the bourgeoisie refused (1927) to be subverted by this stratagem,
Moscow began the switch to the peasants as the primary base.

The Comintern operation at that time (1928) did not exceed a hundred
thousand party members in the whole of Asia, most of them on the China
mainland. But Asian communism, having developed a political elite force
and an operational strategy more nearly adjusted to Asia, began to grow
at an accelerated pace.

Communist guerrilla warfare was limited exclusively to mainland China
until the fortunes of World War II opened up new opportunities in Southeast Asia. The use of guerrillas in Southeast Asia was made possible by the
Japanese disruption of that area, by the weapons sent in by the Allies to all
sorts of irregular groups, and the lack of foresight on the part of the Chinese Nationalists, who allowed the Vietnamese Communists to arm and
organize under their very noses—because the Kuomintang was there more
anti-French than anti-communist.

Communist policy in Southeast Asia has often been made up after the
fact. The Communists lack an accurate appraisal of the sociological and
political struggle in terms of their own theories. They have shown themselves to be opportunistic as well as tenacious, but they have sometimes
been very haphazard in conducting their campaigns. In Southeast Asia
communist victories have come only after they acquired massive conventional military power to provide the thrust behind their paramilitary activities. Dien Bien Phu, which gained North Vietnam for them, was just
such a large-scale communist military operation.

Communism in China contributed a technique whose full implications
are only now being perceived: highly politicized large-scale guerrilla
warfare. Asia, with its poor transportation and communications, vast areas,
starving and desperate populations, loose and corrupt governments, contains ideal territory for this intermixture of ideological and physical force.
All that was lacking were trained organizers.

As long as communist organization focused upon the big cities as the
decisive centers rather than the peasants, large, army-size guerrilla operations could not develop. Only when the social base for the operation was

changed to the peasants did the new combat system evolve. Thus guerrilla warfare based upon the peasants became the core of the Party's organization.

The misery of Asia, which facilitates communist guerrilla recruiting, does not stem from the oppression of "imperialism" of the recent past. Imperialism, with all its faults, sought to nudge Asia away from its antiquated techniques of production, and the new "nationalism" itself starts with the tools and some of the ideas of the modern world. The enormity of the task, however, is such that even if *all* industrialized countries would combine to assist Asia, it would take decades to raise the standard of living to Japan's current levels.

Japan Opens Pandora's Box

Although in several South and Southeast Asian countries (notably India, Indonesia, and the Indochinese peninsula) the aftermath of World War I had given an impetus to the Communist Party, it was not until after World War II that communist influence in this area became important.

With the notable exception of India, there was no very strong feeling of nationalism in most of these regions before World War II. Following the war, however, the colonial powers faced a different situation. In the first place, many of the colonies had lost respect for the colonial powers because the latter had been unable to protect their possessions from the Japanese.[3] Moreover, in most colonies the spirit of nationalism had been quickened or developed by the Japanese allowance of a measure of symbolic independence. Thirdly, the Japanese conquerors had often been brutal and had therefore increased local disenchantment with all forms of colonialism. In many cases, national leaders had come to power under the Japanese and were in consequence suspect by the colonial power. Often the colonial power faced financial and economic difficulties at home as a result of the war and did not wish to give up lucrative dependencies. In many colonies, there was a hiatus in time between the departure of the Japanese and the arrival of the Allies—or at least the colonial power concerned. The nationalists took advantage of this vacuum, and whenever possible the Com-

3. Genevieve C. Linebarger presents this thesis in some detail, together with references to additional literature, in her chapter "The Aftermath of Japanese Colonialism in Southeast Asia," in Robert Strausz-Hupé and Harry W. Hazard (eds.), *The Idea of Colonialism*, pp. 187-229.

munists tried to make common cause with them.[4] Nationalists who had
collaborated with the Japanese for the sake of nationalism were not averse
to collaborating with the Communists for the same reason, without realiz-
ing that these newer allies might not be so easily abandoned.[5]

The remainder of this chapter surveys how communism came into the
region and what the prospects are for communist success.

Vietnam, Cambodia, and Laos

Communism was introduced into Indochina by a young Vietnamese
leader named Nguyen Ai-Quoc (who later took the name Ho Chi Minh).
Unlike some other Asian leaders who were unsure of their role in communism or of their ideological viewpoint, Ho has been a dedicated Communist since the early 1920's and was in fact one of the organizers of the Communist Party of France.

After having studied for a year (1923) in Moscow, Ho returned to the
Far East with the intention of introducing a two-stage revolution in Indochina, the first stage of which was to use all anti-imperialists to win independence, the second to conduct a revolution against the bourgeoisie. He
formed the Association of Revolutionary Youth, based in South China, as
a preliminary step. After Chiang Kai-shek broke with the Communists in
1927, Ho had to leave China, going to Moscow for further training as a
Comintern agent.

During World War II, Ho reappeared in China as an organizer of Vietnamese resistance. His resistance group was called the League for the Independence of Vietnam (*Viet Nam Doc Lap Dong Minh Hoi*), known as the
Viet Minh for short. Although the Chinese (at this time under the Kuo-

4. This story is told from the British point of view by D. G. E. Hall, *A History of
South-East Asia,* pp. 698-726, and restated in part in F. C. Jones, Hugh Borton, and
B. R. Pearn, *The Far East, 1942–1946,* especially in the detailed survey of the Allied
return to Southeast Asia given in B. R. Pearn's section, pp. 221-307. The curious point
at issue was the fact that the United States supported three different positions simultaneously: first, the communist thesis that all colonialism was wrong per se and that any
government was better than the former government; second, the colonial argument that
our allies should have all their territories restored; and third, the nationalist argument
that immediate independence, whether the country was prepared or not, should be the
order of the day. Dutch troops were transported to Indonesia with U.S. weapons, on
U.S. credit, in U.S.-assigned ships, to put down a revolution which U.S. diplomacy supported. The same thing happened in French Indochina. The contradictions of this three-
headed policy in Washington have never been explored.

5. See Rupert Emerson, *From Empire to Nation: The Rise to Self-Assertion of Asian
and African Peoples,* and G. Almond and J. S. Coleman, *The Politics of Developing Areas,*
for further discussion of these points.

mintang) attempted to prevent communist domination of the Viet Minh, this proved impossible. In 1944, Ho set up a Vietnamese provisional government. By this time the Vietnamese Communist Party was using a number of genuine nationalists in the Viet Minh to establish a popularly based government. Ho's League was thus much earlier than most of the other communist movements of the area in using nationalism as a front.

There was a considerable gap between the time of the Japanese surrender and the arrival of Allied troops—British in the south and Chinese Nationalist in the north—and by then Ho's government had declared its independence. When Ho experienced a reversal after the Allied arrival, he adroitly "abolished" the Indochinese Communist Party in order to gain wider support for his "Government of National Union and Resistance," established in March, 1946.

Because of the French lack of understanding on the one side and steady, genuine nationalist pressures on the Vietnamese side, relations between the French and the Annamese deteriorated steadily. Shortly after the adoption of the DRVN constitution, fighting broke out in earnest between the Viet Minh organization and the French, rapidly turning into guerrilla war.[6] Ho, backed by Communist China, finally won a major victory at Dien Bien Phu, ultimately resulting in control over the northern half of Vietnam in the 1954 Geneva Settlement.

After the Geneva Settlement, North Vietnam was, of course, a communist state and began to prepare for the 1956 elections, which the Communists believed would bring South Vietnam into unity with it. Ho protested the inclusion of Laos, Cambodia, and South Vietnam as protected states under the SEATO treaty, as well as limited American military assistance to the other Vietnamese state.[7]

The 1956 elections did not, however, go as planned by Ho because Ngo

6. The military story of Vietnam has nowhere been better told than in Bernard B. Fall's outstanding treatment, *Street Without Joy: Indochina at War, 1946–1954*. The same author gives the political background of the Viet Minh in *Le Viet Minh, 1945–1960*. See also *Communist Revolutionary Warfare* by George K. Tanham. This handbook on the military aspects of communist revolutionary warfare analyzes the successful struggle the Viet Minh waged against the French in Indochina. Supplementing his firsthand knowledge of the country with French military documents, he examines the Viet Minh concept of protracted conflict, formulated and practiced over the eight years of this war, and describes the military organization of the revolutionaries and their tactics and logistics.

7. The Geneva Settlement and its aftermath are told from the American point of view in the authoritative book by Russell H. Fifield, *The Diplomacy of Southeast Asia: 1945–1958*, especially pp. 274-395.

Dinh Diem, who had become Premier of South Vietnam in 1954, proved to be a strong leader who was able to establish a republic and to depose Emperor Bao Dai. Ngo's government was both nationalist and anti-communist; he refused to be railroaded into all-Vietnam elections—which would have been won by the communist north by sheer arithmetic if Vietnam had voted in one block—by correctly pointing out that his government had not signed the Geneva Settlement and that he therefore did not have to abide by it.

Ho's government attempted to use the underground communist groups, called Viet Cong, to infiltrate the newly created South Vietnamese government. Although the Viet Cong groups achieved tactical successes, Ngo's government remained relatively stable. Then began the slow, careful build-up of communist guerrilla forces according to the strategy devised by Mao Tse-tung and redefined by General Vo Nguyen Giap, who is Vice Premier, Defense Minister and Commander-in-Chief of the North Vietnam forces. In the meantime, Ho's government was suffering some difficulties because of too-rapid land reforms, and the DRVN was forced to reappraise its program and to go more slowly in some of its measures.[8]

North Vietnam has been more in the orbit of Communist China than of Moscow since the Geneva Settlement. In 1955, Communist China presented 800 million yuan to North Vietnam in goods and services. This was followed in 1959 by a gift of 100 million yuan and a credit of 300 million yuan for the construction or expansion of some forty-nine projects.[9]

In South Vietnam there was an attempted coup against President Ngo in November, 1960. The armed forces remained loyal, however, and neither the civilian opposition to Ngo nor the general public supported the coup. The rebels claimed that Ngo had lost touch with the people and was not sufficiently anti-communist.

By early 1962, large areas of South Vietnam were under the control of communist guerrillas. Giap's "peasant's war" led by infiltrated Communists had shifted from a political war to an armed conflict. The Viet Cong

8. For details of the Communist Party in Indochina, see references in Note 6 above and Bernard B. Fall, *The Viet-Minh Regime: Government and Administration in the Democratic Republic of Vietnam.* See also Richard W. Lindholm (ed.), *Viet-Nam: The First Five Years,* and J. H. Brimmell, *Communism in South East Asia: A Political Analysis,* pp. 96-99, 150-51, 176-85, and 294-303. For the communist viewpoint, see Joseph R. Starobin, *Eyewitness in Indo-China.*

9. The figures are from *Far Eastern Economic Review,* Vol. XXI, No. 3 (January 19, 1961), pp. 84-85. Figures for 1960 and 1961 are not available.

were beginning to mount open, sizeable attacks against South Vietnamese troops. Only a major effort by Ngo, backed by strong U.S. support, could save the country from communist take-over.

Laos, in the meantime, had become independent in 1949. The Lao Issara, or "Free Laos" movement, had been established during World War II, led by two half-brothers of Souvanna Phouma The Lao Issara divided into factions when the two leaders disagreed. One opposed the Pathet Lao group as being communist dominated, while the other became a leader of the Pathet Lao and enlisted Viet Minh co-operation. At the Geneva conference the Viet Minh attempted to get the Pathet Lao group recognized as a military if not a political organization.

At the time of the Geneva Settlement, an international commission consisting of a Canadian, a Pole, and an Indian was established to oversee matters in Laos.[10] An agreement was eventually signed in November, 1957, after three years of negotiation, that the Pathet Lao would participate honorably in the royal government. Meanwhile, a group of young Laotians formed the "Committee for the Defense of National Interests" in order to combat communism on the one side and corruption on the other.[11]

Difficulties continued between the Lao government and the Pathet Lao, and in January, 1959, Viet Minh army units moved into Laos. Laos appealed to the United Nations. Phoui Sananikone had, in the meantime, become Premier, and he appealed for extraordinary powers. The Communists stated that Phoui was being pushed into aggressive war by the United States. At Phoui's request, a United Nations inquiry subcommittee was formed and gave official recognition of foreign aggression on the part of the Viet Minh.

10. This was one of the least satisfactory of all mixed commissions. The Pole refused to "intervene" in anything which might possibly embarrass the Communists; the Indian, leaning over backward not to be "provocative" to the Communists, fell neatly into the communist trap; and the Canadian, sensitive to Commonwealth ties, could do nothing but complain occasionally. Communist "warfare by cease fire" was not understood in Laos. The situation was complicated by French resentment over American interference and the general loss of Indochina, which many French laid partly at America's door.

11. The Lao movement was a counterpart of the young colonels in Burma, the Ayub Khan change-over in Pakistan, the Magsaysay crusade in the Philippines, and the Korean coup of 1961. Finding the old religious rationale of the monarchy inadequate, these young men discovered in military discipline a concept of modernity and order which might take their country partway out of chaos. The Communists often seem to appreciate this reaction more than do the Americans. Americans often reject patriotic young officers, suspecting them of fascism or militarism; the communists, sensitive to the play of power, never fail to attack young patriots who side with the West as agents of the American Secret Service.

Since 1959, the war in Laos has continued, with the Pathet Lao being supported by the Viet Minh, while South Vietnam and Thailand have looked on the Laos attacks as a preliminary to attacks on them. In August, 1960, Captain Kong Le, though trained by the United States, blamed American intervention for the continued war with the Pathet Lao and took his troops over to the Pathet Lao.

In December, 1960, after a battle for Vientiane, Prince Boun Oum took over the government. Throughout early 1961, negotiations continued in Geneva in an attempt to protect Laos by neutralization, since it was argued that it was impossible to protect her independence by other means. There has never been any popular sentiment toward any particular party in Laos, and various members of the elite, almost all of them related to one another, have been the leaders of various factions. For this reason it has been relatively easy for the Viet Minh-influenced Pathet Lao to expand by means of guerrilla warfare based on the terrorism of villagers.

The pro-Western Laotians were accused of a lack of the will to fight. United States military advisers operating at the end of a long supply line had no U.S. military commitment behind them. The communist advisers, on the other hand, were reinforced by the conspicuous Soviet airlift and the on-the-scene backing of North Vietnam and Communist China. In Laos, as elsewhere, communist guerrilla warfare owed its success to the exploitation of Sino-Soviet military power.

Except for the fact that Cambodia has not been terrorized to the extent that Laos has and that there is a somewhat more stable government there under the leadership of Prince Norodom Sihanouk, much the same situation has obtained in that country. It is for this reason that Prince Sihanouk proposed the neutralization of Cambodia and Laos. U.S. policy in 1961 also favored neutralization as a means of preserving the independence of these states.[12]

Cambodian neutrality, however, is an asset on the communist side of the ledger. Prince Sihanouk rarely disguises his moves in behalf of communism, but because of his avowed neutralism he must be treated as a quasi-friend rather than an active enemy. This state of affairs complicates government efforts in adjacent South Vietnam to block communist guerrilla infiltration via Cambodian territory.

Real neutrality for Laos appeared at the start of 1962 to be almost im-

12. See Sisouk Na Champassak, *Storm over Laos: A Contemporary History*.

possible to obtain. The cease-fire commission was ignored and humiliated in almost every possible way, and the Pathet Lao advanced even after a so-called truce was arranged. At the instigation of the communist bloc the Pathet Lao was consolidating its take-over of the country while not permitting the commission to make any on-the-spot inspections. Mr. W. Averell Harriman, the American delegate to the fourteen-nation Geneva convention on Laos, told the other delegates that the control commission had to be made effective first and the question of neutrality for Laos taken up only after that had been done. He said: "To talk about neutrality under current circumstances in Laos is like talking about where to store the harvest while the locusts are swarming over the fields."[13]

Even if the control commission could operate, unless tangible safeguards were established to guarantee the internal security of a neutral coalition government, the transformation of Laos into a communist area would be inevitable.

Thailand

The almost complete lack of indigenous Thai communism may to some extent be considered an indication of how communism has ridden the coattails of nationalist movements against colonial powers. Thailand is the only country of the area which has never been subjected to colonialism. Until a *coup d'état* in 1932, it was an absolute monarchy. Following this coup and another in 1933—though other leaders came and went—two men see-sawed in and out of the dominant role in Thai politics. These men were Phibun (or Pibul) Songkhram and Pridi Phanomyong. Some of Pridi's "plans" in this early period, notably his economic plan, were declared "communistic," and he was forced to leave the country for a brief period. In June of 1953 Pridi appeared in Communist China as a full-fledged communist supporter. At this time he organized a "Free Thai" movement. In August, 1954, the "Free Thai" movement shifted its head-quarters from Communist China to Northeast Burma. Since that time most communist forces in Thailand have been underground, and there are no communist Thai leaders of relative political importance.

A revolutionary group led by Field Marshal Sarit Thanarat achieved a coup in 1957 against Field Marshal Phibun Songkhram and abrogated parliamentary government in October of 1958. Sarit's government, however, remained anti-communist. The Thai government has continued to

13. *Washington Evening Star*, July 12, 1961, p. 16.

uphold SEATO and has been quite willing to send support against the
Pathet Lao and North Vietnamese troops in Laos.[14]

Nevertheless, in July of 1961, Prime Minister Marshal Sarit Thanarat
announced that Thailand was willing and ready to accept Soviet aid if it
were offered without conditions, particularly if it were offered in the form
of loans or investments. The Thais are realistic political manipulators—as
attested by their ability to retain their independence by playing competing colonial powers against each other throughout the nineteenth century.
Their continued adherence to SEATO will depend in large measure on
American determination and ability to stop the cancerous spread of communism from Laos into the remaining free countries of Southeast Asia.

Burma

With Burma one moves into an area in which the Communists have
long been active. There was little Comintern interest in Burma until
shortly before World War II broke out in the Far East. In part, this was
because Burma was regarded as a province of India (following British administration), and only in 1939 was the Burmese Communist Party
formed.[15]

In 1943, Burma was granted "independence" under Japanese auspices.
Only the desire not to allow the Japanese to split Burmese leaders into
numerous ideological factions held the Burmese government together. As
the war progressed, one Burmese leader, Thakin Than Tun, former Executive Secretary of the Burmese Communist Party, made contact with
the Chinese Communists. At the same time, Aung San was preparing to
take his Burmese Independence Army over to the Allies. The new name for
his resistance group was the Anti-Fascist People's Freedom League. Its
goals were to rid the country of the Japanese and to achieve complete independence from Britain.

After the end of the war, when the British had reoccupied Rangoon

14. For more detailed studies (up to 1957), see J. H. Brimmell, *op cit.*, pp. 111-16,
153-55, 240-46, and 344-54. See also Frank N. Trager (ed.), *Marxism in Southeast Asia:
A Study of Four Countries,* Chapter 3, "Thailand and Marxism," by David A. Wilson,
pp. 58-101.

15. On the development of the Communist Party in Burma, see Brimmell, *op. cit.*,
pp. 116-21, 155-58, 185-94, and 308-20, and Trager, *op. cit.*, "Marxism in Burma," by
John Seabury Thomson, pp. 14-57, as well as Hugh Tinker, *The Union of Burma: A
Study of the First Years of Independence,* and Geoffrey Fairbairn, "Some Minority Problems in Burma," *Pacific Affairs,* Vol. XXX, No. 4 (December, 1957). On Burmese
socialism, see U Ba Swe, *The Burmese Revolution,* and U Nu, *Towards a Welfare State.*

with the help of Aung San and his military group, now called the Burma National Army, British policy remained confused because the British did not believe in the existence of a nationally organized resistance group which opposed not only the Japanese but also the British in Burma. The first British proposals were to place Burma in a political position of even less independence than before the war.[16]

Aung San and the British, however, carried on negotiations, and finally, in 1947, the British agreed that the new Burmese Constituent Assembly, which was to be elected in April, 1947, should devise a government for an independent Burma. The Burmese Communist Party decided to trust the British, after initial confusion, and participated in the elections, but another faction, the Communist Party (Burma) did not. The Constituent Assembly met in June, 1947, and elected Thakin Nu (who later returned to the title U Nu) as President of the Assembly. Aung San, who might have been an effective national leader, was murdered by a political rival in 1947.

U Nu attempted to bring the factions of Burmese politics together, but they resisted his efforts. The factions included, in addition, some Chinese anti-communist troops who had been left in northern Burma and were living off the countryside; armed bands of Muslims, called Mujahids, roaming in Arakan; and Red Flag communist groups (called "Trotsky-ists"), led by Thakin Soe, and White Flag communist groups (called "Stalinists"), led by Thakin Than Tun, both agitating separately for the overthrow of the "British-imperialist-dominated" government of Burma.

In May, 1948, U Nu issued a program for leftist unity which went a long way in an attempt to conciliate the feuding Marxist groups. Among its points were: (1) the securing of political and economic relations with Soviet Russia and the "democratic countries of Eastern Europe in the same way as we are now having these relations with Britain and the United States"; (2) the nationalization of capitalist undertakings and redistribution of land, with abolition of all private ownership of land and the land being distributed "only among the tillers of the soil"; (3) the transformation of the government from a bureaucratic to a "democratic" one; and (4) the

16. The developments of this period are the subject of a doctoral dissertation by Oliver Edmund Clubb, Jr., now of the staff at the Brookings Institution, who compiled a careful summary of the concrete events and alliances of the Burmese independence movement on the basis of interviews with the surviving revolutionaries in Rangoon. He expects to publish this study. The dissertation is on deposit at the School of Advanced International Studies of The Johns Hopkins University, Washington, D. C.

formation of a "league for the propagation of Marxist Doctrine, composed of Socialists, Communists, *Pyithu Yebawa* (People's Volunteer Organization members or PVOs) and others who lean towards Marxism and to read, discuss and propagate the writings of Marx, Engels, Lenin, Stalin, Mao Tse-tung, Tito, Dimitrov and other apostles of Marxism."[17]

The Communists refused to accept this friendly hand and continued to call for open insurrection. In early 1951, Than Tun announced a program leading to a victory of a "People's Democratic Government" which was to start on the Chinese frontier and spread south. As a first step the Communists tried to force the government to accept the Burmese Communist Party in a coalition government, with the intention of infiltrating the administration. Fortunately, however, U Nu resisted the offer. Although the Communist Party was outlawed in 1953 it continued its agitation, leading almost to civil war; factionalism, combined with Chinese Communist pressure, finally brought a cessation of fighting in 1956. The fact that in 1956 Chinese Communist troops flowed into a number of Burmese border areas, particularly in the Wa state and the Kachin state, helped to give rise to a feeling of antipathy toward Communist China and in effect strengthened the government's position.

In 1958, General Ne Win assumed governmental power after the army discovered what was believed to be a communist plot to take over the government and assassinate the leaders. U Nu resigned as Premier. Although Ne Win denounced the communist actions within Burma, in January, 1960, he made a trip to Peking, where he signed two agreements: one was a treaty of friendship; the other was a settlement of the Burma-China border dispute with the 1941 line being accepted. U Nu then returned to the government following a victory in the February elections, and in October, 1960, the treaty with Communist China was signed.

Despite the internal difficulties which Burma has had to face since World War II, she might have achieved a relatively stable socialist government were it not for outside influences. The Burmese were shocked at the defection of Aleksandr Y. Kaznacheyev from the Soviet Embassy in Rangoon and granted him political asylum. Kaznacheyev has stated that his mission in Burma, and the mission of others sent as technical experts or Soviet Embassy members, was and is to subvert the nationalist political forces and

17. Thakin Nu, *Towards Peace and Democracy,* p. 94.

politicians and to gather up secret information about the Burmese government.

The Kaznacheyev findings could have educated a more modern and responsive audience than that of Rangoon. Though highly sophisticated in terms of their old Buddhist civilization, the Burmese are unprepared to believe that the modern world employs conspiracies as complicated and as murderous as the clouds of sedition which used to envelop their own ancient dynastic courts at Ava and Pegu. They have been taught by their British ex-masters that the modern world is a kindly and law-abiding place, and it is in their national temperament and tradition to attempt to believe the best of everyone. They therefore missed the plain truth which Kaznacheyev was trying to tell them. In Southeast Asia, the communist movement has found parties unreliable in many cases. *The Communists therefore use their own government channels as direct instruments of intervention and subversion.*

The communist movement in Burma did not have to wait for its local communist party to mature. Given the caliber of the cadres available, that might have taken a long time. The Communists used their own people, acting through the Soviet and Chinese Communist embassies, and they employed increasingly open weapons of seduction and penetration. Loans and intergovernmental "gifts" on the surface supplemented the work of secret agents scattered among the population.

One of the goals of the secret agents has been to undermine genuine neutrality in Burma. One method has been the planting of falsified articles and letters in Burmese newspapers, purporting to show that the United States supported the rebels against the Indonesian government. Other such articles portray various Southeast Asian leaders as corrupt or as tools of colonial nations. Ne Win, after taking over the government, was termed a Fascist and an imperialist, and the next immediate goal of the Soviet agents was to split and weaken and drive out pro-Western officers from the army. The treaties accorded Ne Win by Peking may have been further evidence of these attempts to weaken the army.[18]

Burma appears to be less and less able to resist increasingly stronger Communist influence on her internal and external affairs. Whether this country will become a kind of communist protectorate remains to be seen.

18. Aleksandr Y. Kaznacheyev, "Soviet Operation Burma," *The New Leader,* January 18, 1960.

Such a development would, of course, have an adverse impact on Thailand's orientation.

Malaya and Singapore

The former British Federation of Malaya, from which Singapore was recently separated, has long been a hotbed of communist machinations. The Indonesian communist leader, Tan Malaka, introduced communism in 1925 by inducing the Chinese Communist Party to engage in activities there. Most communist activities in Singapore and Malaya were carried on by the Chinese or by the Indonesian Communists passing through this key communications center. They organized trade-unions among the Chinese and did some teaching in the schools, as well as organizing a Malayan revolutionary committee. After Chiang Kai-shek broke with the Communists in China in 1927, the Communists operating in Malaya had to abandon the cover of the Kuomintang Party, and so they organized a "South Seas (*nan yang*) Communist Party," which was to foment "nationalist" revolutionary movements in Indonesia, the Indochinese peninsula, Siam, and Burma, as well as Malaya.

It was the opportunity for guerrilla fighting during World War II which gave the Malayan Communist Party its greatest impetus. Although some Malay resistance groups were formed, most of the guerrillas and guerrilla supporters were Chinese and were in turn communist or communist-supported. The British built up many of their own later difficulties by supporting the Chinese Communist guerrillas against the Chinese Kuomintang guerrillas, to the point that the latter were almost completely wiped out.[19]

After the return of the British to Malaya at the end of the war, there was a brief carryover of the wartime co-operation of the Malayan Communist Party with the British. While ostensibly co-operating with the British by allowing the General Labor Union and other communist affiliates to become members of the Singapore Advisory Council at British invitation, the Communists were actually using all possible methods to obstruct the British military administration. Communist newspapers began openly

19. This policy parallels British support during World War II of Communist Tito in Yugoslavia to the net detriment of the West. On the guerrilla campaigns of the Communists during World War II, see F. Spencer Chapman, *The Jungle Is Neutral*. On the general history of the Communist Party in Malaya, see Gene Z. Hanrahan, *The Communist Struggle in Malaya*, and Victor Purcell, *The Chinese in Malaya*, which covers the Chinese part of the Communist influence in Malaya through the immediate postwar years.

calling the British government "fascist" and saying that the British were worse than the Japanese. After a series of increasingly violent communist-instigated strikes which crippled recovery in Malaya, the Communist Party went underground.

It became evident that the one real goal of the Communists in Malaya was the disruption of government. They continued a terrorist campaign of murder and intimidation, as well as setting up parties in opposition to genuinely non-communist nationalistic parties, and the penetration of the genuine parties.

By 1948, the guerrilla war carried on by the Communists (mostly Chinese) broke out in earnest. With the failure to register in 1949, the Malayan Communist Party became illegal. The China Democratic League, which was linked to the Chinese Communist Party, was also banned. However, since the Chinese Communist Party and the Kuomintang proper were not Malayan parties, membership in these parties was not banned, a fact which made checking on the Communists difficult for the British.

In 1948, the British had decided on the form of a federation for the government of Malaya. Although good government was being provided, this was not sufficient. Many non-communist Malays desired self-government, and the nationalistic propaganda used by the Communists was their chief weapon in gaining mass support. The fact that complicated regulations regarding citizenship made it difficult for a Chinese to become a Malayan citizen was another propaganda weapon. The Communist Chinese in the area were using the Chinese schools, taught in the Chinese language, as centers of communist propaganda and as recruiting centers for guerrillas. Not until Lieutenant General Sir Harold Briggs inaugurated the "Briggs Plan" for removal of the squatters and villagers who were giving food and shelter to the guerrillas did the British army, aided by the Malays, begin to win.

High Commissioner Sir Gerald Templer also carried out a vigorous campaign against the guerrillas. When in 1957 Malaya became independent, the death knell began to sound for the guerrilla army. With Malayan independence, the Communists lost one of their chief means of gaining popular support. The fact that there was closer co-operation with Thailand in policing the borders from 1958 on also helped in wiping out the guerrilla forces.

The new state of Singapore is another focal point of communist efforts. It is strategically located. It remains a British colony largely because the peninsula of Malaya does not want it as a part of independent Malaya: the large number of Chinese living in Singapore, combined with the Chinese of the peninsula, would make the Chinese the most numerous single group in a combined Malaya and Singapore. In the first election held in the self-governing colony of Singapore in April, 1955, the communist-supported People's Action Party won three of the four seats for which it put up candidates. In 1957, when Singapore became an autonomous state within the Commonwealth, riots and difficulties continued, but there was increased co-operation among non-communist groups.

Although the Communist Party as such is illegal in the colony, Singapore remains vulnerable to communist penetration, if not control.[20]

Indonesia

Communism was introduced into Indonesia by a Dutch Marxist, H. J. F. M. Sneevliet, who, with others, organized a Marxist party in the Indies in 1914—the Indies Social-Democratic Association. A few years later, the Association split and a faction formed in 1920 called the Communist Union of the Indies. This party joined the Comintern. Tan Malaka (mentioned in the discussion of other Southeast Asian countries above) went to Russia, where he became a member of the Comintern organization.

The fledgling Communist Party decided to concentrate on trade-unions, although the Comintern attempted to direct the Communists to make temporary common cause with the nationalists and the People's Associations. Extremists in the Indonesian Communist Party decided on a revolution immediately. Tan Malaka felt that this revolution was premature, but he was unable to prevent it and the abortive attempt occurred in 1926. The consequent failure meant a setback of many years for the Indonesian Communist Party.

Concurrently, the idea of independence was advanced by a group of Indonesian students in the Netherlands who had formed the *Perhimpunan* ("Association") *Indonesia* and were willing to associate with the Communists for the sake of nationalism, although they were not themselves communists. By 1927, a new party led by a young engineer, Sukarno, had been formed; it was called the Partai Nasional Indonesia (PNI) or Indonesian

20. For further discussion of post–World War II developments in Malaya and Singapore, see Arthur Campbell, *Jungle Green*, J. B. Perry Robinson, *Transformation in Malaya*, M. C. A. Henniker, *Red Shadow over Malaya*, and Brimmell, *op. cit.*, pp. 77-88, 146-50, 194-212, and 320-40.

Nationalist Party. Sukarno and other nationalist leaders were eventually arrested and exiled to the outer islands in the early 1930's. There they remained until released by the Japanese during World War II.

Sukarno and Hatta, when released by the Japanese, collaborated with them to further the nationalist movement in Indonesia. They were successful in this, setting up an Indonesian government as Japan was falling in 1945. Not until the end of World War II did the Partai Komunis Indonesia (PKI) or Indonesian Communist Party become active again.

The Dutch-Indonesian War culminated in independence for Indonesia in 1949. During this period, the PKI was still weak, but the People's Democratic Front was established, a group which had a definitely leftist orientation. This front exhorted the people to continue the struggle against Dutch imperialism. Rivalry between the various communist leaders, however, prevented any concerted effort, and when in 1948 the Communists attempted an uprising at Madiun, they were put down by Sukarno's forces.

Only after this failure did the Indonesian Communist Party regroup and really begin to gain power. In part, the Party's rise appears to have been fostered by the deteriorating economy. The Communists also seized on the question of West "Irian" (Western New Guinea), which the Netherlands retained and which Indonesia claimed as her own. They were able to use anti-imperialist slogans to advantage to inflame Indonesian nationalism.

In the 1955–1956 national elections, the PKI was estimated to have polled 20 per cent of the votes, making it one of the four largest parties. The others were Sukarno's Nationalist Party and two Muslim parties, the Masjumi and the conservative Nahdatul Ulama. In the 1957 elections, the PKI polled more than 25 per cent of the votes in the local and regional elections. From almost nothing the PKI had increased in less than a decade to a membership estimated at between 1.5 million and 1.8 million, making it one of the largest parties outside the actual communist bloc.

Since the Bandung Conference in 1955 and Sukarno's visit to Moscow in 1956 the Indonesian government has been increasingly less Western-oriented, and this may have been a factor in the growth of the PKI. Soviet-bloc aid to Indonesia has also increased. Between 1954 and 1959, communist-bloc aid to Indonesia in the military field is estimated to have been $163 million, and economic assistance $239 million, as against U.S. assistance of $189 million.[21]

21. Willard Hanna, in his *Bung Karno's Indonesia*, pp. 4-6, estimates the total of communist-bloc aid as being about $259.2 million for more or less the same period.

President Sukarno's program of "guided democracy" has been an encouragement to leftist groups who saw in it a reflection of Soviet thinking. In his appointed cabinet of June, 1960, the PKI had the largest representation of any group, and PKI leaders Aidit and Njoto (both Politburo members) were appointed members of the Supreme Advisory Council. Sakirman (also a Politburo member) was appointed a member of the National Planning Council, as was Wikana (a Central Committee member). The program of the PKI has evidently been to make the Indonesian economy so dependent on Soviet-bloc aid that it cannot afford to alienate the Communists.

In the wake of Khrushchev's February, 1960 visit to Indonesia, Russia extended a credit of $250 million for economic aid. The one Indonesian group which had appeared to be still firmly anti-communist was the army, headed by General A. H. Nasution. In January, 1961, however, General Nasution, Minister for National Defense and Chief of Staff of the Army, visited Moscow and accepted an offer of $400 million worth of arms.[22]

The amount of Russian aid pledged to Indonesia is second only to that given to Communist China. By this aid the Soviet Union hopes, perhaps, to buy off the Indonesian army, as earlier the Russians had provided military aid for the Indonesian air force and navy. It appears almost certain that the Soviets have promised moral if not military support in the event that Indonesia launches the frequently threatened military attack against the Netherlands forces in Western New Guinea.

The conclusion that the Soviet Union supports the Indonesian intent to "liberate" West Irian[23] is borne out by the fact that although the National Front for the Liberation of West Irian, which was created as an anti-communist instrument by Nasution in 1958, was eradicated by Sukarno's order as of January 31, 1961, a new body for the same purpose was created in March, 1961, with Sukarno as Chairman, and includes Nasution and Aidit, the PKI leader.[24]

22. Much of the information in regard to the $400 million arms agreement is from two articles by Guy J. Pauker in *Asian Survey*. These are "General Nasution's Mission to Moscow," Vol. I, No. 1, pp. 13-22, and "Current Communist Tactics in Indonesia," Vol. I, No. 3, pp. 25-26.

23. Indonesia claims West Irian, though there is no ethnic base for the claim, on the historical basis that this area, Java, and Sumatra were all once under Dutch rule.

24. On earlier developments in Indonesia, see John O. Sutter, *Indonesianisasi: Politics in a Changing Economy, 1940–1955*, George McTurnan Kahin, *Nationalism and Revolution in Indonesia*, Brimmell, *op. cit.*, pp. 77-88, 144-46, 219-40, and 354-77, and Saul Rose, *Socialism in Southern Asia*, pp. 144-75.

If the PKI is able to maintain its legal existence and Soviet influence continues to grow, it is possible that Indonesia may be the first Southeast Asian country to be taken over by a popularly based, legally elected communist government. This is not to say that communism is popular outside Java, but if Indonesia remains a unitary state, the fact of Java's overwhelmingly more numerous population would be enough to carry an election. The anti-communist rebel government, which had some of Indonesia's most able leaders, appears to have dwindled almost to the vanishing point. Unless there is some drastic and unforeseen change, Indonesia may slip into the communist orbit.[25]

The Philippines

Communist activity began in the Philippines following World War I. Tan Malaka, who played an important part in Indonesian communism and was the chief Comintern agent for the Southeast Asian area, was sent to the Philippines in 1925 and gained the sympathy of some Filipinos. A few Filipinos took part in the Sixth Comintern Congress in 1928, and in 1930 the Communist Party of the Philippines was founded.

The Japanese invasion and the guerrilla activities of the Hukbalahap (the fighting arm of the Communists in the Philippines) gave new impetus to the movement. By the end of World War II, the Hukbalahap was a trained, armed, organized guerrilla army.

On July 4, 1946, the Philippines became independent. The Communists could therefore not pose as liberating the country from the colonialists, though they claimed to be protectors of the people and stated a desire to eliminate "fascism" in the Philippines. Unfortunately, some of the early days of independence in the Philippines lent color to the communist claims: there was some corruption, usury, and absentee-landlordism. Also, it was some time before Filipino authorities recognized the seriousness of the situation. After Ramon Magsaysay was appointed Secretary of Defense in 1949, and particularly after his election to the presidency in 1953, the situation improved rapidly. Magsaysay's honesty and his obvious inten-

25. A recent book on Indonesia written by an American long in Indonesian government employ takes a more heartening view of the future. Jeanne S. Mintz in her *Indonesia: A Profile*, points out that communism is handicapped in Indonesia by its close association with Chinese power—long a subject of dread to the Javanese and their neighbors. The conflicts between Indonesia and the communist bloc derive chiefly from the attempts of the Peking Embassy to use local Chinese as a politico-economic beachhead, pp. 170-75.

tions of improving the lot of the common people, combined with his military efficiency, his protection of villages from communist terrorism, and his willingness to give surrendered Huks a chance at a new life under better conditions, made the continuance of the Hukbalahap of short duration. After the surrender of Huk leader Luis Taruk in 1954, the army rapidly disintegrated.

The legal status of the Communist Party in the Philippines continued in doubt. President Magsaysay had wanted it outlawed; the Committee on Un-Filipino Activities maintained that it had been outlawed in 1932 and remained outlawed. When the Communist Party put up candidates for the 1955 elections, a new Committee recommended outlawing the Party once more. The law had not been passed at the time that President Magsaysay was killed in an airplane crash in 1957. Although some of the difficulties existing in the early days of Philippine independence recurred after President Magsaysay's death and although communist and some non-communist leaders have deplored the continued close association with the United States as a disguised form of colonialism, the revolutionary army of the Hukbalahap has not regained its strength or its appeal. If corruption can be kept minimal in the Philippine government, the program for improvement of the people's conditions expanded, and elections carried on honestly and without terrorism, it is unlikely that the Communists will regain any degree of popular support, although there still exists a group of hardcore Communists. The land-settlement program started by President Magsaysay provided an effective answer to many of the communist claims.[26] It would appear that constructive and adroit political leadership rather than exclusive reliance on economic palliatives may be the best antidote to communist political warfare.[27]

India

Although the communist bloc and the United States are the main protagonists contesting for the ultimate orientation of Southeast Asia, both India and Japan[28] can exert significant influence on this communist-Free World type of war. For this reason, communist political-warfare efforts

26. See Alvin H. Scaff, *The Philippine Answer to Communism,* and Brimmell, *op. cit.,* pp. 99-111, 151-53, 212-19, and 340-44.

27. The relation between economic and opinion appeals has been discussed in Charles A. H. Thomson, "Western Influence and Asian Opinion," a chapter contributed to Philip W. Thayer (ed.), *Nationalism and Progress in Free Asia,* pp. 329-45.

28. There is not space here to describe the long and tortuous history of the Japanese communist movement and the infighting between Communist China and the Soviet

designed to guide the policy decision of these two major Asian nations are important.

The history of communism in India would require several volumes, but the early story of the Communist Party in India parallels that of many of the countries of Southeast Asia. Communism followed World War I and was admixed with idealism and with nationalism in the minds of the people. From the beginning in India, however, communism has been largely intellectual. In part, this has been caused by the kind of Indian thinking of which Gandhism was an expression—and in part by the inoculation of socialism, which seems to have been Burma's earlier means of warding off communism's social medicine.

The close intellectual ties between Britain and India far surpassed those which obtained between Indochina and France or between the Netherlands and Indonesia. Because of this closeness, the Indians mirrored every shift and fragmentation in British left-wing opinion. To a considerable degree, they continue to do so to this day. One of the results of this contact was to duplicate almost the entire history of the secession of communism from the main stream of British Laborite socialism. British contacts were the chief ones in making the first communist connections, although in later years American Communists—with the help of American passports and relative immunity from the British police in India—were able to do a great deal. Furthermore, even where communist agents did not penetrate, British publications did. The wide use of English in India made possible the duplication on Indian territory of almost every shift in either the socialist or the communist lines. It must never be forgotten that much of the apparent "pro-communism" of the Indians is the ill-tempered left-wing "Marxism" of the Labor intellectuals; seen from America, it looks communist; to the sectarians themselves, there is always a gulf between them and the Communists. John Strachey provides an example of this type of non-Stalinist Marxist.

The fragmentation of India by history and geography means, as Overstreet and Windmiller have pointed out in their *Communism in India* that communism is an intellectuals' movement which has spent forty years trying to reach the masses, without much success if it is indeed true

Union for its control. There is an enormous amount of literature on the subject. The manifold extent to which Japanese society has been weakened by Soviet political warfare and subversion is, however, imperfectly understood. The example of the Japanese Teachers' Union, whose 500,000 members staff Japan's public schools, illustrates the problem. The power of the pro-communist forces was drastically illustrated by the severe rioting which forced the cancellation of President Eisenhower's projected 1960 visit to Japan.

that "poverty breeds communism." Nowhere else in the world is there so explosive a combination of civilized, sensitive people living through decades of deprivation and want. It is in the cultural field, rather than the economic, that one must seek the answer to Indian adherence to non-communism after China had fallen to Red control.

M. N. Roy was the first great pioneer in representing the Communist International in India. In July, 1924, on Roy's advice, it was decided that the Communist Party of India should be established as a branch of the Communist International. Shortly thereafter, however, the Comintern evidently decided to work through the British Communist Party in dealing with India.

In 1929, the Indian Communist Party was organized into five departments: trade-unions, peasants, propaganda, organizational and secretariat (political control). Soon afterward, the arrest of some thirty of the leading Indian Communists rendered the Party impotent. The Indian National Congress, launched by Gandhi in 1930, largely filled the vacuum left by the Communists. The latter deprecated Gandhi's work and said that he was a tool of capitalism and imperialism because he advocated non-violent means of winning concessions from the British.

World War II brought some abrupt changes in the communist line. When Hitler and Stalin were allies, the war was one between peace-loving Germany and Russia on the one side, and the warmongering imperialist British and French on the other. When Germany attacked Russia and Russia was allied with the West, the West became "peace-loving by association" with Russia. Because of its patent opportunism, after World War II, the Indian Communist Party found itself relatively discredited.

Although the Communists called a number of strikes in 1949 and 1950, none of these was very successful and Russia attacked the Indian government as an agent of Anglo-American imperialism. This line later changed, but it was obvious, even to Moscow, that there was no widespread popular support for the Communist Party in India. Prime Minister Nehru has attempted to follow a policy of neutralism which seems genuine to him, even when it leans to the communist side, and this is a line which appears to achieve popularity against the background of indigenous Indian political thought.

From the beginning, the Communist Party of India has been connected with Moscow, and it has received outside aid and direction. It has also been clear that the Party's interests were not motivated by concern for India or the best interests of Indians. The motivation has always been the best interests of Moscow and of international communism, as may be discerned in the close following of the Moscow party line by the Indian Communist Party. It has always been a small hard-core group of Communists who have carried on the work of the Party in India, rather than a broad-based popular group.

One of the few effective propaganda lines of the Communists in India since the war has been the reiterated stress on peace. This, of course, fits well with India's neutralism and with Nehru's compulsive role to act as a mediator in international disputes. However, the Communists are still arguing with the dead Gandhi, whom they correctly blame as a major obstacle to the advance of communism in India. Acharya Vinobha Bhave's scheme for the voluntary distribution of land (the Bhoodan Yagna scheme) has been denounced by the Communists on the grounds that it signifies "charity in land," whereas they claim that land distribution should be a movement of the people's seizing the land from the landlords. This kind of protest, of course, makes it clear that the Communists are much less interested in the peasants' receiving the land than they are in having them use communist methods to achieve the end.[29]

The Indian government is considerably more stable than the Burmese government, but there is a definite parallel in the fact that, left alone, internal communism has little strength. Moreover, since November, 1959, when Communist Chinese troops violated the McMahon Line, the border between the two countries, the leadership of the Indian Communist Party has been split between the nationalists, who support Nehru on the border issue, and the others, who unreservedly support China.

Conclusion

This chapter paints a dismal picture, from the Western point of view, of communist inroads into Southeast Asia.[30] There are grounds for optimism,

29. On the Indian Communist Party, see Democratic Research Service, *Indian Communist Party Documents 1930–1956,* and M. R. Masani, *The Communist Party of India: A Short History.* See also Margaret W. Fisher and Joan V. Bondurant, *Indian Approaches to a Socialist Society,* Indian Press Digest Monograph Series, No. 2, July 1956, which discusses at length Nehru's schemes and economic programs, which have in many cases foiled Communist objectives. A scholarly treatment, making extensive use of both academic and field research, is to be found in Gene D. Overstreet and Marshall Windmiller, *Communism in India.* The authors disagree fundamentally with the thesis *op. cit.,* that Maoism is a different and rival kind of communism. They give an excellent presentation of the extraordinary linkages set up between Moscow and the policy-making apparatus of the Communists in India.

30. President Kennedy's notable speech to the United Nations on September 25, 1961, concurred in the seriousness of this threat when he stated: "The first threat on which I wish to report is widely misunderstood: the smoldering coals of war in Southeast Asia.

however, provided the leaders of the area, in concert with the United States and other Free World nations, undertake countermeasures that are politically attuned to the needs of the region. The Communists have nothing to contribute except enforced industrialization. They marched into the area under the banners of nationalism tinctured with shadings of Marxism, but they had, and have, no sociological insight for transforming the peoples of Southeast Asia into Communists. Now that independence has muted the appeal of nationalism, the Communists have relied on guerrilla-warfare terror and power politics as the main forces behind their campaign of expansion. Communist practitioners of political warfare are technically proficient, but they are handicapped by the absence of a real ideological *rapport.*

For the past eleven years, mainland China has been the main proving ground of what Communists can do in tackling the Asian problem. Thus far they have shown that is political banditti, they have retained much of their skill, but as economic organizers they have surpassed the Russian Communists in incompetence. Communist China has slid down to a condition of outright famine. Mao's man-made famine (worse than the famine resulting from collectivization in Russia from 1930 to 1935), the result of the imposition of silly policies, should be thoroughly exposed. From the point of view of political counterwarfare the time is ripe for a reappraisal of Red China's internal problems with a view to exploiting them. In political warfare, an adequate presentation of the enemy's failures, particularly signal ones, may be even more important than the advertisement of our own successes.

In the meantime, with Western help, Free Asian political leaders—together with the military—must not only hold on and manage, but reform and advance while liquidating the enemy's political and guerrilla armies.

Marxism-Leninism started in Asia with a doctrine which had little correlation to the realities, but it was an effective doctrine of opposition. Now a new, better, and more seasoned program of political development is needed, one that combats and impedes the advance of Asian despotism, creeping back in new forms, and is constructive at the same time. The West, with its superior means, could stimulate and champion such a program.

South Vietnam is already under attack—sometimes by a single assassin, sometimes by a band of guerrillas, recently by full battalions. The peaceful people of Laos are in danger of losing the independence they gained a short time ago." *Philadelphia Inquirer,* September 26, 1961, p. 10.

CHAPTER XIII

THE LATIN AMERICAN WAY

THE COMITERN'S FIRST EFFORT TO PENETRATE SOUTH AMERICA began in the early twenties. The Communist Party of Argentina was established in January, 1918, and those of Chile and Uruguay three years later. A Latin American secretariat was set up at Comintern headquarters in Moscow under Palmiro Togliatti, the 1961 Secretary of the Italian Communist Party. Trained personnel from the American, Russian, and other communist parties, as well as subsidies from Moscow, began to flow into Latin America.

In the 1920's, the first group of Latin Americans arrived at the Lenin School in Moscow, where they received training in all the arts of subversion. Their number increased from year to year. Communist strength developed rapidly after World War II, following the establishment of Soviet diplomatic and commercial relations with many Latin American countries. The Latin American communist parties have long since outgrown the Communist Party, U.S.A., which initiated the original penetration at Moscow's direction.[1]

The Communists have made substantial advances in Latin America during the past decade, culminating in their successful rise to power in Cuba. If their strength in the area makes a comparable advance in the next ten years, the precarious stability now prevailing will be gone, and Latin America might become a more dangerous focal point of Moscow's manipulations against the United States. The communists view the United States

1. August 13, 1959 hearing of the Senate Internal Security Committee, published as Part 2 of the "Communist Threat to the United States Through the Caribbean" Series. See also Robert J. Alexander, *Communism in Latin America*, pp. 75, 136, 154, and 157.

as the giant which must ultimately be struck down before capitalism as a social system can be buried.

Lenin's Strategy in a South American Setting

When Lenin first conceived of operating in Latin America, both his objectives and his ideas on how to realize them were vague. Thus for Latin America there was no single strategy, but different strategies adopted by the Kremlin at different times. From 1917 to 1923, Lenin felt that Europe was about to be bolshevized in a wave of revolutions and civil wars, and he thought that shortly thereafter the proletariat of the United States might also rise.[2] While there is no evidence that Lenin believed the United States could be communized via Latin America, he certainly regarded Latin America as an extremely important base for future operations.

Lenin's over-all theory and methods were able to attract at least part of the Marxist and radical elements already present in Latin America. The task was not too difficult, since the difference between Lenin and Marx was not as much in general theory as in method of application. Lenin's ideological authority, backed by the successful seizure of power in Russia, strengthened the appeal of communism to Western Hemisphere radicals.

In Latin America, where, with few exceptions, parliamentary democracy was always fragile and dictatorships common, the Communists came with promises of salvation. Many Latin American radicals, mired in their imitations of European methods, were ready to try something new. That something new combined familiar schemes with new methods of conspiratorial organization, infiltration, mass agitation, and use of force.

The Communists thus began in Latin America by splitting the old radical movements, just as they had wrecked the old Socialist Party and the I.W.W. in the United States. The Comintern spent the first ten years in South America forming a vanguard of country-wide national communist parties and infiltration groups. The standard techniques of penetration into the various social strata were used with but minor variations. The development of a specific strategy and tactical pattern applicable to Latin America did not take place until the early 1940's.

Until at least 1942, there was uncertainty as to the over-all strategy to be applied. Stalin was too busy with internal Soviet problems to study Latin America specifically. Lenin's political-warfare concept embodied two

2. See his "A Letter to the American Workers" in *Collected Works*, Vol. XXIII, pp. 192-204.

main variants: (1) the "socialist revolution" concept applied to the advanced countries and (2) the "bourgeois democratic revolution" concept applied to backward countries, such as China. The Moscow high command hesitated in deciding which of the two strategies to apply to the South American continent. It was not an easy decision to make. Latin America was obviously considerably ahead of China in its social and economic development, yet considerably behind the more advanced countries of Europe and North America. The problem was complicated by the proximity of the United States, a major factor in Latin America commerce and industrialization.

While Lenin might have solved such problems competently and quickly, it took Stalin nearly two decades after the initiation of operations to decide, finally, to apply the strategy for backward countries to Latin America.[3] In the meantime, Latin American communist operations had been proceeding, based on a European-style strategy, and many tactical opportunities were lost.

The Democratic Revolution Concept as Applied in Latin America

The Communists, under their "bourgeois democratic revolution" strategy, do not aim at the improvement of democracy. On the contrary, their long-range aim is to do away with democracy, although outside the hard core there are many politically naïve Communists who believe in the idealistic trappings of the movement. The bourgeois democratic revolution has been successful so often that it is high time that it be understood. In this connection, a 1953 warning by John Foster Dulles is important:

I have the feeling that conditions in Latin America are somewhat comparable to conditions as they were in China in the mid-1930's, when the communist movement was getting started. They, the Reds, were beginning to develop a hatred of the Americans and British, but we didn't do anything adequate about it. It went on and on, and then finally it came to a climax in 1949. Well, if we don't look out, we'll wake up some morning and read in the newspapers that there happened in South America the same kind of thing that happened in China in 1949.[4]

Throughout the world the Communists recruit their leaders from power-seeking members of the middle class and the intelligentsia. Recruit-

3. Eudocio Ravines, *The Yenan Way*, pp. 148-59.
4. As quoted in the August 13, 1959 hearings of the Senate Internal Security Committee. Published as Part 2 of the "Communist Threat to the United States Through the Caribbean" Series, p. 73.

ment of shock troops to carry out the programs of this elite varies from country to country. Political warfare in advanced industrial countries is adapted for the industrial workers. In Latin America, the Communists look for support among the peasants as well as industrial workers. But for each the strategy of the bourgeois democratic revolution is indispensable.

In a few Latin American countries where there are large Indian populations, the peasants own land according to traditional collectivized tribal patterns. In situations like this, the communist collectivist approach does not have the same hurdles to leap since among such groups the mentality of a property owner is absent. In Mexico and Bolivia the governments have distributed lands, not to the individual peasant, but to the community.[5] In these countries communist appeals for collectivism at the point of production are made to receptive ears. This is true also with the majority of industrial workers, who own no productive property.

Communist efforts to win over the rural worker in most parts of Latin America have met with little success. While the rural movement headed by Francisco Juliao in northeast Brazil has received considerable publicity, the Brazilian Communist Party is urban-based, with most of its members in Rio, Sao Paulo, Porto Alegre, Recife, and a few other centers. The city and province of Buenos Aires, the urban centers of Rosario, Mendoza, Cordoba and Santa Fe account for the great majority of Argentine Communist supporters. Again, as in the case of Brazil, the Argentine party draws its strength from the middle class and the urban workers. Certainly Uruguay is "agrarian," yet what has been said concerning the source of communist strength in Brazil and Argentina is even truer in the case of Uruguay. Chile follows the same pattern. In brief, the Latin American rural workers, theoretically speaking, should be receptive candidates for communist exploitation; recognizing this potential, party propaganda efforts designed to harness this force have been appreciably stepped up in recent years. Yet, as a practical matter, these potential candidates have proved to be difficult subjects in view of their isolation, illiteracy, and general apathy. In short, communist efforts in the rural sector are targetted more *against* the conservative landowner than *for* the rural worker, and

5. There is a difference, of course. In Bolivia and Peru, Indian collective property has survived in vestigial form across the centuries; in Mexico, the *ejido* was an artificial and conscious reconstruction of the pre-Spanish past. The Mexicans are proudly quick to point out that their rural socialism antedated the Russian revolution of 1917 by some months and that they, not the Communists, are the world's pioneers in collectivized agriculture.

have as an added objective general disruption of the target economy.

The Communists devise tactics to attract all social elements except the big landowners and the big bourgeoisie. In Latin America, where their effort is now concentrated against the United States, they pose as the champions of the masses, but promise to reward all others who go along with them, except the owners of the so-called imperialist enterprises and their indigenous collaborators. These are to be expropriated and liquidated as a power-holding class, though not necessarily killed as individuals.

This formula permits the Communists to operate, not as "Communists," but as revolutionary Jacobins of the 1792 French revolutionary variety. Under this plan, individuals who are not overtly known as Communists can pose as "liberators" or "democrats" of the left, as in Cuba and previously in Guatemala. With these tactics, they can in the initial stages unite with a wide variety of other elements and more easily neutralize them. They need not ride into power overtly as a party at all. It is sufficient initially to take the state out of the hands of their opponents, crush them, and, by availing themselves of the opportunities afforded by a "friendly" government, gain power. Of course those in the upper layer of non-communists are viewed as expendable pawns. The non-communists among the revolutionary coalition can later be eliminated one by one. The bourgeois democratic revolution strategy, which enables the Communists to pose as nationalists, anti-imperialists, revolutionary liberators, and reformers, is the key to understanding communist operations in Latin America.[6]

Lenin developed the doctrine in his *Two Tactics* (1905),[7] where he pointed out that in backward countries a bourgeois revolution must precede the socialist one. Lenin later changed his mind, not about the nature of this bourgeois democratic revolution, but about Russia's readiness for a socialist one. However, the concept was retained, and Stalin wrote about a bourgeois democratic revolution under a dictatorship of the proletariat and peasantry in which "capitalism fundamentaly remains" and the "democratic bourgeoisie" shares power with the masses.[8]

The analysis of Latin America contained in the "Program of the Communist International," adopted by the Sixth World Congress of the Comintern (1928), stated the concept very clearly. Section IV, 8 of that program

6. August 13, 1959 hearings of the Senate Internal Security Committee, Part 2, pp. 50-51.

7. See especially pp. 18-22 of V. I. Lenin, *Two Tactics of Social-Democracy in the Democratic Revolution*, Vol. X.

8. See especially Stalin's advice to Dmitriev: "Concerning the Question of Workers' and Peasants' Government," *Works*, Vol. IX, pp. 182-93.

divides the capitalist world into: (1) highly developed nations, such as the United States and the United Kingdom; (2) countries of medium development, such as Portugal and Hungary; (3) colonial and semicolonial countries (China, India) and dependent countries (Argentina, Brazil); and finally, (4) "still more backward countries" (primitive Africa). With reference to the colonial and semi-colonial countries, the program notes that industry is usually too underdeveloped for socialist revolution, that "medieval, feudal relationships" exist, and that the chief task is to fight against the latifundia and against imperialism. It goes on to argue for development of "the peasant agrarian revolution" and the fight against foreign imperialism to gain "national independence." The program also declares that, generally, "a series of preparatory stages" must be passed through before the bourgeois democratic revolutionary task can be supplanted by the task of socialist revolution.[9]

Essentially, the bourgeois democratic revolution is a form of deceit designed to lure the peasants and the middle class into communism. It should be fairly noted, however, that the concept of the bourgeois democratic revolution has been expounded by the Communists at great length and with considerable candor as a transitional stage toward proletarian dictatorship and the liquidation of the middle classes. Far from trying to keep these writings secret, the communist parties distribute millions of copies of their program in those countries where bourgeois democratic revolutions are to be launched. Hence we are not dealing with a deception in the usual meaning of the phrase. Those middle-class people who abet such revolutions could possibly save their property, their freedom, and their lives if they would read communist publications at their face value.[10]

We quote from the 1954 program of the Communist Party of Brazil, a leading Red party in Latin America, as an example:

The poverty of the people in a country so rich as ours is the result of the predatory policy of the American monopolies, the result of the rule of the owners of the latifundia[11] and big Brazilian capitalists.

9. Jane Degras, *The Communist International, 1919–1943: Documents*, Vol. II, pp. 505-507.

10. The open confession of an aggressive design is not unknown in modern history. *Mein Kampf* is one example, and the Tanaka Memorial another. In cases such as this the programmer denounces his own program as being misunderstood by its victims and then goes on to carry it out in real life. There is no reason to suppose that the public men of the 1960's are inherently more intelligent than their predecessors of the 1930's; evolution does not move that fast. One can only hope that they might learn a little from recent experience.

11. The latifundia are the large family estates. The word usually carries the implication that much of the land involved is poorly used or not used at all.

Thus, the entire national economy of Brazil is being turned into a mere appendage to the United States war economy. The American imperialists directly interfere in the entire administrative life of the country; they have taken over the state apparatus of Brazil in order ruthlessly to exploit and oppress our people, to plunder the country's natural resources, and to extract maximum profit.

Industrialists and traders are unable to expand their business because of the competition from American goods. American monopolies control entire branches of Brazilian industry and use all the means at their disposal to strangle and retard development of home industry, to prevent the founding of basic branches of industry needed to free Brazil from the economic dependence in which it now finds itself.[12]

The Communist Party of Brazil is convinced that the democratic transformations needed by our people can be achieved only by a democratic government of national liberation, by a government in which along with the working class there would participate the peasantry and intelligentsia, the petty bourgeoisie and the national bourgeoisie.

The Communist Party is fighting for Socialism, but it is convinced that in the present economic, social, and political conditions in Brazil, socialist transformations are impossible. But it is quite possible to fulfill the task of replacing the present antinational and antipeople's government by a people's government which would free Brazil from the domination of the United States imperialists and their lackeys—the owners of the latifundia and the big capitalists.

The democratic government of national liberation will not confiscate the enterprises and capital of the national bourgeoisie. It will, however, confiscate and nationalize the capital and enterprises belonging to big capitalists who have betrayed the interests of the nation and who have aligned themselves with the United States imperialists.

Independent development of the national economy and the creation of conditions for intensified industrialization of the country utilizing for this purpose the confiscated capital and enterprise of the American imperialists. For this it will be necessary to invite private capital which must be guaranteed profits and protection in accordance with a special law.

Confiscation of all land belonging to big landlords and its transfer, free of charge, to landless and land-hungry peasants, and to all who care to till it. Distribution of the land shall be recognized by law, and each peasant given title deeds. The possession and seizure of the lands, belonging to both landlords and the state, already effected by the peasants shall also be recognized by law, and the peasants will receive necessary title deeds.[13]

The programs and statements of the other Latin American communist parties generally follow the same line.[14]

12. PETROBAS, the Brazilian government oil monopoly, is perhaps the most concrete outcome of the appeal of this type of propaganda. By law, no foreign interests may participate in the development of the oil industry in Brazil.

13. All excerpts from "Draft Programme of Communist Party of Brazil," published in *For a Lasting Peace, for a People's Democracy,* pp. 3-4.

14. If the reader, however, wants to consult more documentation, he can find it in the August 13, 1959, hearings of the Senate Internal Security Committee, Part 2, pp. 56-69.

Playing Both Ends Against the Middle

Communist employment of the bourgeois democratic revolution strategy should not lead to the illusion that the Communists, even for the sake of expediency, aim to be real democrats for a decade or so. When they speak of democracy, they mean a dictatorship which claims to be operating in the interests of the majority. They can play with dictators when it serves their purpose and against them when it does not. They played opportunistically with Juan Peron in Argentina, with Fulgencio Batista in Cuba, with Hitler during the Nazi-Soviet alliance, and now with semidictators like Nasser of Egypt.

Their bourgeois democratic revolution formula is an example of communist "revolutionary opportunism." They can thus approach an ambitious dictator and sell him much of their technique as a way of staying in power and becoming the idol of the masses. If he accepts their offer, they can build their movement under his authority, making him dependent upon their superior skill in organization.[15] If the dictator becomes aware of what is happening and opposes them, or if he is about to be overthrown, they can turn on him, posing as ultra-democrats, as they did with Batista in Cuba. In spite of their opportunism, there is unity in their apparently contradictory method that comes from striving for a total goal.

Guerrilla Warfare

Because of the instability of the governmental structures, guerrilla warfare for political purposes was important in Latin America long before the Communists had a hand in it. It is imbedded in the revolutionary lore and romanticism of Latin America, a tradition which the Communists utilize to the utmost. Latin America is, as a colonel teaching guerrilla warfare in Moscow said, "a terrain which is politically and otherwise ideal."

Guerrilla warfare in Latin America has often been the forerunner of a revolution.[16] In the early part of the twentieth century, Emiliano Zapata, never a Communist, unleashed a peasant revolution in Mexico under the

15. See Robert J. Alexander, *Communism in Latin America*, pp. 13-14.

16. The Iberian conquest of America was itself guerrilla warfare on a spectacular scale; the Indian resistance was also guerrilla warfare. The Spanish American struggles for independence involved both guerrilla warfare and positional war. The tragic, endemic military turmoil of the nineteenth century bred shiftless *soldatesca*—pseudo-soldiery—all over the Spanish portions of the two continents. One could almost go so far as to say that guerrilla warfare is normal in the Latin American environment. That it happens to coincide with current communist doctrine is a pure accident—one, however, which may help decide future history.

banner of land reform. With few ideals, Juan Vicente Gomez of Venezuela, leading his Andino peasants, swept away a fragile effort at democracy and established a thirty-year dictatorship lasting until his death in 1935. Luiz Carlos Prestes, then a colonel in the Brazilian army, conducted guerrilla operations from 1924 to 1927; in 1961, Carlos Prestes was the head of the Communist Party of Brazil. There were other wildcat attempts at guerrilla warfare in the early stages of the communist penetration of South America which Moscow chose to ignore or even denounce as futile "putschism." One of these was the abortive attempt to land a guerrilla force (Fidel Castro fashion) in Venezuela in 1929. This attempt was led by Gustavo Machado, the present head of the Communist Party of Venezuela.[17]

A more recent and far more serious and protracted use of guerrilla warfare followed the assassination of Jorge Elicier Gaitan (1948), leader of a wing of the Liberal Party of Colombia. Who actually engineered the assassination is not known. The assassin was killed on the spot. It occurred at a time when the internecine political warfare between the Liberals and the Conservatives, who controlled the government under President Ospina Pérez, was at a boiling point. The assassination was the sparking match in a situation loaded with political gunpowder. Both sides apparently saw possibilities in a civil war.

The Communists, with a membership of ten thousand in a nation of about eleven million, controlled the Student Federation and the Confederation of Labor of Colombia. Just prior to Gaitan's assassination, they were in the midst of preparations to dramatize their antagonism to the Inter-American Conference of States, then meeting in Bogota. The means chosen was a demonstration aimed at the United States. Ideologically and organizationally, the Colombian Communists were ready for a major protest demonstration, but not yet quite ready for a civil war.

Gaitan, whose left-wing backers were a powerful minority in the Liberal Party of Colombia, had been collaborating with the Communists since the early thirties. His assassination was blamed on the Conservatives. In a matter of hours, violent conflict between the Liberals and the Conservatives exploded. There was widespread discontent in Colombia, but communist-directed squads, assisted and abetted by leftist Liberals, seized strategic points in the city, including the headquarters of hostile organizations, and began to call for a revolution over the radio.

17. See Alexander, *op. cit.*, pp. 93-134 and 253-55. See also Alfred B. Thomas, *Latin America*, pp. 666-69.

The communist core made one major mistake, they failed to seize the Presidential Palace from which counterorders poured. The army, insufficiently infiltrated, responded to the government's call for rescue and in a matter of days crushed the rebellion. The Communists, in their hurry to take advantage of Gaitan's assassination, had overlooked a lesson taught at the Lenin School, namely, that guerrilla groups by themselves cannot defeat a loyal army. Nor were the Communists sufficiently organized to control the rampaging mobs set loose by the rebellion. In fact, they encouraged the mobs to act as blind auxiliaries. The result was that every thug and scoundrel helped himself in a tragic sacking and devastation of the city. Although the Bogota events did not proceed according to the communist book, the Inter-American Conference was adversely affected.[18]

The crushing of the revolt in Bogota did not end the civil war sparked by Gaitan's assassination. Many of the insurgents fled into the Colombian interior and regrouped. Virulent hate propaganda, originating with the Communists and rebroadcast in but slightly modified form by Gaitan's left-wing Liberals, had been spread for years, preparing the masses for a showdown. Gaitan himself had been a master agitator and an idol of the people. His assassination contributed the necessary emotional element for the explosion. Thus the revolution, although crushed in the capital, was transferred to the countryside. The government continued to hold the major cities, but in rural areas guerrilla warfare raged for nearly ten years. According to the Colombian government's estimates the civil war took 100,000 lives.[19] After the brutal dictatorship of Rojas Pinilla, it was settled by a compromise between the principal elements in 1958. However, rebel

18. The Conference was interrupted for several days, its meeting place badly damaged, and for a time the delegates considered premature adjournment. However, they voted to reconvene at a suburban estate and continued their discussions. The final result was the Pact of Bogota, which established the Organization of American States. The Conference delegates also signed the American Declaration of the Rights and Duties of Man. A good, brief summary of the happenings of the Bogotazo appears in the August 26, 1960 staff study of the Senate Internal Security Subcommittee "Communist Anti-American Riots," pp. 1-11. This account includes important quotations from many contemporary sources. See also Willard L. Beaulac, *Career Ambassador*, pp. 234-56. Beaulac was U.S. Ambassador to Colombia and saw, perhaps, as much of the actual events before, during, and after the riots as any American. Further, see Matthew B. Ridgeway's account in his autobiography, *Soldier*, pp. 177-82. General Ridgeway was present as a member of the American delegation and was instrumental in saving the lives of a number of his American colleagues.

19. If the same percentage of deaths as occurred in Colombia's population were to be suffered by the people of the United States, the toll would approach 1,500,000.

bands, many thought to be communist controlled, still roam the country-side and engage in general pillage, plunder, and murder.[20]

A situation like the one prevailing in Colombia after April, 1948, is an advantageous one for the Communists, even if they are only a minority in the total revolutionary combination. They excel not only in organizing techniques, but also in guerrilla warfare. The Communists considered it feasible to apply Mao Tse-tung's Chinese pattern of organizing a guerrilla force mainly among the peasants for eventual capture of the big cities. After Bogota, they had no alternative. As the allies of the left-wing Liberals, they had either to surrender to the Conservatives or to continue the fight together with the Liberals. In view of the strength displayed by the coalition in the prolonged struggle which took place, it must be admitted that the gamble was tempting. If they had had the kind of open support that Mao in China had from neighboring Russia, their chances of winning would have been good. In that case a pro-Communist regime would have been established right next to the Panama Canal, the aim of Moscow and its Bogota Embassy. As it was, the compromise settlement achieved between the Conservatives and the rightist Liberals was a real if temporary defeat for the Communists. But the situation in Colombia remains unstable and vulnerable to Communist penetration.

The Cuban Revolution

In spite of only partial success in Colombia, Moscow's adventures with guerrilla warfare in Latin America were not ended. While the fighting in Colombia was still going on, Moscow was helping in the preparation of still another guerrilla-type effort aimed at Cuba. This adventure was to be an invasion by Cuban nationals organized outside the country. This successful thrust, led by Fidel Castro, a Cuban intellectual of unusual political skill, had its beginning in Mexico. A training camp to develop Castro's initial force was set up there under the command of Alfred Bayo, Castro's military brains and a former colonel in the Spanish Loyalist Army, noted as an expert on guerrilla warfare. How many of those trained were card-holding Communists is not known, but a number

20. Testimony of William D. Pawley, September 2 and 8, 1960 hearings of the Senate Internal Security Subcommittee. Published as Part 10 of the "Communist Threat to the United States Through the Caribbean" Series, p. 726. See also Eugene K. Culhane, "Red Pocket in Colombia," *America*, March 12, 1960, pp. 701-704, and the July 1, 1961 issue of the *New York Times*.

of them, including the principal leaders, were ideological Communists. Che Guevara, Raúl Castro, and Armando Hart are and were Communists and few informed persons deny this today. The same applies to Celia Sánchez and Vilma Espín, who seemed to have Soviet liaison functions, and to the OGPU operative Victor Trapote. All of these people were part of the force which launched the movement from Mexico.[21]

Castro's band of communist radicals, Socialists, and idealists was welded together by an anti-Batista, anti–United States hatred. Once the group was trained. the invasion was begun. The landing was accomplished, although not without loss, and the small guerrilla force established itself in Sierra Maestra, a high mountainous area in Eastern Cuba, far from the centers of governmental power in Havana. Batista's government obviously underestimated this operation and made no serious effort to liquidate Castro until it was too late.

Officials in Washington, insensitive to communist political-warfare techniques of the Latin American variety and anti-Batista in sentiment, apparently accepted Castro's alleged non-communism, underestimating the extent to which Moscow was behind him. The rebels initially received a good press in the United States and support from Latin American quarters in New York and Miami.[22] At the time of his move to full power in January of 1959, Castro was widely viewed as the liberator of his people. Hopes ran at full crest. Realization of the disastrous deception which had been effected came later.

The official United States government view of the Red take-over in Cuba, as late as April, 1961, was that Castro was not a Communist or Soviet agent prior to his conquest of power, although it was acknowledged that some of his chief lieutenants were ideologically Marxist-Leninists. The State Department White Paper on Cuba argued:

It is not clear whether Dr. Castro intended from the start to betray his pledges of a free and democratic Cuba, to deliver his country to the Sino-

21. Che Guevara, *Guerrilla Warfare*, p. 44; testimony of Salvador Díaz-Versón, May 6, 1960 hearings of the Senate Internal Security Subcommittee, published as Part 7 of the "Communist Threat to the United States Through the Caribbean" Series, pp. 426-31. See also the testimony of Colonel Manuel A. V. Carrillo, *ibid.*, pp. 374-76.

22. The favorable press in the United States is best exemplified in the articles by Herbert L. Matthews in the *New York Times* in 1957. The series was widely influential. See especially the issues of February 24, p. 1; February 26, p. 7; February 26, p. 13; June 16, p. 1; and June 17, p. 3. See also "The *Times* and Cuba," *Time*, July 27, 1959, pp. 47-48. The reaction of Matthews to Castro's admission that he was and is a communist is not known. See wire service report *Philadelphia Inquirer*, December 2, 1961, p. 1, regarding Castro's admission.

Soviet bloc, and to mount an attack on the Inter-American system; or whether he made his original pledges in all sincerity but, on assuming his new responsibilities, found himself increasingly dependent on ruthless men around him with clear ideas and the disciplined organization to carry those ideas into action. What is important is not the motive, but the result.[23]

Although Castro boasted in December of the same year that he had been a Communist since 1953 and would remain one "until the day I die" the issue remains important, since communist success in Cuba, as well as elsewhere, resulted partially from the United States' failure to understand whom Moscow was backing and what kind of people Castro and his associates were.

Assume for the sake of argument that Fidel Castro was an idealist and a believer in democracy until some undetermined period after he took power at which time he became a Communist. This might presuppose a sudden, total, and almost miraculous ideological conversion, perhaps analogous to that of Saul on the road to Damascus. If, however, miracles are excluded, the process of conversion would necessarily have been gradual and Castro's conduct would have reflected that fact in many hesitations, inconsistencies, and retreats. Nothing of the sort occurred. When revolutionary politicians are merely in opportunistic alliances with communism, they take steps to build up independent organizations of power which can be used against the Reds in case of a showdown. Nasser in Egypt, Kassem in Iraq, and Chiang Kai-shek in China in the 1920's chose this path. Fidel Castro, on the other hand, as was noted in the State Department White

23. State Department White Paper on Cuba as printed in the *New York Times*, April 4, 1961, pp. 14-15. The White Paper ignored much evidence on this point including information long available in quantity in the State Department. According to the testimony of Robert C. Hill, former U.S. Ambassador to Mexico (1957-61) and Foreign Service Officer in Costa Rica and El Salvador there was a continuous flow through the 1950's of official talk and correspondence in Embassy and State Department circles concerning Castro's strong ties with communism. Officers in the field were mostly anti-Castro because of this and repeatedly spoke their minds. Reports coming out of the State Department ignored their warnings. See June 12, 1961, hearings of the Senate Internal Security Subcommittee, published as Part 12 of the "Communist Threat to the U.S. Through the Caribbean" Series, pp. 794-807. The Administration had the essence of Hill's testimony in January of 1960 well before the White Paper was released. *Ibid.*, pp. 809-14. On December 2, 1961 Castro boastfully revealed to the Cuban people that he was a dedicated "Marxist-Leninist" follower of Communism and had been at least since the beginning of his revolutionary movement in 1953. He explained that he had disguised his Communism, "because otherwise we might have alienated the bourgeoisie and other forces which we knew we would eventually have to fight." This should have been obvious to any realistic student of Communist political warfare.

Paper on Cuba, has consistently destroyed all power organizations and political groups in Cuba which stood in the way of the communist monopoly of power. Moreover, in every political decision he has faced, he has acted in accordance with the ideological line of the Soviet bloc. This alone should have been sufficient to show a strong communist bent at the time he took power.

Powerful groups in both the United States and Cuba tried to conceal and distort basic facts concerning his position. Cuban politicians, who bear grave responsibility for the destruction of the basic freedoms of the Cuban people, naturally wish to disseminate the line that the revolution was suddenly "betrayed" precisely at the point where they abandoned it. In the United States, those publicists and politicians who consistently misinterpreted the Castro movement, influenced American policy, and helped to inflict a disastrous diplomatic defeat on the United States understandably wish to restore their reputations and to create a mythology of the Cuban revolution under which their blunders seem to have been unavoidable.

There is considerable evidence that Castro was closely associated with communist activity for at least twelve years prior to his seizure of power in Cuba. His role as a Soviet agent in the Bogotazo in 1948 was denounced at the time by then President of Colombia Ospina Pérez and by the Liberal security chief of Colombia, Alberto Niño, in a noteworthy book.[24] He was further identified in another book on the Bogota riots which appeared in 1949,[25] in published reports of the surveillance of Castro in Bogota in 1948, and in a detailed dossier which the Colombian government says it gave the U.S. delegation at the time. The most charitable conclusion that can be drawn is that this documentation and these events made virtually no impact on official minds.

The communist activities and affiliations of Fidel Castro in the 1940's have been described in detail by Salvador Díaz-Versón, who was a counterintelligence chief for President Prío and who went into exile when Batista seized power, but these disclosures were published in Spanish and were apparently overlooked by our Latin American "experts."[26] Photographs of Fidel Castro taking part in communist gatherings at about this time have been published in the Cuban exile press. When the Mexican police

24. Alberto Niño, *Antecedentes y secretos del 9 de Abril.*
25. Francisco Fandiño Silva, *La Penetración Sovietica en America y el 9 de Abril.*
26. Testimony of Salvador Díaz-Versón on May 6, 1960, before the Senate Internal Security Subcommittee. Published as Part 7 of the "Communist Threat to the United States Through the Caribbean" Series, pp. 423-39.

raided Castro's revolutionary training camp and headquarters in 1956, they reported that the movement contained known Communists and was heavily communist infiltrated. Ambassadors William D. Pawley, Arthur Gardner, Earl E. T. Smith and Robert C. Hill warned the State Department that Castro's movement was infiltrated by Soviet forces to a dangerous extent, but these warnings were brushed aside by middle-echelon officials in Washington.[27]

In addition to infiltrating the rebels with trained leaders, Moscow sent supplies and arms, including some that were smuggled into Cuba by submarine. Not wishing to alert the United States and having in mind failures with such ventures, the Soviet Union stayed in the background and gave no intimation of supporting Castro until his success became obvious.[28]

The fact that the Cuban Communist Party did not support Castro at first has been submitted as evidence that Fidel was not really a Communist and that his movement was essentially a non-communist one until he moved to power, at which time the Reds opportunistically took over. Analysis of the over-all picture leads to a different conclusion. The Popular Socialist Party (Cuban Communist Party) had become demoralized and discredited because of factionalism, police torture of individual leaders, abject subservience to Moscow, and, paradoxically, a several years' alliance with Batista. Because of this, the Castro movement relied on the secret Soviet apparatus, on those of the intellectual communist youth who had not been exposed and rendered useless by open party activity, and outstanding leaders of the Communist Party, such as Carlos Rafael Rodriguez, who were revolutionary realists capable of grasping and pursuing a new strategy.[29] After all, Cuba is not the only instance in which the official local communist-party leadership has been left uninformed concerning the broad Soviet strategy applicable to its country. The communist underground in Germany in 1939–41, for example, was sacrificed to the Gestapo at a time when Stalin was desperately attempting to maintain his alliance with the Third Reich. Moreover, the presence of multiple communist parties in the Latin American countries, pursuing different tactics

27. Testimony of William D. Pawley, September 2 and 8, 1960, in *ibid.*, Part 10, pp. 723-26, 738-39, and 751; testimony of Arthur Gardner, August 27, 1960, and Earl E. T. Smith, August 30, 1960, in *ibid.*, Part 9, pp. 663-80 and 681-710.

28. Testimony of Pedro Diaz Lanz July 14, 1959, before the Senate Internal Security Subcommittee. Published as Part 1 of the "Communist Threat to the United States Through the Caribbean" Series, p. 15.

29. Testimony of Salvador Díaz-Versón, *ibid.*, Part 7, pp. 426-31.

but all serving Moscow, suggest that the official pronouncements of the various politbureaus do not necessarily disclose actual communist strategy. As it turned out, the Party's absence from the public scene helped to deceive the middle classes, as well as many others inside and outside Cuba.

Batista's repressions during the rebellion made Castro in Sierra Maestra a magnet which attracted the anti-Batista opposition, and his last-minute savageries before he fell only accelerated the trend in favor of the rebels.[30] Castro, in turn, encouraged the entire anti-Batista opposition to rally to his side by disclaiming any affiliation or association with the Communists. However, significantly, shortly before and after Castro's breakthrough, the entire communist apparatus dropped its caution to acclaim vociferously Castro's revolution as almost their own.

Thus a small, pro-communist guerrilla force played the role of a catalyst to take over a non-communist nation of nearly eight million inhabitants next to the shores of the United States. The Cuban anti-Batista revolution started like many a Latin American revolution, but like the one in Russia, it was derailed into communism. The mechanics were somewhat different and hence more confusing, but the end result—a communist dictatorship—is the same.

The complexity of the Cuban socio-economic-political kaleidoscope of the 1950's, culminating in the Castro-communist victory, has given birth to a myth, a myth which has been disseminated by Communists and by confused non-communists. Certain important facts have been lost in the maze. An example is the essential nature of the Cuban revolution. It was a middle-class movement set in a middle-class environment. Cuba, contrary to a main theme of the pro-Castro mythology, was not *the* giant rural slum of the Western Hemisphere. It did have serious social problems and its standard of living was not as high as those of the United States or Western Europe. However, among Latin American nations it was one of the most industrialized, most urbanized, and most middle class. Its per capita income was fourth highest of the twenty southern republics. The anti-Batista movement within Cuba, initially democratic in character, sprang from the middle classes, vocally represented by the intelligentsia and most noisily by the students. The result was Castro's guerrillas, amongst whom were but a few workers and not many peasants.[31]

30. Theodore Draper, "Castro's Cuba: A Revolution Betrayed?" *The New Leader*, March 27, 1961, p. 8.
31. The most complete analysis is in Nathaniel Weyl, *Red Star Over Cuba*, pp. 196-200. See also Theodore Draper, "Castro's Cuba: A Revolution Betrayed?" *The New Leader*, March 27, 1961, pp. 11-12.

The Marxist-Leninist dogma is based on the universal conflict of classes, with Marxism-Leninism claiming to represent the over-all and long-range interests of the working class. In fact, contrary to Lenin, the preconditions for this type of revolution did not exist in Cuba. Lenin postulated an economic and political crisis as a prerequisite for revolution, plus a party to carry the action through. In Cuba, only the political sickness existed, which, in the absence of economic crisis, could have been cured. Further, contrary to Lenin's dicta, the Cuban party apparatus did not play the role of the indispensable "living force" activating the revolution. That role was played by Castro's artfully camouflaged July 26 Movement and its allied underground in the urban centers. In May, 1961, the Partido Socialista Revolutionaria was still in search of the complete fusion of party and state which is the most typical feature of a communist regime.

The Cuba pattern, with all of its variations, however, fits into Lenin's grand strategy for backward countries, that of the bourgeois democratic revolution manipulated by the Communists. For this reason the Castro approach (which utilizes the middle classes as the primary base for seizing power) may, with minor variations, be applied in other countries with a development level comparable to that of Cuba.

The Lessons of Cuba

History is one thing; to analyze and to heed its lessons is another. In Cuba, Moscow, with a blundering assist from Washington, obtained a major base of operations in the Americas ahead of schedule, and indications are that the Soviets intend to utilize it to the utmost. Cuba has been turned into the Number One Latin American political-warfare base. Strategically located in the heartland of the enemy, it is being used to infect surrounding areas at a time of apparent maximum concentration on the United States. The island is also unique because it is the first firmly established Soviet satellite in an area not adjacent to the Sino-Soviet bloc. If Moscow's political-warfare machine can thus establish satellites thousands of miles away and *hold them,* it may well be later than we think. The Red beachhead in Cuba is the beginning, not the end.

The Moscow high command and its specialists on guerrilla warfare are studying the Cuban action with great care from the point of view of its possible use and application in other countries, particularly in Latin America. It is noteworthy that Mikoyan and his party, in their 1959 visit, inspected the Cuban guerrilla headquarters in the Sierras. In January, 1959, the Cuban Communist Party sent an agent, Severo Aguire, to Moscow to report to the Central Committee of the Soviet Communist Party. A statement he made is significant:

What have the events in Cuba shown? The events in Cuba . . . have refuted the claims of those who try to prove that, because of the closeness of the United States, a successful battle is impossible in the Latin American countries. When the entire people rises in armed struggle and takes the fate of the country in its hands victory is assured.[32]

Che Guevara concluded similarly. In *Guerrilla Warfare*, he argued that the three "fundamental lessons" of the Cuban revolution were that "popular forces" can win against a regular army, that the insurrection itself can create revolutionary conditions, and that the countryside is the basic exploitable terrain in the less developed countries of the hemisphere.[33]

The West, accustomed to looking upon war only in its traditional international form, has seeemingly, underestimated the new factors in communist guerrilla warfare, just as it has not understood political warfare in general. Hitherto guerrilla warfare has, in the main, been used as an auxiliary to harass the enemy during major military conflicts.

Something of significance is Khrushchev's threat to protect his new satellite, in our midst, with nuclear firepower. At the time it was uttered, it was a bluff, no doubt, or "symbolic," as he said months after. The purpose behind the threat, however, is not symbolic at all. It is an old problem and operationally not an easy one.

The problem is the uniting of physical and ideological power. In Lenin's and Stalin's time this was a difficult and cumbersome proposition often discussed in the Lenin School.

Originally it was necessary to use bribery, smuggling, and raids on arms depots, stores, caches, and the like. All action was on a small scale. Today this is done at a state level on a much larger scale by arming governments like the one in Cuba or by arming "neutrals" on the side of Moscow and using them to pass on arms and experts to the various communist-led undergrounds. Air power can be used for the same purpose, as has been seen in Laos, and so can the large Soviet submarine fleet. It is a vast and growing operation proceeding in secrecy, with only a small part visible in the surface. If the West loses will power, Moscow will be increasingly brazen in

32. Translated from *Pravda*, February 1, 1959, and printed in the August 13, 1959 hearings of the Senate Internal Security Subcommittee. See the "Communist Threat to the United States Through the Caribbean" Series, Part 2, p. 71.
33. Che Guevara, *Guerrilla Warfare*, p. 15.

arming its ideological armies. Eventually, this adroit combination of the
military and the ideological may tip the balance of power in favor of Russia. The climactic stage may well see paramilitary political armies, supplied,
organized, and protected by Moscow, taking power in countries all over
Latin America. The fact that the first forcible conquest of this sort in Cuba
has not been overthrown thus far opens up opportunities for more.

Since the "perfect failure" of the Bahia de Cochinos invasion, the idea
has grown in influential United States circles that nothing more can be
done in Cuba at the present time.[34] Further, Castro is viewed as a destructive bore who is sometimes ridiculous and can be made more so if he is
ignored. This avenue to a solution has many dangers. Castro does talk
interminably and his speech frequently sounds ridiculous to American
ears, yet he cleverly appeals to all less educated and disgruntled elements
in Cuba and Latin America and has become known to every Latino and
idolized by many. Stalin was not a "normal" man, psychiatrically speaking,[35] nor were many lesser communist figures. It is unwise to underestimate
Castro. It would be more prudent to treat him as an avowed enemy rather
than a sort of expendable clown.

It is quite possible that the Castro regime, if not overthrown soon, will
liquidate or politically incapacitate the entire middle and propertied
classes, all non-communist intellectuals, and all politically unreliable elements and that it will, in the meantime, build an effective internal-terror
and security apparatus under communist-party control. If Castro and his
communist allies succeed in destroying all potential sources of revolutionary opposition, they may be able to mold the Cubans as Lenin and Stalin
did the Russian people. The Latin American precedent would be Francisco
Lopez, a nineteenth-century dictator of Paraguay. He retained power by

34. Perhaps the most eloquent spokesman for this point of view was Ambassador Adlai
E. Stevenson. See the *New York Times,* June 26, 1961, p. 13, and July 24, 1961, p. 12.
Since July, 1961, however, the Kennedy Administration has taken an increasingly
stronger stand vis-à-vis Castro. Following the January 1962 Punta del Este meeting of
the Organization of American States, Ambassador Adlai E. Stevenson pledged U.S.
opposition to Fidel Castro's communist-backed regime in Cuba "until the happy day
when the Cuban people themselves are again able to walk in freedom." *Philadelphia
Inquirer,* February 6, 1962.

35. Physically, Stalin was a near-dwarf, maniacally sensitive about his height. He
seems to have been irreparably resentful about his damaged, pock-marked complexion.
In his later years he became paranoid, obsessive, and homocidal far beyond the call of
communist duty. Clinically, he represents a late-degenerative personality of the type so
brilliantly analyzed by the Spanish physician Dr. Gregorio Marañon in his *Tiberio:
Historia de un Resentimiento,* translated into English as *Tiberius: A Study in Resentment.*

terror and propaganda despite a suicidal war against Brazil, Argentina, and Uruguay, as a result of which the population lived on wild roots, and at the end of which only 30,000 able-bodied men remained alive.[36]

The Reach for the Middle Class

It would take at least a book in itself to examine the status and role, actual and potential, of the middle class. Communist attitudes toward it have varied considerably. Marx's greatest misjudgment, perhaps, was his negative attitude toward the middle classes. He saw them only as a perishing species to be squeezed out of existence between big capital and the proletariat. Neither did Lenin, fifty years later, seriously preoccupy himself with the problem. All he sought was temporarily to neutralize what he also considered to be a moribund class while the battle for power between the two great contending classes proceeded. The middle class, however, refused to perish; on the contrary, it grew apace.

In fact, the middle class has, beginning with the Reformation and the English and French revolutions, a more stormy history than any other class. Although because of its great diversity of interests it seldom shows a cohesion like wage-hungry workers or land-hungry peasants, it can, in periods of great social and economic disturbance, become a decisive force if united behind an organization and a leader.

In a condition of impending or actual social disturbance of consequence, the middle class is a more accurate barometer than any other group because large numbers of the class live on the edge of an economic precipice with no reserve capital to speak of nor any large trade or professional organization as protection. The shopkeeper and proprietary element in particular, even in semi-normal times, face superior competition, depression, inflation, taxes which they cannot repeal, price shifts they are unable to cope with, and so forth. In the volatile and unstable Latin American situation, they are a receptive element for the unscrupulous social demagogue to work on, as Castro, Peron, and others have proved again and again.

Many of the Latin American countries are on the verge or in the midst of their period of industrial expansion, a period in which the middle classes grow rapidly. The current communist emphasis on the "bourgeois democratic revolution" is the Soviet invitation to the middle classes. This idea represents the gradualistic element in the communist strategy as applied

36. Watt Stewart and Harold F. Peterson, *Builders of Latin America*, pp. 178-87.

to underdeveloped countries. In Dmitri Manuilsky's words, "for backward countries, backward politics."[37]

The Chinese Communist Role

It is not yet known what the role of Mao Tse-tung's Peking apparatus is in communist Latin American operations. The Chinese interference in the area has a long history. Eudocio Ravines gives a revealing account of his meetings with Chinese Communist leaders in Moscow in 1935, where they instructed him to apply Chinese strategy and tactics to Latin America. The Chinese spokesmen were able to take this initiative because a few days previously Stalin had decided, according to the French communist writer Barbusse, that the way to success in Latin America was the "Road of Yenan."[38] The events in Cuba have given a great stimulus to the future application of this strategy.

The Chinese Communists maintain a substantial mission in Cuba and are rapidly expanding their trade, cultural, propaganda, and subversive activities all over Latin America. Their shortwave broadcasts in obscure dialects to Indian leaders in the interior of the South American continent indicate careful planning and long-range ambitions. An agreed Russo-Chinese division of labor could serve the purpose of letting Mao play the role of trouble-maker while Khrushchev occasionally acts as pacifier with the United States, a Janus-faced arrangement at which both Mao and Khrushchev are expert. In any event, the approach through the bourgeois democratic revolution gives both of them full room for maneuver.[39]

General Implementation

The organizational implementation of the "bourgeois democratic revolution" strategy proceeds via the cluster of communist methods described in preceding chapters: formation of quasi-patriotic fronts; operation of captive organizations, such as student groups, peasant leagues, and labor

37. See the August 13, 1959 hearings of the Senate Internal Security Subcommittee, published as Part 2 of the "Communist Threat to the United States Through the Caribbean" Series, p. 51.

38. Eudocio Ravines, *The Yenan Way*, pp. 148-59.

39. Jose J. Santa Pinter, "China Communista en America Latina," *Estudios Sobre el Communismo*, July-September, 1961, pp. 101-105. See also the testimony of General C. P. Cabell, Deputy Director of the CIA, on November 5, 1959, before the Senate Internal Security Subcommittee, published as Part 3 of the "Communist Threat to the United States Through the Caribbean" Series, pp. 165-67, and the testimony of Colonel Manuel A. V. Carrillo, May 4, 1960, *ibid.*, Part 7, pp. 376-77.

unions; and the formation and interlinking of secret party cells. The secret networks inside the government include the army, the police, and the civilian apparatus. The last group may be interlinked with the communist-party factions inside the recognized political parties. The three networks are meshed only at the top, either through the Party's high command or the Soviet underground operating out of the Embassy or both. The members of the army and police networks seldom know each other. This is also partly true of the civilian network. A considerable number of the members of the civilian group may participate in the pro-communist activities of the deceptive fronts and captive organizations, since this network, or parts of it, is the least secret of the three. Thus in Latin America, what shows above ground is of comparatively minor importance and may even be uninformed and treated by the Kremlin as expendable, as was the case in Cuba.

The Communists' aim is subtle promotion of the idea that the system of private initiative and democratic government is an antiquated institution which impedes the rapid development of a country. The progressive penetration being practiced by the Communists and their extreme leftist allies is geared toward the opportune moment when the social and political structure will fall, either from guerrilla or other outside pressures or, in some cases, without any special additional effort. While this process is developing, they continually campaign to make the people believe that all who talk against communism, especially those who are most reasonable and effective, are ultra right-wing reactionaries or worse.

Yankee Imperialism

Out of all of Moscow's probings in Latin America, there eventually emerged two potent slogans: "Anti-Yankee Imperialism" and "Anti-Latifundism" (plantation ownership). Of the two, Moscow concluded that anti-Yankee feeling was the better emotional lever needed to launch the revolution. Therefore, under the current communist strategy, the attack is not centered on the domestic bourgeoisie but against alleged Yankee imperialism. Few Latin American politicians will reject the anti-imperialist bandwagon in seeking their political fortunes. Extreme nationalism, also aimed at Yankee imperialism, is incited at the same time. Even the plantation owners, except for those with large holdings, are offered a moderate treatment. Thus the Communists in Latin America seek to make friends with everyone except the "imperialists" and their alleged stooges, and a stooge is anyone who is against communism. Their efforts are undertaken in the name of liberating Latin America from Yankee imperialism, and under this strategy, the Communists can collaborate with nearly everyone.

Yankee imperialism in the oppressive sense conjured up by the Communists rarely ever existed, and the record of the United States in the area since the 1930's has been generally good. Actually, Latin America liberated itself some generations ago from the centuries-old imperialism of Spain. The United States viewed this trend favorably in keeping with her tradition of support for self-determination movements. What the Communists are trading on is not today's reality but the residue of the European imperialism of decades past. They seek through propaganda to use this distant legacy for a rise to power. Unfortunately, propaganda does not have to be true to be effective. It only has to *seem* true to those being propagandized. Communist political warfare has never been inhibited by facts.

The communist high command knows the realities, of course, as well as anyone. That is why they intermix their anti-Yankee drive in Latin America with all sorts of immediate demands. They expect to sell their anti-imperialism on the strength of their reformist requests and promises. They promise much, especially to those they consider susceptible to their strategy.

If left to themselves, the Latin American Communists would probably prefer to concentrate on the domestic enemy, but anti-imperialism reflects Moscow's primary orientation. Like Communists elsewhere, those in Latin America must work for the defeat of the United States as a precondition for their own victory. They do not necessarily expect to convince a majority of their fellow countrymen to accept their anti-imperialism. According to communist strategic calculations, 15 per cent on their side, plus twice that many deceived or confused, may be sufficient for their purposes, provided the ruling circles are divided. Such a division, plus infiltration in the strategic sectors of the government apparatus, may throw the balance of the *active forces* to their side. What counts is not the formal number but the active, mobile force applied against the live core of the enemy at the right place and the right time.

Communist Success to Date

The Communists have succeeded with fictitious slogans before. For years they convinced many liberals that their system was a real democracy, and even now these permanent war-makers pose as the champions of peace. Their current over-all success in Latin America is difficult to judge. Extreme pessimism leads to panic and only contributes to the communist cause. A realistic appraisal is essential. The following 1961 view by an astute and responsible Colombian indicates that the hour is late:

It is not necessary to go into the details of how communist penetration has affected our daily life already in Colombia. Suffice it to say that technicians whom we have employed have pointed out that, when Castro entered Havana from the Sierra Maestro, Cuba was not as well penetrated and prepared as is Colombia now, at this time, for a communist revolution. There is violence and death in several rural mountain areas; our schools and universities have become a hot-bed of leftists, advanced marxists, and confused "useful idiots" (in Lenin's own words). When we woke up we found that our labor unions, judicial system, the press, the national security organizations, Congress, were all well penetrated by Marxists and by paid or fervent fellow travellers, effectively bent on disruption, Marxist anarchy and the "revolution" that comes before the period of "order" and communist peace and slavery. Even many of our friends without knowing were repeating fragments of Marxist doctrine in their daily expressions.[40]

Political Avenues to Power

The Communists have specialized in the take-over of backward or underdeveloped countries. They have shown, in parts of the world other than Latin America, that in economically backward areas it is possible to seize political power first and then use that power to impose their brand of totalitarian socialism. Their thrusts in the twentieth century have demonstrated the predominance of political power over economic determinism, a fundamental repudiation of Marxism but not of the communist power drive.

Thirty-five years ago, when the Communists began operations in Latin America, they were preoccupied with the penetration of the radicals, the workers, and the peasants. The idea of a Communist serving in the government, in order to penetrate it, was not considered. It took years before their tactics became opportunistic, and even then their effort at entering the government apparatus was, in the main, via the non-conservative or liberal parties or in coalition with them, if and when these parties came to power.

The political systems in Latin America are a major source of weakness. These countries seem never to have quite decided between dictatorship and democracy and often alternate between the two. The tendency to hold to the absolutist methods inherited from more than three centuries

40. Written in June of 1961. The source is withheld for protection of the writer.

of Iberian rule has been dominant. The unsteady trend towards authentic democracy appears to be gaining ground but is not yet predominant. Too many times in Latin American history forces seemed to work toward democracy, only to stumble into dictatorship. The growing power of the Latin American middle class is the prime force on which the democratic current is based. This force has already ushered out a number of dictatorial regimes and will, granting the likelihood of temporary setbacks here and there, gradually introduce a stabilizing influence in traditionally turbulent Latin American politics. The Communists, as a party dedicated to a new type of dictatorship, are exploiting this struggle between democracy and old forms of dictatorship in their endeavor to establish their own form of totalitarian rule. The confusing complexities of the political situation permit the communist medicine men, with their false panaceas, to operate freely as they side first with one group and then with the other.

The penetration of the established government apparatus which exists in most Latin American countries is a long and tedious process. Yet since a configuration of events and circumstances like the one in Cuba occurs rarely, penetration of the government apparatus to the point of saturation can be the only calculated communist strategy. Superficially, the odds would seem to be against Soviet penetration because the government as a superior force-in-being should be more than able to cope with the Communists. In reality, however, as experience shows, the Communists do have a chance. Their strength lies in greater political homogeneity and greater flexibility, plus ambiguous methods, which make them a difficult target for counter-operations.

In any event, in the last ten years the Communists have pursued the tactic of stepped-up penetration of the government apparatus. In Venezuela, for instance, under the dictatorship of Perez Jimenez, they divided their roles openly. One faction, the so-called "black" Communists, worked with the dictator, while the other, the "red" Communists, anticipating the overthrow of Jiminez, worked with the bourgeois liberal underground. Thus they were on both sides of the fence, uniting again after the overthrow.[41] In 1961, a comparable situation appeared to exist with regard to labor representatives in the National Senate and Assembly of Ecuador. Similar strategies are being applied, especially in pivotal countries like

41. Alexander, *op. cit.*, pp. 265-69.

Argentina, Mexico, and Brazil. In August of 1961, Cheddi B. Jagen, a dentist with communist leanings, came to power through election in British Guiana.

The Military Factor

In many countries in Latin America the hard core of the government apparatus is the military, which still plays a major role in politics. The more unstable the government, the greater the army's role. For many years, various Latin American armies have made and unmade presidents. Preliminary to the seizure of power, the Communists are confronted with this hard-core formation of the enemy. For a long time the Reds adhered to the idea of winning sufficient civilian components of a country to topple the government, but the Colombia experience indicated the need for a new approach. In Guatemala, too, they gained the first place in government, the presidency, but were unable to hold on. Their organization in Guatemala was too weak and lacked depth. They did not have sufficient time to penetrate the old political apparatus and the army, nor did they obtain the necessary arms from the outside to create a reliable coercive force of their own.[42]

Given time, the problem of penetrating at least the lower ranks of the military-bureaucracy combine may not be insoluble. Recruitment in the army is mostly from the peasants, and in the lower ranks a turnover occurs every few years. In a decade the change-over in officer personnel is also considerable. What is a reliable force today may not be reliable in ten years. In some Latin American countries, the officer personnel is largely recruited from young people educated at colleges and universities, themselves targets of communist penetration. Communist indoctrination successes there have brought an increasing number of new officers, either to the army or the police, who are, if not outright Communists, at least ideologically susceptible. In other countries, Brazil and Argentina in particular, the indoctrination of the officer corps is generally effective in immunizing its members against communism.

Communist supporters inside the military are, of course, kept very much underground. The cells among the officers are separate and super-secret, a sleeper apparatus kept for the day of decision. The officers, thus organized individually or as groups, are not supposed to participate in any overt pro-

42. Ronald M. Schneider, *Communism in Guatemala, 1944–54*, gives the best single-volume view. See especially pp. 301-22.

communist activity until directed to do so. While "sleeping," their main service to the party is in supplying intelligence information about the situation inside the government.

The Educational Equation

Not only the officer corps but the government apparatus and indeed all aspects of national life depend on the universities as their source of new leadership. If these sources are penetrated ideologically, the entire nation is fundamentally weakened. As long as the Communists in Latin America stuck to their original doctrinaire orientation, infiltration of the colleges proceeded slowly. Only after the application of the bourgeois democratic line did their impact on Latin American students and faculties become important. This switch greatly multiplied their influence in all university circles. The impact of this change explains much of the communist progress in the area in recent years.

Of course the student body in Latin America, as elsewhere, changes continuously, yet the Communist Party cleverly maintains control of student associations through permanent officials who are not really students but men thirty to forty years of age with many years of communist training. This seasoned influence is extended by the average Latin American university administrative organization, which follows the medieval Italian pattern, in which students have real, extensive, and sometimes almost overwhelming power in the actual running of the school. Students sit—and vote—with deans on the governing bodies. The degree of control exercised is far beyond that of any North American student-council system and seems almost incredible to some American observers.[43]

Because of the economic immaturity of most of the Latin American countries, a business career is not as attractive there as in the United States or much of Western Europe. Therefore, governments generally draw a higher percentage of talented persons, and many of them start their immersion into politics early, while still in college. In addition, it is traditional in Latin America for the students to be the leaders of social-reform movements. While European scholars hike and fence and American students swallow goldfish, go on panty raids or jam telephone booths, their Latin American counterparts take to the streets and build barricades as

43. For an impressive brief survey of the Latin American University system, see William E. Benton, "The Voice of Latin America," in *The 1961 Britannica Book of the Year*, pp. 3-64 and, especially, the details at pp. 46-52.

a form of political protest. Sometimes their actions result in lasting changes. The APRA movement of Peru, the largest indigenous left-wing movement to arise in Ibero-America, originated in the universities. And it was an earlier generation of Cuban students who overthrew Machado and placed Grau San Martin in power for a short time.

In the present context, communist "student" leaders effectively introduce their methods of connivance, intrigue, and conspiratorial organization. These have an extraordinary attraction for ambitious youngsters as a short-cut to power. These methods, coupled with promises of real social change, appeal to their youthful enthusiasm.

Although the pattern is not always finished as neatly as planned, it is a dynamic blueprint. Given a sufficient penetration of the civilian components of a country, the government apparatus eventually succumbs. It is a case of an aggressive force penetrating a more static one. In the long run, nothing but a thorough anti-communist education of the vital elements of the population, especially the youth, can prevent this. Needless to say, the Communists and their sympathizers are trying to do their utmost to block counterindoctrination. Against such a pattern of conquest of Latin America, many of our conventional ways of dealing with the Soviet challenge are obsolete.

Organized Labor

In Latin America, as elsewhere, the Communists started with the creation of the Party and the penetration of established labor unions and the organization of new ones. In most areas outside the Iron Curtain the Party and party-controlled or influenced labor unions are still the most massive instrument of internal conquest. The penetration of Latin American labor is considerable, though spotty as yet in most countries. There have been some heartening union elections during the past two years which have reduced the number of communist officers.[44] However, with the forcible capture of the Cuban Confederation of Labor, a renewed effort in this field under Cuban auspices must be expected. *Trud*, central organ of the captive Soviet unions (published in six languages, including Spanish), has given the lead to the new drive.

44. *Inter-American Labor Bulletin*, issued monthly by ORIT (AFL-CIO). See the January, February, June, and July, 1961 issues.

Communist Vulnerabilities

Communist successes over the years are numerous, but so are communist failures. Communist strengths, stemming largely from decades of activity, are impressive, but communist weaknesses are real and fundamental. In short, Latin America is still very much a battleground. The issue stands in doubt. Even in Cuba, where the Communists have made a major advance, not all is lost. A successful guerrilla action and interminable speech-making are hardly a substitute for the art of governing. An economic and political crisis is boiling in Cuba. Revolutions in a hurry may be made to appear attractive through propaganda. For Moscow, they may even be useful to stimulate unrest elsewhere, but they seldom pay off for the people.

Castro's mistakes reflect the fundamental error of communism, which is to seek social solutions through force. The Communists' obsessive fanaticism in favor of forced solutions applies especially to things economic, about which Communists have always displayed a massive ignorance. Castro has repeated in Cuba all of the blunders of the early years of bolshevism and even doubled on some of them. According to some reliable reports, the standard of living for millions in the island was in 1962 about half of what it was before Castro came to power.[45] Aggravating the economic situation is the compulsiveness of Communists to spend far too much on the creation of a huge military and police machine, both as political insurance for themselves and as preparation for further expansion. They build their glittering shows for propaganda purposes, but the end result thus far is the creation of a militarized poorhouse.

Of the nearly two hundred thousand refugees from Castro's Cuba, the overwhelming majority are middle class, most of them former Castro supporters or sympathizers. The exodus includes trained agriculturists, engineers, technicians, managers, directors, professors, teachers, shopowners, and others. It is generally conceded that even a much larger number of professionals are anxious and willing to leave Cuba at great sacrifice—if they could. Among the refugees, there is also a sizable group of skilled workers, and 1961 reports indicate that exile ranks are steadily broadening.[46] By antagonizing the middle class, which included the "new class" elements of modern industrial society, namely, the technological and man-

45. *Inter-American Labor Bulletin*, April, 1961, p. 1.
46. *New York Times*, September 8, 1961, p. 8.

agement intelligentsia—the most difficult to develop and acquire for any country—Castro has lost the skills essential for economic recovery and progress for many years to come. The vast departure of these skilled elements from Cuba is in itself a first-class calamity for Cuba's economy, not to mention the loss of the American sugar trade, the lucrative tourist trade, and so forth. It took the Bolsheviks twelve years to alienate the peasants. It took Red China's Mao nearly ten years to do the same. Castro's political hooliganism toward the middle classes alienated this vital group in Cuba in just two years. Their hostility creates a major economic and political vulnerability for Castro to deal with.

Other vulnerabilities include Castro's default on his promises of a general distribution of cultivated land to the peasants and failure to keep his pledge to hold democratic elections. What could be the worst vulnerability for Castro, however, is the proximity of a strong United States intelligently pressuring Cuba's militarized tyranny. If the United States would turn to political counterwarfare and take the Cuban situation as the first item to practice on, it could liquidate Castro and discredit Castroism in the eyes of Latin America.

It might be argued that in view of the importance of the Cuban beachhead to the communist empire, Khrushchev will support Castro with economic and other kinds of aid. Yet he would have to do so at the end of a line thousands of miles long. If so, Cuba might become far too expensive for Moscow. The Kremlin has never before operated in an area with the odds so much in the favor of the United States. With the Soviet coalition short on food, consumer goods, and shipping, the contest for Cuba could be brief and interesting, but disastrous for the Kremlin. It is time that we look upon Castro as an inviting target within easy range.

Beyond Cuba, across Latin America in general, there are many communist weaknesses to probe. Communist blindness toward the small owner and producer may yet prove to be the movement's downfall. Addiction to force is the main reason why Russian housing and agriculture remain substandard after more than forty years under an allegedly "superior" system and why China under the communists is starving.

The captured middle-class revolution in Cuba only proves once more, and in a vivid way, what has been obvious to many close observers of this twentieth-century social phenomena, namely, that contrary to all of its allegations, the Communist Party does not represent and is not loyal to any class. It merely uses a class or classes to ride into power, after which it be-

comes independent of the classes whose aid it sought and betrays them—
and the country—at its own convenience. No matter what maneuvers and
promises the Party resorts to as it pursues its road to power, it is a party
dedicated to wiping out all classes based on private property. Realistic
ideological counterwarfare can and should take full advantage of these
facts.

Although the Communists have offered to "march with the bourgeoisie"
as an essential feature of their strategy, the bourgeoisie has not offered to
march with them. There is a basic contradiction between what the bourgeoisie wants and what the Communists want, regardless of any temporary
coincidence of interests. The Communists, for example, are interested in
rooting out all North American political economic influence in Latin
America and replacing it with Soviet influence. Communist anti-imperialism calls for the nationalization of the so-called imperialist and other major
enterprises, a measure of dubious interest to the bourgeoisie, since it rules
out private ownership.

Even guerrilla warfare can be contained and turned to positive ends.
The conditions in Cuba in the last stages of the Batista regime which made
Castro's victory possible—corruption and ignorance, amoral and demoralized political management and United States' blindness, need not be dupli-
cated in other countries. Guerrilla warfare has many applications under
the conditions of a maturing political and economic crisis. While in communist hands it can be used to move in on a revolution under the pretense
of bringing more rapid reform, it can also be used against the communist
regime in Cuba and against pro-communist movements in other parts of
Latin America.

Genuine reform is necessary, of course, and here the communist menace
may be supplying an impetus which has never been present before. Political warfare includes all factors of the economic equation. Although discussion of this topic lies beyond the scope of this study, a brief recapitulation is in order. A first priority is avoidance of the misconception that Latin
America is an area where virtually no middle-class leadership exists. This
view sees a mass of poverty-stricken Latin Americans leading a hopeless
life while a handful of incredibly wealthy, predatory families rule the nation. Such a picture distorts reality, weakens faith in evolutionary change,
and increases the attraction of violent social solutions. Poverty is a problem, one which cannot be ignored, yet a balanced study of Latin America
today must not ignore the large and growing middle class, which has

exerted and is exerting positive leadership. From this group there is emerging a substantial number of young men and women who are socially as responsible as their counterparts in any country in the Free World. Devoted to the system of private initiative, which has contributed so much to the development of the United States, they see the future of their continent in terms of real social responsibility and substantial economic growth. While spending an impressive amount of time and energy in halting the spread of communism in the hemisphere, they are also making every effort to bring their nations into full social maturity. The *Alliance for Progress* can only be effected in close and continuing co-operation with this democratic leadership.

Until now, those who have expounded upon the *Alliance for Progress* have focused attention almost exclusively upon government-to-government aid. Certainly this type of assistance is essential to get the job under way, but government-to-government aid represents only a fraction of the total panorama of possibilities, and a minor fraction at that. The tremendous amount of capital involved is not understood except in the most informed circles. Responsible United States and Latin American economic experts estimate, for example, that for steel and electric power alone, the area needs an amount of capital investment far greater than the entire Marshall Plan. When other priorities are considered, the total sum is completely beyond the willingness of the United States or any other government to supply. The major portion of this development capital must come from non-government sources both inside and outside Latin America. In a hemisphere where governments have at their disposal a small fraction of the total available current production, the predominant role which must be played by private economic activity in expansion of trade and the processes of over-all growth should require no elaboration. There is a corollary to the attraction of large amounts of new private-capital investment. It is incumbent upon the foreign enterprises already operating in Latin America to pursue policies which will make them fully acceptable.

Housing, even more than land reform, is the most pressing problem confronting the mass of the people in Latin America. Furthermore, it is a problem which can be solved without arousing the kind of political opposition from landowners which so often delays social progress.

A large-scale housing program would have several advantages. It would bring genuine social gains which could be felt by the people; hence it would diminish the attractiveness of drastic socio-economic solutions. Housing, too, is a unique sector of the economy where the satisfaction of consumer desires and the stimulation of productive growth meet. Housing programs create not only jobs and purchasing power but whole new industries. Forest products, metals, plastics, factories for the production of prefabs, furniture, electric-power plants, appliances, and many other lines of production are greatly stimulated by the building of homes in large numbers. Housing is politically attractive to all government sectors involved—local, regional, and national. Finally, housing programs, by making human existence more attractive for large numbers of people, provide an incentive to construct stable political communities in which freedom and legal rights are respected. Both governmental and private-capital programs should be directed toward the building of small homes for individual owners or cooperative units in which each family could purchase its own apartment.

Housing is crucial, but so are agrarian problems in most of Latin America. Housing programs must always be integrated with parallel programs of rural improvement, expansion of educational facilities, industrial development, administrative efficiency, and social modernization.

Communist planners do not see Latin America as it is but as they want it to be. In Latin America the major metropolitan areas are more modern and exceed in number the large cities in Russia. Most of Latin America is in the midst of its take-off period towards full industrialization and is currently far ahead of Russia forty-two years ago when the Communists took over. It is one of the strangest phenomena of our times that crude experimenters, operating in the name of communism, arrogate to themselves the role of advisers to a superior civilization, and, more impertinent yet, seek to impose their ideology upon peoples who, whatever their shortcomings, are way ahead in the practices of humanism and freedom.

Communist propaganda should not be permitted to make its way unburdened by the story of the unfavorable and contrary communist record. All that needs to be done is to open the eyes of the multitude to the vast discrepancy between propaganda and performance. Communism can lose its potency as an alternative to Western society if it is properly exposed.

Avenues to Success

This exposure must take full advantage of all the means of political warfare legitimately open to the West. If communism is receding in the developed free countries but still advancing in the underdeveloped ones, it is because no force comparable to the international communist party is ready to combat it. Political countereducation, when present at all, is still on the back pages of the press and the off-hours of radio and TV. Unfortunately, because of modern communications, the mass mind can indeed be manipulated for either good or evil. The West has the necessary means and resources to catch up with the Kremlin, but it requires a major orientation and a major effort.

The theory that man is primarily motivated by his stomach has always been a half-truth. Man is also motivated by transcendental ideas. Ideas penetrate the mind, regardless of the condition of the stomach, and once lodged there, they stay for a long time and are passed on to others. The Communists do not distribute powdered milk in their pursuit of power. They distribute and engender hope. Nor is it necessary that the hope be based on reality. Our culture confines us to the use of the truth; the Communists have no such limitation. Because of the furious pace of our times, ideas can become dominant before man can reflect on the consequences, thus creating a condition difficult to reverse. All that is needed is for these ideas to appear plausible during the time necessary to take power in their name. Thus what in the past took centuries can now be done in decades. The danger to the superior civilization of the West, including Latin America, comes from underestimation of the conquering force of ideas, whether good or bad, true or false. Today key ideas are manipulated by an organization which fights with no moral restraints. When Nikita Khrushchev said that "in another forty years, your children shall live under communism," it was not a mere boast. Behind his confidence was an empire of over one thousand million inhabitants built in forty-two years on postponed promises and ideological deception. It is time to cut through the deception.

For the purposes of counterpolitical warfare and in the interests of an objective scientific study of modern tyrannies and their antecedents, the great and mysterious voids in Marxism-Leninism must be explored and exposed. What, for example, is "imperialism" to the average politically ignorant mind in Latin America? In the absence of an effective counter-effort, it is what the active propagandists on the subject say it is. If the active propagandists say that investments from and trade with the advanced countries is imperialism while similar relations inside the Soviet bloc constitute fraternal aid, many of the politically uneducated come to believe it. Such misconceptions cannot be combatted with vast expenditures of money or the piling up of aid to these countries, but only with effective counter-propaganda. It is a matter of the mind and can be coped with only on that level.

There is considerable evidence that the present generation of Latin American leaders is more aware of this fact than their counterparts in the United States. In many of the twenty republics to the south, well-directed, comprehensive efforts are being made to defeat the Communists by counter-political warfare. No doubt their activities have been sparked by the realization that their countries are in the immediate target area and, indeed, under heavy fire. Still, this does not alter their accomplishments. The groups are, in the main, private organizations loosely confederated with those in neighboring countries. Their objective has been to have an impact, through organized effort, on the educated and influential classes. They fight communism by showing that its record indicates clearly its opposition to Christian moral values, Western systems and institutions, concepts of personal dignity, traditional family structures, property, and, in a word, human freedom. They have had some impact on the Church, professions, the press, labor, business, political parties, some sectors of education, and the governments as a whole. However, much remains to be done.

Furthermore, they conclude from serious thought and technical appreciation of the problem that the communist approach is more effective in Latin America than that of the United States. The Russians, with the Communist Party as their means, work directly with the people in private areas of national life. The United States, working through government bureaucracy in the country involved, has much of its impact wasted or filtered out before it reaches the citizens. Though Latin Americans are saddened by this realization, it in no way lessens responsible Latin American desires for further United States effort. They realize that they cannot win the fight alone, and they look to the north as the only place from which they can receive the necessary additions to their strength.

The forces against communism in the Western Hemisphere could be potent if they were brought to bear upon the problem. An ideological force must be fought with another ideological force, a political attack by political countermeasures. This task must be co-ordinated and executed by persons trained for the purpose. If it is not, Castro's Cuba could be the New World prologue for the absorption of our rich and varied civilization into Khrushchev's tyranny, in which freedom tops the long list of items in short supply.

PART THREE

Counterattack

COUNTERATTACK

IT IS GENERALLY RECOGNIZED BY NOW THAT THE UNITED STATES and the Free World face a profound crisis which could result in the collapse and ruin of the free societies. According to Senator J. W. Fulbright, Chairman of the Senate Committee on Foreign Relations:

> We must now focus our efforts on the insidious challenges of psychological penetration, of political subversion, of economic conquest, of the use of foreign aid and trade as political weapons. To meet these threats we have already begun to devise, and we must now go on to perfect, new and varied instruments of foreign policy that go far beyond containment and military alliances.[1]

Among the new and varied instruments the United States might perfect would be political warfare in an American context. Yet certain attitudes block the perfection and American use of the political warfare instrument.

---

1. From a speech in "Public Policy and Military Responsibility" delivered to the National War College on August 21, 1961. See the *Congressional Record*, Vol. 107, No. 144, pp. 15358-59. Senator Fulbright is a very complex individual. His brilliant article, "For a Concert of Free Nations," which appeared in *Foreign Affairs* in October, 1961, sets forth an inspiring concept of Atlantic unity which, if adopted, would give a tremendous boost for the free world. On the other hand, Fulbright opposed the American intervention in Cuba, as well as any commitment to defend the neutrality of the Laotian people. Fulbright also suggested, in early August, 1961, that the East Germans had the right to seal off East Berlin from West Berlin. Subsequently, Senator Fulbright, in speaking of the September, 1961 Commonwealth Parliamentary Association advised our British allies that "the West is not entirely blameless for the development of the Berlin crisis." Senator Fulbright's recognition of the new dimensions of the East-West conflict could be most significant if he would simultaneously grasp the fact that political warfare can be as ruthless and as decisive as armed conflict.

The most fundamental obstacle to the United States' prosecution of political warfare is the illusion that we may soon achieve a general settlement with the Communists. Such hopes are inspired by two mistaken beliefs—one, that we can (in the short run) encourage the emergence in the Soviet Union of new leaders and groups who stand for moderation; the other, that the Kremlin leaders basically think as we do.

The first of these ideas ignores the evidence which indicates that what we call moderation is, on the Soviet leaders' part, merely a temporary "retreat" resulting from our opposing pressure, without any change in their over-all intent. One may contrast, for example, the Korean armistice, the backdown at Quemoy, and the end of the Berlin blockade with the aggressive Soviet penetration of the Middle East and Latin America following our 1955 efforts toward a settlement at Geneva. As for the second belief, we can only say that the Kremlin is merely fostering our illusion that they think as we do.

Another factor limiting American use of political warfare is a failure to "see the picture big." Traditionally, Americans "think big" only about economic problems. In matters political, they tend to conservatism and caution. By contrast, the Soviet-communist leader is trained to think big in all things. Nathan Leites, a well-known Soviet specialist, has pointed out that when faced with a new problem, the Russian Communist considers the extreme alternatives first, while Americans concentrate on weighing "middle" compromise solutions.

Examples of the Soviet tendency to "think big" are many, not alone in the field of economics, but in science, military matters, and politics as well. The Soviets have largely neglected the highway age in Russia, preferring to resort to airplanes in order to save the vast capital costs of highway construction. They turned to automation at a remarkably early stage of development. In 1946–47, when we postponed the development of the intercontinental missile because the nuclear warhead we then foresaw seemed too large to be efficiently propelled, the Russians, facing the same problem, simply built more powerful missile engines. Their political proposals and actions are timed to compel Western attention to shift back and forth from the Far East to Europe to the Middle East, and from military challenges to economic competition to political gambits, at a pace and scale designed to keep our policy-planners off balance and too preoccupied to plan major political initiatives.

If the United States accepts the necessity for waging political warfare, it must initiate a major training program for political-warfare operatives, and devise a better system for developing and co-ordinating an integrated Cold War strategy. Implicit in such a strategy will be the exploitation of the basic vulnerabilities of communist-dominated countries and the world-wide communist parties.

Political warfare requires untold thousands of skilled specialists who must not only know their specialty, communist political-warfare techniques, the language of the country to which they are sent, but be sufficiently familiar with its culture to gain influence.

The pace of today's struggle allows no time for gradual maturing. We, too, need to take a "great leap forward"—in preparing America for national service throughout the world. The Soviets have had such training for forty years.

Better and more training might also overcome one of our most serious deficiencies: the incapacity of most Americans to articulate our ideology. The basic principles of democracy provide just as comprehensive guidelines to action as does communism. But as citizens and students we rarely learn to distinguish the basic from the derivative or even trivial aspects of democracy. We find ourselves unable to select those elements of our ideology which have immediate relevance for each particular foreign culture and to adapt them to concrete ends. Not only do we not translate our ideology into concrete forms, we tend to view it negatively, as a set of American values to be defended rather than as a positive guiding force. Perhaps America, and indeed democracy, needs a secular Thomas Aquinas who can distill philosophical order from our democratic practices. As a world power, we must lead through the example of ideas as well as behavior.

The question of training is examined in the chapter which follows.

Our greatest post-war actions, the Marshall Plan and the Korean War, were immediate responses to unambiguous challenges. They did, however, bring in their train a new sophistication about the interrelationship of economic and political realities and new wariness about the seriousness of the communist challenge.

These and other experience have prepared us to devise a clear informing theory of action to deal with communist conflict strategy. Such a theory must provide for: (1) analysis of Soviet moves in terms of Soviet doctrine, resulting in a strategically planned political warfare of appropriately long range; (2) the formulation of concrete, phased objectives; and (3) the co-ordinated and dynamic use of the instruments of political warfare on the scale appropriate to the challenge.

With strategic theory must go organization. We must improve the planning co-ordination between the field activities of different departments of our government and interlink them with private organizations. This is an extremely difficult task in a large bureaucracy, and we do not suggest that there have not been efforts to make that co-ordination more effective. The organizational issue will be surveyed in the second chapter of this section.

The final chapter examines the weaknesses of those who are seeking our destruction and suggests how to take advantage of them, as we are able, to reduce the pressure of communism's unremitting attack against freedom.

CHAPTER XIV

TRAINING FOR POLITICAL WARFARE

"EVERYONE WILL AGREE," WROTE LENIN, "THAT AN ARMY which does not train itself to wield all arms, all means and methods of warfare that the enemy possesses is behaving in an unwise or even criminal manner. . . . Unless we are able to master all forms of warfare, we stand at the risk of suffering great and sometimes decisive defeat."[1]

Lenin gave this advice in 1920, when his fledgling Bolshevik Party was weak and ill equipped to fight a major struggle with the bourgeoisie. Training has ever since been one of the vital mainsprings of communist expansion via political warfare. Because of their emphasis on trained conflict managers, the Communists have gained a forty-year lead in political warfare. Now it is the West's turn to "train itself to wield all arms, all means of warfare that the enemy possesses."

The Communists are assaulting the Free World with an extraordinary variety of conflict instruments. They use every promising avenue to approach their objectives and are demonstrating superlative organizational capabilities in penetrating and manipulating a wide range of political parties, institutions, and organizations in Latin America, Africa, the Middle East, and Far East.

A remarkable research, development and training program in conflict technique and management has been carried on in the Soviet Union for more than forty years. This program has enabled the Communists to develop and integrate the full spectrum of conflict instruments and to train "conflict managers" capable of arranging all of these instruments in carefully orchestrated aggression.

1. Quoted from *Selected Works*, Vol. X, p. 139.

Forty years of intensive preparation are paying off. It is conceivable the communist bloc can substantially isolate the United States and its allies in a hostile world in a few years—unless we develop a far greater capacity in the full range of countermeasures available to us.

What must be done? What are the requirements for preparing an open, pluralistic society to meet the non-military sectors of the communist Cold War attack on a global basis?

Requirement No. 1

The public must have greater understanding of communism, especially communist conflict technique, and the nature of the global struggle. This is necessary to maintain the will to victory and to overcome apathy in a long and tedious struggle. In a free society, policy must have public support to be effective. A widening fissure between public knowledge and policy can spell disaster. For defensive purposes alone this knowledge is essential, if public opinion is not to be confused and manipulated by the deception and lures of skilled propagandists who understand us and our desire to be left alone too well.

Requirement No. 2

The public must participate in the global struggle in a sustained and systematic manner. America has a huge reservoir of talent, ingenuity, and strength which can be utilized in the Cold War. Whether this is done or not done can spell the difference between victory and defeat in a contest in which the enemy has mobilized his entire society to win the "conflict of systems."

Requirement No. 3

Policy-makers and government personnel at many levels must acquire a better understanding of communism, particularly of its conflict techniques. Especially must they understand deception and be able to defend their thinking against propaganda. It is not enough to have experts available for consultation. Basic "battle knowledge" must be widely understood in the government if planning and implementation are to be geared to the conflict we are in.

Requirement No. 4

Policy-makers and those who advise them must understand the *full* range of measures, public and private, potentially available to meet the entire communist attack and to work toward our national objectives systematically. This means they will have to master a broad range of non-military measures which have yet to be thought through and systematized. They must be able to devise an integrated strategy to attain national objectives.

Requirement No. 5

At all levels, government personnel must be trained to understand and implement a sophisticated strategy. Unless there is a substantial "common fund of knowledge" about the nature of the enemy, the global conflict, the competitive technological environment in which it takes place, and the array of negative and positive measures available to us, there cannot be the team play necessary to compete with vigor and *élan* with a dedicated and skilled enemy.

There are other requirements, but the above are basic. In part, we have failed to meet these because we have not understood the need for systematic, large-scale research and training programs required in political warfare. Nor have we understood the range of organizational and operational means required. But if political performance is the payoff, our research and training program in the area of non-military conflict, considered as a whole, is grossly inadequate.

The problem of adequate research and training in non-military conflict has been approached on a piecemeal basis. Fifteen years ago, when we first recognized the existence of the Cold War, American policy-planners began formulating some ideas and programs for meeting the non-military challenge. As the crisis deepened and the massive nature of the communist assault on our civilization became evident, various research projects were instituted at our universities and within governmental agencies; there was an increase in language study at the Foreign Service Institute and greater emphasis was placed on the non-military area at the War Colleges.[2] However, there is little evidence that anyone believed that an over-all national research and training program would be necessary.

The governmental training available to meet Requirement No. 3 is far from adequate. The War Colleges devote from two weeks to a month to coverage of the Soviet bloc. Within that period the *specific* treatment of communism and communist conflict techniques rarely exceeds *two or three days*. Yet this difficult subject, which requires considerable, systematized

2. The National War College, under the JCS, as well as the Army, Navy, and Air War Colleges, the Industrial College of the Armed Forces, and the Armed Forces Staff College.

study, is absolutely essential to an understanding of the protracted conflict. It is true, of course, that the rest of the instruction is related to the communist threat. But even this instruction presupposes a more complete understanding of communist operations than the War College student actually possesses.

The Foreign Service Institute of the Department of State has a *two-week* seminar on communism and the Soviet Union. This is one of the best courses of the kind offered in the U.S.A., yet because of time limitations, this broad survey course can give only light treatment to communism and communist conflict technique. Limited to ten days of actual training, the course provides one and one-half hours of lecture-discussions each on communism in the Far East, South Asia, Africa, Southeast Asia, Western Europe, Eastern Europe, Latin America, and the United States. There is *one* lecture-discussion on such involved, encyclopedic subjects as subversion. Considering the very few points even a first-class teacher can get across in one lecture, the superficiality of the course is self-evident.

The State Department's Basic Foreign Service Officer's Course (nine weeks), required of all junior officers on appointment, and the Mid-Career Course in Foreign Affairs (thirteen weeks) offer almost nothing on the "Conflict of Systems." The Basic Course has *six hours* of lectures by CIA experts "covering" the Soviet Union, the international communist movement, the organization and strategy of communism, Soviet global propaganda, and how to answer criticisms abroad originating from Communists. The Mid-Career Course includes only a *two-hour* lecture on communist doctrine and practice, *two hours* on the role of behavioral science in Soviet strategy, and *two hours* on Soviet political organizations.

In 1958, the State Department inaugurated the Senior Seminar in Foreign Policy, a nine-month course, for about twenty senior officers at a time, which is the Foreign Service Institute counterpart to the War Colleges. This course devotes *five days* to "Communist Strategy," and a good part of the time is spent in discussion groups or attending optional films. Again, much of the remainder of the course relates to the communist threat, but, as in the case of the War Colleges, it presupposes more operational knowledge about communist political warfare than the student usually possesses. The United States Information Agency training program has no course on communism, but does send a limited number of its officials to the two-week State Department Seminar.

Dr. Stefan T. Possony, a leading authority on communism, lecturer at the National War College, and adviser on Soviet affairs to the Department of Defense, has stated: "There is, to the best of my knowledge, no school within the government which *specializes* in communism, let alone operational communism." He further commented:

Without detracting in the slightest from the value of the War Colleges and the agency trade schools, it cannot be seriously argued that these schools provide an adequate coverage of communism. There is indeed a coverage in broad outline, but no intensive study and there are large gaps in the coverage. This cannot be otherwise because literature dealing with communism also shows wide gaps; furthermore, there are no textbooks which allow a student to tackle the whole problem matter within two covers. Instead, anyone who wants to be knowledgeable on communism is compelled to read and analyze carefully a minimum of two or three dozen books, and such an undertaking simply is not in the cards within a ten-months course [length of War College courses], most of which deals with other subjects, let alone courses lasting only a few weeks.

Regarding adequate public knowledge about communism and the global struggle, there is no evidence of an existing organized effort which can hope to fill the gap. It should be emphasized here that even adequate generalized knowledge about communism and communist conflict technique can only be obtained through a systematic training program or a heavy amount of organized reading. It is no answer to say that our news media give excellent coverage of world events. They present a hodgepodge of uncorrelated facts which leave the untrained individual with a blurred image of communism. Nor is it any answer to say that many good books about communism are stacked in our libraries, when no significant number of people are reading these books, or reading them in sufficient quantity.

It should be kept in mind that there is little in the experience of our people to prepare them to understand the present struggle. The type of enemy we face, the dazzling and confusing array of methods and means used against us, the skillful deception, the ambiguous nature of enemy moves, the misleading vocabulary, the slow and often obscure erosion of our position, the seemingly disconnected events in all parts of the globe, subversion raised to an art—all are foreign to our experience.

Our secondary schools and universities are an obvious place to make a beginning in organized instruction about communism and the world conflict, yet by and large, they offer almost nothing. A former Director of CIA, Allen W. Dulles, in a speech given to the Veterans of Foreign Wars at Detroit on August 22, 1960, commented:

In our schools and colleges we can find many courses in ancient history, in philosophy, courses on the great movements of the past, the conquests of ancient times from Alexander the Great to Napoleon. Courses on Communist theory and practices are few and far between.

By and large, however, in our educational institutions, except in the graduate field or in specialized schools and seminars, these subjects are not generally taught.

There is a real urgency to build up our knowledge on the entire background of the Communist threat against our civilization.

The people of this country are and will continue to be basically opposed to Communism in general. This opposition is based more on instincts than on knowledge. This is not enough. Our people should be sufficiently educated in all of the ramifications of communist intrigue and its historical background, its purposes and programs adequately to contribute toward an effective answer. . . . The initiative for new knowledge comes more often from those of us who want to learn than from those who teach. But let us also call on our educators, and on those in authority who have influence over the development of our educational system to begin to expand the realistic teaching of the history and policies of Communism.

A course covering political philosophy in the nineteenth and twentieth centuries in which the student reads the *Communist Manifesto* and *State and Revolution,* does practically nothing to prepare him to understand the global conflict, nor do a few chapters on Russia since 1917 in a modern European history course. Yet this is about all that most colleges offer.

Some instruction on the communist challenge should begin in our secondary schools. Here the gap is immense. Public pressure is developing to inaugurate courses on "Communism *versus* Democracy" in our high schools. However, even if our schools wanted to do this, and some now do, they are stymied because *almost no teachers have been trained to give such a course* or to treat the subject in adequate form in social science and history courses.

Nothing demonstrates our research and training failure better than this failure to teach the teachers. Again and again civic organizations, the American Bar Association, for example, have urged such instruction. And each time they run up against the same roadblock. There is little evidence that our teachers' colleges and state universities are doing anything to remedy the situation or that they have instructors themselves who are prepared to teach these subjects. There is no organized effort to cover the ground. It is unrealistic to expect our busy teachers to educate themselves in this difficult subject. Even if courses begin to appear in our high schools, their quality, in the absence of thoroughly trained teachers, will leave much to be desired.

If we ask how private citizens can contribute to winning the global struggle, then the absence of research and training becomes even more fully apparent. The very idea that private citizens can or should engage to the extent of their ability and opportunities in the Cold War may be a novel one to many Americans. If one looks at the comparative commitment of the communist-dominated nations to the "conflict of systems" compared to that of the democracies, the value of private participation should be obvious. As we have stated previously, the Communist Party of the Soviet Union has at its disposal all of the material human resources of the Soviet Union in the waging of the conflict. The United States government, on the other hand, has available to it for all purposes about 20 per cent of the resources of the American nation. About half of the federal resources can be considered as being involved in the Cold War in one form or another.

Consciously or unconsciously, private American institutions, as well as private American citizens, have a direct influence on attitudes and decisions made by other nations—American movies, educational exchange programs, tourists, missionary activities, etc., all weigh heavily in projecting the American image abroad. These activities never can or should be fully coordinated to the extent that the Soviet Union integrates Tass, its state trading agencies, and external propaganda. But if those Americans who participate in these activities have a better understanding of communist techniques, as well as more ability to articulate the fundamental political principles on which our pluralistic society rests, their effectiveness in meeting the communist challenge abroad can be increased manyfold.

Many of our most difficult Cold War problems are susceptible to partial solution by private groups, *provided* that our private institutions and civic organizations have among their members some who have received systematic training concerning the global conflict. Yet, as in the case of school teachers, we have neglected training programs which would enable any significant number of private citizens to learn about these things.

Responsible citizens who showed little concern even a year or two ago are now crowding forward to ask: "What can we do to help win the Cold War?" They sense that the business-as-usual civic projects now engaging their time are a little remote in terms of the present world situation. Many display eagerness to work on worth-while projects that have some real bearing on winning the Cold War. By and large, however, this increasing desire to participate has been frustrated by lack of trained leadership at the community, state, and national levels and responsible knowledge as to what the private citizen can do.

It will require a concentrated, systematic research program involving a broad cross-section of experts with much experience to think through the many methods and means the private citizen can employ—if the millions of private citizens who are in some kind of contact with people all over the world are to participate on a sustained and systematic basis.

A number of private organizations are making contributions overseas. Certain foundations are spending substantial sums abroad on a range of projects that have at least an indirect bearing on the outcome of the struggle. The AFL-CIO has done considerable work in Latin America, Africa, Europe, and Asia attempting to bolster free labor against the communist onslaught. Several universities offer short courses to businessmen going overseas. At first glance the list of private participation appears impressive. But only a tiny fraction of the ingenuity, talent, and strength that could be brought to bear here and overseas is being utilized. Much of what is being done is mediocre in terms of what could be done if we had *trained* people to carry out these programs.

Turning now to Requirement No. 4, we find that we have developed few true generalists capable of devising an integrated national strategy. Many of the shortcomings in our national structure for strategy (discussed in the next chapter) can be traced to the inadequate training of our key officials in the nature and techniques of the present conflict.

At the higher levels we need conflict managers on the side of freedom who have assimilated a wide range of background information and operational knowledge and can visualize, organize, and manage the range of measures and countermeasures by which the global conflict will be decided. The field is so vast, the interrelationship between programs so sophisticated, that it cannot be mastered except through systematic and intensive study.

Lacking an adequate training program, our Cold War strategists have had to learn on the job, with tragic consequences. This stands in marked contrast to the preparation of Soviet conflict managers, who have been schooled in long-term planning and political warfare throughout their careers. Henry Kissinger has commented on this crucial issue:

Whatever the qualities of Soviet leadership, its training is eminently political and conceptual. Reading Lenin or Mao or Stalin, one is struck by the emphasis on the relationship between political, military, psychological and economic factors, the insistence on finding a conceptual basis for political action and on the need for dominating a situation by flexible tactics and inflexible purpose. And the internal struggles in the Kremlin ensure that only the most iron-nerved reach the top. Against the Politburo, trained to think in general terms and freed of problems of day-to-day administration, we have pitted leaders overwhelmed with departmental duties and trained to think that the cardinal sin is to transgress on another's field of specialization.[3]

Without intensive, systematic study of a vast array of subjects, how can a U.S. strategist possibly hope to develop strategy attuned to the world conflict? To say that specialists are available to advise him on these matters is like saying experts on strategy and tactics are available to a field commander who has never studied these things himself. Washington advised Braddock about the unconventional Indians, and that well before the ambush. Unless the policy-maker has himself mastered these central subjects and can think conceptually about the global conflict, the availability of specialists will not make a strategist out of him.

When these grave deficiencies are pointed out, the stock answer is: "We know government training programs are inadequate, but this is supplemented by sending regular quotas of higher civil servants to schools of international studies at our universities." As one State Department official put it, "We like our people to get the Harvard viewpoint, the Johns Hopkins viewpoint, the MIT viewpoint." The urgent need is for rounded Cold War strategists. Our universities are attuned to developing scholars and specialists. The urgent need is for operational-organizational competence in the new dimensions of struggle.

We are constantly told that the Communists work harder and with more dedication than their opponents. This, if true, is so because the communist training program, the whole process by which they mold their cadres, concentrates on achieving a complete personal commitment. Our armed forces understand its importance. Paratroop, Marine Corps, and Ranger units have it, and it has been carefully cultivated in training because their tough combat missions require it. Yet non-military conflict tests the human will in more subtle and deadly ways than military combat, and the will to win is equally crucial. The university atmosphere is simply not conducive to developing a complete personal commitment. Sometimes it will, but this is by accident rather than by design. To win the "conflict of systems" we must have men and women who are ready to accept any financial sacrifice or physical rigor if it contributes to victory, who will not permit themselves

3. Henry Kissinger. *Nuclear Weapons and Foreign Policy,* p. 434.

to be affected by the apathy of their associates or the psychological pressures of the enemy.

We must keep constantly before us the distinction between studying communism and the languages, institutions, economies, and histories of foreign countries, on the one hand, and exploring and developing the operational-organizational skill and the conceptual framework for non-military conflict, on the other hand. This will make it possible to understand the conflict in all its dimensions and to apply the full range of means potentially available in an integrated, sustained, and consistent fashion. But such operational-organizational knowledge and a realistic conceptual framework for a global struggle between freedom and communism is not a main concern of our universities.

The Soviets also engage in extensive area and language studies. But what gives them their great advantage is the systematic way in which they have thought out and mastered the organizational forms and operational techniques which are possible in a total power struggle. They apply these, flexibly, yet systematically and consistently, with clearly understood purpose, within an all-encompassing conceptual framework.

President Kennedy's April, 1961 speech gave his understanding of the inadequacy of our strategy and the means of implementation for non-military conflict.

We dare not fail to see the insidious nature of this new and deeper struggle. We dare not fail to grasp the *new concepts, the new tools,* the new sense of urgency we will need to combat it, whether in Cuba or South Viet Nam. And we dare not fail to realize it is this struggle which is taking place every day without arms or fanfare, in thousands of villages and markets and classrooms all over the globe. . . . No greater task faces this nation or this Administration. . . . Too long have we fixed our eyes on the traditional military needs. . . . We intend to profit from this lesson. We intend to *re-examine and reorient our forces of all kinds, our tactics and our institutions* here in this community. We intend to intensify our efforts for a struggle in many ways more difficult than war.[4]

The capability for non-military conflict is not developed easily or quickly. If the enemy is given enough lead time, as he has been given in the production of missiles, we may never stop him. Further, we can pass the point of no return without being aware of it. We can leave the enemy uncontested in the villages, the classrooms, the markets just so long.

4. Italics added.

The most alarming aspect of the unfolding world situation is not the Communists' gains to date, but their over-all *capacity* for conflict vis-à-vis the West. The question must now be asked, in all seriousness, whether communist capabilities are such that they can complete the isolation of the West before we can develop sufficient countercapabilities. The communist research, development, and training program, beginning with Lenin's three bolshevik schools of revolution in Italy and France prior to 1914, and expanding during the twenties into the most massive research and training program in all history, has given them truly frightening capabilities.

We cannot offset communist advantages with half-measures. A program backed by the full weight and prestige of our government will be most realistic in terms of the challenge we face. A group of patriotic and knowledgeable citizens in Orlando, Florida (The Orlando Committee), have developed the concept of a "Freedom Academy" to conduct both research and training in the many aspects of the Cold War. Legislation to implement their concept was passed by the Senate in 1960 and reintroduced in 1961.[5]

The purpose of the proposed Freedom Academy is to develop our over-all capacity in the new dimensions of struggle. It would bring under one roof the necessary range of knowledge and experience to consider non-military conflict as a whole. The operative language of the bill, Section 6, reads:

The principal functions of the Commission and Academy shall be—
(1) to carry on a research program designed to develop an integrated, operational science that benefits and bespeaks the methods and values of freemen and through which the free world will be able to meet and defeat the carefully patterned total aggression (political, ideological, psychological, economic, paramilitary, and organizational) of the Communist bloc, and through which we, as a nation, may work in a systematic manner for the preservation and extension of freedom, national independence, and self-government. To achieve this purpose the full range of methods and means is to be thoroughly explored and studied including the methods and means that may best be employed by private citizens and nongovernmental organizations and the methods and means available to the Govern-

5. Senate Bill 822, 87th Cong., 1st Sess.: A BILL to create the Freedom Commission and the Freedom Academy to research and develop an integrated, operational science to win the nonmilitary part of the global struggle between freedom and communism and to train Government personnel, private citizens, and foreign students in this science. By Mr. Mundt, Mr. Douglas, Mr. Case of New Jersey, Mr. Dodd, Mr. Smathers, Mr. Goldwater, Mr. Proxmire, Mr. Fong, Mr. Butler, Mr. Hickenlooper, Mr. Miller, and Mr. Keating. February 9, 1961. Read twice and referred to the Committee on Foreign Relations.

ment other than the methods and means already being used. This research program shall include the study of our national objectives and the development of proposals for intermeshing and integrating the full spectrum of methods and means into a coordinated, short and long range strategy for victory, seeking the utilization of our full potential in the public and private sectors; and

(2) to educate and train Government personnel, private citizens, and foreign students concerning all aspects of the international Communist conspiracy, the nature and dimensions of the global struggle between freedom and communism and the full range of methods and means that free men should employ to meet and defeat the entire Communist attack in the non-military areas and to work systematically for the preservation and extension of freedom, national independence, and self-government.

The Freedom Academy would train men and women in the conduct of non-military conflict in accordance with the requirements and needs of the Free World. Those who think we cannot do this without aping the Communists have lost faith in themselves, this country, and freedom. And those who are unwilling even to try are already defeated.

Of special interest is a letter from then Senator John F. Kennedy to Dr. Blair O. Rogers dated September 9, 1960. Dr. Rogers, in a letter to the *New York Times* had proposed that a "Free University of the West" be established on Ellis Island. In commenting on Dr. Rogers' proposal, Senator Kennedy said:

You will likewise have read of a bill passed recently by the Senate proposing a Freedom University for training our people in techniques for fighting the Cold War. I feel certain that something will come out of this proposal.

Presidential support for the Freedom Academy could be a turning point in the Cold War. On the other hand, there is opposition to the Freedom Academy concept on the grounds that the type of operational training suggested in this chapter is not necessary. In other words, our governmental officials and those of our private citizens whose activities bring them into frequent contact with foreign nationals know all they need to know about communist ideology and operational techniques and know how to articulate the American way of life and how a free society operates. The gradual advance of communist influence during the Cold War, however, does not confirm the adequacy of our training for engaging in "the conflict of systems."

There are also many who recognize the need for greater education of our citizens in communist doctrine and conflict techniques and yet who believe that the Freedom Academy proposal is not the most desirable instrument for overcoming these deficiencies. There is no question that the existing agencies of the government could undertake a far more intensive and thorough training of their personnel in the subjects discussed in this chapter. There is no question that many of our universities could support far more systematic and thorough research into the problems covered in this book. There is no doubt also that our large foundations could promote and support research and training in this area far beyond the miniscule level of effort which they currently sponsor. In short, the objectives of the Freedom Academy could be obtained in other ways. At this writing, however, training within the government is inadequate, research and investigation within the universities is insufficient, and the amount of interest displayed in this area by our major foundations is almost nil. Consequently, the Freedom Academy proposal seems to be the most effective means of overcoming, in a comparatively short time, the political-warfare lead the Communists have achieved during the course of the past forty years.[6] The immediate need for the Freedom Academy program can only be eliminated by vigorous and large-scale action taken *now* by appropriate government departments and agencies, American universities and foundations.

Our national survival requires highly trained men and women who will dedicate themselves to winning the global struggle between freedom and communism. Such men and women can shatter forever the image of America as a complacent, self-satisfied, *status quo* power unwilling to give up its soft ways to contest the Communists in the villages, the market places, the classrooms, the labor unions, and wherever else this struggle is being fought.

If the challenge we face is as revolutionary and potentially destructive to our values and way of life as it appears to be, some major innovations in the conduct of the struggle are necessary. The American people are ready to respond to leadership. In President Kennedy's own words:

6. Whatever steps are taken to improve the training of our citizens in the general subject of political warfare, indispensible though they are, they will by no means solve all of the national-security problems confronting the United States. It should also be recognized that it may be many years before the full impact of the creation of the Freedom Academy will be felt in the conduct of American foreign affairs. Nevertheless, unless we take long term steps to improve our position after the present crisis, we are not likely ever to seize the initiative.

"We shall pay any price, bear any burden, meet any hardship, support any friend, oppose any foe to assure the survival and success of liberty."

The words of the President of the United States do not have the force of dogma in our democratic society. Yet when the President's solemn words are widely consented to, then they do commit him and they commit the country. . . .

The climax of the struggle with Communism will come—soon. It has begun, and it is probable that in the present decade we shall either have negotiated our own surrender or Communism will have become a disrupted, discredited and disintegrating force.

The time has come then for the United States to take its stand—unambiguously and implacably.[7]

Training Americans to fight communism's challenge to freedom could be the beginning of this stand.

7. Quoted from a *Life* magazine editorial entitled "We Must Win the Cold War."

CHAPTER XV

CONFLICT MANAGEMENT

MANY AMERICANS LACK A CATEGORICAL BELIEF THAT THE Cold War is a part of a long life-or-death conflict for the United States and that the U.S. government should treat it as such. The reluctance of the American people and their leaders to accept this macroscopic, gigantic fact might itself lead to an American defeat.

The communist threat is no simple challenge. Historically, it is persistent; organizationally, complex; operationally, multiphase; planning-wise, deliberate; intellectually, systematic; ethically, ruthless; and politically, dynamic. It must be understood in terms of the history of our fathers' lifetimes and our own. It must be calculated along trajectories stated by the Sino-Soviet leaders—courses of declared action which no American should any longer dismiss as "mere propaganda." We must acknowledge the inroads already made by the threat, admit to new penetrations of our borders, and evaluate the emerging dangers on the scale of whole continents.

To fight the Cold War successfully, we need some changes on our side, changes will not impair democracy but sharpen its performance. We need, first of all, a new conception and evaluation of the communist threat. Secondly, we need an underlying doctrine, developed from our own free traditions and practical national experience, to meet this threat, together with the management structure to work out the doctrine in practice.

Indecisiveness and halfheartedness in accomplishing these changes— whether motivated by escapism, wishful thinking, political or budgetary convenience, or the reluctance of allies—could eventually prove disastrous to our national existence. A continuing failure to recognize the real nature of the threat or to accept the risks and costs of meeting it successfully gives to the Sino-Soviet leaders enough reassurance to warrant their retention of initiative. Resignation to the present state of affairs, moreover, will not even assure the durability of the present state, undesirable as it may already be. Instead, our fortunes will deteriorate in a continuing pattern of retreat and attrition through subversion, civil conflict and limited aggression. Any permanent concession of the initiative to the communist leadership could set in motion disintegrating forces which could not only destroy the confidence of allies and the hopes of uncommitted nations but which would finally destroy the will and capacity to defend our own borders.

The Organization Problem

Because of its global nature and the complexity of its strategy, tactics, and weapons, the Cold War exerts ever changing pressures upon Washington. The attention of members of high U.S. strategy councils has been distracted as the Communists shifted their initiative from one area to the other or reopened old trouble spots. When Berlin is on the center of the stage, the Congo or Southeast Asia receive inadequate attention.

President Kennedy clearly recognized the global interactions of the communist challenge in his July, 1961 address to the nation. Calling for increased military strength, the President said:

The immediate threat to free men is in West Berlin, but that isolated outpost is not an isolated problem. The threat is world-wide. Our effort must be equally wide and strong, and not be obsessed by any single manufactured crisis. We face a challenge in Berlin, but there is also a challenge in Southeast Asia, where the borders are less guarded, the enemy harder to find, and the dangers of communism less apparent to those who have so little. We face a challenge in our own hemisphere. And indeed wherever else the freedom of human beings is at stake.[1]

This challenge derives from three major factors: Sino-Soviet military power, superior leadership for conflict, and sophisticated, massive political-warfare capabilities. Regarding the leadership factor, Harry Schwartz, Soviet-affairs specialist for the *New York Times,* had this to say:

Much of the growth in relative Soviet power and prestige as against the United States since 1945 has basically been the product of superior Soviet leadership. The test of history has shown that Stalin and Khrushchev were more imaginative, planned more wisely for the attainment of their goals, and organized their resources far more skillfully for the cold war than did the leaders of the United States. Any shift of world power in the Communists' favor during 1961–75 comparable to that which took place from

1. *New York Times,* July 26, 1961.

1946 to 1960 might turn into reality Khrushchev's dream of world communism. Defeat for the United States in the world struggle is not yet a foregone conclusion. But in 1961 such defeat is far more threatening than could possibly have been foreseen—even by Stalin, we suppose—in 1945.[2]

The question of leadership is closely related to U.S. and Western deficiencies in the conduct of the Cold War. Although the conflict is an organic whole and is so conducted by the Communists, recognition of this state of affairs is not reflected in the U.S. governmental structure for coping with it. The radical adjustments required to meet a revolutionary challenge will be made only when our leadership obtains a profound personal understanding of how the communist conflict system works. Our leaders must come to know intimately the tested communist doctrine of conflict. The Communists, their recent achievements in missiles notwithstanding, do not have a "master weapon" on which they place all their reliance. Their skill lies, rather, in their ability to vary tactical combinations constantly. Tactical innovation is more important to them than technical innovation.

If the existing mechanisms of the U.S. government were adequate to cope with the challenge, the crisis of freedom in its present magnified form would not exist. There are two chief reasons why the government's organizational approach for the development of a positive national concept has not succeeded: There is the inescapable fact that the highest-level officials are bogged down in the operations of their respective departments and agencies, and, since they are held personally accountable for these operations, necessarily give them their personal priority. Secondly, interdepartmental policy-planning agencies are representational in nature and correspondingly narrow in outlook. Their policy proposals and action programs consequently represent a summation of compromise of various departmental points of view and at times result in the government working at cross-purposes. Since a truly national strategy is far more than the sum total of the various components that go into it, policy and strategy achieved through either addition or compromise are inadequate. Dean Rusk, prior to becoming Secretary of State, wrote:

The departments and agencies of government are each concerned about a part of the whole. The President, assisted by his White House staff and the Executive Office, must weld the parts into an effective national effort. He cannot hope to achieve nice consistency in leading a vigorous and diverse people concerned with conflicting interests and aspirations, but

2. See Harry Schwartz, *The Red Phoenix: Russia Since World War II.*

he can try to achieve a broad political consistency in the main directions of movement and to limit the waste and frustration which occur when one hand tears down what the other is laboriously trying to build.[3]

An Evolving System

The background of our present National Security Council and its sub-structure begins with the improvised machinery for governmental co-or-dination during World War II. Recognizing the need for improvement in this area, Ferdinand Eberstadt, in a report in 1945 to Secretary of the Navy James Forrestal on the nature of the post-war organization for na-tional security, first proposed the establishment of a "National Security Council." As Mr. Eberstadt conceived it, the National Security Council would link foreign, domestic, and military policy through a membership to include the Secretaries of State, War, Navy, and Air, the Chairman of the Joint Chiefs of Staff, and the President. It was to perform policy-formulation and advisory functions, including advice on the combined military budget. A Central Intelligence Agency was to be formed and placed under the National Security Council's immediate jurisdiction, and the Council was to be staffed by a permanent secretariat.

President Truman incorporated the essentials of Eberstadt's proposals for the new organization for national security in legislation which became the National Security Act of 1947. There was little disagreement on the need for, as well as the basic form of, the National Security Council.

Although membership of the National Security Council has been changed frequently, the statutory functions of the Council have remained the same since its creation. The National Security Act states them as follows:

The function of the council shall be to advise the President with respect to the integration of domestic, foreign, and military policies relating to the national security so as to enable the military services and other departments and agencies of the government to cooperate more effectively in matters involving the national security.

The period from 1947 to 1953 was one of inception and slow growth. President Truman recognized the Council's potential, fostered its devel-opment, and used it in the development of some of his most important

3. Dean Rusk, "The President," *Foreign Affairs*, Vol. XXXVIII, No. 3 (April, 1960), p. 356.

foreign policies. Yet Truman attended very few NSC meetings and did not consult with the NSC on thrusting us into the war in Korea. President Eisenhower, upon his election, proceeded to reconstitute the National Security Council mechanism, principally by adding to its supporting structure.

Between the time of its inception and the present, many studies of the National Security Council have been conducted. In summary, the criticisms of its performance reduce to these: The National Security Council appeared deficient in planning long-range policy and anticipating developments. The Council, instead of actively resolving issues arising between segments of government, too often acted as a referee. Once policy had been determined, no means of assuring execution in the intended fashion existed other than the assignment of the task to one of the departments or agencies involved in carrying out the decisions.

To correct this last-named deficiency, the Operations Coordinating Board was created in 1954. The Operations Coordinating Board occupied a position subordinate to the National Security Council and operated under the chairmanship of the Under Secretary of State. The Operations Coordinating Board was composed of representatives of those departments and agencies which have operating functions in the national security area (with the exception of its vice-chairman, who was a special assistant to the President). Assisting in its functions were an Operations Coordinating Board assistants group and Operations Coordinating Board working groups, both standing and *ad hoc,* all composed overwhelmingly of personnel representing the operating agencies.

There has never been a single presidential staff member responsible for the execution of national-security policy. The Operations Coordinating Board was a co-operative structure; it lacked a directive power of its own. Robert Cutler has pointed out that:

The Board is a coordinator and an expediter and follower-up and a progress reporter. . . . Its membership consists of the Under-Secretary of State, the Deputy Secretary of Defense, the Director of Central Intelligence and certain others. Such officers are obviously without authority, individually or collectively, to interpose their views between the President and his responsible Cabinet members. The O.C.B. can assist, follow up, report; but it cannot initiate or change policy.[4]

4. See Robert Cutler, "The Development of the National Security Council," *Foreign Affairs,* Vol. XXXIV, No. 3 (April, 1956), p. 449.

During 1959 and 1960, the Committee on Government Operations of the United States Senate, whose Subcommittee on National Policy Machinery was chaired by Senator Henry M. Jackson, conducted an extensive review of the effectiveness of U.S. policy-making organizations. In several reports made by his Subcommittee, Senator Jackson presaged the Kennedy Administration revisions of the NSC structure when he argued:

> The real worth of the council to a President lies in being an accustomed forum where he and a small number of his top advisers can gain that intellectual intimacy and mutual understanding on which true coordination depends. Viewed thus, the Council is a place where the President can receive from his department and agency heads a full exposition of policy alternatives available to him, and, in turn, give them clear-cut guidance for action.[5]

Changes in the National Security Structure

In keeping with this point of view the National Security Council structure and functioning were fundamentally reorganized by the Kennedy Administration shortly after President Kennedy took office. The Operations Coordination Board, admittedly an abortive attempt at co-ordination of policy implementation, was discontinued. The NSC Planning Board, an interdepartmental co-ordinating agency, has not functioned since the advent of the new administration. As a result of these changes, the Department of State was charged with initiating *co-ordination* on foreign-policy *formulation,* co-ordinating with the other departments, including the Department of Defense, in matters where co-ordination was, in the opinion of the State Department, necessary. In other words, the organization for insuring co-ordination of "strategic hot" war and "cold" war policy planning was disbanded and the initiative transferred to the Department of State. A special assistant to the President for NSC affairs and his small executive staff are charged with monitoring co-ordination in carrying out policy. Further, instructions to ambassadors "to take charge overseas" have been more forcefully emphasized than in the past.

Some contend that the formal mechanism for handling National Security matters, abolished by President Kennedy, did not work because of the key position of the Department of State and its concern in attaining domination over foreign-policy. The feeling of the Department of State toward

5. *Organizing for National Security—The National Security Council,* a study submitted to the Committee on Government Operation, U.S. Senate, by its Subcommittee on National Policy Machinery (Pursuant to Senate Resolution 248, 86th Cong.), pp. 2-3.

the intrusion of five or more agencies in determining the policy guidance going out to the field was made pointedly evident in the Operations Coordinating Board working groups—the hundred-odd interagency meeting groups formed to work on individual-country operations plans, each chaired by a State Department country expert. State generally preferred that these be talking rather than meaningful working groups.

The Department of State had been observing foreign affairs from the outside during World War II and immediately thereafter. Any long-range political thought which might have come to the front was subordinated to military considerations at that critical time.[6] After 1947, the creation of boards made up of five or more agencies, each of which attempted to influence national policy in foreign affairs, primarily in terms of narrow, vested agency interests, could not avoid being opposed by State in its efforts to assume its statutory responsibilities.

The Department of State, charged with the conduct of foreign affairs, carries a tremendous responsibility in policy formulation and co-ordination of policy implementation. Basically, however, the questions involving other agencies are less controversial than those involving the use of military power. The basic task of the diplomat is to keep the peace— through inducement and persuasion. Benjamin Franklin wrote candidly *On the Means of Disposing the Enemies to Peace:*

Warres, with whatsoever prudence undertaken and conducted, do not always succeed. . . . Northerne People . . . are ofttimes more easilie to be governed and turned by Skill than Force. There is, therefore, always Hope that, by wise Counsel and dexterous Management, those Advantages, which through cross Accidents in Warre have been lost, may again with Honour be recovered. In this Place I shall say little of the Power of Money secretly distributed among Grandees, or their Friends or Paramours; that Method being in all ages known and practiced. If the minds of Enemies can be changed, they may be brought to grant willingly and for nothing what much Gold would scarcely have otherwise prevailed to obtain.[7]

The task of the soldier, in contrast, is to keep the peace by making war unattractive to prospective enemies. Obviously, the roles of the statesman and the soldier both have the same aim: national security. This fact was

6. Walt W. Rostow, *The United States and the World Arena,* pp. 33-34, 45-47, and 146. Rostow subsequently became Deputy Special Assistant for National Security Affairs to President Kennedy, and later head of the Policy Planning Council, Department of State.

7. *The Complete Works of Benjamin Franklin,* compiled and edited by John Bigelow, Vol. III, pp. 133-37. The paper, written in 1760, was addressed to the King of England.

formally recognized in the 1947 creation of the National Security Council.

Formerly, the Department of Defense entered automatically and actively into the process of formulation of national-security policy through the National Security Council Planning Board. The outcome of the 1961 changes which eliminated the NSC Planning Board has been to downgrade the Defense Department, or military position, in the development of national strategy.

Yet by its very nature the Cold War cannot be the province of any single department. The Cold War is many things. It is a diplomatic battle in that the dignity, the sensibilities, the intense national pride of even the smallest countries may dictate whether they will align themselves with the United States and the Free World or on the side of the communist bloc. Diplomacy and negotiation play a major role in the battle to maintain the advantage in Free World alliances confronting potential and actual enemies.

The Cold War is a power struggle. Communist armed forces have been held in check in Europe, not through diplomatic negotiations, but only because they are faced by an American soldier looking down the sights of a heavy tank gun—or by a British ally in a dug-in observation post with communications leading to a fire-control center in constant 24-hour contact with American dual-purpose conventional or atomic artillery—backed up through a network tied into SAC's ICBMs.

The Cold War is an economic fight to help raise living standards and to help peoples in order that they may help themselves in resisting communist inroads.

The Cold War is an ideological battle for the minds of men. In the Korean War, for example, we decided that to repatriate against their will the Chinese and North Korean prisoners of war would be a psychological blow to free men's principles. Further, we believed that if given a choice, large numbers of these prisoners would refuse to return to their homelands. Such rejection would be a severe blow to the prestige of the Communists, a blow which would be felt throughout the communist bloc. For seventeen months we held fast to this point at the Panmunjom armistice negotiations, and the Communists finally yielded. At least 23,000 communist troops taken prisoner chose not to return. Large numbers of the Chinese prisoners settled in Taiwan; representatives from this group promptly visited overseas Chinese communities in Southeast Asia to tell the story of their suffering under communism. On the other hand, only twenty-one

American prisoners chose not to return to the United States. This, then, was action damaging to the Communists which resulted from a policy—the policy of "voluntary repatriation"—worked out jointly by the State and Defense departments.

Collaboration between the two departments has not always been so successful. In fact, a central U.S. Cold War organizational problem is the difference in concept as to the day-to-day conduct of foreign affairs, a problem which has long existed between the Departments of State and Defense. The two departments entertain widely divergent views about how to deal with emerging crises. The Department of Defense has consistently pressed for more planning to meet the foreseeable, while the Department of State prefers to "play it by ear." Repeatedly, Defense, on behalf of our military commanders abroad, has asked State for guidance for positive action should this or that specific situation arise, but State is reluctant to allow itself to be drawn into what it feels might be premature policy decisions. The answer, the Foreign Service officers tell their frustrated opposite numbers in the Pentagon, would always depend on the "situation then obtaining."

Between the personnel who man the two departments there are underlying divergencies in background, training, and methods of operation. High value is attached to the Foreign Service officer's ability in conversation and debate, his mastery of the technique of influencing people, and the art of negotiating documents, while the key criteria used in judging the military officer, who spends most of his career in the type of work that calls for concrete, practical activities, is "ability to obtain results or some form of action."

The soldier is impatient with the diplomat's cautious approach to the military's recommendations for pursuing Cold War objectives which involve other governmental agencies. Involved as the soldier is in eighty-odd foreign countries throughout the world, he considers his cold war efforts and ideas significant.

The philosophy, the environment, and the training of the two proponents are poles apart. Trite, demagogic description exaggerates the characteristics of the State Department career officer and the military officer. Neither one is the stereotyped "cookie pusher" or "military mind" some sensationalists would have the public believe. They are, for the greater part, capable men who would place truly national considerations first if the environment in which they work would permit them to do so and if they could still be loyal to their immediate departmental or service interests.

Western diplomats, however, hold the traditional view that negotiations, even with the Communists, should lead to accommodation and compromise. They believe, too, that democratic publics expect their leaders to make genuine efforts to negotiate in order to settle controversies. The Communists capitalize upon these Western attitudes. Most military men, for example, believe that the endless disarmament and nuclear-test negotiations are Soviet political-action maneuvers aimed at exploiting such Western predilections, maneuvers designed to puzzle and divide the West. As of 1962, many State Department people advocated that the United States try to outbid the Soviets by pressing for some kind of general and complete disarmament. Most U.S. military men took Khrushchev's statement that he intended to use disarmament to degrade Western military power at its face value, and they look suspiciously at this scheme. These considerations point out the difficulty of reconciling two widely divergent points of view.

Although the respective approaches of U.S. diplomats and soldiers to the solution of problems frequently appear to be at opposite ends of the spectrum, a combination of their talents and approaches has often resulted in effective and workable solutions. This is particularly true when our soldiers and diplomats have had a chance to get to know each other through daily working contacts or attendance at the National War College and other war colleges. It also points up the value of training of government officials in special warfare along the line of suggestions made in previous chapters. The aim should be to develop an operational environment in which they can work things out together, rather than one in which one group's intellectual contribution to the conflict is regarded as inferior or contrary to the others.

The State Department's Role

The State Department sets policy and *initiates co-ordination* on foreign-policy formulation with other departments, including the Department of Defense, in matters where co-ordination is, in the opinion of the State Department, necessary.[8]

8. Defense Secretary McNamara, in testimony before the U.S. Senate Armed Services Committee stated: "Every speech with foreign policy implications is submitted for comment to the State Department, the agency which has the basic responsibility. We do not want to usurp the State Department's functions any more than we expect the State Department to usurp ours." Hearings before the Committee on Armed Services, U.S. Senate, 87th Cong., 1st Sess., on Senate Resolution 191, September 6 and 7, 1961, p. 6.

The Department of State made some organizational changes in 1961 to discharge its increased co-ordination function. A new office, or operations center, nicknamed the "flap house" or "rumpus room," was created.[9] The center provided the Secretary of State with an instrument for following up government-wide action in the field of foreign affairs and for conducting informal interdepartmental analyses of emerging foreign-policy problems and potential crisis areas. Interdepartmental "task forces," the 1962 Washington vogue, were created to handle particularly thorny problems.

An emerging or potential crisis was placed under special watch. An embryonic interdepartmental task force was thus established as the permanent Defense, CIA, and USIA members of the operations center worked informally with the departmental officers concerned.

This procedure was a useful organizational advance within the State Department. It was not, however, a high-level headquarters for managing conduct of the Cold War. In fact, for a number of reasons the operations center was discarded in January 1962.[10]

John Foster Dulles, as Secretary of State, established a pattern of ambulatory diplomacy which has been emulated by his successors. During his first six months in office, for example, Secretary Rusk was away from Washington well over half the time. Whether the absence of the Secretary of State from Washington is desirable or not, there is little indication that this pattern will be changed. Consequently, State Department co-ordination of foreign operations will not always be effected personally by the Secretary of State, although he can influence actions from abroad.

The implication of this is that policy co-ordination undertaken in the name of the Secretary of State is often actually performed by relatively low-level officials. As Senator Dodd expressed it:

A master architect is heavily dependent on his draftsmen. And the fact is that, to a very large degree, those who are responsible for our policy are dependent on the publicly unknown, but tremendously important, subor-

9. See Chalmers M. Roberts, "New Operations Unit Is Crisis Nerve Center," *Washington Post*, August 14, 1961, p. 1. Launched after the Cuban invasion became a total failure, the operations center "has become a sort of Kennedy Administration version of the Eisenhower Administration's Operations Coordinating Board."

10. As this book was in galleys, a report in the *New York Times* on January 11, 1962, indicated that this "crisis center" was already going out of business. During its short period of existence it was found that many of its expectations were never fulfilled. Those task forces that were established tended to become virtually autonomous and other bureaus of the State Department saw the center as a threat to their functions. Furthermore, the around-the-clock watch was duplicating the work of other watches. Thus the present Administration is still searching for the best means of coping with non-military emergencies.

dinates whose task it is to sift all information that comes in from the field, to present the salient facts to their superiors, and to indicate general policy lines. This dependence is particularly heavy when our policy makers are called upon to deal with remote places like the Congo, about which they have little or no personal knowledge.[11]

Actually, the Deputy Under Secretary for Political Affairs has been given a major role in interdepartmental co-ordination. Under the current administration, this office has grown from a very informal and small staff to approximately sixty foreign-service officers. It is the top professional office in the department and is particularly responsible for co-ordinating State Department decisions and actions with those of the Department of Defense and the Central Intelligence Agency. The Deputy Under Secretary of State monitors the actions of the Assistant Secretaries for the various geographical areas. His office also follows up, when requested by the Secretary of State, any interdepartmental action in the field of foreign affairs, whether it originated in the department or in the National Security Council or in some other interagency decision.

Within State's sphere of responsibility the emphasis is on informal, *ad hoc* task forces to deal with a permanent crisis. The informal approach has advantages, as well as some very definite limitations. The practice of regular, informal top-level meetings is suited to the development of ideas on general organization and broad policy, to call attention to and prompt emphasis in critical areas, to expedite matters requiring immediate action, and to surface problems that could too readily become submerged in interdepartmental channels. The informal, high-level approach to policy formulation and implementation has limitations in the number of problems that can be handled, and in the scope and *expertise* of considerations. It is no substitute for fixed organizational procedures in the continuous and regular planned evaluation of basic policy governing hundreds of countries and programs. In the majority of cases, lower-level layers, if given support and properly monitored, can work out the answers to problems. In fact, only they know the "grass roots" operational problems that must be faced to make a solution workable.

In this age of "total diplomacy," where not only the conventional diplomacy of negotiating but every national asset and every "cold" war and "hot" war weapon must be brought into play, where our totalitarian opponents respect only the power behind the threat; when propaganda, espion-

11. Statement of Senator Thomas J. Dodd on the floor of the Senate, September 16, 1961.

age and sabotage, agitation, mass movements, and civil war are proclaimed and exploited as communist instruments in attaining their ultimate goal; when the Communists openly use the United Nations as a propaganda medium, the Cold War is too important a matter to be entrusted exclusively to diplomats.

The conduct of the Cold War requires something more than short-lived task forces or pragmatic action. The ability to project isolated and obscure facts concerning the global conflict into meaningful patterns is essential to our needs. Our strategy should be devised at least in part by those who have the training and ability to generalize from many complex particulars. We must have men with the capacity to determine accurately the nature of the final goals of our enemy, as distinguished from his immediate, piecemeal aims, and to project a comprehensive strategy of our own.

Who is to develop this doctrine and strategy? Those responsible for daily operations are naturally concerned with the immediate—what Dean Acheson has called "the thundering present." They lack both the time and the vantage point necessary to abstract conceptions of what the long-range impact of a particular communist maneuver may be. They are concerned only with putting plans for immediate action into effect and with accomplishing short-range projects. Their preoccupation with day-by-day events is essential. Danger becomes real, however, when their *ad hoc* viewpoint dominates the agency—the State Department—which plays so dominant a role in over-all and long-range policy formulation. Today, in our highest policy-making institutions, those who are to carry out policy have the predominant—if not always the only—voice in making it.

There is no question that the Department of State must play a major role in the conduct of America's Cold War strategy. It remains to be seen whether its personnel, trained to practice the functions of diplomacy—representing, negotiating, and reporting—can actually plan, direct, and monitor the integrated Cold War operations required. For one thing, the State Department has too few officials, according to Senator Jackson, who "possess the background and experience required for executive tasks. Increasingly, the administration of foreign policy is 'big business' which must be run by skillful administrators."[12] Furthermore, the State Department has long been reluctant to undertake imaginative long-range planning,

12. *Organizing for National Security: The Secretary of State and the National Security Process*, a study submitted to the Committee on Government Operations, U.S. Senate, by its Subcommittee on National Policy Machinery, pp. 7-8.

although, as former Secretary of State Acheson has indicated, "the true problem lies in determining the emerging future and the policy appropriate to it."[13]

The State Department has had fifteen years to align its structure for dealing with the Cold War. It has never relished the tough and tedious task of program integration and concise direction of day-by-day operations. In fact, it has been inclined to sabotage existing interdepartmental mechanisms through a variety of measures, including passive resistance. " 'Control or divert' is the State's guiding strategic principle; when it cannot gain the upper hand, it tries to occupy committees with 'busy work,' while getting key decisions through informal arguments with its adversaries or directly from the President."[14]

The Cold War, or "conflict of systems" as the Communists describe it, engages all the resources of the nation. Its conduct requires skillful integration of political, military, economic, and psychological factors. If one agency, the State Department, continues to have primary responsibility for the conduct of the Cold War, its operations will necessarily cut across the responsibilities of all others. It will have to move in on the planning and operational responsibilities of the other departments, including the Department of Defense. Inevitably, military and psychological and other considerations will be subordinated to diplomatic factors. By the very nature of the executive branch, only the President is in a position to reconcile the many factors that must go into a truly integrated national strategy. Consequently, the path of progress does not lie in a return to the pre–World War II status but in a continued effort to project the line of development initiated in 1947 with the creation of the National Security Council.

The Presidency

Effective direction of U.S. Cold War efforts can be given by the President. Richard E. Neustadt, whose persuasive book helped inspire President Kennedy to dismantle much of the executive machinery established by Presidents Truman and Eisenhower, nevertheless saw the convergency of problems and power in the White House:

In the American political system the President sits in a unique seat and works within a unique frame of reference. The things he personally has

13. *Ibid.*, p. 8.
14. *Ibid.*, p. 4.

to do are no respecters of the lines between 'civil' and 'military,' or 'foreign' and 'domestic,' or 'legislative' and 'executive,' or 'administrative' and 'political.' At his desk—and there alone—distinctions of these sorts lose their last shred of meaning. The expectations centered in his person converge upon no other individual; nobody else feels pressure from all five of *his* constituencies; no one else takes pressure in the consciousness that *he* has been elected 'by the Nation.' Besides, nobody but the President lives day by day with *his* responsibility in an atomic age amidst cold war. And he alone can claim unquestionable right to everybody's information on the mysteries of that age and that war.[15]

It is worth recalling that in the communist system all major political-warfare decisions are made in the Kremlin and implemented either by the Soviet state apparatus or communist parties abroad. All Soviet government agencies which by nature of their operations (foreign affairs, intelligence, radio, foreign trade, etc.) interlink with political warfare outside Russia have "special sections" or trained "conflict managers" whose orders come direct from conflict-management centers in Moscow. The conflict-management activities are separated from the normal operations of these agencies.

We have earlier discussed the high degree of centralization in communist policy, strategy, and commitment of resources characteristic of the Soviet and other communist conflict systems. The Western world has consistently underestimated advancing Soviet capabilities in many fields and has almost totally neglected the power the communists derive from their effective system of conflict management. In planning and managing the global struggle which the West calls the Cold War and the Communists describe as the "conflict of systems" the United States does not need to concede organizational superiority to the Communists. It is doubtful, however, that under present governmental arrangements the State Department can create an effective mechanism for marshalling and employing the full range of U.S. resources. Unless the United States is to lose out by default in the vital area of Cold War generalship, the alternative is to create such a mechanism within the office of the presidency. If the United States is to wage political warfare effectively, it must organize its machinery to do so.

Political warfare is a systematic activity designed to influence the policies of other nations. It cannot be a sideshow, a hideout in some agency or department, or farmed out in disjointed tidbits to more than a dozen departments. Political warfare has to do with the full range of Cold War activities. Since effective political warfare demands integration of effort

15. Richard E. Neustadt, *Presidential Power: The Politics of Leadership*, pp. 183-84.

that cannot be achieved solely through co-ordination, its locus must be in the White House.

If the various parts of our government are to move in unison in dealing with the communist challenge, the government's top policy advisers, planners, and decision-makers must work from a commonly accepted foundation. The President needs a total and integrated picture of our relative strengths and weaknesses vis-à-vis the communist bloc.[16] Only on the basis of such a continuing net balance sheet can he assess the weight and impact of new factors, such as technological innovations or unanticipated political developments. Only in this light can an effective Cold War strategy be devised. This task calls for men, working directly for the President, who have sufficient perspective to be able to see our problems in their entirety and to utilize every available means, public and private, in flexible combination in their solution.

The curiously fragmented pursuit of what should be an integrated approach to a national Cold War strategy was revealed June 29, 1961, in a bill introduced in Congress (HR 7936) to establish a United States Disarmament Agency for World Peace and Security. Among its particulars, this bill stated that "the formulation and employment of United States disarmament policy in a manner which will promote the national security requires a *central organization* charged by statute with primary responsibility for this field." The bill provided resources and supergrade personnel far in excess of those ever given to the National Security Council, let alone any non-existent mechanism for developing an integrated national policy and a Cold War strategy related thereto. In September, 1961, this legislation was approved by Congress.[17] For one relatively small area of a total na-

16. "Broadly speaking, there is virtually no important matter on which any one agency clearly has sole jurisdiction, can implement a program with its own resources, or even has all the relevant facts. Because of the large number of agencies with conflicting interests or competing jurisdictions, the interrelationship among agency programs, and great imbalances in the bargaining power of the various departments, it cannot be assumed either that the advice of agency heads is complete and objective or that Presidential decisions will automatically be implemented with speed and vigor. Unless there is a staff directly and immediately responsible to the President, with no competing loyalties, with no task other than that of providing an adequate framework for Presidential action, the President—any President—will be handicapped in discharging his responsibilities to the nation." From National Planning Association Pamphlet No. 112, "The Presidential Staff," by Joseph I. Coffey and Vincent P. Rock, April, 1961.

17. An impressive list of supporters was rallied behind this bill, among them Robert A. Lovett, former Secretary of Defense and Under Secretary of State. He also endorsed the bill's purpose. He expressed concern, however, that "this would be an ideal place for the Communists to infiltrate. It would be regarded as a mecca for a wide variety

tional strategy, thus was provided more "central organization" than for the total U.S. security effort of which it should be a part. The far more imperative need for some central organization for American management of conflict remains to be met.

A Presidential Command Post

There is widespread recognition that the U.S. presidency has grown bigger than the capacity of any given President. To do his job, the President requires a host of assistants—advisers, planners, implementers, expediters, investigators, and administrators. A part of the President's tasks are farmed out to the powerful departments and agencies which comprise the executive branch of the government. The heads of these departments and agencies necessarily administer segments of the President's responsibilities. In addition, the existing system requires that these men be the principal advisers and planners for the executive branch as a whole. Preoccupation with their own vital responsibilities makes it virtually impossible for them to give the kind of integrated advice which the President requires. Efforts to decentralize planning and review, as distinguished from operations, prompted President Kennedy in the troubled summer of 1961 to take a second look at the government's machinery for waging the Cold War.

Eight months ago [President Kennedy] and his Administration set out to capture the initiative in the "cold war." Today he finds himself waging a defensive battle on Berlin, compelled not only to cope with the unceasing assaults of Premier Khrushchev but also to justify himself to "neutral" opinion for doing so.

In this extremity he has turned for advice, as Presidents Harry S. Truman and Dwight D. Eisenhower turned before him, to a group of men with experience in politics, diplomacy, military affairs and human relations.

It is an informal group comprising at the moment Gen. Maxwell D. Taylor, the President's military representative; Attorney General Robert F. Kennedy, Secretary of Labor Arthur J. Goldberg and U. Alexis Johnson, the Deputy Under Secretary of State for Political Affairs.

The President's advisory group is not directly concerned with practical matters like these in the world at large, but with the Government's machinery for waging the "cold war."

In this connection, General Taylor has under consideration a paper proposing the appointment of a special assistant to the Secretary of State with a mandate to keep watch on the entire Government's "cold war" performance.

of screwballs. It would be a great pity to have this launched and then become a sort of 'bureau of beatniks.'" *New York Times,* August 15, 1961, p. 16.

Robert Kennedy, it is said, would prefer to have the official in the White House.

What seems certain is that somebody will get a new "special assistant" and that the United States will continue its hit-or-miss performance in the power struggle with the Communists.[18]

The tendency toward policy centralization within the executive branch has grown apace since World War II. The Executive Office of the President, and particularly the over-all planning required to formulate the federal budget, is set up to take an all-inclusive view of the vast federal governmental machine. Unfortunately, however, the efforts of the Executive Office of the President to achieve more effective co-ordination among the governmental departments and agencies break down because there is no over-all planning to guide the actions of the separate departments.

The Director of the Bureau of the Budget, Mr. David Bell, had this to say in testimony before the Jackson Subcommittee of the Committee on Government Operations:

Our budget for national security must reflect, and can only be as good as, our strategy for national security, and I think everyone would agree that the United States has much to do to develop a fully satisfactory strategy for our security.

What is the proper mix of military and nonmilitary measures?

How can we guide the inevitable processes of change in Asia, Africa, and Latin America to produce free institutions and not communism?

How can we step up the rate of economic growth?

On these, and many other issues affecting our national security, our budgeting can only be as good as our underlying strategy. Much of what is needed is quite beyond budgetary consideration, and improvement must come from analysis of our situation in the world, and imaginative thinking about the courses of action that are open to us.

In this same testimony, Mr. Bell stated:

Logically, budgeting and planning are two sides of the same coin, two aspects of the same process. A budget is the financial expression of a plan.

Unfortunately, there is no organized U.S. national-security plan, no scheme to capture initiative in the Cold War. U.S. strategy for national security is devised by *ad hoc* task forces set up in response to specific crises

18. Wallace Carroll, "Waging the Cold War," *New York Times*, September 16, 1961, p. 8.

and under the direction of one or another of the government departments. The government departments are instruments for carrying out the jobs assigned to them, but if they are to operate in unison, someone above them must establish the general course of their actions. Under the American system, this determination of broad course of action can only be made by the President.

The President, of course, requires assistance in the conduct of his office. A number of proposals have been made to give him the assistance he needs. Each President will naturally adjust the machinery of the executive branch to suit his own temperament as well as his own concept of operations. The National Security Council structure has functioned differently with each of the three presidents who have been in office since its formation.

It has been suggested by some experienced men that the management of our foreign affairs be vested in an "Assistant President." This individual would be the President's alter ego, in much the same fashion that Mr. James Byrnes acted as general co-ordinator in the executive branch for President Roosevelt during the latter stages of World War II. Nelson Rockefeller, for one, has advocated the creation of such an office.

Others believe that the same results could be obtained, without any formal organization change, by the President's placing his personal confidence in an individual who would be able to act and speak for him in most cases. Such a person would be comparable to Colonel House in the Wilson Administration or Harry Hopkins during various phases of Franklin Roosevelt's tenure in office. But the problems confronting this country in its interaction with the rest of the world have grown far too complex for any one man, however gifted, to handle. Skilled staff assistance would be required.

Another device proposed to inspire more effective and integrated U.S. action abroad is to create regional co-ordinating centers in various locations overseas. The examples of the British High Commissioner for Southeast Asia or the Resident Commissioner for the Middle East come to mind. In this system there would be, perhaps, a U.S. region co-ordinator for Europe, Africa, the Middle East, Southeast Asia, Latin America, and other areas where events in one country have a direct impact on developments in near-by nations. This solution would approach the problem from the other end by establishing unity in the field. The effect of co-ordinated or integrated action would then eventually be felt in Washington. It would produce immediate results and would force the agencies in Washington to deal with the total problem rather than with bits and pieces of it, as they do now.

There are doubtless many other variants as to how the office of the presidency might best be organized to plan, conduct, and audit U.S. operations in the Cold War. Based on the thesis that there must be presidential co-ordination in execution of plans as well as in their development, the following proposals for a Presidential Security Staff are advanced.

A Presidential Assistant for National Security Affairs, with Cabinet rank, would be provided, by Congressional act, in the Executive Office of the President. He would be approved by the Senate and supported by an administrative structure to be established by act of Congress, but in very general provisions, in order to give flexibility to the staff agency. This structure would have the following characteristics:

(1) The Presidential Assistant for National Security Affairs would sit on the National Security Council as a full member by act of Congress and would be Chairman in the absence of the President and the Vice President.

(2) The National Security Council structure would be supported by a new staff organization to be headed by the Presidential Assistant for National Security Affairs. Under the Assistant would be a Director for Plans and Policy, a Director for Operations, and a Director for Review, responsible respectively for formulating plans and policies, co-ordinating operations, and for review and analysis of the results obtained. In each staff element, members of the Presidential staff would be teamed with representatives of the departments and agencies involved in the Cold War. The Director for Policy and the Director for Review would both be Presidential-staff appointees, whereas the Director for Operations would be, as was the case recently with the Chairman of the Operations Coordinating Board, a designee of the Secretary of State.

(3) A "situation center" using techniques for a net Free World–Communist Bloc situation analysis would be established in the Executive Office.[19]

(4) An Office for Review would be established in the Bureau of the Budget. It would evaluate Cold War performance independently of operating agencies. By imaginative review and analysis of the execution of our national-security program, the Bureau of the Budget could help fashion those management tools required to make the organizational machine within

19. It is understood that such a center was finally established during the latter part of 1961, under the Special Assistant to the President for National Security Affairs.

the executive branch function more effectively. An audit of past perform-ance that goes beyond cost accounting could have a "feedback" on policy by revealing explicit examples of success or failure. In this way, the Bud-getary Review could become a real aid to the decision-makers. The Office for Review would be responsible to the Presidential Assistant for National Security Affairs for evaluating substantive achievements and to the Bureau of the Budget with respect to fiscal matters.

(5) The chiefs of diplomatic missions in each country would be pro-vided, whenever necessary, with additional staff personnel to conduct the United States programs within their jurisdiction. As is presently the case, United States agencies in each foreign country would be supervised by and come under the leadership of the particular United States ambassador.

The effect of these proposals is not to create a gigantic superstaff in the White House, but to give the President the backup which he requires in order to supervise the entire executive branch in the interests of our na-tional security. The Secretary of State would still play the primary role in foreign relations; his voice would still be the most important in advising the President regarding the range of possible choices of policy. But foreign policy, as well as the security of this country, rests, in the final analysis, with the President. The organization changes suggested here would permit the President to discharge his duties with more comprehensive support than he has been given thus far.

Most Americans now recognize our struggle with the communist world for what it is, a war in which the ultimate stake is national survival, yet many officials resist the requisite of changing our attitude toward the con-flict and governmental procedures for coping with it.

There is a continuing and imperative need to overhaul our present na-tional mechanism for waging the Cold War. Unity of purpose must be preserved so that departmental parochialism, zeal, misunderstanding, and deliberate deviation can no longer undermine established policy. Co-ordi-nation solely by co-operation will not work, nor will integrated operational plans, no matter how soundly formulated, alone suffice. There must be Presidential co-ordination in execution of plans as well as in their develop-ment.

It would be erroneous to believe that the most effective organization in the world, manned by the most astute men available, would auto-matically solve the serious problems confronting us abroad. Effective political warfare must be supported by a wide array of programs and actions,[20] including adequate armed forces, technological competence, economic vitality at home and appropriate economic development abroad, dynamic cultural and artistic achievement, and effective communications with other peoples. Both the U.S. government and American citizens are deeply involved in these activities, but the full impact of such programs is lost because of faulty direction or inadequate co-ordination. Only over-all guidance can co-ordinate a global "conflict of systems" fought as bitterly in the realms of ideas or economics and in the "underground" contests for many nations as in open battle. Such guidance will not be forthcoming until the office of the presidency becomes the operational planner and co-ordinator for the Cold War.

History awards no prizes for failure. If our system for waging the Cold War is to be spared some future post-mortem examination conducted by the communist opponents of freedom, we must do everything we can to insure that our high command for the Cold War is more than equal to its tasks.

---

20. For a full discussion of the elements which might be considered in a comprehensive U.S. strategy, including the relationship between foreign affairs and domestic programs, see *A Forward Strategy for America*, previously referred to. Particularly pertinent to the discussion in this chapter is Chapter 11, entitled "Structure for Strategy," which sets forth the operational criteria which must be satisfied if the United States is to respond effectively to the communist challenge.

CHAPTER XVI

TARGET: COMMUNIST VULNERABILITIES

THE OPPONENTS OF COMMUNISM HAVE WAVERED BETWEEN belittling it and panicking at the mention of it. The Communists distort their own size—always in the direction of enlargement—because of their emotion-centered belief that anything which is sufficiently emphasized will eventually become fact. In the areas they dominate, preaching of communism is mandatory. Marxist and Leninist literature is spread all through the Soviet Union, and every bit of it suggests and inferentially breeds rebellion against the conditions that exist under communism. Contradiction between ideology and performance colors every facet of life in Communist-dominated countries.

After forty years of communist rule, communism has defaulted on all its essential social promises and merely replaced the old class rule with a new and far worse one.

There are many faults in the world outside: there always will be. But there are faults in the communist world as well. Communist extremism is caused by a malfunction of the social conscience in which hate becomes a substitute for honor. Communism has its surpassing virtue—incessant activity; communism has its own perennial target—the faults of our world. How tall has it grown in relation to us? How really strong is a system which systematically employs coercion to rule?

There is no perfect human society. The communist political-warfare attack is designed to detect and magnify the stupidities, the blunders, and social schisms of our world. Yet the communist system is also rife with inherent ideological, political, and economic weaknesses. Despite the sputniks, the Communists face an ever present crisis in food production, and in many areas of the communist domain people are hungry. In the communist world, man's inhumanity to man flourishes untempered by a justice

317

wedded to law. Finally, the Soviet Union is today the major colonial pro-
prietor of the world.

Considering the stakes involved in the present global conflict, the failure
to attack effectively the weaknesses of communism must be viewed as a
colossal omission of Western policy and strategy. Why?

There are people who argue that the firm hold of the Communists on
the peoples they rule belies the existence of any inherent weakness in communist society and deny any real structural weakness within the communist
bloc. Modern totalitarianism is hard to crush. The relatively short histories
of the Soviet Union and Communist China have so far revealed that it is
nearly impossible to dislodge a totalitarian dictatorship by an uprising
from *within*.

It has been equally difficult to overthrow police states from within by
conspiracy, sabotage, and other clandestine operations. In Germany during
World War II, there were millions of foreign slave laborers, hostile to the
Nazis, yet there were virtually no acts of sabotage nor any major political
demonstrations. Even in Nazi-occupied Europe, merciless retribution
against any infraction served as a remarkably effective deterrent. The communist rulers of the Soviet Union and Communist China, do not, moreover, simply rely on terror. They also "educate" by manipulating psychologically the minds and souls of their subjects.

People tend to tolerate even the harshest governments as long as their
achievements satisfy national pride. Tyrannies weather internal storms so
long as they appear to be winning striking victories externally and making
minimal progress domestically. There are few today in the West who
expect that communist totalitarianism will be overthrown by internal upheavals. Yet twenty-five years ago very few men thought that Italian fascism
could disappear and that the Italians could revert to lively parliamentary
government.

In recent years, a comforting theory has gained ground in academic
quarters. According to it, communist regimes are bound to undergo a
"natural" process of erosion and gradual "softening." As the general level
of living standards and education rises, so the argument goes, the people's
demands for greater freedom and further easing of living conditions can
no longer be disregarded by the party elite. The party leaders themselves,
moreover, are supposed to become less militant and increasingly more
"civilized." Their resolve will presumably be weakened by the relative comforts they enjoy as a privileged class.

Khrushchev's style of rule, which, indeed, differs considerably from that of Stalin, has been pointed out as evidence that the humanization of the regime has, in fact, begun. If one compares Khrushchev to Lenin, however, it becomes difficult to maintain that the present leadership is more humane, more cultured, and in any respect less resolved than the original one. A certain amelioration of conditions following Stalin's death testifies not to the mellowing of the regime but to its growing confidence in its final victory over the Free World.

Nevertheless, the communist regimes do suffer basic structural weaknesses. One, for example, is their tendency to gravitate toward a one-man dictatorship. Another is the absence of a legitimate way of transferring power from one dictator to another. The problem of communist succession is strikingly similar to that which Imperial Rome never really solved. Each time a dictator dies is a time of crisis for communism.

For a long time to come the best the capitalist nations can hope to obtain from communism is not peace but an armed truce. And whether the latter abides will depend entirely on the actual array of power which the West is willing to maintain. The central thrust of communist political warfare is to erode Western willingness to support and use the forces it needs to survive. The outcome of the struggle—however long it may continue—is likely to hinge on the ideological commitments and resolve of the peoples living under the competing systems. The side that holds out the longest may win.

Some Westerners who oppose any efforts to turn communist weaknesses against the Communists point to the "apparatus," especially the bolshevik kind based on a monolithic party and all powerful political police. According to them, the Soviet system is destined—unless destroyed by war from the outside—to rule forever. History does not bear out this point of view. The Hungarian Revolution, for example, was an authentic popular struggle for freedom. We should not ignore its implications. On October 23, 1956, hostile demonstrations against the Hungarian communist government began in Budapest. These demonstrations were intended to lend support to the anti-communist trends then unfolding in Poland. In the vanguard of the Budapest revolt were intellectuals, students and workers— the very groups on which the Communists had concentrated their greatest indoctrination efforts. Soviet emblems were ripped from the Hungarian flag. The statue of Stalin was pulled down. The conflict spread like wildfire through towns and villages all over the country. A new regime was installed, headed by Imre Nagy, whose goal was to declare his country's independence of the Communist bloc and to remove the vestiges of foreign military rule.

The Hungarian army quickly went over to the side of the rebellion, and even some Soviet military forces joined the freedom fighters against the detested local communist secret police. By the end of October, Soviet armies were withdrawing from Budapest. Long-suppressed political parties sprang up and joined Nagy's coalition. Hungarian Communism was rapidly disintegrating. For five glorious days, the Hungarian people experienced a freedom unknown for many years in Eastern Europe. Freedom of speech returned; newspapers with real news began to appear on the streets. But Hungary's elation was short-lived. November 2, the Soviets invited a delegation from the Hungarian government to a meeting outside of Budapest to make final arrangements for the withdrawal of the Soviet troops. According to a subsequent United Nations report, the Chief of the Soviet Security Police appeared and arrested the Hungarian delegation. At 5:20 A.M. on the morning of November 4, 1956, Premier Nagy made his last address over the radio. He said: "Today at daybreak, Soviet troops attacked our capital with the obvious intention of overthrowing the legal Hungarian democratic government." Throughout that day, hundreds of Stalin tanks descended upon Budapest. The valiant youth, boys and girls, who went out to meet the Soviet tanks armed only with a few home-made "Molotov cocktails" joined the ranks of those heroes who, in the words of Pericles, "have the whole earth as their sepulchre."

Revolutions are made by long accumulations of discontent. Organization plays the role of a *catalyst* in bringing them about. Organization begins when people are stirred by ideas—the prime organizers. The more potent the ideas, the more effective are the organizations built in their name.

Nor does man need the printed word to embrace ideas; man is born to observe, compare, and deduce—in short, to think. All that the printed word does is to *accelerate* that process, as do also radio and television. It is the thinking man who makes communication possible, not vice versa. The Russian revolution of 1917 had its origin in the preceding Western European revolutions; it was delayed but inevitable.

Another theory even more widely accepted is the one about the invincibility of the party-created governing apparatus. This myth still has a strong hold on our intellectuals, though it has been shaken by the succession struggle and the discontent of the satellites, especially Hungary. Here, too, we can learn from history. If absolutism were invincible, then the fearful terror-apparatuses of the great empires antedating private capitalism would be still with us. The fact is that rank or position—or uniform— is not an absolute barrier against transcendental ideas (witness the Roman Empire), and the disintegrating forces inherent in man and society, such as paranoiac tendencies, jealousies, ambitions, intrigues, and other manifestations of his divergent drives, are continuously at work. Once they combine with catalytic ideas and fuse into a new rationale, then a new revolution is on the march. These factors, at least in embryonic form, are already present behind the Iron Curtain.

Stalin, who built the most notable terror-apparatus of our century, certainly did not believe in the absolute reliability of the apparatus under his command; hence the constant purges.[1]

The relation between spontaneity and organization has been under constant study at the Lenin School, with the emphasis on organization. The art of agitation and propaganda is to stimulate and run ahead of "spontaneity," and the art of organization is to push the revolution from behind. In free countries the mastering of the art is relatively simple; in closed countries it is a more difficult problem. The problem of organization is, essentially, a technical one. One must establish what resources for potential organization exist. It does not seem possible to start organizing a revolutionary movement in the Soviet Union (and in the satellites) via shortwave broadcasts. That would be too easy. Such an organization to be genuine and successful must originate within the communist countries themselves, not abroad, although some initial "push" (and, of course, a more substantial support of the opposition once it materialized) might, and should, come from the West.

1. "We must assume that the Soviet hierarchs know their political sitution. . . . Even an absolute police-state wouldn't assign a major portion of its budget, brains and manpower to the job of *internal* security unless it felt itself seriously *insecure*. . . . Otherwise why would they maintain, in the 42nd year of total power, a political-police establishment without match for size and ruthlessness in modern history? Why would they surround the country with barbed-wire/and minefields/and death decrees/to keep their happy and loyal citizens from escaping? Why would they train and pay hundreds of thousands of full-time 'agitators' to *sell* their system if the peoples were already *sold* on it?" Lecture by Mr. Eugene Lyons, "Soviet Vulnerabilities," at the National War College, July 22, 1959.

The main point, however, is not the technical one of organization, but the fact that the weaknesses inherent in the communist system can become fatal to its very existence, provided the Free World has the wisdom and energy to take advantage of them. Sustained assaults on the philosophical foundations of communism can be launched from the non-communist world. Seeping through the Iron Curtain, it will help to erode the twisted pillars of faith on which communism rests.

Crisis in Philosophy

The Communists claim that they have the true vision of the future for humanity. They promised well-being for all citizens of the communist dictatorship. Their chief accomplishment, however, has been to suppress active internal opposition and to make the communist empire militarily strong. Beyond this, the Communists assert that their solution will be valid for all times and everywhere. By implication the Communists presume to know what the problems of the future will be and that all social and historical processes, hitherto experienced by mankind, will continue after their work is done. Their ideology assumes that history, as we have known it, will come to a standstill. But history is not static; nor is the permanence of communism any more assured than the perpetuity of the divine Pharaohs or the millennial span of Hitler's *Reich*.

The Kremlin regards its relations with the West not only as a power struggle but also as a competition between two cultures. Moscow maintains that socialist institutions and culture are destined to spread throughout the world until all of mankind will live under a "socialist" and eventually a "communist" system. However, unless their redemptory scheme is backed by brute military force, this prospect is unlikely for three reasons: (1) the fragile base of communist philosophy; (2) the oppressive character of communist imperialism; and (3) the wide discrepancy between communist ideology and practice.

Communist philosophy rests on what is called historical materialism, a concept of purposeful matter first conceived by Karl Marx. According to Gerhard Niemeyer:

Before any Communist program of action was ever planned, Karl Marx thus developed a world view, a comprehensive explanation of human existence, social development, and the meaning of historical change. The basic tenets of this world view can be summarized as follows: (1) Life is fundamentally not a relation between man and God, but a relation between man and matter. (2) There are laws of history; they can be scientifically determined; and the Marxist interpretation of change in terms of developing modes of economic production is the only "scientific" key to the knowledge of history. (3) Because history is essentially a process in which the inherent logic of human affairs works itself out, one can find general truth about human affairs only by participating in historical change, not by abstractly speculating about it—so that the point of philosophy is not to interpret but rather actively to change the world.[2]

Communism is a pseudoscientific product of the nineteenth century. Its basic concepts are materialistic and mechanistic.[3] Since the death of Stalin the Communists have explored many new areas of science; they remain, however, moored to a philosophical base that appears to be less and less scientific. The more deeply man explores matter, the more probabilistic and less predetermined does the basic substance of the universe appear to be. Hence a system which asserts that the process of history unfolds according to determinate forces inherent in the very structure of matter rests on a precarious foundation. Likewise the communist concept that the human personality is solely the product of external environment is, in the light of modern investigation, more questionable than it has ever been. The communist concept conflicts with all spiritual belief—that in the noble language of the Declaration of Independence holds that all men are "endowed by their Creator with certain inalienable rights." The science of biochemistry has unveiled the structure of the nucleus of the living cell. It now appears that each individual human being's cell plasm is coded differently so that each person is a unique creature and is inherently beyond the reach of even the most drastic application of external manipulation. Thus science, as well as theology, supports the belief in the dignity of man, because each person is a unique unrepeated center of life.

The underlying philosophical structure of communism, in conflict with the idea-base of the rest of the world, is fundamentally insecure. One day the communist elite, operating on outmoded assumptions regarding the universe and man's place within it, will stumble over the tenacity of

2. Gerhard Niemeyer, "The Ideological Core of Communism," in Walter F. Hahn and John C. Neff (eds.) , *American Strategy for the Nuclear Age*, pp. 56-57.
3. One of the best critiques of the communist structure of thought may be found in H. B. Acton's *The Illusion of the Epoch, Marxism-Leninism as a Philosophical Creed*. Acton, a professional philosopher, furnishes a technical guide more detailed than the dramatic and persuasive recitation of personalities, insights, and issues given in the appropriate chapters in George G. Catlin's *The Story of the Political Philosophers*. A marvelous tour de force showing the communist rationale being turned against itself is provided by John Robinson Beal, *The Secret Speech*.

human nature and scientific exploration for closer approximations of truth. Meanwhile, we can assist the process by turning the professed values of Communists against the Communists themselves.

The Crisis of Communist Imperialism

The imperialistic nature of the Soviet Union and Communist China manifested itself when the communists seized power in those countries. We must distinguish, however, between suppression of nationalist aspirations of the minorities *within* a communist state, imperialistic policies toward satellite states ruled by proxy from the two centers of communist power, and the non-communist world. While the latter clearly belong to the field of international relations and power politics carried out by a combination of traditional and revolutionary means, the first two forms of imperialism are peculiar to the communist system alone. In our age of disintegrating colonial empires and universal trend toward national independence even among the most backward nations of the world, the communist insistence on retaining in political bondage alien national bodies inevitably leads to strains and frictions within the communist world.

Suppression of minorities within a communist state possesses characteristics substantially different from those which existed in old-fashioned multinational empires. According to Walter Kolarz

The Soviet Russian colonizer considers that he is entitled to abolish all institutions of a given nationality; to impose every possible reform if this is in line with the communist programme. Thus Russian Bolsheviks never hesitated to introduce the principles of class struggle into the most backward atmosphere. They discovered an equivalent to the Russian "kulaks" everywhere, from the oasis of the Kara Kum desert in Turkmenistan to the Lapp settlements of the Arctic coast. The most violent measures of coercion against the guardians and symbols of primitive national traditions, the chiefs and tribal elders, were always justified in the eyes of Soviet colonizers.[4]

The minorities problem of Soviet Russia or Communist China cannot be viewed in isolation from the colonial problem presenting itself in other parts of the globe. In the modern world of mass communications the struggle for the fulfillment of national aspirations among the colonial peoples proceeds everywhere on a fairly similar pattern. Four lessons may be drawn from the general trend in the colonial territories outside the Soviet Union.

4. Walter Kolarz, *Russia and Her Colonies*, p. 310.

First, the more advanced dependent peoples will appreciate material achievements only if such go hand-in-hand with political progress. . . .

Secondly, the peoples of the colonial territories in order to fulfill their national aspirations create political movement and ideologies corresponding to their own national and tribal traditions. . . .

Thirdly, national aspirations can be properly defined only if the colonies enjoy at least a certain measure of democracy and freedom of discussion . . . towards self-government and national independence.

Fourthly, recognition of self-government as a desirable political aim on the part of a progressive colonial power does not mean unlimited recognition of all national aspirations of a colonial people. . . .

If one admits that the essence of a modern colonial policy lies in the encouragement of self-government, then every colonial system, including the so-called "Soviet nationalities policy," must be judged on the basis of this fourfold standard.[5]

If such is the general trend among peoples striving to assert their national identity, "Soviet nationalities policy" runs against it. Within the Soviet Union, however, the situation is not all black and white. The non-Russian communist elites in the Soviet Union enjoy the same privileged status as that of the Great Russian majority. At the same time, the less fortunate groups of population on the Russian periphery are often, at least economically, better off than the corresponding groups in the strictly Russian areas. Such visible equality of treatment tends to corrupt nationalist elements, and it is not accidental that throughout Soviet history genuine nationalists could usually be found only among native intellectuals.

There is, however, a notable division of expert opinion as to whether the chief enemy inside the Soviet Union is Russian nationalism in communist dress or communist ideology covered with Russian veneer. Actually there is an element of each involved. The Russian people, particularly the workers and peasants, have themselves been victims of the communist system while at the same time serving as tools in the hands of the Moscow leadership whenever it needed to displace or to dilute the more hostile populations in non-Russian areas. Consequently, the anti-Russian feelings among the minorities have often been less intense than have been the feelings of subjugated peoples against colonial powers in Asia or Africa. This is why some authors stress:

To incite the non-Russian nationalities of the Soviet Union against the Russian people and to aim at the disintegration of the Russian Empire

5. *Soviet Russian Nationalism,* Frederick C. Barghoorn, p. 269.

would be a short-sighted policy. . . . In other words, the Western nations should not become the splitters of Russia by attaching more importance to the local nationalities than to the Russian people. Those peoples of the USSR who for geographical, historical, cultural, and economic reasons will not fit into a new Russian Federal State will leave Russia anyway, in the process of tremendous political upheavals which are likely to accompany a change of regime. Responsibility for this action, however, should rest with these people alone.[6]

Quite distinct from the internal situation of Russia are conditions in the satellite states of Eastern and Central Europe. There, with a possible exception of Bulgaria and, to a lesser extent, Czechoslovakia, the anti-Russian sentiment runs high, mixed as it is with contempt for and resentment against native communist regimes subservient to Moscow. The relations between the center of power in the Soviet Union and the satellites fit more accurately the old imperialist pattern so much discredited in the non-communist world. In the West, the colonial powers voluntarily—or under pressure—continue to disband their empires and strive to re-create their relationships with former colonies on a more tolerable and mutually beneficial basis. The Soviet and Chinese imperialist powers persist in preserving and strengthening their hold over alien and hostile populations of other countries:

We can probably expect continuation of the effort to Sovietize the captive countries of Eastern Europe, and, in a different fashion, of China. If and when it becomes expedient, some captive countries may be incorporated into the Soviet state. Some of the most powerful weapons of Soviet policy consist in the dissemination of translations of Soviet technical and political material, as well as of the classics of Russian culture, and a systematic program of instruction in the Russian language.[7]

Inside both the Soviet Union and Communist China bourgeois nationalism is the supreme crime against the totalitarian communist state. In both systems the satellite nations are subject to absolute central authority, regardless of what benefits they may receive from enforced incorporation into the communist paradise. In both areas the peoples subject to central communist domination detest it:

Clandestine public opinion polls shows that the satellite populations are overwhelmingly hostile to the Russians and only awaiting the time

6. *Ibid.*, p. 316.
7. *Ibid.*, p. 269.

when Russian attention is engaged elsewhere to mount open resistance.

The polls, conducted by Western intelligence agencies, indicate that resistance to Russia is apparently the strongest since the East Germany uprising of 1953 and the Hungarian revolt of 1956.

However, the vast majority (82 per cent) of pollees said it was "useless" to mount open resistance to the Russians as in East Germany and Hungary "unless we can be certain in advance of Western support."[8]

In both Communist China and the Soviet Union, the communist rulers take the line:

Resist us and we shall annihilate you, do exactly as we tell you, however different it is from what you want to do, and we shall share with you everything we have. It may not be what you want, but it will be good for you. There may not be much to share now, so that you have to give more than you receive; but one day, if you do what we tell you, we shall all be rich together.

This is a point of view. But it is not the point of view of the hundreds and thousands of martyrs who struggled for so long, who in lesser numbers still struggle, against Russian domination. And Mr. Khrushchev knows it.[9]

Perhaps the communist leadership is aware that its efforts to "Sovietize" the satellites may one day backfire and that in the event of a major war the subjugated areas east of the Elbe would prove to be a great liability. It can also be guessed whether actual incorporation of the East European nations into the Soviet Union is under any active consideration in Moscow. Deciding such a move, if it is indeed to be made, would be postponed until such time as the great majority of Poles, Hungarians, Czechs, Slovaks, Rumanians, and others will have themselves adjusted completely to communist rule and abandon all hope for liberation. Yet the nature of communism prevents Moscow from considering withdrawal even from the most "difficult" countries. Any reduction of territories under its domination would undermine the basic thesis of inevitability of communism's victory on the global scale. This thesis has become such an important pillar of communist ideology that any setback in East Central Europe would acquire, in the minds of the leaders and the peoples alike, the dimensions of a catastrophe. This fact of communist life is the underlying meaning of the Berlin crisis. The ideological commitment to preserve the empire and to expand it further greatly reduces Soviet maneuverability and forces Moscow to carry out often-unprofitable and sometimes irrational policies with the sole purpose of saving the ideological face of communism.

8. *Washington Evening Star,* August 28, 1961, p. A-7.
9. Edward Crankshaw in the *London Observer,* July, 1956.

This determination to preserve its possessions and to expand them regardless of the costs leaves the communist system wide open to a political offensive. Local conflicts between the puppet governments and population; frictions between satellite countries and between the satellites and Moscow; cultural, economic, political, and religious conflicts—all of them offer *unlimited opportunities* to an imaginative political warfare waged by the West.

The Crisis of Communist Performance

Frederick C. Barghoorn has said:

> The old Russian characteristic of external conformity combined with a stubborn effort to maintain a measure of personal integrity, has not been eliminated by the pressure of life in a totalitarian state.
> Soviet escapism manifests itself in such diverse ways as the tendency to "go overboard" for foreign novelties, craving for "decadent" forms of entertainment, tendencies toward alcoholism, about which the Soviet press has had a good deal to say since the death of Stalin, and, on a higher plane, an effort on the part of able young people to avoid political pitfalls by "retreating into the past," or by entering technical occupations as little connected as possible with ideological or political responsibility.[10]

In the light of this portrayal of Soviet society how can the social promises of Marxism might be turned against communist rulers?

Marxism-Leninism was conceived as a "science": a science for the destruction of a given society. The very methods of criticism and organization embodied in its doctrines could, with some modification, be used with greater effect against communism than against private capitalism. To be exploited by a monolithic state is potentially and often actually much worse than to be exploited by private capital. Legal servitude, abolished under capitalism, has been replaced by the even worse servitude to the state in the Soviet Union, its satellites, and Red China.

The average Soviet citizen resents strongly the fact that the state robs and exploits him all the time and in every possible way. Yet, this kind of "impersonal" state exploitation doesn't seem to be so offensive to his human dignity and pride as, *he believes,* would be the "exploitation" by one individual. His refusal to be made a "servant" to another man is a purely psychological phenomenon resulting from forty years of biased propaganda. Notwithstanding such psychological conditioning, rights for

10. Barghoorn, *op. cit.,* p. 261.

the working class and freedom do not exist behind the Iron Curtain; they have advanced far more in the pluralistic economies than in the communist system.

Marxist and Leninist literature is available throughout the communist world, and every bit of it suggests protest and could breed rebellion against the conditions that exist in the Soviet empire. The contradictions between ideology and performance colors every facet of communist-dominated life.

After forty years of rule, communism has defaulted on all of its essential social promises and has merely replaced the old class rule with a new and far worse one. The Soviet regime is as vulnerable to tactical assault as it is to philosophical attack. Though they tout theirs as a "superior" society, the Communists have produced a monstrous state and political barbarism.

If we keep in mind that the communist movement is built on ideology and the criticism of the "capitalist" society, we should conclude that its default in performance is its major vulnerability, a contradiction which if skillfully exploited, might become a decisive factor in the disintegration of communist regimes. The ideological superiority of the West, sometimes obscured by propaganda generated in Moscow, is reflected in a society which, with all of its faults, has a far better performance record.

Contradictions in Soviet Society

It is always easier to criticize than to build anew. Men found it difficult to come to grips with Marxism-Leninism when it was an opposition theory promising a new day on earth. The man in the street, aggrieved with things as they were, could always long for and speculate about something better. Marxism-Leninism, the most comprehensive social opposition theory in depth and scope, acquired its force as a critique of what existed. The Communists did not have to worry about the correctness of their doctrine, but only whether its propagation exerted a cumulative effect in preparations for the overthrow of traditional society. Its strength lay in its negatives. Their protest "science" rested on irresponsibility. One need not wonder that when its advocates came to power, only the destructive part of the "science" worked. Instead of the classless society they promised, they created a new kind of class society in aggravated form, replacing the old proprietary groups with a single new group. The collective ownership they promised, upon which the theoretical abolition of classes was based, was turned into oligarchic ownership by the new upper stratum, the bureaucratic elite. All the mystifying socialist phraseology aside, there are in present-day Soviet society the same main class categories as exist elsewhere—the industrial workers, or proletariat, the peasantry, and the intellectuals. But Communists imposed upon their society a new class of the party bureaucracy, and, dramatizing the contradictions of the whole structure, they have one element which does not exist anywhere else: the class of state-managed forced labor. Thus we have two new phenomena in Soviet society, the new upper party class and, at the bottom, the forced laborers.

Under the communist system, any worker or peasant or any member of the managerial bureaucracy and intelligentsia may lose his status as a free servant of the state and be reduced to the low grade of a forced laborer. Forced labor in the Communist is no respecter of rank or status; it is political.

Admittedly, some changes have been made in the forced-labor system since Beria's administration. The whole Soviet economy was geared to slave labor then, and the slaves were numbered in the millions. Those who were sentenced to long terms in concentration camps seldom survived. This was not only because their sentences could be extended arbitrarily, but also because of the severity of exploitation and mistreatment in the camps.

Khrushchev has "modernized" the system. Many camps have been closed down, although a large number of inmates were forced to continue working in the old places as "free" laborers. But the old system of mass deportations —on a somewhat reduced scale—is still in operation. Under cover of cultivating the "virgin lands," hundreds of thousands, if not millions, have gone into the traditional exile areas of Soviet Asia, where men would not go voluntarily. In addition, despite noticeable liberalization of the old labor laws, the so-called free labor is still not quite free; many obstacles to changing one's place of employment continue.

The Country of Forbidden Thoughts

The contradictions in Sino-Soviet society dealt with thus far, even if not generally known outside the communist bloc, are in part admitted by the Communists—witness the speech on "Contradictions" delivered in 1958 by Mao Tse-tung. The greatest of all contradictions in communist society, and the least understood in the outside world, is not that of the various classes, however, but that between the system and man as a thinking being; between freedom, the natural urge of man, and the suppression of all freedoms. That the Western type of freedom does not exist in the communist dominated lands is fairly well known, but somehow other freedoms supposedly exist. The Western mind cannot fathom life without freedom. It is like imagining life without air.

The communist suppression of freedom started with, and was supposed to terminate with, the liquidation of the old propertied classes. From the beginning the Bolsheviks classified their enemies as (1) the objective enemy, that is, those who by the nature of their class status and property interests would or should oppose them; and (2) the subjective enemy, that is, those hostile to them ideologically, regardless of class status or property.

The concept of an objective opposition can be illustrated. The Ukrainians were considered by tradition violent nationalists and hence were subject to continuous and all-pervasive purges, the Communists among them included. The Volga Germans were suspect during the war with Hitler's Germany and hence were rounded up *in toto* and scattered. The Jews were suspect as a "race" even prior to the war, and after it they were arrested as "cosmopolitans."[11]

The major consequence of the objective-enemy formula has been to drive all dissent underground. Double-faced behavior has become general. Each citizen must learn to lead a double life, one in relation with his superiors, and the other unto himself.

In the past a Soviet citizen could not express dissent on anything of political consequence, and he avoided even being suspected of harboring dissenting thoughts. He remains insecure, for some time in his past he may have expressed an adverse attitude or had the wrong parents or talked too freely—all of which has gone into his dossier. Denunciation under such a system flourishes. A man may even improve his lot thereby. He must, above all, never deviate from the official propaganda line. If the line says there are no classes in Soviet society, he must pretend to believe, even if all around him he sees the opposite. Regardless of what he thinks, he must deny what he sees and say what the official propaganda desires. Thus the people living within the Soviet Union have been made to live the life of fictitious propaganda, not that of reality. They exist in a condition of sustained psy-

11. "The Soviet Jewish community of three million is officially deprived of major cultural and religious rights guaranteed to all ethnic and religious groups by the Soviet Constitution, laws and practice, and is subjected to discriminatory practices in education and employment." For a fuller exposé of anti-Semitism throughout the Soviet Union and the degree of support given this movement by the Soviet government, see "Facts" (from which this note is quoted), *Foreign Report*, Vol. 13, No. 11 (October, 1960), published by the Anti-Defamation League of B'Nai B'Rith.

chological irritability with the unending distortion of human experience.

Judging by the Soviet press over the past several years, the people have now begun to express their criticism—mostly camouflaged, but sometimes even openly (letters to editors, literature, particularly poetry, statements on various meetings, etc.). After 1961's "De-Stalinization" this process may become even more manifest.

The contradiction between distortion and reality in Soviet society is part of the consciousness of every thinking being. Mao Tse-tung says that the contradictions under communism are but partial and short lived. The contrary is the truth; they are deep and all-pervading. The all-pervading state police system is not the cause, but the result. The contradiction is between man the family-builder, man the thinking being, and the system.

Vulnerabilities of Communist Theory

The nurturing of a new revolution in the communist world could begin by stressing the unfulfilled promises of the old. Unfulfilled revolutions stand as accusers against the demagogues who initiated them. The Communists would like us to believe that their revolution is the terminus of all revolutions, a convenient concept which has nothing to do with practical fulfillment. Indeed, they themselves fear nothing more than a new revolution.

Modern means of communication and the organizational techniques of Marxism-Leninism created the huge empire of the Soviets in a short time, too short, in fact, to erase its promises from the memory of man. The old revolution beckons the new one in a single lifetime. Thus the Communists of yesteryear can be used against the communism of today, Marxist socialism against the communism of Khrushchev and Mao Tse-tung.

A Marxian Boomerang

Marxism-Leninism as a social theory and a method of action was built around the class and social relationships developed in the nineteenth century. It was partially false even then and has long since been completely outdated. The spearhead of that theory was aimed at the property-owning classes and meticulously avoided all other experiences in the history of man. It stressed the idea of collective ownership as an alternative to private ownership, but only to produce a bureaucratic class ownership by a one-party state.

Modern political history, however, is not keyed solely to a series of class struggles, as Marx thought he discovered; it is even more a history of accumulation or dispersal of power by the state. The bourgeois system of society is competitive; it tends to disperse political power, not to concentrate it. The tyrannies of antiquity, and today, were built not by private property owners (the bourgeoisie) but by talented military organizers and leaders, theological hierarchies, or military leaders and ideologies combined.

If any law of political motion is discernible through history, it is not the law of class struggle, but the law of concentration and dispersal of power. The tendency toward accumulation of power at all levels is inherent in man, as is also the tendency to oppose it.

Potent ideologies, both religious and secular, have been and are the driving force to undermine great empires as well as to build and stabilize them. Whereas in past centuries the religious ideologies have been predominant, ours is the age of conflict between religious and secular ideologies, the age of political ideologies, science and political power accumulation, with the anti-religious elements as the aggressors.

The current menace to man's freedom comes from the ideologies of total centralization, particularly Marxism-Leninism. Centralization is a process which, if unrestrained, shifts the power relationships in society from the many to the few. Once it reaches the stage of totalitarianism it becomes enslavement maintained by force.

Before the advent of totalitarian centralization, the concept of freedom, with all of its imperfections, was spreading over the earth. Marxism-Leninism began as a criticism of the faults of Western society, promising even greater freedoms, only to carry out a counterrevolution against liberty. Thus it reversed within its own domain the centuries-old struggle of man against autocratic government and is striving by subterfuge and force to chain the rest of the world.

The State of Soviet Society

In a free society, the power urges of man can be restrained or limited through the free interplay of competition and public surveillance. In short, they are driven outward. In a closed, centralized society, the contrary takes place: they are driven inward. A totalitarian society can be totally corrupt and still cover up the fact, whereas in a free society even partial corruption will be exposed and thus fought and done away with. In a free society the accumulation of wealth is a manifold process; it does not have to take

place at the expense of the state. The Soviet state, with its claims to infal-
libility, cannot admit that any large-scale corruption exists in its ruling
circles, no matter how extensive it might be; even if there are some cases
that it chooses to reveal, it will do so strictly for political reasons—reasons
of state.

Corruption is a social cancer which has been a prime factor in the destruction of great empires. Corruption in the communist world does not
yet seem to have reached a stage where it is beyond control. But a system
that has to tolerate dishonesty and use it as an element of rule is already
sick.

In climbing the communist ladder, ability counted, to be sure; but first
came political cunning and pliability. To succeed was to belong to the right
faction at the right time, stepping over one's friends and denouncing them.
Under Stalin that was the price one had to pay to be of the communist
power elite and stay there.

Today the elite is much stronger and determined to maintain its privileged status and personal security. This fact, perhaps, also explains the
second "De-Stalinization" which, in reality, is a re-endorsement of the
"Magna Charta" issued to the elite at the 20th Party Congress. At the
same time, the new elite has lost now all ideological justification for its
superior status.

Thus we have an upper class which must constantly debase itself, whose
status is insecure, and whose temporary rights exist only at the pleasure
of the summit of the party bureaucracy. The question arises: How strong
can such a regime be? If we also consider the condition of the masses, who
through their labor must pay for the cost of misrule, then we have a
glimpse of the vulnerability of the communist system.

Reaction to the sickness of Soviet society by its members has not been
uniform. Among the peasantry, which still comprises one-half of the
Russian population, it takes the form of a deep resentment toward all
things communist. The resentment of the peasants manifests itself in their
refusal to exert themselves in tilling the land: they have come to believe
that the all-powerful state robs them of the fruits of their labor and is
unable to assure them even the standard of living their parents and grandparents enjoyed before the revolution. A chronic agricultural crisis and the
resultant shortage of foodstuffs is one of the major headaches of the Kremlin leaders for which they can find no remedy. Both threats and incentives—
those few incentives that the bureaucratized state can spare for the peas-

antry without lowering the standard of living of the new class—fail to encourage production. It is unlikely that anything short of an old-fashioned free-market system would satisfy the Russian peasant.

The industrial working class is almost as unhappy over the state of affairs in the Soviet Union as are the peasants. The labor is hard, the working hours long, the wage scale low. Only a small minority of the skilled industrial workers, usually the party members and the Komsomol "activists," enjoy a somewhat higher standard of living. They get better housing, an occasional vacation in some resort area at low cost, better working conditions, and higher wages. While the peasantry has given up hope that the state may improve their well-being, many workers still look to it for improvement of theirs. They are not aware that the huge overhead imposed on the Soviet economy by the necessity to keep happy the ruling bureaucracy, by enormous military expenditures and by outlays for promotion of the communist cause the world over, make any significant improvement impossible. Along with the army of underpaid civil servants in the lower echelons of the bureaucracy, the workers represent a brooding mass shifting from despair to hope and from hope to despair. They have no ideas as to how the situation could be remedied and tend to see the source of evil, not in the system itself, but in what they consider to be local aberrations. There is no real search for solutions.

Despite a relatively high degree of political sophistication, these predominant groups of the Soviet population have no knowledge of and little interest in political democracy. Their attitudes toward political matters are negative. Yet, they would be receptive to explicit criticism of the existing system if the criticism were supplied them from the outside.

And even though the Soviet population as a whole has had no experience in democratic self-government in the last forty-four years, there still is an amazing degree of intuitive understanding of its principles and workings. During the initial stage of World War II, the people in the Nazi occupied areas showed a surprising ability to organize local self-government by classical democratic methods. Only upon the installation of Nazi civilian control were these locally elected authorities replaced by appointed officials.

The Soviet intelligentsia are a mixed group. On the whole, they tend to support the regime, which offers an opportunity for advancement in social and economic standing. Those who have succeeded in reaching the higher steps of the ladder, whether party members or not, appear quite content with their lot. If they belong to the older generation and remember harsh realities of life in the Stalin era, they tend to abstain from vocal criticism of Soviet shortcomings as a measure of self-preservation. But the younger ones, who are still at the start of their careers, are, as a rule, more daring and more inclined to explore forbidden areas of thought. They have less to lose if they get into trouble with the regime, and they are often willing to take risks. One characteristic of contemporary youth in the Soviet Union is its impatience with the slowness of whatever progress takes place in the country. The skepticism of the young generation toward standard and all-too-familiar propaganda, its search for facts, and its receptiveness to new ideas contain great promise. Younger people everywhere are more sensitive and more idealistic, and they are apt to notice and to react more quickly to injustice observed around them; reports confirm that those living under communism are no exception. While most are likely to direct their thinking toward the search for ways to improve the communist system, with only a minority rejecting it altogether, all appear receptive to criticism of the system and willing to exercise their own judgment—partly because of the greater leeway increasingly given by the regime. As it is, this trend among the youth does not yet represent a serious threat, but it contains certain potentialities which could and should be explored in the course of political warfare. Many of Marx's and Lenin's writings, particularly the latter, are replete with advice on how to fight a social enemy and how to organize against him. Although the present regime guards against the hostile use of these Leninist methods by suppressing liberties, still there is much in them that an anti-Soviet rebel or a dissident may utilize in the way of practical guidance.

An orientation theory, presenting the "how" of organization against totalitarianism, may either come from the West or be born inside the communist world. Writings by critics of the Soviet regime could be used to attack the practice of Marxism—Leninism. Trotsky's "Leninist" writings, particularly the passage written after his break with Stalin, and some of Tito's statements could be used as a starting point.

By stimulating ideological infighting within the enemy camp it may be possible to penetrate the enemy's ideology and explode it from within. It may require a complete contrary ideology to do this effectively. Dissident Communists cannot do it, but once their faith is shaken, many of them can render real service. The most effective ones are those who, although versed in communist theory and practice, would be inclined to reject historical materialism and its associated ideas.

There are many sectors of potential dissent. The Soviet trade-unions, whose power was whittled down to zero during Stalin's reign, want to regain at least the power they had under Lenin. The industrial managers, who have become a force in the last thirty years, want to manage and are set against bureaucratic overcentralization. The discontent in the agricultural sphere is notorious, as is that with shortages in other consumer goods. The various national and local soviets want to be more than mere rubber stamps for the bureaucracy in Moscow.

The top leaders seek alternately to manipulate, neutralize, or suppress these forces. Right now Khrushchev and his faction are in the stage of manipulation and neutralization, with suppression used but sparingly. If and when he reaches the point of being able to suppress dissensions physically, as Stalin managed to do, he will make himself absolute ruler.

Khrushchev's yielding to internal pressures has thus far been a policy of method rather than of substance. The methods of the political police are now more restrained and concealed. There has been some relaxation of bureaucratic centralization, particularly in the economic sphere. There has also been a renewal of promises to the masses for a better standard of living. All of this happened—off and on—under Stalin and represented the customary maneuverings of the leading autocrats when a show of relaxation was deemed necessary. These concessions help to create new illusions, but actually, no basic reforms are thus far on the horizon. The "unanimity" rule in the Party continues, as under Stalin; labor and the peasants remain in a strait jacket tailored by the Party. Whatever relaxation there is, however, indicates that the pressure against the top bureaucracy from the lower ranks is both persistent and continuous. It is prompted by necessity as well as personal ambition. This does not mean that it is revolutionary, *but it may become so if it congeals into an ideology opposed to the regime as a whole.* It is in this process that the outside world can be of immense assistance. Discontent exists in width and depth, far exceeding anything existing in the West, but no way has been found to counter the oppressive apparatus which holds it down. Communist dialectic maintains that there cannot be an antithesis to the communist regime and that the communist social system is the ultimate in human endeavor, but the Communists are not sure of this themselves, hence their huge police apparatus to see that no counterthesis ever crystallizes and becomes a force.

What is needed to create a counterforce is an orientation theory which serves as a comprehensive goal for action, a theory which advocates values and goals opposite to those of communism and is appealing enough to unite the opposition. Let us illustrate some of the elements of such a theory:

(1) A return to individual rights, including free speech, freedom of assembly, the abolition of a one-party monopoly, etc.

(2) Destatification of Soviet economy, which means a return of property to ownership by the people co-operatively, either as profit-sharing enterprises or in some other form.

(3) Return of the land to the peasants, to be owned individually or as co-operatives.

(4) Restoration of nationality rights, including the right of secession.

These are but some points of a broadly designed program which stands for liberty and representative government, a program which rejects the fraudulent collective ownership by the state. It could vest such ownership, collectively if desired, in the hands of those who work and operate the various enterprises that are now state owned. It represents a compromise between the individual ownership in the West and total statism. This would be good for both sides and would, at the same time, give the lie to the oft-repeated accusation that the West aims at the restoration of the former factory owners and big landowners, most of whom are no longer alive.

The major points in this program can be broken down into more limited objectives which appear to be realizable under the Soviet system itself. These objectives could be: (1) restoration in full of democracy inside the Communist Party; (2) abolition of party control of the labor unions, which would restore to the workers some of the authority they were supposed to have under the Soviet system; (3) a return to voluntary participation in Soviet collectives, which would do away with compulsory servitude to the state and restore to the peasants the status of allies that they were to have under Lenin's concept of the workers' and peasants' state; and (4) abolition of the political police and its system of forced-labor camps.

Since opposition of any sort is forbidden inside the U.S.S.R., the initial problem is to give it cohesiveness, first ideologically, by providing goals, and then organizationally, by furnishing methods likely to succeed even under conditions of heavy suppression. Even a Khrushchev and a Mao swear by Lenin and Marx, and even in the Soviet Union it is easier to dissent or advocate change in the name of the prophets than to oppose them.

The guiding theory for crystallizing opposition can be presented by the

West as news and interpretation of news. The Communists' suppression of adverse news is now such that we on the outside often know more about what is going on behind the Iron Curtain than do the people who live there.

The reader should note that the major goals here enumerated guide the *strategy* to be pursued in the *abolition of the totalitarian state,* while the minor or immediate demands, aiming at its amelioration of the tyranny, inspire the *tactics.* As tactics and strategy, they are not inconsistent with each other; together they are aimed against the despotism of the communist state.

A concerted use of the vulnerabilities and contradictions of the communist regime for purposes of ideological counterpenetration and organization would also have an extremely deleterious effect on the communist movement outside the Iron Curtain. This, in fact, is the key to its extinction. The Kremlin is fully aware of its own vulnerability. Gone are the days when it stressed social betterment within its own domain. Now it advertises its gross military power, its atom bombs, submarines, missiles, and Sputniks, plus its foreign adventures. It pretends to catch up with the West, not in social progress, but in technology, particularly military technology. Khrushchev draws attention away from the inner vulnerabilities of communism toward the alleged war danger, self-created, as did Stalin during most of his reign.

The Ideological Spark

Dissatisfaction alone, no matter how widespread and deep, does not produce a counterorganization; it is merely the objective prerequisite to it. To organize an opposition one must have an *ideology* which synthesizes the dissatisfaction into a positive goal sufficiently worth while to risk sacrifice. In short, to the objective factor there must be added the *subjective* one: ideology.

When Marxism started over a hundred years ago, Marx had to invent a social theory. He presented unproven theories as supremely desirable and at the same time discredit existing theories and practices. Western society, in the meantime, has improved on precisely those things on which communism has defaulted, namely, the humanities, greater freedoms, and living standards. A countermovement may thus draw inspiration from the effective contrasting of the two. Nor does the new countermovement need to base itself on unproved theories. On the contrary, it can take the best accomplishments of the West, adjust them to Russian conditions as of now, and proceed from there. It can thus, if ably supported from the West, proceed at a twentieth-century pace to effect great changes behind the Iron Curtain, and do so in our lifetime. In fact, if a new catastrophe, such as a world war, is to be avoided or its consequences minimized, this must be done. Dialectically, the theory and practice of Western freedom and standards of living would thus become the counterthesis to that of the Kremlin; the communist-party expropriators thus would be in turn expropriated.

Ideologies have been the prime movers in all historical epochs. Ideological forces are frequently instruments for the manipulation of power; they can change institutions, command people, and destroy and create societies. The competition of sociopolitical ideologies is thus a critical factor in the over-all contest for power. The development of a general philosophy of freedom, liberty, and dignity of man is an essential part of Free World efforts to meet the challenge of communist imperialism—and of its ideological appeal.[12] There appears to be a consensus on the essential nature and future goals of the free society sufficient to permit the formulation of a philosophy which would be widely accepted.[13] Some of the principles[14] of a modern philosophy of freedom would be:

(1) The concept that government should not exist for the purpose of securing the privileges of the few but should be subjected to the test of whether it serves the community as a whole and does so effectively and successfully. A government which works for the benefit of the rulers, and not for the benefit of each member of the community, is a bad government and must be improved.

(2) It will be necessary to explain the position of property and economic security in a free society. Marxists have been able to distort the real meaning of property and to make it the very foundation of poverty and even slavery. Property is generally not considered to be a vital ingredient of free-

12. The development of such a philosophy is feasible, despite the oft-repeated argument that in an open and pluralistic society such as ours there are many attempts to formulate a comprehensive and universally acceptable ideology but no known methods for ratifying or enforcing them.

13. The literature on democratic goals is too vast to be cited in a single footnote. There have been many statements, ranging from that of President Eisenhower's committee on the subject to the various declarations from the Council of Europe and other bodies. It is not too much to hope that a single vivid statement of democratic goals may emerge from a common position on selected fundamentals.

14. These principles were suggested by Dr. Stefan T. Possomy.

dom; it is cursed as a tool of oppression and symbolizes everything that is bad about the "rich." We must make it clear that economic security can be achieved only by the joint application of several methods, including the right to own property, and that this right is designed to increase and not to reduce the importance of the individual.

(3) This philosophy will also distinguish clearly between freedom from oppression and freedom to do things one wants to do. Too often the concept of freedom has been misinterpreted abroad to overemphasize the role of the individual and to give the stronger the right to do whatever he wants, often at the expense of society. This interpretation often links freedom to nineteenth-century capitalism and imperialism. It must be emphasized that life, liberty, and the pursuit of happiness are rights in the sense that no state should hinder individuals in the achievement of their personal aspirations so long as these do not conflict with the aspirations of other individuals. But they are also tasks to be accomplished jointly by the individual, various co-operative social groups, and the government.

The role of ideology in the creation of a cohesive organized opposition is here emphasized because (1) it is the inspirational factor most lacking behind the Iron Curtain; (2) the West has now certain technical means with which to create ideological ferment within the communist domain; and (3) a concerted ideological effort of that sort will also clarify the issues confronting the West and bring about a closer alliance between the West and the multitudes behind the Iron Curtain.

Communist psychological warfare has been concentrated for decades, not on advocating the Communists' theory and demands, but on discrediting the capitalist system. It is their way of sterilizing the nascent opposition behind the Iron Curtain and carrying on their demoralization work in the West. The greater their failures, the more intense the smearing of Western society, while their own system is presented as the epitome of progress. The technique has proven effective, and we must not ignore it. The discrediting of their system is a *sine qua non* of effective counterstruggle, and since there is much to discredit, we could probably, in five years of concentrated effort, accomplish what took them fifty years. Furthermore, we have the advantage of using the truth and of turning their lies about us against them. Discrediting a barbarous tyranny which poses as a benefactor of humanity is not merely expedient but an essential part of building up an opposition.

Accent on the Negative

The main purpose of conducting political warfare against the communist bloc is, of course, to undermine its strength and to render it less dangerous to the free nations of the world. A communist system forced to concentrate on solving its internal problems, with few energies left for aggressive expansionism, would be easier to live with. If in addition some kind of transformation would take place as a result of which the communist society would lose its present characteristics and be replaced by a less dynamic, less totalitarian, and more Westernized society, most of the formidable problems we are facing today, including the threat of all-out nuclear war, would disappear.

It follows that by its nature Western political warfare must be primarily a negative or destructive operation. The urgency of the present danger dictates the primacy of weakening the adversary over the need of promoting different, non-communist societies in the present Soviet empire. We must also be conscious of the fact that a destructive operation is much more simple. There is no need for a particular consistency in criticism which can be advanced from different viewpoints. There is no need for offering remedies or trying to "sell" the Western way of life to the Russians. If we are aware that our purpose is to undermine a self-avowed enemy, the choice of means to accomplish this purpose are wide.

Nevertheless, the negativistic approach should be combined with a positive program to be offered to the communist-dominated world as an alternative to what it has today. New ideas must be presented, around which dissident elements might be able to unite. It would be better if such ideas were born on communist soil. It is well to reiterate the points that should be an integral part of practically any opposition theory: (1) a return to individual rights, including free speech, freedom of assembly, the abolition of a one-party monopoly; (2) destatification of Soviet economy, which means a return of property to ownership by the people collectively, in whichever form they find to be most suitable; (3) return of the land to the peasants, to be owned individually or as co-operatives; and (4) restoration of self-government to non-Russian republics of the Soviet Union, with the rights of self-determination and dissociation. These are major principles which would secure representative government and a return to liberty. A more elaborate program is undesirable, since particulars tend to create dissension rather than contribute to unity. Besides, the development of a specific program for reconstruction of a society is an inalienable privilege of a sovereign nation which liberates itself from tyranny; it is not something to be imposed from outside.

Ever since Stalin's death a view has developed in the West that we should aid and promote a process of liberalization of the communist society which presumably has been under way under the enlightened leadership of Mr. Khrushchev and his associates. This view helps to obscure realities rather than to clarify the issues.

Without basic change any "mellowing" of the communist system internally will not mean that this system would stop being a threat to the rest of us. Foreign policies of the Soviet Union and Communist China are seldom dependent upon domestic developments—which allows the communist leadership a freedom of action undreamt of in democratic societies. In other words, promoting liberalization of the communist system may not really serve our needs. History reveals many cases in which truly enlightened societies were simultaneously cruel oppressors of other nations and carried out imperialistic policies toward the outside world. There are no reasons to expect that the ideologically motivated communist powers would display more tolerance toward their opponents than they display toward the subjects they control.

The War Issue

There is only one issue on which the leadership is sensitive to the mood of the population: the threat of a major war. This sensitivity is based on fear, fear born on the battlefields of the Second World War. Russian experience has shown that an armed nation, with many millions of soldiers constantly risking their lives, tends to become unmanageable. In the first year and a half of the last war, approximately five million Soviet soldiers surrendered to the enemy without much of a fight—a degree of defection unthinkable in peacetime. An armed soldier under wartime conditions is inclined to defy his military and political superiors; the maintenance of the famed "Soviet State Discipline" becomes a problem with which state, party, and police apparatus, designed for "normal" conditions, cannot cope satisfactorily.

In the next war the communist powers would have few allies; they would have to rely entirely on their own resources. Instead of a relatively homogeneous army of "tamed" Soviet people, Moscow would also have to depend on loyalties and good will of the nations which compose the so-called Warsaw Pact. There are strong reasons to believe that such loyalties and good will exist only until the first military setback. The present-day Soviet allies might easily start acting as enemies. The communist leadership is keenly aware of this possibility.

There is another factor which makes all-out war a dreaded development for the Kremlin. Unlike elected leaders in the democratic West, whose mission is to serve their respective peoples but who do not regard the people as their wards and do not identify the national wealth with the contents of their own pockets, the communist leaders consider their country as a kind of personal preserve. They view the growth of economy of the nation as their personal achievement. They also know the almost unbelievable efforts which went into that growth, the sacrifices of the five-year plans and the over-all difficulties in building what they view as the basis of communist society. The loss—inevitable in case of war—of what they have created is to Soviet leaders a very personal matter, comparable to the loss of one's only house in a fire—without any fire insurance to lean back on. This psychological factor must always be taken into account by the West whenever the threat of nuclear war looms in some recurrent crisis.

Finally, a war that the communist side might conceivably lose threatens the Moscow leaders in the most intimate way. A Western leader, if his country is taken over by the enemy, might go into exile to another Allied country and attempt to weather the storm. Individual leaders, with or without means, can emigrate and end their days in peace in another corner of the globe, adjusting to new conditions and finding their place in a different but nevertheless familiar society. To the Soviet leaders, such prospects must be terrifying. For one thing, they live by power, which constitutes the essence and the meaning of their whole existence; *they would be deprived of that power everywhere outside the land they now rule.* For another, despite international characteristics of communism, the Soviet leaders are intensely Russian, with no interest, knowledge, or experience in living outside Russia. Some leading Communists from elsewhere have in the past gone to Moscow and lived there, without much happiness or satisfaction. But to imagine the leaders of Soviet communism living in exile in China, Cuba, or Yugoslavia is impossible and, in their own view, unthinkable. Their fear of war is very real, and it is not by accident that the 1961 communist-party program makes prevention of the nuclear war the first order of business for all Communists of the world.

So long as there exists a danger that a major war against the West might be lost, so long as there are no reliable means to assure that the Western bombers and rockets would be shot down at the borders of the communist empire, such a war would never be initiated by the Communists. Moreover, we can reasonably assume that the communist leaders would do everything in their power to prevent it.

Warlike gestures and rocket-rattling emanating from Moscow, reflect the communist estimate of Western resolution—or irresolution—to fight. Combined with protestations of peaceful intentions, these belligerent declarations are aimed at scaring Western public opinion in order to produce pressures which could undermine Western resolution to resist communist political onslaught. Rather than engage in a popularity contest and try to appeal to pacifist and "neutralist" elements, the communist leadership put increasing reliance on a display of strength, calculating that such a course may pay off better in a world where people are more and more inclined to think that communism is the wave of the future.

In this instance we see how a basic weakness of communism—its very genuine fear of nuclear war—is being turned into a powerful weapon against democracies solely because the latter allow themselves to become trapped. Whether Western statesmanship is able to institute policies which appreciate the operational significance of the Soviet attitude toward war remains to be seen.

Conclusions

The first condition for successful psychopolitical warfare directed against communism is a determination to fight to win, eventually to destroy this totalitarian phenomenon which endangers the very existence of Western civilization. A part of this determination is an abandonment once and for all of all the notions of lasting compromise, accommodation, or coming to terms with present-day communism. Unless such a determination becomes the cornerstone of Western policy, it is quite useless to start a search for technical means for accomplishing the purpose and to go into details of the political-warfare program in order to convince the "right people." The unfortunate thing is that the "right people" need to be convinced, even at this late hour.

It is an interesting paradox that as Soviet power has grown and as the announced determination of the Soviet leaders to destroy the American system of government has been repeated with increased frequency, the U.S. government has progressively modified its policies toward the Soviet bloc from those aiming at elimination of the power of the Communist Party within the Soviet Union to one of tacit accommodation with the leadership of the international communist conspiracy. Shortly after the beginning of the Korean War, a much publicized paper, National Security Council No. 68, recognized the life-and-death nature of the struggle with Communists and set as a U.S. goal the eradication of the international communist apparatus. In subsequent statements of basic national security, the objective has been progressively refined until all that we seem to aspire toward is a continuation of the kind of unpeaceful coexistence which has characterized the last decade. Meanwhile, the fact that Khrushchev[15] asserts that communism "will bury" us is regarded with academic detachment by many of those who have been responsible for U.S. policy.

Only when the seriousness of the Western predicament is wholly appreciated will the search for means to defeat the enemy begin in earnest. It is realistic to launch a program aimed at making communist regimes more responsible to the wishes of the peoples they rule. The evidence indicates that the majority of people living under communism is, at least potentially, on our side. But as isolation of the communist world from Western influences continues and the incessant propaganda keeps driving into everybody's mind that any affinity with the West is a major crime, the opposition to communism tends to dissociate itself from ideas and policies originated in the West. This is particularly true in the original communist domain, Russia, and, to a lesser degree, in China. The ancient dictum that the "enemies of our enemies are our friends" must be applied discriminatingly in the case of idealistically minded Communists who criticize shortcomings of the communist system. We must always be on guard against obviously supplying such Communists with facts and ideas because in their eyes the West remains Enemy Number One; anything addressed to them has to be presented with the acme of sophistication.

We would be on much surer ground dealing with those who oppose the very essence of the communist system and are willing to admit it to themselves. As a rule, we do not find such people among those who occupy key positions in communist society and can influence important events directly.

15. "It is perfectly obvious that the establishment of the world system of socialism, the quick progress of the disintegration of the colonial system, the unprecedented upsurge of the struggle of the working class for its rights and interest—that all this undermines the support for capitalism, intensifies its general crisis. The losses of capitalism as a result of these blows are irreparable. This refers both to the entire system of capitalism and to its main power, the United States." Cited in an analysis of the Khrushchev speech of January 6, 1961. Hearing before the Commitee on the Judiciary, U.S. Senate, 87th Cong., 1st Sess., June 16, 1961, p. 56.

Yet those disenchanted with communism constitute a majority, or at least a potential majority, of the population. From this great mass the true fighters for freedom from communist oppression will eventually emerge. It is they who need our message, our ideas, and our information.

Up to the present time, the Western propaganda effort has been directed primarily toward those "who count" in the communist world. Such orientation of Western efforts has been wrong, for those "who count" have vested interests in preserving and strengthening and expanding communism. Communicating with them has practically the same effect as appealing to Khrushchev directly and does not need costly and complicated operation of mass communications media. An "improvement" of the communist system will not solve our problems; neither would it provide a satisfactory answer to the question of freedom *versus* slavery for the masses of people living under communism.

The communist leadership goes to extraordinary efforts to keep its subjects isolated from outside influences. A radical change in tone and direction of Western propaganda will undoubtedly induce it to double these efforts. But it will be up to Western technological superiority and ingenuity to find ways of reaching the population of the communist world and making sure the message goes through.

Perhaps the guiding political principle of the nineteenth century was the concept of Freedom of the Seas, championed by Great Britain and espoused by the United States. It was the guarantee of this freedom which made possible the massive movements and exchange of people, culture and capital which laid the foundations for the twentieth century world. The modern world is separated by artificially imposed barriers to the exchange of persons and ideas. If the cleavages rending our globe are ever to be closed, freedom of communications between peoples must be the guiding operational concept underlying international relations. Mikhail Suslov, chief theoretician of the Communist Party of the Soviet Union, declared as late as February, 1962, that in the realm of ideology, peaceful coexistence will be impossible. Artificial barriers to communications have been erected by communist regimes to prevent the erosion of their dogmatically hostile ideology—which asserts that the world must remain divided until communism conquers. To help the cause of freedom, to help the peoples living under communism, we must find means to reduce artificial barriers to communications between nations.

For many years the best people under communism—our true allies—

have been systematically rendered impotent through imprisonment, or destroyed physically. Their sacrifices have so far been in vain. For those unfortunates, for the good of their nations, and for the good of humanity, it would have been better if they had died on barricades rather than in secret-police dungeons and remote concentration camps. At the same time, we should always remember that every open and forceful challenge the Communists meet in their realm leaves lasting, often ineradicable scars, and cuts deeply into communist power.

Instead of discouraging the discontented population and displaying hypocritical friendliness toward communist oppressors, we in the West should identify ourselves with fighters for freedom and the dignity of man everywhere, recognize them as heroes worthy of imitation, and do everything in our power to aid them in their struggle.

One key to communist successes lies in the fact that the Communists have introduced idealistic elements in their appeal to those who fight their battles against the West. They have created a long list of heroes—most of whom have been regarded as criminals in the West—and they boldly keep extolling them and urging everyone to follow their example. The Communists never hesitate to support any movement, any cause which promises to undermine Western positions, and they frankly admit it.

They do so because they believe that their cause is right. Do we have a corresponding belief in the righteousness of ours? Without such conviction we are doomed, with or without a nuclear war. If we do, we have to abandon perennial doubts and hesitations and treat communism as our enemy and the enemy of freedom.

We should recognize war as the Communists wage it today. There are still ways of avoiding a general clash of arms, but it cannot be done merely by staying on the defensive and by purchasing more and better weapons. We must weaken the enemy ideologically, both inside and outside the Soviet empire, by helping to counterindoctrinate and organize the masses against him. Modern military strength is not simply a matter of arms, but one of ideological and moral strength on both sides.

The hardest way to wage the conflict is to have the people behind the Iron Curtain solidly against us, and the easiest way is to have them on our side. Taken in reverse, that is the operational formula of the Kremlin.

We cannot be secure until freedom reigns in all of the decisive areas of the globe. Nor can Khrushchev and Mao end their warfare against us until freedom is obliterated from this earth.

The most active element in Soviet expansion is not the military, but the vast trained group which captains the communist parties and organizes and stimulates the dissident elements in the West. The Communists seek to capture our masses. Soviet diplomacy is conceived of as an aid in the process of conquest. The military plays the role of a backstop to that operation. The more powerful the military, the more aggressive is communist political-warfare. The different parts are woven into a consistent whole, each part playing the role called for at a particular time. The Kremlin feels strong enough to threaten Berlin, to arm dissident nations in the West, and to resort to guerrilla warfare in the other soft areas of the West. Tomorrow we may have other Koreas, Congos, or Cubas, and then some more "peace and coexistence" campaigns while the Communists digest the conquest.

According to Soviet plans, this is a method which cannot fail, against which they consider our diplomacy to be both senile and fumbling. They discount the West's willingness or ability to take advantage of Soviet vulnerabilities. If the Kremlin should prove wrong on this, it would be the biggest surprise to them since they came to power, bigger than the thermonuclear bomb. With faith in freedom's ultimate triumph we could more than match the Soviet political-warfare machine. And tyranny as vulnerable as communism would not long endure.

BIBLIOGRAPHY

Acton, H. B. *The Illusion of the Epoch, Marxism-Leninism as a Philosophical Creed.* London: Cohen & West, 1955.

Alexander, Robert J. *Communism in Latin America.* New Brunswick: Rutgers University Press, 1957.

Almond, G. and Coleman, J. S. *The Politics of the Developing Areas.* Princeton: Princeton University Press, 1960.

Ball, W. Macmahon. *Nationalism and Communism in East Asia.* Melbourne: Melbourne University Press, 1956.

Barghoorn, Frederick C. *Soviet Russian Nationalism.* New York: Oxford University Press, 1956.

Barghoorn, Frederick C. *The Soviet Cultural Offensive.* Princeton: Princeton University Press, 1960.

Barnett, A. Doak. *Communist Economic Strategy: The Rise of Mainland China.* Washington: National Planning Association, 1959.

Barnett, A. Doak. *Communist China and Asia.* New York: Harper (for the Council on Foreign Relations), 1960.

Beal, John Robinson. *The Secret Speech.* New York: Duell, Sloan & Pearce, 1961.

Beaulac, Willard L. *Career Ambassador.* New York: Macmillan, 1951.

Bechhoefer, Bernard G. *Postwar Negotiations for Arms Control.* Washington: The Brookings Institute, 1961.

Bertram, James M. *First Act in China: Story of the Sian Mutiny.* New York: Viking, 1938.

Bigelow, John (ed.). *The Complete Works of Benjamin Franklin,* Vol. III, New York: Praeger, 1961.

Bland, J. O. P. *China: The Pity of It.* London: Heinemann, 1932.

Brandt, Conrad, Schwartz, Benj., and Fairbank, J. K. *A Documentary History of Chinese Communism.* Cambridge: Harvard University Press, 1952.

Brimmell, J. H. *Communism in South East Asia: A Political Analysis.* London: Oxford University Press, 1959.

Brzezinski, Zbigniew K. *The Permanent Purge.* Cambridge: Harvard University Press, 1956.

Budenz, Louis F. *The Techniques of Communism*. Chicago: Regnery Co., 1954.

Byrnes, James F. *Speaking Frankly*. New York: Harper, 1947.

Campbell, Arthur. *Jungle Green*. Boston: Little Brown, 1953.

Catlin, George E. G. *The Story of the Political Philosophers*. New York: McGraw-Hill, 1939.

Chapman, F. Spencer. *The Jungle Is Neutral*. New York: Norton, 1949.

Ch'en Po'ta. *Stalin and the Chinese Revolution*. Peking: Foreign Language Press, 1953.

Cheng Tien-fong. *History of Sino-Russian Relations*. Washington: Public Affairs Press, 1957.

Collective Defense in South East Asia. London: Royal Institute of International Affairs, 1956.

Crankshaw, Edward. *Cracks in the Kremlin Wall*. New York: Viking, 1951.

Dallin, David. *Facts on Communism* ("The Soviet Union: From Lenin to Khrushchev." Vol. II, Committee on Un-American Activities, House of Representatives, 86th Congress, 2nd Session, December, 1960.) Washington: Government Printing Office.

Dedijer, Vladimir. *Tito*. New York: Simon & Schuster, 1953.

Degras, Jane (ed.). *The Communist International, 1919-1943: Documents*, Vol. II. London: Oxford University Press, 1960.

Dinerstein, H. W. *War and the Soviet Union*. New York: Praeger, 1959.

Djilas, Milovan. *The New Class*. New York: Praeger, 1957.

Dyer, Murray. *The Weapon on the Wall*. Baltimore: Johns Hopkins, 1959.

Emerson, Rupert. *From Empire to Nation: The Rise of Self-Assertion of Asian and African Peoples*. Cambridge: Harvard University Press, 1960.

Fall, Bernard B. *Street Without Joy: Indochina at War, 1946-1954*. Harrisburg: Stackpole, 1961.

Fall, Bernard B. *Le Viet Minh, 1945-1960*. Paris: Colin, 1960.

Fall, Bernard B. *The Viet-Minh Regime: Government and Administration in the Democratic Republic of Vietnam*. Ithaca: Cornell University Press, 1954.

Fandino Silva, Francisco. *La Penetracion Sovietica en America y el de Abril*. Bogota: Ed. ABA, 1949.

Feis, Herbert. *The China Triangle*. Princeton: Princeton University Press, 1953.

Feis, Herbert. *Churchill, Roosevelt, Stalin: The War They Waged and the Peace They Sought*. Princeton: Princeton University Press, 1957.

Fifield, Russell H. *The Diplomacy of Southeast Asia, 1945-1958*. New York: Harper, 1958.

Garthoff, Raymond L. *The Soviet Image of Future War*. Washington: Public Affairs Press, 1959.

Guevara, Che. *Guerrilla Warfare*. New York: Praeger, 1961.

Gunther, John. *Inside Asia*. (War edition.) New York: Harper, 1942.

Hahn, Walter F. and Neff, John C. (eds.) *American Strategy for the Nuclear Age*. Garden City: Doubleday, 1960.

Hall, D. G. E. *A History of South-East Asia*. (2nd ed.) London: Macmillan, 1960.

Hanna, Willard. *Bung Karno's Indonesia*. New York: American Universities Field Staff, 1960.

Hanrahan, Gene Z. *The Communist Struggle in Malaya*. New York: Institute of Pacific Relations, 1954.

Hennikar, M. C. A. *Red Shadow over Malaya*. Edinburgh and London: Wm. Blackwood & Sons, 1955.

Hirsch, Richard. *The Soviet Spies*. New York: Duell, Sloan, Pearce, 1947.

Hudson, G. F., Lowenthal, Richard, and MacFarquhar, Roderick. *The Sino-Soviet Dispute*. New York: Praeger, 1961.

Jones, F. C., Bortin, Hugh, and Pearn, B. R. *The Far East, 1942-1946*. New York: Oxford University Press, 1955.

Kahin, George McTurnan. *Nationalism and Revolution in Indonesia*. Ithaca: Cornell University Press, 1952.

Kennan, George F. *Russia and the West Under Lenin and Stalin*. Boston: Little Brown, 1961.

Khrushchev, Nikita S. *For Victory in Peaceful Competition with Capitalism*. New York: Dutton, 1960.

King, John Kerry. *Southeast Asia in Perspective*. New York: Macmillan, 1956.

Kintner, William R. *The Front Is Everywhere*. Norman, Okla.: University of Oklahoma Press, 1950.

Kissinger, Henry A. *Nuclear Weapons and Foreign Policy*. New York: Harper (for the Council on Foreign Relations), 1957.

Kolarz, Walter. *Russia and Her Colonies*. London: Philip, 1952.

Korbonski, Stefan. *Fighting Warsaw: The Story of the Polish Underground State, 1939-45*. London: Allen & Unwin, 1956.

Kulski, Wladyslaw W. *Peaceful Co-Existence*. Chicago: Regnery, 1956.

Leites, Nathan. *A Study of Bolshevism*. Glencoe: The Free Press, 1953.

Lenin, Nicolai. *Collected Works*. New York: International Publishers, 1927.

Lenin, V. I. *Two Tactics of Social Democracy in the Democratic Revolution*. New York: International Publishers, c. 1935.

Leonhard, Wolfgang. *Child of the Revolution*. Chicago: Regnery, 1958.

Levenson, Joseph. *Confucian China and Its Modern Fate*. Berkeley: University of California Press, 1958.

Linebarger, Paul M. A. *The China of Chiang Kai-shek*. Boston: World Peace Foundation, 1941.

Lindholm, Richard W. (ed.) *Viet-Nam: The First Five Years*. East Lansing, Mich.: Michigan State University Press, 1959.

Lippmann, Walter. *The Communist World and Ours*. Boston: Little Brown, 1957.

Liu Shao-ch'i. *Internationalism and Nationalism*. New York: Committee for a Democratic Far Eastern Policy, 1948.

Tse-tung, Mao. *Selected Works*. London: Lawrence & Wishart, 1954.

Tse-tung, Mao. *La Nouvelle Democratic.* Paris: Editions sociales, 1951.

Maranon, Gregorio, *Tiberius: a study in resentment.* London: Hollis & Carter, 1956.

Masani, M. R. *The Communist Party of India.* New York: Macmillan, 1954.

Michael, Franz H. and Taylor, George E. *The Far East in the Modern World.* New York: Holt, 1956.

Millis, Walter (ed.). *The Forrestal Diaries.* New York: Viking, 1951.

Mintz, Jeanne S. *Indonesia: A Profile.* Princeton: Van Nostrand, 1961.

Neustadt, Richard E. *Presidential Power: The Politics of Leadership.* New York: Putnam, 1904.

Nino, Alberto. *Antecedents y secretos del 9 de Abril.* Bogota: Ed. Paz, 1949.

North, Robert C. *Kuomintang and Chinese Communists Elites.* Stanford: Stanford University Press, 1952.

Overstreet, Harry and Bonaro. *This War Called Peace.* New York: Norton, 1961.

Pavlov, I. P. *Conditioned Reflexes.* London: Oxford University Press, Humphrey Milford, 1927.

Phillips, Morgan. *East and West.* London: Lincoln-Praeger, 1954.

Possony, Stefan T. *A Century of Conflict.* Chicago: Regnery, 1953.

Purcell, Victor. *The Chinese in Malaya.* London: Oxford University Press, 1948.

Ravines, Eudocio. *The Yenan Way.* New York: Scribner, 1951.

Ridgeway, Matthew B. *Soldier.* New York: Harper, 1956.

Robinson, J. B. Perry. *Transformation in Malaya.* London: Secher & Warburg, 1956.

Rose, Saul. *Socialism in Southern Asia.* New York: Oxford University Press, 1959.

Rostow, Walt W. *The United States in the World Arena.* New York: Harper, 1960.

Rubinstein, Alvin Z. *The Foreign Policy of the Soviet Union.* New York: Random House, 1960.

Sargant, William. *Battle for the Mind.* Garden City, N. Y.: Doubleday, 1957.

Scaff, Alvin H. *The Philippine Answer to Communism.* Stanford: Stanford University Press, 1955.

Schneider, Ronald M. *Communism in Guatemala, 1944-1954.* New York: Praeger, 1959.

Schwartz, Harry. *The Red Phoenix: Russia Since World War II.* New York: Praeger, 1961.

Sisouk Na Champassak. *Storm over Laos.* New York: Praeger, 1961.

Starobin, Joseph R. *Eyewitness in Indo-China.* New York: Cameron & Kahn, 1954.

Stewart, Watt and Peterson, Harold F. *Builders of Latin America.* New York: Praeger, 1942.

Strausz-Hupé, *et al. Protracted Conflict.* New York: Harper, 1959.

Strausz-Hupé, Robert and Possony, Stefan T. *International Relations,* 2nd edition. New York: McGraw-Hill, 1954.

Strausz-Hupé, Robert, Kintner, William R. and Possony, Stefan T. *A Forward Strategy for America.* New York: Harper, 1961.

Strong, Anna Louise. *Dawn Out of China.* n.p. Indian edition of *Tomorrow's China.* New York: Committee for a Democratic Far Eastern Policy, 1948.

Sutter, John O. *Indonesianisasi: Politics in a Changing Economy, 1940-1955.*

Tang, Peter S. H. *Communist China Today.* New York: Praeger, c. 1957-58.

Thakin, Nu. *Towards Peace and Democracy.* Rangoon: Supt. of Govt. Printing and Stationary, Govt. of Burma, 1949.

Thayer, Philip W. (ed.) *Nationalism and Progress in Free Asia.* Baltimore: Johns Hopkins, 1956.

Thomas, Albert B. *Latin America: A History.* New York: Macmillan, 1956.

Tinker, Hugh. *The Union of Burma: A Study of the First Years of Independence.*

Trager, Frank N. (ed.) *Marxism in Southeast Asia: A Study of Four Countries.* Stanford: Stanford University Press, 1959.

U Ba Swe. *The Burmese Revolution.* Rangoon: Pyidawsoe, 1957.

U Nu. *Towards a Welfare State.* Speech at Third All-Burma Congress of AFPFLn.p., 1958.

United States Relations With China (with special Reference to the Period 1944-1949). Publications of the United States Department of State No. 3573. Washington, D. C.: Government Printing Office, 1949.

Vandenbosch, Amry and Butwell, Richard. *Southeast Asia Among the World Powers.* Lexington: University of Kentucky Press, 1958.

Weyl, Nathaniel. *Red Star Over Cuba.* New York: Devin-Adair, 1960.

Whiting, Allen S. *China Crosses the Yalu.* New York: Macmillan, 1960.

Wittfogel, Karl A. *Oriental Despotism.* New Haven: Yale University Press, 1957.

Yen, Maria. *The Umbrella Garden,* New York: Macmillan, 1954.

INDEX

357